CONTENTS

Principles of
Services Marketing

Adrian Palmer
De Montfort University
Leicester Business School

McGRAW-HILL BOOK COMPANY

London · New York · St Louis · San Francisco · Auckland
Bogotá · Caracas · Lisbon · Madrid · Mexico · Milan
Montreal · New Delhi · Panama · Paris · San Juan · São Paulo
Singapore · Sydney · Tokyo · Toronto

Published by
McGRAW-HILL Book Company Europe
Shoppenhangers Road, Maidenhead, Berkshire, SL6 2QL, England
Telephone (0628) 23432
Fax (0628) 770224

British Library Cataloguing in Publication Data

Palmer, Adrian
  Principles of Services Marketing
  I. Title
  658.8

  ISBN 0–07–707746–6

Library of Congress Cataloging-in-Publication Data

Palmer, Adrian
   Principles of services marketing / Adrian Palmer.
      p.   cm.
   Includes bibliographical references and index.
   ISBN 0–07–707746–6:
   1. Marketing – Management.   2. Service industries – Marketing.
   I. Title.
   HF5415. 13.P3242   1994
   658.8 – dc20   94–4289
                                                                CIP

Copyright © 1994 McGraw-Hill International (UK) Limited. All rights reserved. No part of this publication may be reproduced, stored in a retrieval system, or transmitted, in any form or by any means, electronic, mechanical, photocopying, recording, or otherwise, without the prior permission of McGraw-Hill International (UK) Limited.

  2345 CUP 97654

Typeset by Datix International Limited, Bungay, Suffolk
and printed and bound in Great Britain at the University Press Cambridge

THE CONTRIBUTORS

Writing a book that is both comprehensive and up to date can be a daunting task. *Principles of Services Marketing* only became a reality because of the invaluable contributions of colleagues who shared a vision for this book.

Tony Conway, Principal Lecturer in Management Development, University College, Salford, contributed chapters on product policy and the promotion of services.

Ian Clark, Senior Lecturer in Industrial Relations, De Montfort University, Leicester, provided input relating the importance of Human Resource Management to Services Marketing.

Jasmine Williams and **Phil Megicks**, Senior Lecturers in Marketing, University of Plymouth Business School, used their knowledge and experience of market research techniques within the service sector to good effect in Chapter 5.

My thanks go to all the contributors for their patience and diligence in bringing this book together. Inevitably, I have edited their contributions, and any subsequent misrepresentations of their original intentions are my responsibility.

Adrian Palmer
De Montfort University,
Leicester

PREFACE

The service sector today occupies a pre-eminent position in the economies of most western countries. Not only are we producing and consuming more services than ever before, the manner in which services are made available to the final consumer is changing. As private sector service companies face increasingly fierce levels of competition, a further group of public services are beginning to experience the realities of competitive markets for the first time. Service producers have to be increasingly sure that they are producing the right services in the right places at the right time for the right price. In short, marketing within the service sector is more important than it has ever been.

Many of the familiar principles of marketing were first developed when the fast moving consumer goods (fmcg) markets experienced a great growth in competitive activity. This legacy has been handed down to marketers who are engaged in the current growth in services marketing. Yet it is now recognized that services can be quite different to goods in how they should be marketed, and some of the tried and tested frameworks for analysis cannot sensibly be stretched to cover services. The intangibility and inseparability of the service offer are just two factors which call for new approaches.

This book provides the student with a framework for understanding the key issues of services marketing. It does not assume that the reader has any prior knowledge of marketing principles. However, the reader who has developed his or her marketing skills in the context of consumer goods may find the contrasts presented in this book a revelation.

It could be argued that in a truly market-oriented service organization, marketing is so fundamental that it cannot be separated from the other basic functions of a business. Indeed, many have argued that services marketing can only be sensibly understood as the bringing together of the principles of marketing, human resource management and operations management. This is acknowledged in this book, where emphasis is placed on the management of personnel as a vital element in marketing a service offer and the importance of operations management is recognized in tackling such problems as the peaked pattern of demand which faces many service organizations.

As with most marketing books, the arrangements of the chapters in this book is to some extent arbitrary. The first chapter sets the scene by trying to define services and assessing their importance to national economies. A number of core marketing concepts are then introduced, followed by a discussion on services marketing management. Subsequent chapters examine aspects of marketing mix planning. Some of these chapters are based loosely on the traditional 4 'Ps', but are supplemented by analysis of issues which are quite unique to the service sector. In this respect, a chapter deals with analysing service encounters while another looks at the topical issue of service quality. The traditional 'P' for place is redefined in terms of accessibility to services and a fifth 'P' for people is added. Finally, problems and opportunities in the internationalization of services are discussed.

This book is ideal for students who have followed a basic principles of marketing course and wish to specialize in the area of services marketing. Such readers may wish to pass quickly through Chapter 2, which summarizes some of the most important characteristics of marketing philosophies and practices. By reading this chapter, the newcomer to marketing will gain the full benefit of this book. Considerable attention is given within the book to the particular needs of public sector services marketing.

Adrian Palmer
De Montfort University,
Leicester

ONE

WHAT ARE SERVICES?

OBJECTIVES

After reading this chapter, you should be able to understand:

- The essential characteristics of services and their implications for marketing
- Bases for classifying the diverse range of services according to marketing needs
- The importance of the service sector in national economies and the reasons for its emergence

1.1 INTRODUCTION

The idea that the service sector should be worth study in its own right is a relatively recent phenomenon. Early economists paid little attention to services, considering them to be totally unproductive, adding nothing of value to an economy. Adam Smith, writing in the eighteenth century, distinguished between production that had a tangible output—such as agriculture and manufacture—and production for which there was no tangible output. The latter, which included the efforts of intermediaries, doctors, lawyers and the armed forces, he described as 'unproductive of any value' (Smith, 1977 [1776], p. 430). This remained the dominant attitude towards services until the latter part of the nineteenth century, when Alfred Marshall (1890) argued that a person providing a service was just as capable of giving utility to the recipient as someone producing a tangible product. Indeed, Marshall recognized that tangible products may not exist at all were it not for a series of services performed in order to produce them and to make them available to consumers. To Marshall, an agent distributing agricultural produce performed as valuable a task as the farmer—without the provision of transport and intermediary services, agricultural products produced in areas of surplus would be of no value. Today, despite some lingering beliefs that the service sector is an insubstantial and relatively inferior sector of the economy, considerable attention is paid to its direct and indirect economic consequences.

Modern definitions of services focus on the fact that a service in itself produces no tangible output, although it may be instrumental in producing some tangible output. A contemporary definition is provided by Kotler and Armstrong (1991):

A service is an activity or benefit that one party can offer to another that is essentially intangible and does not result in the ownership of anything. Its production may or may not be tied to a physical product.

There has however, been no consistent definition of what constitutes a service. In his study of

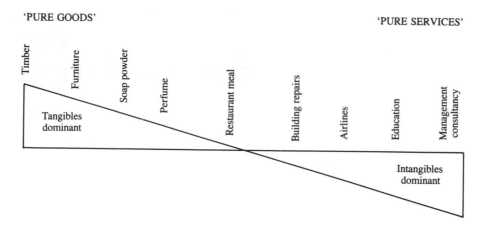

Figure 1.1 The goods and services continuum

the US service economy, Fuchs (1968), for example, excluded transport and communication, arguing that they formed an integral part of goods. Stanton (1981) included activities such as entertainment and tourism, but excluded delivery services and credit facilities where these are essentially attached to a tangible good offered for sale.

In practice, it can be very difficult to distinguish services from goods, for when a good is purchased there is usually an element of service included. Similarly, a service is frequently augmented by a tangible product attached to the service. In this way, a car may be considered to be a good rather than a service, yet cars are usually sold with the benefit of considerable intangible service elements, such as a warranty or a financing facility. On the other hand, a seemingly intangible service such as a package holiday includes tangible elements in the purchase—use of an aircraft, a transfer coach and a hotel room, for example. In between is a wide range of outputs that are a combination of tangible good and intangible service. A meal in a restaurant is a combination of tangible goods (the food and physical surroundings) and intangible service (the preparation and delivery of the food, reservation service, etc.). Figure 1.1 shows schematically that considerable diversity exists within the service sector. In fact, rather than describing the service sector as a homogeneous group of activities, it would be more appropriate to speak of degrees of service orientation. All productive activities can be placed on a scale somewhere between being a pure service (no tangible output) and a pure good (no intangible service added to the tangible good). In practice, most products fall between the two extremes by being a combination of goods and services.

There is argument about the extent to which services should be considered a distinctive area of study in marketing. On the one hand, some have argued that a service contains many important elements common to goods which makes services marketing obsolete as a separate discipline. Thus Levitt (1972) observed:

... there is no such thing as service industries. There are only industries where service components are greater or less than those of other industries.

On the other hand, many have pointed to the limitations of traditional marketing principles when applied to the marketing of services. Gronroos (1978), Lovelock (1981), Shostack (1977), Berry (1980) and Rathmell (1974) are among the critics who have argued that the differences that exist between goods and services mean that the marketing tools used for goods marketing cannot easily be translated to services marketing.

The purpose of this book is to analyse and refine the basic principles of marketing to allow them to be operationalized more effectively in the services sector. Many of these principles will be familiar to those involved in the marketing of goods and can be applied to services with relatively little refinement. In some cases—such as the analysis of service encounters—a new area of marketing thought needs to be opened up.

There are many definitions of what constitutes a service. The definition that will be used for the scope of this book is '*The production of an essentially intangible benefit, either in its own right or as a significant element of a tangible product, which through some form of exchange satisfies an identified consumer need.*'

This definition recognizes that, in addition to the grey area between a pure good and a pure service, some marketing activities do not easily fit on this scale at all. The first of these which has attracted growing interest is the marketing of ideas, whether these be the ideas of a political party, a religious sect or on a specific subject, such as road safety. The second—and related—area is the marketing of a cause, such as famine relief in Africa or a campaign to prevent the construction of a new road. Both types of activity are distinguished from normal goods and services marketing as there is no exchange of value between the producer and the individuals or organizations to whom the marketing effort is aimed. To take an example, the consumer of transport services enters into an exchange and pays for a transport service either directly and willingly—as in the case of a train fare—or indirectly—and possibly unwillingly—through general taxation, as in the case for the use of roads. On the other hand, when a pressure group mounts a campaign to bring about the building of a new road, the concept of exchange of value becomes extremely tenuous, only really occurring where—for example—a member of the public subsequently contributes to a cause—either financially or by their actions. Generally, the concept of services does not offer an appropriate framework for analysing the marketing of ideas and causes.

This book will focus on distinct services aspects of marketing activities, rather than on the generality of marketing decisions for tangible products of which service is just one element. In this way, distribution is an activity that, for example, surrounds building materials. As an activity, it can be seen as an integral element of the tangible product which is essential for securing its sale. Alternatively, it could be regarded as a discrete activity that delivers an intangible benefit—movement—the payment for which the purchaser has nothing to show in return. The latter perspective will be adopted throughout this book in tackling the marketing of products which are a combination of goods and services.

1.2   DISTINGUISHING FEATURES OF A SERVICE

'Pure' services have a number of distinctive characteristics which differentiate them from goods and have implications for the manner in which they are marketed. These can be described as intangibility, inseparability, variability, perishability and the inability to own a service. As these characteristics will be a recurrent theme throughout this book, their nature is introduced below.

1.2.1   Intangibility

A pure service cannot be assessed using any of the physical senses—it is an abstraction which cannot be directly examined before it is purchased. A prospective purchaser of most goods is able to study them for physical integrity, aesthetic appearance, taste, smell, etc. Many advertising claims relating to these tangible properties can be verified by inspection prior to purchase.

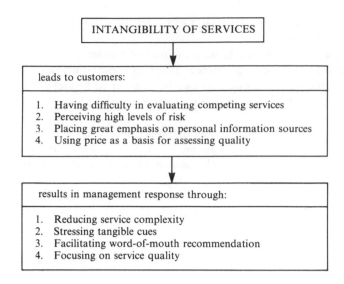

Figure 1.2 Some implications of service intangibility

On the other hand, pure services have no tangible properties which can be used by consumers to verify advertising claims before the purchase is made. The intangible process characteristics which define services, such as reliability, personal care, attentiveness of staff, their friendliness, etc., can only be verified once a service has been purchased and consumed.

Intangibility has a number of important marketing implications which will be examined in more detail in subsequent chapters. The lack of physical evidence that intangibility implies increases the level of uncertainty which a consumer faces when choosing between competing services. An important part of a services marketing programme will therefore involve reducing consumer uncertainty by such means as adding physical evidence and the development of strong brands. It is interesting to note that pure goods and pure services tend to move in opposite directions in terms of their general approach to the issue of tangibility. While service marketers seek to add tangible evidence to their product, pure goods marketers often seek to augment their products by adding intangible elements such as after-sales service and improved distribution (Figure 1.2).

1.2.2 Inseparability

The production and consumption of a tangible good are two discrete activities. Companies usually produce goods in one central location and then transport them to the place where customers most want to buy them. In this way, manufacturing companies can achieve economies of scale through centralized production and have centralized quality-control checks. The manufacturer is also able to make goods at a time which is convenient to itself, then make them available to customers at times which are convenient for them. Production and consumption are said to be separable. On the other hand, the consumption of a service is said to be inseparable from its means of production. Producer and consumer must normally interact in order for the benefits of the service to be realized—both must meet at a time and a place which is mutually convenient in order that the producer can directly pass on service benefits. In the extreme case of personal care services, the customer must be present during the entire production process—a doctor cannot provide a service without the involvement of a patient.

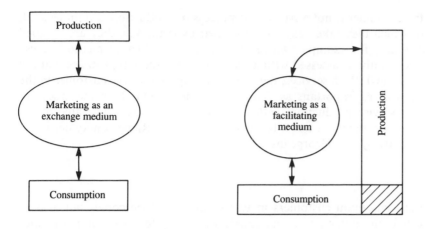

Figure 1.3 Services marketing as a facilitating medium

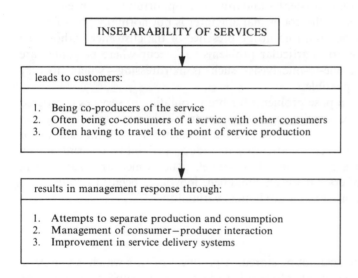

Figure 1.4 Some implications of service inseparability

For services, marketing becomes a means of facilitating complex producer–consumer interaction, rather than being merely an exchange medium (see Figure 1.3).

Inseparability occurs whether the producer is human, as in health-care services, or a machine, as in the case of a bank ATM machine. The service of the ATM machine can only be realized if the producer and consumer interact. In some cases, it has been possible to separate service production and consumption, especially where there is little need for personal contact.

Inseparability has a number of important marketing implications for services. First, whereas goods are generally first produced, then offered for sale and finally sold and consumed, inseparability causes this process to be modified for services. These are generally sold first, then produced and consumed simultaneously. Second, while the method of goods production is to a large extent (though by no means always) of little importance to the consumer, production processes are critical to the enjoyment of services (see Figure 1.4).

In the case of goods, the consumer is not a part of the process of production and, in general, as long as the product of which they take delivery meets their expectations, they are satisfied (although there are exceptions—for example, where the ethics of production methods cause concern, or where quality can only be assessed with a knowledge of production stages that are hidden from the consumer's view). With services, the active participation of the customer in the production process makes this as important as defining the end-benefit. In some cases, an apparently slight change in service production methods may totally destroy the value of the service being provided. A person buying a ticket for a concert by Cliff Richard may derive no benefit at all if it is subsequently by Boy George instead.

1.2.3 Variability

For services, variability impacts upon customers in terms not just of outcomes but also of processes of production. It is the latter point that causes variability to pose a much greater problem for services, compared to goods. Because customers are usually involved in the production process for a service at the same time as they consume it, it can be difficult to carry out monitoring and control to ensure consistent standards. The opportunity for pre-delivery inspection and rejection which is open to the goods manufacturer is not normally possible with services—the service must normally be produced in the presence of the customer without the possibility of intervening quality control. Particular problems can occur where personnel are involved in providing services on a one-to-one basis—such as hairdressing—where no easy method of monitoring and control is possible.

The variability of service output can pose problems for brand building in services compared to tangible goods—for the latter it is usually relatively easy to incorporate monitoring and quality control procedures into production processes in order to ensure that a brand stands for a consistency of output. The service sector's attempts to reduce variability concentrate on methods used to select, train, motivate and control personnel, issues which are examined in Chapter 9. In some cases, service offers have been simplified, jobs have been 'de-skilled' and personnel replaced with machines in order to reduce human variability.

1.2.4 Perishability

Services differ from goods in that they cannot be stored. A producer of cars which is unable to sell all its output in the current period can carry forward stocks to sell in a subsequent one. The only significant costs are storage, financing and the possibility of loss through obsolescence. In contrast, the producer of a service which cannot sell all its output produced in the current period has no chance to carry it forward for sale in a subsequent one. An airline which offers seats on a 9.00 a.m. flight from London to Paris cannot sell any empty seats once the aircraft has left. The service offer disappears and spare seats cannot be stored to meet a surge in demand which may occur at, say, 10.00 a.m.

The perishability of services results in greater attention having to be paid to the management of demand by evening out peaks and troughs and in scheduling service production to follow this pattern as far as possible. Pricing and promotion are two of the tools commonly adopted to tackle this problem and these are analysed in detail in Chapter 7.

1.2.5 Ownership

The inability to own a service is related to its intangibility and perishability. In purchasing goods, buyers generally acquire title to the goods in question and can subsequently do as they want with them. On the other hand, when a service is performed, no ownership is transferred from the seller to the buyer. The buyer is merely buying the right to a service process such as the use of a car park or a solicitor's time. A distinction should be drawn between the inability to own the service act and the rights that a buyer may acquire to have a service carried out at some time in the future—a theatre ticket gift voucher, for example.

The inability to own a service has implications for the design of distribution channels—a wholesaler or retailer cannot take title, as in the case with goods. Instead, direct distribution methods are more common and where intermediaries are used, they generally act as a co-producer of the service.

1.3 ANALYSIS OF THE SERVICE OFFER

The extent to which these five features can be used to distinguish between goods and services marketing has been questioned by many. Wyckham *et al.* (1975), for example, have argued that intangibility, variability and perishability are not sufficient to explain the differing marketing needs of services. For example, on the subject of variability, there are some non-service industries—such as tropical fruits—which have difficulty in achieving high levels of consistent output, whereas some service industries such as car parks can achieve a consistent standard of service in terms of availability and cleanliness, etc. Similarly, many tangible goods share the problem of intangible services in being incapable of full examination before consumption. It is not normally possible, for instance, to judge the taste of a bottle of wine in a supermarket before it has been purchased and (at least partially) consumed. Also, 'Just-in-Time' (JIT) methods of delivery goods exhibit many of the problems of perishability associated with services.

Much of the usefulness of this list of distinguishing features is in understanding the nature of the service offer, in particular the extent to which it includes tangible goods elements. Shostack (1977) attempted to analyse the elements of a service in terms of a molecular model of interrelated services and goods components. Thus an airline offers an essentially intangible service—transport. Yet the total service offering includes tangible elements such as the aircraft as well as intangible ones such as the frequency of flights, their reliability and the quality of in-flight services. When many of these intangibles are broken down into their component parts they also include tangible elements. Thus in-flight service includes tangible elements in the form of food and drink. A hypothetical application of the molecular model approach to the analysis of the complex output of a theatre is shown in Figure 1.5.

1.3.1 Goods as 'self-services'

A distinction can be drawn between a service that is delivered directly by an organization to consumers and services that are delivered by means of the goods that are purchased. Conceptually, many goods purchases effectively result in a consumer buying a stream of internally produced services. Gurshuny (1978) uses the term 'intermediate services' to describe complex manufactured equipment which private and industrial buyers purchase in order to provide services that may otherwise have been supplied as a direct service activity. In this way, an automatic washing machine provides indirect service benefits that may otherwise have been supplied directly by a launderette and a car provides benefits otherwise available from taxis and public transport.

1.4 CLASSIFICATION OF SERVICES

It is too simplistic to divide the economy into goods and services sectors, for the service sector itself covers a diverse range of activities. The contrast between a small, local window-cleaning

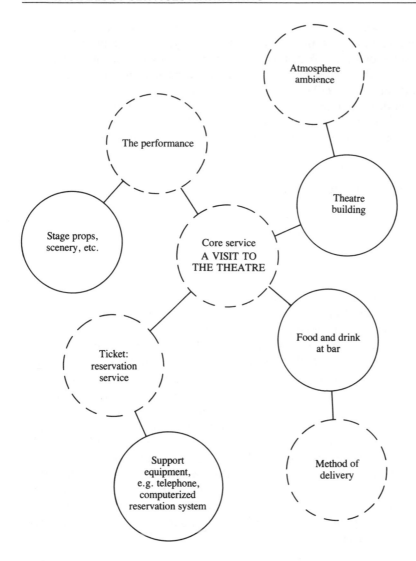

Figure 1.5   An application of Shostack's molecular model of service components to the analysis of a theatre. Unbroken circles—tangible elements; broken circles—intangible elements

service and a complex international banking facility illustrates this contrast. Because of this diversity, any analysis of the service sector will prove to be very weak unless smaller categories of services can be identified and subjected to an analytical framework which is particularly appropriate to that category of service.

The most common basis for classifying services has been the type of activity which is performed. Statistics record service activities under headings such as banking, shipping, hotels, based largely on similarity of production methods. Thus banking is used to classify all organizations whose main activity is the circulation of money, and shipping is defined in terms of organizations which are largely engaged in movement by sea, even though freight movement between, say, Dover and Calais is quite different from the operation of a cruise ship in the Caribbean.

Such simple classification systems are not particularly helpful to marketers. In the first place, a single production sector can cover a very diverse range of activities with quite different marketing needs—small guest houses and international hotels may fall within the same sector, but their marketing needs are likely to be quite different. Second, most services are in fact a combination of services—retail stores, for example, often go beyond their traditional sectoral boundaries by offering banking services. Third, the marketing needs of a particular production-based subsector may share more in common with another unrelated subsector rather than other areas within its own sector.

Marketers should be more interested in identifying subsectors in terms of similarity of marketing requirements. In this way, the provision of hotel services may have much in common with some shipping operations in terms of the processes by which, for example, customers make purchase decisions and interact with a company's employees.

Defining categories of services is arguably more complex than for manufactured goods, where terms such as fast-moving consumer goods, shopping goods, speciality goods, white goods, brown goods, etc. are widely used and convey much information about the marketing requirements of products within a category. The great diversity of services has made attempts to reduce services to a small number of categories difficult to achieve. Instead, many analysts have sought to classify services along a number of continua, reflecting the fact that products cannot be classified into dichotomous goods and services categories to begin with.

Many bases for classifying services have been suggested over the years. Some of the more frequently quoted ones are discussed below.

1.4.1 Marketable versus unmarketable services

This first classification distinguishes between those services that are considered marketable and those where the social and economic environment of the time considers it desirable that benefits should be distributed by non-market-based mechanisms. Among the latter group, many government services are provided for the public benefit but no attempt is made to charge users of the service. This can arise where it is impossible to exclude individuals or groups of individuals from benefiting from a service. For example, it is not possible in practice for a local authority to charge individuals for the use of local footpaths—the benefits are essentially external in that it is not possible to restrict the distribution of the benefit to those who have entered into some form of exchange relationship. Furthermore, many public services are said to result in no rivalry in consumption in that one person's enjoyment of a service does not prevent another enjoying the same service. One person using a footpath does not generally prevent another from using the same path.

A second major group of services that many cultures do not consider to be marketable are those commonly provided within household units, such as the bringing up of children, cooking and cleaning. While many of these services are now commonly marketed within Western societies (for example, childminding services), many societies—and segments within them—would regard the internal provision of such services as central to the functioning of family units. Attempts by Western companies to launch family-based services in cultures with strong family traditions may result in failure because no market exists.

As with all service classifications, a whole range of services lies between these two extremes and the classification of any service is dynamic, reflecting changes in the political, economic, social and technological environments. Attempts are often made to internalize many of the external benefits of public services, turning them into marketable services. The provision of road facilities in the UK may have been considered until recently to be totally unmarketable, for the reasons described above. Since then, proposals for toll roads based on marketing principles of selling relatively uncongested road space to motorists have appeared. Similarly, attitudes towards which household-produced services should be considered marketable have changed over time and government social policy has had the effect of forcing trade-offs between home-produced and bought-in services—for example, in relation to the buying-in of care services for elderly relatives.

1.4.2 Producer versus consumer services

Consumer services are provided for individuals who use the service for their own enjoyment or benefit. No further economic benefit results from the consumption of the service. In this way, the services of a hairdresser can be defined as consumer services. On the other hand, producer services are those that are provided to a business so that it can produce something else of economic benefit. In this way, a road-haulage company sells services to its industrial customers so that they can add value to the goods that they produce, by allowing their goods to be made available at the point of demand.

Many services are provided simultaneously to both consumer and producer markets. Here, the challenge is to adapt the marketing programme to meet the differing needs of each group of users. In this way, airlines provide a service basically similar to both consumer and producer markets, but the marketing programme may emphasize low price for the former and quality and greater short-notice availability for the latter.

While this is a very common basis for classifying service sectors, it could be argued that a private household may act as a production unit in which services are bought not for their own intrinsic value but in order to allow some other benefit to be produced. Thus a household mortgage is not so much consumed, rather it is used to produce the benefit of homemaking. There is also evidence that industrial buyers of services do not simply judge a service on its ability to profitably add value to their own production process, but the personal, non-organizational goals of individuals within an organization may cause some decisions to be based on personal consumption criteria. A car telephone service may be judged for its personal status as well as productive value.

1.4.3 The status of the service in the product offering

It was stated above that most products are a combination of a goods and a service element. Services can be classified according to the role of the service in that total offering and three principal roles can be identified:

1. A pure service exists where there is little (if any) evidence of tangible goods—for example, an insurance policy or a management consultancy service. With this group, where tangible elements do exist, their primary function is to support an intangible service, in the way that a tangible aircraft supports the essentially intangible service of transport.
2. A second group of services exists in order to add value to a tangible product. This can occur where a goods manufacturer augments its core tangible product with additional service benefits, such as after-sales warranties. In other cases the service is sold as a discrete product which customers purchase to add value to their own goods—in this way, a car-valeting service is purchased to add to the resale value of a used car.
3. A third group of services may add value to a product more fundamentally by making it available in the first place. Such services can facilitate delivery of a tangible good from the point of production to the place where it is required by the consumer, or can provide the means through credit arrangements which allow tangible goods to be bought. In this way, mortgages facilitate house purchase and road-haulage services assist delivery of goods.

1.4.4 Tangible versus intangible services

Intangibility has been seen by many as a defining characteristic of services. However, it was noted earlier that a grey area exists between pure services at one extreme and pure goods at the other. Much of the intermediate greyness can be explained in terms of the extent to which the offer includes tangible elements.

The level of tangibility present in the service offer derives from three principal sources:

- Tangible goods which are included in the service offer and consumed by the consumer
- The physical environment in which the service production/consumption process takes place
- Tangible evidence of service performance

Where goods form an important component of a service offer, many of the practices associated with conventional goods marketing can be applied to this part of the service offer. Restaurants represent a mix of tangibles and intangibles and, in respect of the food element, few of the particular characteristics of services marketing are encountered. Thus, production of the food can be separated from its consumption and its perishability is less significant than the perishability of an empty table. Furthermore, the presence of a tangible component gives customers a visible basis on which to judge quality.

The tangible elements of the service offer comprise not just those goods which are exchanged but also the physical environment in which a service encounter takes place. Within this environment, the design of buildings, their cleanliness and the appearance of staff present important tangible evidence which may be the only basis on which a customer is able to differentiate between one service provider and another. While some services are rich in such tangible cues (restaurants, shops), others provide relatively little tangible evidence (telephone sales operations).

Tangibility is further provided by evidence of service production methods. Some services provide many opportunities for customers to see the process of production, indeed the whole purpose of the service may be to see the production process (for example, a pop concert). Often this tangible evidence can be seen before a decision to purchase a service is made, either by direct observation of a service being performed on somebody else (watching the work of a builder) or indirectly through a description of the service production process (a role played by brochures which specify and illustrate the service production process). On the other hand, some services provide very few tangible clues about the nature of the service production process. Portfolio management services are not only produced largely out of sight of the consumer, it is also difficult to specify in advance in a brochure what the service outcomes will be.

Some of the marketing management implications of intangibility will be explored in later chapters of this book. However, it should be noted here that intangibility tends to increase the level of uncertainty that consumers perceive in making purchase decisions. Marketing management seeks to compensate for this by focusing attention on the management of the tangible evidence of the service offer. Heightened uncertainty resulting from intangibility is often also addressed by attempts to develop strong brands to provide reassurance.

1.4.5 Extent of customer involvement

Some services can only be provided with the complete involvement of customers, whereas others require them to do little more than initiate the service process. In the first category, personal-care services, almost by definition, require the complete involvement of customers during the service production and delivery process. This is often of an interactive nature, as where a client of a hairdresser answers a continuous series of questions about the emerging length and style of his or her hair. For such a customer, the quality of the service production process as well as of outcomes assume importance. For other services, it is not necessary for the customer to be so fully involved in the production process. Customers listening to music on a radio do not need to be involved for the service to be delivered—they can receive the service quite passively.

Customer involvement is generally lower where the service is carried out not on the mind or body directly but on customers' possessions. The transport of goods, the cleaning of a home or office or the operation of a bank account do not involve a service being carried out directly on the customer, whose main task is to initiate the service and to monitor performance of it. Monitoring can take the form of examining tangible evidence of service performance, such as whether a carpet has been cleaned to the required standard, or examining intangible evidence of performance, such as a statement about an investment that has been made on the client's behalf.

Because it is relatively difficult to maintain consistent production standards for services, many services marketing organizations have sought to reduce the level of customer involvement in the production process. Simplification of the service production process and distant communication by mail or telephone have been used to achieve this.

1.4.6 Degree of variability

There are two dimensions of variability that can be used to classify services:

- The extent to which production standards vary from a norm, in terms of both outcomes and production processes
- The extent to which a service can be deliberately varied to meet the specific needs of individual customers.

Variability in production standards is of greatest concern to services organizations where customers are highly involved in the production process, especially where production methods make it impractical to monitor service production. This is true of many labour-intensive personal services provided in a one-to-one situation, such as hairdressing. Some services allow greater scope for quality-control checks to be undertaken during the production process, allowing an organization to provide a consistently high level of service. This is especially true of machine-based services. For example, telecommunication services can typically operate with very low failure rates (British Telecom claims that customers are able to make a connection to their dialled number in over 99 per cent of all first attempts to obtain service).

The tendency today is for equipment-based services to be regarded as less variable than those that involve a high degree of personal intervention in the production process. Many service organizations have sought to reduce variability—and hence to build strong brands—by adopting equipment-based production methods. Replacing human telephone operators with computerized voice systems and the automation of many banking services are typical of this trend. Sometimes reduced personnel variability has been achieved by passing on part of the production process to the customer, in the way that self-service petrol stations are no longer dependent on the variability of forecourt serving staff.

The second dimension of variability is the extent to which a service can be deliberately customized to meet the specific needs of individual customers. Because services are created as they are consumed, and because the consumer usually takes part in the production process, the potential for customization of services is generally greater than for manufactured goods. The

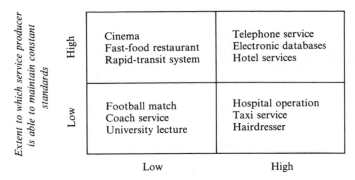

Extent to which service can be customized to individual customers' needs

Figure 1.6 Classification of services by variability in production and adaptability to individual consumers' needs

extent to which a service can be customized is dependent upon production methods employed. Thus services that are produced for large numbers of customers simultaneously may offer little scope for individual customization—the structured production methods of a railway do not allow individual customers' needs to be met by the more flexible methods of a taxi operator.

The extent to which services can be customized is partly a function of management decisions on the level of authority to be delegated to front-line service personnel. While some service operations seek to give more freedom and authority to front-line staff, a common tendency is for service firms to 'industrialize' their encounter with customers. This implies following clearly specified standardized procedures in each encounter. While industrialization normally reduces the flexibility of producers to meet customers' needs, it also has the effect of reducing variability of processes and outcomes.

The two dimensions of variability are clearly interrelated. It is in services with low variability in both dimensions that brand building by services organizations has assumed greatest importance. The two scales of variability are illustrated in Figure 1.6.

1.4.7 The pattern of service delivery

Two aspects of service delivery are distinguished here:

- Whether a service is supplied on a continuous basis or as a series of discrete transactions, and
- Whether it is supplied quite casually or within an ongoing relationship between buyer and seller.

With respect to the continuity of supply, a first group of services can be identified which are purchased only when they are needed as a series of discrete transactions. This is typical of low-value, undifferentiated services that may be bought on impulse or with little conscious search activity (taxis, cafés, etc.). It can also be true of specialized, high-value services that are purchased only as required (funeral services are usually bought only when needed).

In contrast, other services can be identified where it is impractical to supply the service on a casual basis. This can occur where production methods make it difficult to supply a service

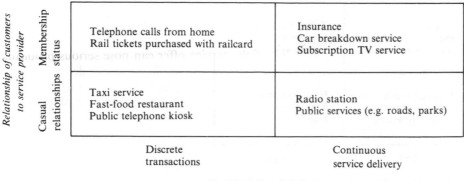

Figure 1.7   The nature of the relationship between producer and consumer

only when it is needed (it is impractical to provide a telephone line to a house only when it is needed—the line itself is therefore supplied continuously) or where the benefits of a service are required continuously (insurance policies).

Continuous service supply is commonly—though not always—associated with a relationship existing between buyer and seller. A long-term relationship with a supplier can be important to customers in a number of situations: where the production/consumption process takes place over a long period of time (a programme of medical treatment); where the benefits will be received only after a long period of time (many financial services); and where the purchaser faces a high level of perceived risk. Supply through an on-going relationship rather than by discrete transactions can also reduce the transaction costs of having to search and order a service afresh on each occasion (an annual maintenance contract on domestic equipment avoids the need to find an engineer on each occasion that a failure occurs).

Sometimes, it is sensible to supply the central element of a service through an on-going relationship but to provide additional service benefits as and when required. In this way, a telephone line is supplied within an on-going relationship, whereas individual calls are provided as and when needed.

Services are classified according to the nature of their supply in Figure 1.7. Service marketers generally try to move customers into the category where service is provided continuously rather than discretely and within an on-going relationship rather than casually. The former can be achieved by offering incentives for the purchase of a continuous stream of service benefit (for example, offering attractively priced annual travel insurance policies rather than selling individual short-term policies as and when required). The latter can be achieved by a number of strategies which are discussed in more detail in Chapter 7. At its simplest, relationships could be developed through a communication programme to regularly inform existing customers of new service developments. It could develop into methods to tie customers to a single service provider by offering a long-term supply contract. In this way a bus company may seek regular custom from individuals by offering season tickets which restrict the consumer's choice to one particular service provider.

1.4.8   The pattern of demand

Services can be classified according to the temporal pattern of demand that they face. Very few services have a constant pattern of demand through time—many show considerable variation, which could be daily (city-centre sandwich bars at lunchtime), weekly (the Friday evening peak in demand for railway travel), seasonal (hotels, stores at Christmas), cyclical (mortgages) or an unpredictable pattern of demand (emergency building repair services which may peak in demand after a heavy storm). The perishability of the service offer can pose serious problems for services suppliers facing a very uneven pattern of demand. Many quite diverse service industries such as electricity supply, hotels and railways have nevertheless recognized common problems and in many cases have responded with quite similar solutions. Some of these are examined in detail in Chapter 7.

1.4.9 People-based versus equipment-based services

Some services involve very labour-intensive production methods. A fortune teller employs a production method which is almost wholly based on human actions. At the other extreme, many services can be delivered with very little human involvement—a pay and display car park involves minimal human input in the form of checking tickets and keeping the car park clean. The management of people-based services can be very different from those based on equipment. While equipment can generally be programmed to perform consistently, personnel need to be carefully recruited, trained and monitored. People-based services can usually allow greater customization of services to meet individual customers' needs. These issues are considered in more detail in Chapter 9.

1.4.10 The significance of the service to the purchaser

Some services are purchased frequently, are of low value, are consumed very rapidly by the recipient and are likely to be purchased on impulse with very little pre-purchase activity. Such services may represent a very small proportion of the purchaser's total expenditure and correspond to the goods marketer's definition of fast-moving consumer goods ('fmcgs'). A casual game on a slot machine would fit into this category. At the other end of the scale, long-lasting services may be purchased infrequently and when they are, the decision-making process takes longer and involves more people. Package holidays fit into this category.

A number of bases for classifying services have now been presented. In practice, services need to be classified by a number of criteria simultaneously so that groups of similar service types can be identified. A number of researchers have sought to use a multidimensional approach to identify clusters of similar services. One example is provided by Solomon and Gould (1991), who researched consumers' perceptions of 16 different personal and household services. A cluster analysis revealed two statistically significant bases for grouping services. The first—called the service locus—was defined along a scale from personal (e.g. doctors' services) to environmental (services performed on a person's possessions rather than on their body). The second—service instigation—referred to the underlying reason for a service being purchased. At one extreme, a service could be purchased for basic maintenance purposes (regular visits to a dentist) while at the other, it is purchased for enhancement (health and fitness clubs).

If the clustering of service types has been carried out in an appropriate manner it could be deduced that all services within that cluster will benefit from a broadly similar approach to marketing strategy. In Figure 1.8 a simple and hypothetical clustering has placed services along three classificatory scales—the amount of customer involvement, the extent to which the pattern of demand is peaked and the degree of variability in production from the norm. Within the sector defined by high customer involvement, a constant pattern of demand and middling variability in production, three service offers can be identified—language tuition in a language

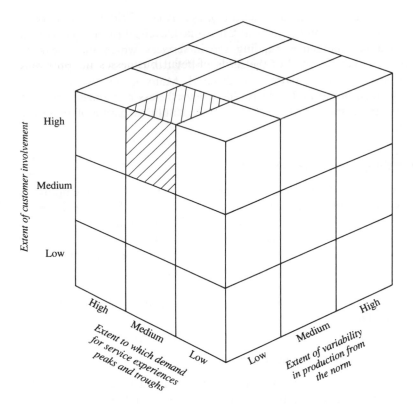

Figure 1.8   A three-dimensional classification of services showing points of convergence

laboratory, eye-testing services and dry-cleaning services. On the basis of this analysis, each of these services could be expected to benefit from broadly similar marketing programmes. These may include stressing the benefit to potential customers of the service's equipment base for reducing variability, developing a strong brand and encouraging word-of-mouth recommendation. In fact, the marketing programmes of three large operators in each field—Linguaphone, Dollond & Aitchison and Sketchley—would appear to converge on these points.

1.5   FURTHER DIFFERENCES BETWEEN GOODS AND SERVICES MARKETING

In addition to the distinguishing features of services described above, a number of environmental differences should be noted which differentiate the marketing of goods from the marketing of services. These comprise differences in the structure of services business units and in their operating environment.

1.5.1   Differences relating to services producers

Although it is impossible to speak of a 'typical' service organization, two key differences when compared to goods manufacturers become apparent. First, a wide range of services are provided on a very small scale where economies of scale are either minimal or non-existent.

Hairdressing, plumbing, legal services, painting and decorating are usually provided by small units employing no more than a handful of people. Even a service activity such as retailing—where the public perception is often of large hypermarkets—is dominated by a very large number of small operators. In the UK, nearly two-thirds of retail businesses in 1989 were single-outlet.

The degree of marketing orientation of small service providers can be questioned, with evidence that, among other things, they may be less likely to undertake marketing research or to have formalized marketing planning processes. The incoming tourism industry is one sector which is dominated by small-scale service providers and was studied by Greenly and Matcham (1986). Out of a sample of 28 members of the British Incoming Tour Operators Association, only 48 per cent of firms claimed ever to have used marketing research in any form, and just under half of these only made limited use of it. Forty-five per cent of the firms modified their service offering without reference to their customers (40 per cent claimed that modifications were made primarily for the internal convenience of the company). The study found that 93 per cent of the sample used a relatively simple cost-plus basis for setting prices, rather than one which took more explicit account of market conditions.

A second feature of services providers is the presence of many public-sector suppliers. While there is usually little rationale for governments supplying manufactured goods, market mechanisms often fail to distribute services effectively. For some essential functions such as roads and rapid-transport systems it is either impractical or undesirable for the private sector to take responsibility for provision, and government organizations assume responsibility for these functions. In the case of many public utilities, the nature of service supply often creates potential monopoly problems which are resolved either by direct government supply or supply through highly regulated private sector organizations.

1.5.2   Differences relating to the marketing environment

It can be argued that the marketing environment of service organizations is subject to much more regulation than the goods sector. The fact that a service is intangible makes it more difficult for a potential customer to examine fully a service before purchase. Service supply involves a greater degree of trust than the supply of goods and, consequently, regulations often seek to ensure that service delivery meets specifications. In the UK, as in most Western countries, highly intangible services such as banking, insurance and holidays are regulated by a combination of voluntary and statutory measures. The Financial Services Act 1986 is an example of legislation that has a profound effect on the range of services offered by financial services companies and the manner in which they are distributed and promoted. In some sectors, customers seek to reduce their perceived risk by selecting only organizations that agree to have their relationship governed by a trade association's code of conduct. In this way, tour operators may find it difficult to distribute their holidays through retail travel agents if they are not a member of the trade association, the Association of British Travel Agents (ABTA). This trade body specifies—among other things—the limits to which a company can amend its service offer (for example, by rescheduling aircraft departure times or changing hotel accommodation).

1.6   THE EMERGENCE OF THE SERVICE ECONOMY

There is little doubt that the service sector is becoming an increasingly important element of most economies. To understand the context in which services are marketed, this section makes an environmental assessment of the role of services within national economies.

1.6.1 The problem of measuring services activity

Before reviewing how important it has become, it is worth noting that measuring the services sector can present as many problems as attempting to define services, for a number of reasons. First, the level of accuracy with which service sector statistics have been recorded is generally less than for the primary and secondary sectors. The system of Standard Industrial Classifications (SICs) for a long while did not disaggregate the service sector in the same level of detail as the other two sectors. Many service sectors do not fall neatly into one of the classifications, making it difficult to obtain an overall picture of that sector. A good illustration of this is provided by the tourism sector and Table 1.1 shows some of the diverse SIC headings under which tourism activity is analysed. Second, the intangible nature of services can make them relatively difficult to measure, especially in the case of overseas trade. Whereas flows of tangible goods through ports can usually be measured quite easily, trade flows associated with services are much more difficult to identify and assess. Furthermore, cutbacks in government collection of statistics have increased the inaccuracy of many series—for example, the trade figures relating to tourism and financial services frequently have to be revised after initial publication. Third, a part of the apparent growth in the service sector may reflect the method by which statistics are collected, rather than indicating an increase in overall service level activity. Output and employment is recorded according to the dominant business of an organization. Within many primary and secondary sector organizations, many people are employed producing service-type activities, such as cleaning, catering, transport and distribution. Where a cook is employed by a manufacturing company, output and employment is attributed to the manufacturing sector. However, a common occurrence during the 1980s was for manufacturing industry to contract out many of these service activities to external suppliers. Where such contracts are performed by contract catering, office cleaning or transport companies, the output becomes attributable to the service sector, making the service sector look larger, even though no additional services have been produced—they have merely been switched from internally to externally produced.

Table 1.1 Standard industrial classifications used for the tourism sector

SIC	Description
6610	Restaurants, cafés, etc.
6620	Public houses and bars
6630	Night clubs and licensed clubs
6650	Hotels
6670	Other tourist or short-stay accommodation
7100	Railways
7210	Urban railways, buses, etc.
7400	Sea transport
7500	Air transport
7700	Travel agents
8150	Credit card companies
8490	Car-hire firms
9690	Tourist offices, etc.
9770	Libraries, museums, etc.
9791	Sport and other recreational services

1.6.2 Key trends in the UK economy

The importance of services to the economy of the UK—and indeed to most developed economies—has been increasing rapidly during the past two decades. Three methods that can be used to assess the changing relative importance of the service sector to the economy are to consider (1) the share of Gross Domestic Product (GDP) for which it accounts; (2) the proportion of the labour force employed in the sector; and (3) the contribution of services to the balance of payments. Most analyses of these indicators divide economic activity into three sectors: the primary sector (i.e. agriculture, mining, etc.); the secondary sector (manufacturing, construction, raw material processing, etc.) and the tertiary sector (services).

In respect of its share of GDP, the tertiary sector saw almost continuous growth during the period 1970–90. With the exception of transport and distribution, where output fell between 1979 and 1981, and public administration, where the same occurred between 1981 and 1986, all subsectors experienced increases in output over the whole period, with banking, finance, insurance, business services, leasing and communications being particularly prominent. In 1990, the tertiary sector accounted for 63 per cent of GDP, up from 53 per cent in 1970. The primary sector held its own during the period, accounting for 4.3 per cent of GDP in 1970 and 5.3 per cent in 1990, largely on account of North Sea oil production. Output in the secondary sector fell during this period from 42 per cent to 32 per cent, reflecting the poor performance of manufacturing industry (CSO, 1991). Given that the secondary sector is a major consumer of the output of the tertiary sector, it seems likely that levels of growth in the service industries during the period would have been higher had manufacturing and construction not suffered the decline highlighted above.

These structural changes are further illustrated by changes in the levels of employment in the three sectors over the same period. The tertiary sector's share of employment grew from 49 per cent to 67 per cent, mirroring changing employment patterns in many other advanced industrial economies. In contrast, employment in the primary sector fell from 3.6 per cent of total employment in 1970 to 2.5 per cent in 1990, largely as a result of the decline of the coal industry and fewer jobs in agriculture. Secondary-sector employment also fell, from 47 per cent in 1970 to only 30 per cent by 1990, with manufacturing suffering the largest number of job losses.

An interesting observation can be made by comparing the share of GDP accounted for by the tertiary sector and its corresponding share of employment. In the UK, the tertiary sector has consistently accounted for a greater share of employment than the proportion of GDP which it contributes. This may give some justification to claims that the services sector as a whole is associated with relatively low earnings.

When the contribution of services to the UK balance of payments is considered, the growing relative importance of the sector can again be seen. During the past two decades it has been usual for the UK to have a deficit in traded goods, made up by a surplus in invisibles, which includes services and dividends, interest and profits remitted from abroad. During the 1980s, while the visible trade balance continued to deteriorate (especially when the oil element is set aside), the net surplus in trade in services was maintained. In 1991, while the UK's visible balance was in deficit by £10 290 million, there was an invisible surplus of £4 871 million.

1.6.3 International comparisons

Although the OECD (1984) reported that the services sector had accounted for most of the worldwide growth in employment since the oil crisis in 1973, there are still significant differences in their impact between countries. There appears to be a high correlation between the level of economic development in an economy (as expressed by its GDP per capita) and the strength of its service sector, although whether a strong service sector leads to economic growth, or is the result of growth, is not clear.

The International Labour Office's *Year Book of Labour Statistics* (ILO, 1991) illustrates the magnitude of these differences in 1990 (or the most recent year for which figures were available at that date). The more developed economies were associated with high percentages of workers employed in the service sector—for example, the United States (75.6 per cent), Canada (75.2 per cent), Australia (74.2 per cent), the United Kingdom (70.6 per cent) and Switzerland (69.0 per cent). Western countries that are considered to be less developed have proportionately fewer people employed in their services sector—for example, Spain (59.7 per cent), Portugal (53.2 per cent), Ireland (53.0 per cent) and Greece (49.9 per cent). The lowest levels of services employment are found in the less-developed countries—for example, Mexico (29.9 per cent), Bangladesh (28.3 per cent) and Ethiopia (9.7 per cent).

1.6.4   The service sector as a vehicle for economic growth

Growth in the service sector can result in economic growth to a nation in three main ways:

1. By offering an exportable activity which results in a net inflow of wealth
2. By reducing the need to buy-in services from overseas that consume domestically produced wealth
3. By combining with other primary and secondary activities, which allows new production possibilities for manufactured goods, increasing exports and reducing imports.

While each of these means of growth is also true of primary and secondary activities, the third category is particularly important in the case of services that are often crucial in facilitating productivity gains in other sectors of the economy. Transport and distribution services have often had the effect of stimulating economic development at local and national levels—for example, following the improvement of rail or road services. The absence of these basic services can have a crippling effect on the development of the primary and manufacturing sectors. One reason for Russian agriculture not having been fully exploited has been the ineffective distribution system available to food producers.

Services can have a multiplier effect on local and national economies in that initial spending with a service producer triggers further expenditure. The first producer spends money buying-in supplies from outside (including labour) and these outside suppliers in turn purchase more inputs. The multiplier effect of this initial expenditure can result in the total increase in household incomes being much greater than the original expenditure. A good example of the multiplier effect at work in Britain is provided by the National Garden Festivals held during the 1980s in Liverpool, Stoke-on-Trent, Glasgow and Gateshead. While these government sponsored events initially created direct employment within the events themselves, demand rippled out to other service sectors, such as hotels and transport. The level of activity generated additional demand for the local manufacturing industry. For example, visitors require food that may be produced locally, the producers of which may in turn require additional building materials to increase production facilities. The multiplier effects of additional service activity will depend on the proportion of the subsequent spending that is kept within the local area. In a study of the regional effects of large firms setting up administrative service centres in an area, Marshall (1985), for example, found that firms frequently bought in many of their supplies from outside the region, or even the country, thus lessening the local benefits of this form of services development.

One approach to understanding the contribution of services to other aspects of economic activity is to analyse input–output tables of production and data on labour and capital inputs. Wood (1987) used these to estimate the effects that productivity improvements in all the direct and indirect supply sectors had on the productivity levels of all other sectors. Thus, some apparently high productivity sectors were shown to be held back by the low productivity of some of their inputs, including service inputs. On the other hand, efficiency improvements in some services such as transport and distribution were shown to have had widespread beneficial effects on the productivity contribution of other sectors.

The service sector should, in principle, be a valuable tool of regional development, for many services can involve a considerable labour-based production element, free from locational constraints imposed by access to raw materials and remote from the point of final demand. Processing work involved in the financial services sector is a good example, where the problem of inseparability of production and consumption has been overcome by using modern means of communication. Government has recognized the social and economic effects of services development in the regions by programmes to transfer many civil service jobs to the Assisted Areas (for example, 3000 jobs within the Property Services Agency were transferred from London to Teesside during the 1980s) and by broadening the scope of regional development grants to put services job creation on a par with manufacturing industry. However, despite the attempts of governments to move operations to Assisted Areas, a number of studies (for example, Allen, 1988) have shown that services development has occurred at a much greater rate in the already highly developed south-east, thus increasing regional imbalances.

During the recession of the early 1980s, the service sector was seen by many as the salvation of the economy. Many politicians were keen to promote the sector as a source of new employment to make up for the diminishing level of employment within the primary and secondary sectors. A common argument during this period was that Britain no longer held a competitive cost advantage in the production of goods and therefore these sectors of the economy should be allowed to decline and resources made available to those services that showed greater competitive advantage. The logic of this argument can be pushed too far, in particular:

1. A large part of the growth in the service sector during the 1980s reflected the buoyancy of the primary and secondary sectors. As manufacturing industry increases its level of activity, the demand for producer services such as accountancy, legal services and business travel rises. The sudden decline of many financial services sectors after 1989 reflected the downturn in manufacturing activity resulting in lower demand for business loans and export credits, etc.
2. The assumption that Britain has a competitive advantage in the production of services needs to be examined closely. In the same way that many sectors of British manufacturing industry lost their competitive advantage to developing nations during the 1960s and 1970s, there is evidence that Britain's once-unquestioned supremacy in certain service sectors is being challenged. Financial services markets, which achieved prominence in London when Britain was the world's most important trading nation, are increasingly following world trade to its new centres such as Tokyo and Frankfurt. High levels of training in some of Britain's competitor nations have allowed those countries to first develop their own indigenous services and then to expand them for export. Banking services that were once a net import of Japan are now exported throughout the world.
3. Over-reliance on the service sector could pose strategic problems for the UK. A diverse economic base allows a national economy to be more resilient to changes in world trading conditions.

REVIEW QUESTIONS

1. To what extent do you consider that the principles of marketing which have been tradition-ally applied to the goods sector are appropriate for the services sector?
2. Outline the reasons why it is useful—from a marketing perspective—to classify services. Identify the most important bases for classification.
3. Briefly summarize the principal marketing implications that flow from the inherent intangibil-ity of service offerings.
4. What is meant by inseparability? Suggest why its existence might pose problems to service organizations and methods by which its impact may be reduced.
5. Explain the reasons why governments are often keen to encourage the service sector within their countries.
6. Identify some of the problems associated with attempts to measure the size of a nation's service sector.

WHAT IS MARKETING?

OBJECTIVES

After reading this chapter, you should be able to understand:

- The importance of marketing as a fundamental business philosophy in competitive operating environments
- The nature of needs, wants and exchanges in market-based distribution systems
- The tools by which marketing management responds to customer needs in the form of the marketing mix, and the appropriateness of these tools to the marketing of services
- The nature of an organization's marketing environment, and frameworks for its analysis
- The nature of internal marketing, network marketing and the importance attached to developing relationships with customers.

2.1 INTRODUCTION

Marketing as a business discipline is becoming all-embracing in Western economies, being adopted by large sections of both the private and the public sectors. There are many definitions of marketing—here are two typical definitions:

Marketing consists of individual organizational activities that facilitate and expedite satisfying exchange relationships in a dynamic environment through the creation, distribution, promotion and pricing of goods, services and ideas.

(Pride and Ferrell, 1991)

Marketing is the management process responsible for identifying, anticipating and satisfying customer requirements profitably.

(Chartered Institute of Marketing)

Most definitions of marketing revolve around the primacy of customers as part of an exchange process. Customer needs are seen as the starting point for all marketing activity, which proceeds to analyse the nature of these needs and to develop products that will satisfy these needs through an exchange process. While customer needs may drive the activities of a marketing-oriented organization, organizational factors constrain the extent to which a company is able to cater for identified consumer needs. Most private sector organizations operate to some kind of profit-related objectives—if an adequate level of profits cannot be earned from a particular group of customers, their needs will not be satisfied. In general, though, the closer an organization comes to meeting customers' needs, the greater its ability to gain a differential advantage over its competitors, thereby allowing it to sell a higher volume and/or at a higher price than its competitors, resulting in it being able to achieve profit objectives within a particular sector where its competitors may have failed.

Within the public sector, where financial objectives are often qualified by non-financial objectives, the desire to meet customer needs must be further constrained by the requirement to conform with these wider social objectives. In this way a public reference library may be set an objective of providing the public with a range of materials that help to develop the knowledge and skills of the population it serves. Therefore the 'quality press' may be the only newspapers purchased, although popular client demand may call for the purchase of tabloids. This apparently centrally planned approach is not incompatible with a marketing philosophy—the library may work within its objectives of developing knowledge and skills by seeking to maximize the number of people reading its quality newspapers. Marketing strategies that might be employed to achieve this could include a promotional campaign, the development of a friendly, welcoming attitude and accessible opening hours.

The purpose of this chapter is to explore some of the key concepts of marketing that are of relevance to services, within both the public and private sectors. Readers who are familiar with marketing concepts can skip rapidly through this chapter and proceed to Chapter 3, which focuses on how these concepts are operationalized in marketing-planning processes. Many items introduced in this chapter are returned to for a more detailed analysis in subsequent chapters.

2.2 THE EMERGENCE OF MARKETING SUPREMACY

As the above example of the public library illustrates, it can sometimes be difficult to define the circumstances in which marketing is considered to be either desirable or feasible. This is particularly true in public sector services, where many previously centrally planned services have sought to become market oriented. Before examining what marketing is in more detail, it would be useful to consider some alternative philosophies by which services have been delivered to the consumer, from both the private and the public sectors. Despite its increasing importance as a business discipline, marketing is neither universal nor has it been with us at all times.

Today, the needs of the consumer assume primary importance in the provision of most services. However, in some circumstances, organizations have been driven more by a need to reduce costs rather than to maximize the benefit of a service to the consumer—companies providing services on this basis are said to be operating in a production-oriented environment. At other times, the business environment has been dominated by the need for aggressive selling of an organization's output—this has been described as a philosophy of sales orientation (see Figure 2.1).

2.2.1 Production orientation

Marketing as a business discipline has much less significance where goods or services are scarce and considerable unsatisfied demand exists. If an organization is operating in a stable environment in which it can sell all that it can produce, why bother spending time and money trying to understand precisely what benefit a customer seeks from buying a product and to anticipate future requirements? Furthermore, if the company has significant monopoly power, it may have little interest in being more efficient in meeting customer requirements. The state monopolies of Eastern Europe are frequently cited as examples of organizations that produced what they imagined consumers might want. Planning for full utilization of capital equipment

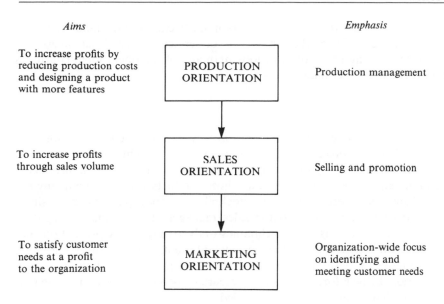

Aims   *Emphasis*

To increase profits by
reducing production costs   PRODUCTION   Production management
and designing a product   ORIENTATION
with more features

To increase profits   SALES
through sales volume   ORIENTATION   Selling and promotion

To satisfy customer   Organization-wide focus
needs at a profit   MARKETING   on identifying and
to the organization   ORIENTATION   meeting customer needs

Figure 2.1   The development of the dominant business environment

was often seen as more important than ensuring that the equipment was used to provide goods and services that people actually needed.

In Britain, it has been argued that production orientation was common until the 1920s, when a general shortage of goods relative to demand for them and a lack of competition resulted in a sellers' market. In the case of many goods markets, the world depression of the 1920s and 1930s had the effect of tilting the balance of supply and demand more in favour of the buyer, resulting in sellers having to address the needs of increasingly selective customers more seriously. Services markets in Britain retained a production orientation longer than most goods markets. This reflected the fact that many key services—post, telecommunications, air, rail, sea and bus travel, electricity, gas and water supply—were dominated by state monopolies which gave consumers very little—if any—choice of supplier. If the consumers did not like the service that they received from their electricity supplier, they could not take their custom to another. Management in these circumstances would have greater freedom to satisfy their own interests rather than those of the consumer and could increase financial returns to their organization more effectively by keeping production costs down rather than applying effort and possibly taking greater risk through developing new services based on consumers' needs.

Large state-owned organizations have frequently been supported by legislation which prevented competition taking place. In the UK, for example, the telephone service was accused of paying insufficient attention to changing consumer needs in—among other things—the standard of installation and maintenance service offered and the lack of choice in telephone handset designs. Before 1980, the Post Office had a monopoly in the provision of telephone handsets, with the result that they were dull and did not do all the things that consumers sought. With the removal of this monopoly, consumers became able to buy or rent handsets that reflected their lifestyle and individual performance requirements.

Production orientation sometimes returns to an otherwise competitive market during periods of shortage. The shortage could be caused by factors such as strikes, bad weather or simply a sudden increase in demand relative to supply. For example, during a public transport strike, private hire car operators realize that there is a temporary massive excess of demand relative to supply and so may be tempted to lower their standards of service to casual customers (for example by allowing longer waiting times and overlooking many of the operational courtesies that would have been provided at other times).

2.2.2 Sales orientation

Faced with an increasingly competitive market, the natural reaction of some organizations has been to shout louder to attract customers to buy its products. No thought had yet gone into examining precisely what benefits a customer sought to obtain from buying a product—product policy was still driven by the desire to produce those products which the company felt it was good at making. However, in order to shift its stockpiles, the focal point of the business moved away from the production manager to the sales manager. The company sought to increase demand by the use of various sales techniques—advertising, sales promotion and personal selling were increasingly used to emphasize product differentiation and branding.

Sales orientation was a move away from a strict product orientation, but it still did not focus on satisfying customer needs. Little effort was made to research customer needs and devise new offerings that were customer-led rather than production-led.

Sales orientation has been evident in a number of areas of the service sector. Supermarkets have often grown by heavy advertising of their competitive price advantage, supported by aggressive sales-promotion techniques within their stores. It was only from the late 1970s that supermarkets in the UK seriously addressed the nature of the needs that customers sought to satisfy in a supermarket, such as the range of goods offered, the availability of car parking, speed of checkouts, quality of after-sales service, etc. Similarly, the UK package holiday industry during much of the 1970s and 1980s was based on a sales mentality—heavy advertising and discounting were used to sell holidays that the companies thought consumers wanted and which were much easier for them to provide. More recently, companies have recognized that selling on the basis of a low price alone is not adequate. They are now responding to identified consumer needs by offering guaranteed standards of hotels, compensation schemes for delayed departures and a better service by representatives at holiday resorts. This is often much more difficult for the company to provide and will cost the customer more, but it represents a shift away from sales orientation to marketing orientation.

If a company had identified consumer needs and provided a product offering which satisfied these needs, then consumers would want to buy the product, rather than the company having to rely on intensive sales techniques. In the words of Peter Drucker (1973):

The aim of marketing is to make selling superfluous. The aim of marketing is to know and understand the customer so well that the product or service fits him and sells itself. Ideally, marketing should result in a customer who is ready to buy. All that should be needed is to make the product or service available . . .

2.2.3 Marketing orientation

Marketing orientation as the dominant business discipline came about as increasingly competitive markets turned to the buyers' favour. It was no longer good enough for a company to simply produce what it was good at, or to sell its products more aggressively than its competitors.

Some of the elements of marketing orientation can be traced far back to ancient Greece, the Phoenicians and the Venetian traders. In modern times, marketing orientation emerged in the relatively affluent countries among products where competition between suppliers had become the greatest. It became an important discipline in the USA from the 1950s and has since become dominant around the world. In a marketing-oriented business environment an organization will only survive in the long term if it ascertains the needs of clearly defined groups in society and produces goods and services that satisfy their requirements. The emphasis is put on the customer wanting to buy rather than the producer needing to sell.

Many people have tried to define just what is meant by marketing orientation. Recent work by Narver and Slater (1990) has sought to define and measure marketing orientation. Their analysis identifies three important components:

- *Customer orientation*, meaning that an organization has a sufficient understanding of its target buyers that allows it to create superior value for them. This comes about through increasing the benefits to the buyer in relation to the buyer's costs or by decreasing the buyer's costs in relation to the buyer's benefits. A customer orientation requires that the organization understands value to the customer not only as it is today but also as it will evolve over time.
- *Competitor orientation*, defined as an organization's understanding of the short-term strengths and weaknesses and long-term capabilities and strategies of current and potential competitors.
- *Interfunctional coordination*, referring to the manner in which an organization uses its resources in creating superior value for target customers. Many individuals within an organization have responsibility for creating value, not just marketing staff, and a marketing orientation requires that the organization draws upon and integrates its human and physical resources effectively and adapts them to meet customers' needs.

It is evident from this analysis that marketing orientation is used to describe both the basic philosophy of an organization and the techniques it uses:

- As a business philosophy, marketing puts the customer at the centre of all the organization's considerations. Basic values such as the requirement to identify the changing needs of existing customers and the necessity to search constantly for new market opportunities are instilled in all members of a truly marketing-oriented organization, covering all aspects of the organization's activities. Thus for a fast-food retailer, the training of serving staff would emphasize those items—such as the standard of dress and speed of service—that research had found to be particularly valued by existing and potential customers. The personnel manager would have a selection policy that sought to recruit staff who fulfilled the needs of customers rather than simply minimizing the wage bill. The accountant would investigate the effects on customers before deciding to save money by cutting stock levels, thereby possibly reducing customer choice. It is not sufficient for an organization merely to appoint a marketing manager or set up a marketing department. Viewed as a philosophy, marketing is an attitude of mind that pervades the whole organization.
- Marketing orientation is associated with a range of techniques. For example, market research is a technique for identifying customer needs and advertising is a technique to communicate the service offer to potential customers. However, these techniques lose much of their value if they are conducted by an organization that has not fully embraced the philosophy of marketing. The techniques of marketing also include pricing, the design of channels of distribution, motivation and control of service personnel and new product development. Application of these techniques to the service sector is described in later chapters.

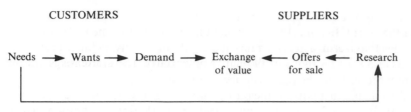

Figure 2.2   Needs, wants, demand and exchange

2.3   KEY MARKETING CONCEPTS

Marketing activity in any organization has no beginning or end. Marketing—oriented organizations continually monitor their operating environments and respond by adapting the organization's output to meet changing needs. Some of the key elements of the marketing process are presented here (these will be returned to in more detail in later chapters).

2.3.1   Needs

The starting point for all marketing activity is the need which consumers seek to satisfy. Needs can be very complex. We no longer live in a society in which the main motivation of individuals is to satisfy the basic requirements for food and drink. Maslow (1943) recognized that once individuals have satisfied these basic physiological needs, they may seek to fulfil social ones—for example, the need to have fruitful interaction with peers. More complex still, Western cultures see increasing numbers of people seeking to fulfil essentially internal needs for self-satisfaction. Services thus satisfy increasingly complex needs. Food is no longer seen as a basic necessity to be purchased and cooked for self-consumption. With growing prosperity, people have sought to satisfy social needs by eating out with friends or family. With further prosperity still, the need simply to eat out with friends becomes satisfied and a higher-order need emerges to experience different types of meals. Thus the great growth in eating out which occurred during the 1970s and 1980s has been followed by a growing diversity of restaurants which cater for peoples' need for variety and curiosity. Hence the emergence in most medium-sized and large towns of Spanish, South American, Malaysian and Creole restaurants.

The term 'need' refers to something that is deep-rooted in an individual's personality. How individuals seek to satisfy needs will be conditioned by the society of which they are a member. Thus the need for team-based competitive physical exercise may express itself in Britain in the form of a wish to play football, whereas in the USA it is more likely to be met by basketball. The latter are referred to as expressed wants rather than needs. Wants are culturally conditioned by the society in which an individual lives. They subsequently become effective demand for a product where there is both a willingness and an ability to pay for the product that will satisfy a particular want (see Figure 2.2).

2.3.2   Exchange

Goods and services can be acquired in a number of ways. One primitive method is by hunting for food or, for some people in some societies, by begging. In socialist economies—and for many services in Western ones—goods and services are acquired as a result of centrally planned decisions. Beds in National Health Service hospitals are acquired by consumers largely on the basis of centrally determined criteria.

For organizations operating in a marketing environment, goods are acquired—and needs satisfied—on the basis of exchange. Exchange implies that one party gives something of value to another. There is a presumption that each party can decide whether or not to enter into an exchange with the other and can choose between a number of alternative potential partners. Exchange usually takes the form of a product being exchanged for money, although the bartering of goods and services is commonly used in some trading systems. In some cases, the value that customers place on a product will be below the cost to the organization of producing it, therefore in the case of profit-motivated organizations no exchange of value would normally take place over the longer term.

There has been debate among marketers as to whether exchange is an essential element of marketing. Thus Oliver (1990) defines marketing as something that 'concerns voluntary, mutually satisfying exchange relationships. Exchange is at the heart of marketing; without exchange, marketing is redundant' while Baker (1979) states that 'marketing is a process of exchange between individuals and/or organisations which is concluded to the mutual benefit and satisfaction of the parties'.

This restricted view that marketing is based on a series of discrete exchanges has been refined, adapted and extended by many writers to try to incorporate the concept of external benefits that are provided by some producers (usually the public sector) but where it is neither possible nor desirable to charge the recipient for the benefits received. Bagozzi (1975) has argued that marketing is concerned with 'generalized' and 'complex' rather than 'restricted' exchanges, stating that the payment of taxes to the government in return for the provision of social services is a form of social marketing exchange, (although it is difficult to identify what sovereignty consumers of government services have in determining the manner or source of their delivery). A number of people, including Alderson (1982), have sought to move the defining characteristic of marketing away from the concept of exchange to one of matching. More recently, marketers have attempted to move analysis of exchange transactions away from a series of discrete exchanges towards on-going relationships (see below).

2.3.3 Value

In an exchange, one party expects to receive something that they value from another party, in return for which they give something that the other party values. For the service supplier, value may be represented by payment received, or in the case of some public services, non-financial factors such as the 'A'-level grades of incoming students to a college. For customers, value is represented by the extent to which a service allows them to satisfy their needs. The basis for customers judging value is how they perceive the benefits adding to their own wellbeing as compared to competitors' offerings. The value they place on an offer may be quite different to that perceived by the service producer. Service organizations succeed by adding value at a faster rate than they add to their own production costs. Value can be added by specifying the service offer in accordance with customers' expectations of its attributes—for example, by providing easy access to the service or the reassurance of after-sales service.

2.3.4 Customers

Customers provide payment to an organization in return for the delivery of goods and services and therefore form a focal point for an organization's marketing activity. The customer is generally understood to be the person who makes the decision to purchase a service, and/or pays for it. In fact, services—like goods—are often bought by one person for consumption by another, therefore the customer and consumer need not be the same person. In these circumstances it can be difficult to identify the focus of an organization's marketing effort.

The nature of the relationship between customers and producers often differs between the manufactured goods and services sectors in two significant ways. First, for many public services, the fact that the service is supplied to individuals may conceal the reality that society as a whole receives the benefit, and may therefore be considered to be the customer. In this way, although a student can be seen as a customer of a school or college, society is an important beneficiary of the skills that the student acquires during the educational process and may also be regarded as an important 'customer'. A second significant difference is that the supplier of a service is often put in a position of trust in relation to their customers, something not so commonly found in the brief transactions that generally occur when goods are sold by a company to its customers. The professional nature of the relationship is often reflected in the names used to describe customers—the term 'patient' implies a caring relationship, 'passenger' an on-going responsibility for the safety of the customer and 'client' that the relationship is governed by a code of ethics (formal or informal).

2.3.5 Markets

The term 'market' has traditionally referred to a place where buyers and sellers gather to exchange goods and services. Economists redefined this to include the abstract concept of the interaction of buyers and sellers. Thus the insurance market refers to the aggregate level of transactions between all buyers and sellers of insurance, regardless of the existence of a formal marketplace. For marketers, 'market' is more commonly confined to describing characteristics of consumers rather than producers. Thus the package holiday market is defined in terms of those people who have the need and want for a holiday and the willingness and ability to pay for it.

Customers within a market vary in the needs that they seek to satisfy. To be fully marketing oriented, a company would have to adapt its offering to meet the needs of each individual. In fact, very few firms can justify aiming to meet the precise needs of each specific individual. Instead, they concentrate on small subgroups within the market, referred to as 'segments'. A segment is a subsection of a market comprising customers who share similar needs, to which a company responds with a product offering designed to meet these specific needs. People or firms within a market can be segmented according to a number of criteria. An example of how a market can be broken down into segments is shown in Figure 2.3, where a three-dimensional criterion for segmenting a market in terms of sex, income level and environmental awareness results in 27 different segments, only some of which are likely be of interest to an organization.

The development of segmentation and target marketing reflects the movement away from production orientation towards marketing orientation. When the supply of services is scarce relative to supply, organizations may seek to minimize production costs by producing one homogeneous product that satisfies the needs of the whole population. Over time, increasing affluence has increased customers' expectations. Affluent customers are no longer satisfied with the basic package holiday, but instead are able to demand one that fulfils an increasingly wide range of needs—not just for relaxation, but for activity, adventure and status associations. Furthermore, society has become much more fragmented—the 'average' consumer has become much more of a myth, as incomes, attitudes and lifestyles have diverged. For the purpose of market analysis, consumers of services can be segmented on the basis of socio-economic, geodemographic and behavioural factors. The bases for identifying market segments are considered in more detail in Chapter 5.

Alongside the greater fragmentation of society, technology is increasingly allowing highly specialized services to be tailored to ever-smaller market segments. Using computerized databases, package holidays need no longer be aimed at broad market segments, but can allow individual customers to put together elements of a holiday that most effectively meets their needs.

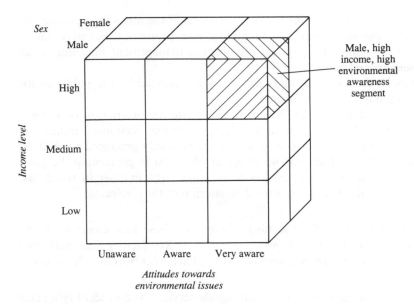

Figure 2.3 Hypothetical segmentation of a population by income, sex and attitudes towards environmental issues

2.4 THE MARKETING MIX

The marketing mix is the set of tools available to the marketing manager to shape the nature of the service offered to consumers. The tools can be used to develop both long-term strategies and short-term tactical programmes. A marketing manager can be seen as mixing a set of ingredients to achieve a desired outcome in much the same way as a cook mixes ingredients for a cake. At the end of the day, two cooks can meet a common objective of baking an edible cake but use very different sets of ingredients to achieve their objective. Marketing managers can similarly be seen as mixers of ingredients that may differ in content but achieve similar objectives. The mixing of ingredients in both cases is a combination of a science—learning by a logical process from what has proved effective in the past—and an art form, in that both the cook and marketing manager frequently encounter situations where there is no direct experience to draw upon and a creative decision must be made.

The concept of the marketing mix was given prominence by Borden (1965) who described the marketing executive as 'a mixer of ingredients . . . who is constantly engaged in fashioning creatively a mix of marketing procedures and policies . . . to produce a profitable enterprise'.

Identifying the ingredients of the marketing mix has caused some debate. Borden initially identified 12 elements of the marketing mix of manufacturers, although these were later simplified by a number of authors. The framework that has endured is that developed by McCarthy (1960), who reduced the marketing mix to four elements—the familiar four Ps of Product, Price, Promotion and Place. Each of these elements would in turn have its own mix of ingredients. Thus the Promotion element involves the mixing of various combinations of advertising, sales promotion, personal selling and public relations.

Borden's initial analysis of marketing mix elements was based on a study of manufacturing industry at a time when the importance of services to the economy was considered to be relatively unimportant. More recently, the four Ps of the marketing mix have been found to be too limited in their application to services:

- The intangible nature of services is overlooked in most analyses of the mix—for example, the product mix is frequently analysed in terms of tangible design properties that may not be relevant to a service process. Similarly, physical distribution management may not be an important element of place mix decisions.
- The price element overlooks the fact that many services are produced by the public sector without a price being charged to the final consumer.
- The promotion mix of the traditional four Ps fails to recognize the promotion of services that takes place at the point of consumption by the production personnel, unlike the situation with most fast-moving consumer goods, which are normally produced away from the consumer and therefore the producer has no direct involvement in promoting the good to the final consumer. For a bank clerk, hairdresser or singer, the manner in which the service is produced is an essential element of the total promotion of the service.

As well as creating ambiguities about the meaning of some of these four elements of the marketing mix, this simple list also fails to recognize a number of key factors that marketing managers in the service sector use to design their service output. Particular problems focus on.

- The problem of defining the concept of quality for intangible services, and of identifying and measuring the mix elements which can be managed in order to create a quality service.
- The importance of people as an element of the service product, as both producers, consumers and co-consumers.
- The oversimplification of the elements of distribution that are of relevance to strategic services distribution decisions.

These weaknesses have resulted in a number of analysts redefining the marketing mix in a manner that is more applicable to the service sector. While many have sought to refine the marketing mix for general application (Kent, 1986; Brookes, 1988; Wind, 1986), the expansions by Booms and Bitner (1981) and Christopher *et al.* (1991) provide useful frameworks for analysis, though they are not empirically proven theories of services marketing. In addition to the four traditional elements of the marketing mix, both frameworks add the additional elements of People and Process. In addition, Booms and Bitner mention Physical Evidence making up a seventh P while the latter adds Customer Service as an additional element.

The principle of the extended marketing mix (as indeed with the traditional marketing mix) is to break down a service offering into a number of component parts and to arrange them into manageable subject areas for making strategic decisions. Decisions on one element of the mix can only be made by reference to other elements in order to give a sustainable product positioning (see Chapter 3). The importance attached to each element of the extended marketing mix will vary between services. In a highly automated service such as vending-machine dispensing, the people element will be a less important element of the mix than a people-intensive business such as a restaurant.

A brief overview of these marketing mix ingredients is given below with more detailed discussion following in the subsequent chapters.

2.4.1 Products

Products are the means by which organizations seek to satisfy consumer needs. A product in this sense is anything that the organization offers to potential customers which may satisfy a need, whether it be tangible or intangible. After initial hesitation, most marketing managers are now happy to class an intangible service as a product. Thus bank accounts, insurance policies and holidays are frequently referred to as products, sometimes to the amusement of non-marketers, as where pop stars or even politicians are referred to as products to be marketed.

Product-mix decisions facing a services marketer can be very different from those dealing with goods. Most fundamentally, pure services can only be defined using process descriptions rather than tangible descriptions of outcomes. Quality becomes a key element defining a service. Other elements of the product mix such as design, reliability, brand image and product range may sound familiar to a goods marketer, but assume different roles, as discussed in Chapter 6. There is also a significant difference with goods in that new service developments cannot be protected by patent.

2.4.2   Pricing

Price-mix decisions are strategic and tactical and concern the average level of prices to be charged, discount structures, terms of payment and the extent to which price discrimination between different groups of customers is to take place. These are very similar to the issues facing a goods marketer. Differences do, however, occur where the intangible nature of a service can mean that price in itself can become a very significant indicator of quality. The personal and non-transferable nature of many services presents additional opportunities for price discrimination within service markets, while the fact that many services are marketed by the public sector at a subsidized or no price can sometimes complicate price setting.

2.4.3   Promotion

The traditional promotion mix includes various methods of communicating the benefits of a service to potential consumers, traditionally broken down into four mix elements—advertising, sales promotion, public relations and personal selling. While the promotion mix for goods may appear similar to the mix for services, the promotion of services often needs to place particular emphasis on increasing the apparent tangibility of a service. Also, in the case of services marketing, production personnel can themselves become an important element of the promotion mix.

2.4.4   Place

Place decisions refer to the ease of access that potential customers have to a service. They can therefore involve physical location decisions (as in deciding where to place a hotel), decisions about which intermediaries to use in making a service accessible to a consumer (whether a tour operator uses travel agents or sells its holidays direct to the customer) and non-locational decisions which are used to make services available (the use of telephone delivery systems). For pure services, decisions about how to physically move a good are of little strategic relevance. However, most services involve movement of goods of some form. These can either be materials necessary to produce a service (such as travel brochures and fast-food packaging material) or the service can have as its whole purpose the movement of goods (road haulage, plant hire).

2.4.5   People

For most services, people are a vital element of the marketing mix. Where production can be separated from consumption—as is the case with most manufactured goods—management can usually take measures to reduce the direct effect of people on the final output as received by customers. Therefore how a car is made is of relatively minor interest to the person who buys it—they are not concerned whether a production worker dresses untidily, uses bad language at work or turns up for work late, so long as there are quality control measures which reject the results of lax behaviour before the car reaches the customer. In service industries, everybody is what Gummesson (1991) calls a 'part-time marketer' in that their actions have a much more direct effect on the output received by customers.

While the importance attached to people management in improving quality within manufacturing companies is increasing—for example, through the development of quality circles—people planning assumes much greater importance within the service sector. This is especially true in those services where staff have a high level of contact with customers. For this reason, it is essential that service organizations clearly specify what is expected from personnel in their interaction with customers. To achieve the specified standard, methods of recruiting, training, motivating and rewarding staff cannot be regarded as purely personnel decisions— they are important marketing-mix decisions.

People planning within the marketing mix also involves developing a pattern of interaction between customers themselves, which can assume great importance where service consumption takes place in public. Thus an important way in which drinkers judge a pub might be the kind of people who frequent it. An empty pub may have no atmosphere while a rowdy one may convey the wrong attitude to important segments. As well as planning the human input to its own production, marketing management must also develop strategies for producing favourable interaction between its customers—for example, by excluding certain groups and developing a physical environment that affects customers' behaviour.

2.4.6   Physical evidence

The intangible nature of a service means that potential customers are unable to judge a service before it is consumed, increasing the riskiness inherent in a purchase decision. An important element of marketing-mix strategy is therefore to reduce this level of risk by offering tangible evidence of the nature of the service. This evidence can take a number of forms. At its simplest, a brochure can describe and contain photographs of important elements of the service product—a holiday brochure gives pictorial evidence of hotels and resorts for this purpose. The appearance of staff can provide evidence about the nature of a service—a tidily dressed ticket clerk for an airline suggests that the airline operation as a whole is run with care and attention. Buildings are frequently used to give evidence of service nature. Towards the end of the nineteenth century, railway companies outbid each other to produce the most elaborate station buildings. For people wishing to travel from London to Scotland, a comparison of the grandeur of the three terminals in London's Euston Road could give some clue about the ability of the railway to provide a substantial service. Today, a clean, bright environment used in a service outlet can help to reassure potential customers at the point where they make a service purchase decision. For this reason, fast-food and photo-processing outlets often use red and yellow colour schemes to convey an image of speedy service.

2.4.7   Process

Pure services are more appropriately defined in terms of their production processes rather than their tangible outcomes. Whereas the process of production is usually of little concern to the consumer of manufactured goods, it is often critical to the consumer of 'high-contact' services who can be seen as a co-producer of the service. Customers of a restaurant are deeply affected by the manner in which staff serve them and the amount of waiting involved during the production process. Issues arise as to the boundary between the producer and consumer in terms of the allocation of production functions—for example, a restaurant may require customers to collect their meals from a counter or to deposit their own used plates and cutlery. With services, a clear distinction cannot be made between marketing and operations management.

2.4.8 Customer service

The meaning of customer service varies from one organization to another. Within the services sector, it can best be described as the total quality of the service as perceived by the customer. As such, responsibility for this element of the marketing mix cannot be isolated within a narrowly defined customer services department but becomes a concern of all production personnel, both those directly employed by the organization and by suppliers. Managing the quality of the service offered to customers becomes closely identified with policy on the related marketing-mix elements of product design and personnel.

The definition of the elements of the marketing mix is not scientific—it is largely intuitive and semantic. In addition to the four traditional Ps, this book recognizes the importance of the fifth 'P' for people and devotes a chapter to this element. The importance of service-production processes is reflected in attention given to the encounter between producer and consumer and a chapter is devoted to analysing service encounters. The importance of quality in customers' perception of a service is reflected in a chapter on the conceptualization and measurement of service quality. The importance of physical evidence is recognized in a number of chapters—for example, it is seen as an important element in the product design and promotional elements.

2.5 THE MARKETING ENVIRONMENT

Marketing orientation requires organizations to monitor their environment and to adjust their offering so that consumer needs are fulfilled, thereby facilitating the organization in meeting its own objectives. Kotler (1991) defines an organization's marketing environment as being 'the actors and forces external to the marketing management function of the firm that impinge on the marketing management's ability to develop and maintain successful transactions with its customers'.

Here, marketing has to look both inwardly within its organization and to the outside world. Within the organization, its structure and politics affect the manner in which it responds to changing consumer needs. An organization which assigns marketing responsibilities to a narrow group of people may in fact create tensions within if that make it less effective at responding to changing consumer needs than one where marketing responsibilities in their widest sense are disseminated widely throughout.

The external environment comprises all of those uncontrollable events outside the organization which impinge on its activities. Some of these events directly affect the firm's activities—these can be described as the immediate external environment. Other events which are beyond the immediate environment nevertheless influence the organization and can be described as the indirect external environment (Figure 2.4).

The immediate external environment includes suppliers and distributors—with some of these the organization deals directly, while others with whom there is currently no direct contact could nevertheless influence the organization's policies. Similarly, an organization's competitors would have a direct effect on its market position and form part of the immediate external environment.

Beyond this environment is a whole set of factors that can indirectly affect the organization's

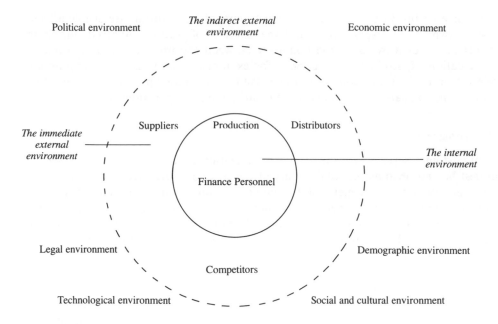

Figure 2.4   The organization's marketing environment

relationship to its markets—the indirect external environment. The organization may have no direct relationships with politicians as it does with suppliers, yet the actions of politicians in passing new legislation may have profound effects on the markets that the organization seeks to serve as well as affecting its production costs. The indirect environmental factors cover a wide range of nebulous phenomena—they represent general forces and pressures rather than institutions to which the organization relates directly.

The indirect external environment has a number of dimensions and can affect a service organization in many ways. Methods of defining these dimensions can vary, and some of the principal elements are described briefly below.

2.5.1   The economic environment

Service development tends to be closely related to the rate of economic growth, with the proportion of Gross Domestic Product (GDP) consumed by services tending to increase as total GDP per head rises. Throughout the economic cycle, service consumption increases during boom periods and declines during recessionary ones. Difficulties in forecasting the level of demand for a service activity is therefore often quite closely linked to those of forecasting future economic prosperity. This is compounded by the problem of understanding the relationship between the economic environment and demand for a service. Most services are positively related to total available income, but some—such as bus services and insolvency practitioners—are negatively related. Furthermore, while aggregate changes in spending power may indicate a likely increase for services in general, the actual distribution of spending power among the population will influence the pattern of demand for a specific service. In addition to measurable economic prosperity, the level of perceived wealth and confidence in the future can be an important determinant of demand for some high-value services.

An analysis of the economic environment will also indicate the level of competitor activity—an oversupply of services in a market sector could result in a downward pressure on prices. Competition for resources could also affect the production costs of an organization which, in turn, will influence its production possibilities and pricing decisions. Rising unemployment may put downward pressure on wage rates, favouring service providers who offer a labour-intensive service.

2.5.2 The political environment

Politicians are instrumental in shaping the general nature of the external environment as well as being responsible for passing legislation which affects specific service providers. At a national level, government is responsible for the nature of the economic environment (through its monetary and fiscal policy), the distribution of income and wealth between the state, the company sector and individuals and also between different groups of individuals. As the legislator, central government passes legislation which can affect market and production possibilities for individual firms, including the competitive framework within which service providers operate.

The political environment includes supra-national organizations which can directly or indirectly affect service providers. The European Community is having an increasing effect on the marketing of services through its directives. These become incorporated into national legislation and can influence the relationship which companies in affected sectors have with their clients. Many other supra-national organizations can have consequences for service providers engaged in international trade—the International Civil Aviation Organization, for example, on international flying agreements.

2.5.3 The social and cultural environment

Attitudes to specific services change throughout time and at any one time between different groups. Those towards healthy living have changed from representing values held by a small fanatical minority to those which now represent mainstream cultural values. Marketers who monitored this emerging value system have been able to respond with a wide range of services, such as fitness clubs and residential health breaks. The dominant cultural attitude towards the role of women has similarly changed, presenting many new challenges for services marketers. The increased acceptability for new mothers to continue working has given rise to a large child- and home-care service sector. New challenges for the marketing of services are posed by the diverse cultural traditions of ethnic minorities, as seen by the growth of travel agencies catering for families wishing to visit relatives or to go on religious pilgrimages.

2.5.4 The demographic environment

Changes in the size and age structure of the population are critical to many service organizations for predicting both the demand for its service output and the availability of service personnel that they will require. Analysis of the demographic environment raises a number of issues which are important to service organizations. Although the total population of most Western countries is stable, their composition is changing. Most countries are experiencing an increase in their proportions of elderly people, and organizations have monitored this growth and responded with the development of residential homes, cruise holidays and financial portfolio management services aimed at meeting the needs of this growing group. At the other end of the age spectrum, the birth rate of most countries is cyclical. The decline in the birth rate in the UK in the late 1970s initially had a profound effect on those services providing for the very young, such as maternity hospitals, kindergartens and babywear retailing. Organizations who monitored the progress of this diminished cohort were prepared for the early 1990s, when there were fewer teenagers requiring high schools or wanting to buy music from record shops. Service providers who had relied on the early 1980s oversupply of teenage labour to provide a cheap input to their service production process would have been prepared for the downturn in numbers by substituting quality of staff for quantity and by mechanizing many jobs previously performed by this group.

Other aspects of the demographic environment which service providers need to monitor include the changing geographical distribution of the population (between different regions of the country and between urban and rural areas), the changing composition of households (especially the service requirements of the growing number of single-person households) and the effects of growing cultural diversity of the population.

BURTON GROUP GROWS OLDER WITH ITS CUSTOMERS

The Burton Group PLC operates many familiar High Street retail clothing stores and has built up a portfolio of brands which can meet the needs of most segments of the population. One of the bases for segmenting its markets is age, with different formats aimed at particular age segments. For the 15–24-year-old segment, Burton Group has developed the Top Shop, Top Man and Radius brands; for the 24–35-year-old segment, Principles, Principles for Men and Burtons, while the 35 + segment is targeted with the Debenhams brand.

The response by the Burton Group to demographic change has been to shift resources to those brands serving segments facing the strongest demographic growth. During the 1970s, when the number of teenagers reached a peak (following the 1960s baby boom), heavy investment was made in expanding the Top Shop and Top Man brands. During the 1980s this bulge of births matured, carrying through with it new attitudes to fashion. In response to both the growing numbers of 24–35-year-olds and their increasing fashion consciousness, the Burton Group channelled resources into its new Principles and Principles for Men brands, both aimed at this group. During most of the 1980s, the Debenhams brand had been the 'cash cow' of the Burton

Group—a relatively static business which had ceased to grow, producing steady but not spectacular profits. Its product offering was geared mainly to the older segments of the population, which had not shown the growth in spending power of younger groups. To bring more business back into the stores, a lot of space within Debenhams was turned into concessions for other brands within the Burton Group—this had the effect of attracting many of the younger segments into the stores.

By the end of the 1980s, however, the teenage market had gone into numerical decline, whereas the number of people aged over 50 was increasing not only numerically but even more so in terms of their spending power. The Burton Group responded to this in a number of ways. The Debenhams chain which had been static during the 1980s received new investment with a series of new store openings. The brand emphasized older age groups' values of quality and durability—as opposed to pure fashionability—in its product offering. The space allocated within Debenhams to the younger Top Shop and Top Man has been reduced. Meanwhile, the group's Dorothy Perkins brand, which had previously targeted 18–40-year-old women, was refocused to meet the needs of the more discerning 30–40-year-old woman.

WHAT IS MARKETING? 39

2.5.5 The technological environment

To the service marketer, technological developments must be monitored for their effects in four related areas:

- First, technological development allows new services to be offered to consumers—telephone chatlines, karaoke bars and fax bureaux, for example.
- Second, new technology can allow existing services to be produced more cheaply, thereby lowering their price and widening their markets. In this way, more efficient aircraft have allowed new markets for air travel to develop.
- Third, technological development allows for new methods of distributing services. Bank ATM machines allow many banking services to be made available at times and places that were previously not economically possible, while modern technology-based control systems allow home-shopping services to be more widely used than hitherto.
- Fourth, new opportunities for service providers to communicate with their target customers have emerged. Many financial services organizations have used information technology to develop databases to target potential customers and to maintain a dialogue with established customers.

2.6 DISTINCTIVE CHARACTERISTICS OF PUBLIC SECTOR MARKETING

Marketing orientation first achieved importance in industries which produced largely undifferentiated goods. With growing competition in their markets, survival meant researching the needs of specific segments of their markets and developing products to meet those segments' needs. The soap powder and cigarette markets were early adopters of marketing orientation for this reason. Over time, more and more markets have become competitive and this has increasingly applied also to much of the public sector. Many non-statutory public services have faced competition for some time—some nationalized industries in particular have faced increasing levels of competition from the private sector. This, combined with the requirement for greater accountability, has encouraged the adoption of marketing orientation by many public services.

Many public sector services such as museums and leisure services are increasingly being given clearly defined business objectives which makes it much more difficult for them to continue doing what they like doing rather than what the public they serve wants. Marketing orientation has been most rapidly adopted by those public sector services which provide marketable goods and services, such as swimming pools and municipal bus services. It is more difficult to adopt marketing orientation where the public sector is a monopoly provider of an essential public service. In the provision of hospitals, the government is moving away from the traditional basis of centralized resource allocation to a quasi-market-based system where funding—in principle—follows patients. Those hospitals that are popular with patients and provide their service at a competitive cost to fund-holding service purchasing authorities will grow, while those that do not will gradually lose resources. Only time will tell if government policies will shift the health service away from its historical acceptance of production orientation.

In other public services, it may be even more difficult to introduce a marketing discipline. The core of the work carried out by the police force, fire brigades and the armed services cannot be easily subjected to the test of market forces. It is difficult for consumers to exercise any choice over who polices their towns and is equally difficult in practice for local authorities to subcontract provision via a competitive tender.

The previous discussion indicates that it is difficult to generalize about public sector services as though they comprise a homogeneous range of activities sharing similar marketing needs. There are in fact many activities, from the pure public service to the pure private one, and the marketing needs of 'pure' public services can differ quite markedly from those of the private sector. Some of the more important differences are summarized below:

1. Traditional definitions of marketing are based on an assumption that a market exists in which buyers and sellers are free to choose with whom they wish to do business. In the public sector, choice is often neither available nor practical. Consumers of social services cannot normally choose to receive their services from a provider other than that which has been designated. Similarly, many public sector service providers are constrained in the choice of clients which they are able to target. While government policy has aimed to create markets to replace central planning, there are limits to the extent to which this can be achieved in practice.
2. The aim of most private sector organizations is to earn profits for their owners. In contrast to these quantifiable objectives, many public sector services operate with relatively diverse and unquantified objectives. For example, a museum may have scholarly objectives in addition to relatively quantifiable ones such as maximizing revenue or the number of visitors.
3. The private sector is usually able to monitor the results of its marketing activity as the benefits are usually internal to the organization. In contrast, many of the aims which public sector organizations seek to achieve are external and a Profit and Loss statement or Balance Sheet cannot be produced in the way which is possible with a private sector organization operating to narrow internal financial goals.
4. The degree of discretion given to a public sector marketing manager is usually less than that given to a counterpart in the private sector. It could be argued that statutorily determined standards affect public sector organizations to a greater extent than the private sector. For example, the marketing of educational facilities is constrained by the need to adhere to the national curriculum. Even where a local authority has a significant area of discretion, the checks and balances imposed on many public sector marketing managers reflect the fact that local authorities are accountable to a wider constituency of interests than the typical private sector organization.
5. Many of the marketing-mix elements which private sector organizations can tailor to meet the needs of specific groups of users are often not open to the public sector marketer. For non-traded public services, price—if it is used at all—is a reflection of centrally determined social values rather than the value placed on a service by the consumer.
6. It can be difficult in marketing non-traded public services to identify the customer. It could be argued that, unlike most private sector services, the recipient is very often not the customer. In the case of state education, the customer could be viewed as the child undertaking the education, the parents of the children, or society as a whole which is investing in a trained workforce of tomorrow.

VICTORIA AND ALBERT MUSEUM DISPLAYS NEW MARKETING ORIENTATION

Museums in Britain have traditionally been seen as guardians of culture and the role of the curator as one who preserves the history of a culture for future generations. Managing a museum has been viewed as a long-term mission with educational objectives, and the idea of basing exhibitions on short-term popularity with visitors has often been met with resistance from curators.

The days of dull exhibits being displayed in dusty glass cases is rapidly disappearing as this sector of the public services takes on board a much greater marketing orientation. The move towards marketing orientation has been brought about by changes in the museums' environment. Visitors' expectations of a museum have changed with the emergence of a wide range of private sector theme museums offering elaborate displays. The relatively high prices charged by museums such as the Jorvik Viking Centre in York indicated that a significant segment of the population was prepared to pay for a museum offering a higher standard of presentation. At the same time, the political environment was changing, with the government trying to move as many public services as possible towards a business-like orientation.

Against this background, the Victoria and Albert Museum in London appointed its first Marketing Manager in 1988. Marketing principles were used to achieve the museum's aim of doubling the number of visitors from 500 000 in 1990 to 1 million in 1995

and then on to 5 million by 2000. A marketing plan was developed after undertaking considerable market research. The strategic plan targeted specific groups by creating highly visible, highly segmented events which would attract new audiences as well as building repeat audiences. One result of this strategy was the creation of the Tsui Gallery of Chinese Art. Market research carried out by NOP into visitor expectations had revealed that visitors were interested in thematic displays rather than the traditional chronological shows.

Carrying marketing practices further, the exhibition earned sponsorship of £1.25 million from Hong Kong businessman T. T. Sui and was supported by a £30 000 poster campaign and the distribution of leaflets in Chinese restaurants throughout London. By adopting these marketing techniques, the Victoria and Albert succeeded in attracting a segment of the population that may not otherwise have visited the museum, as well as generating additional revenue which will contribute towards the long-term cost of maintaining existing collections and acquiring new ones of national importance.

2.7 TOWARDS SOCIETAL MARKETING?

The idea that the overriding purpose of marketing is to satisfy individuals' needs profitably is being challenged. Many have argued that when a consumer buys a good, he or she is today inclined to think of the benefit it will bring not just to him or her directly but also to society more widely. Societal considerations can be manifested in two important ways—in the evaluation of an individual product's acceptability to society at large and in terms of the overall societal credentials of the supplier. Initial interest in societal marketing concepts has focused on the manufactured goods sector, with environmentalism emerging as a major factor affecting consumer purchases during the 1980s. Much of the promotion of environmentally friendly aerosols, babies' nappies and packaging may be dismissed by many as excessively hyped and showing a concern by their manufacturers not so much for the environment but for a unique positioning strategy that will increase product awareness. However, a significant segment of the market for many products has expressed a need to buy products that benefit people other than themselves. Similarly, many consumers have been selective in from whom they make their purchases. They often buy not from the organization best able to satisfy their own narrowly defined personal needs but from one which does more for society in general—for example, by supporting environmental or child-welfare charities, or by refusing to purchase supplies from countries with oppressive governments. There have been a number of well-documented cases of goods manufacturers who have sold socially harmful goods and faced boycotts from consumer groups. The Nestlé Company's exploitation of the market for dried milk products in underdeveloped countries, for example, saw many Western consumers boycotting its products on principle.

As with the development of a general marketing orientation, societal marketing ideas first achieved prominence in the goods sector but have since found application within the services sector. Because of their intangible nature, social costs and benefits of services can be less easy to identify than for goods. Nevertheless, there is evidence that some segments of the population are widening their evaluatory criteria to include the benefits they bring to society (or the social cost they avoid). Within the financial services sector, there is now a wide range of fund-management services available to investors who are concerned about the ethics of their investments. Within the travel and tourism sector, it is now recognized that intensive tourism development can create significant environmental problems—for example, the threat to the breeding habits of the loggerhead turtle on the Greek island of Zakynthos, which has resulted from the intensive development of beaches for recreational purposes. Some customers of package holidays—admittedly a small niche group at the moment—choose their package holiday destinations on the basis of tourism's environmental impact at a resort and their tour operators for their policies towards environmentally benign development of resorts.

It is argued in later chapters that the promotion of service organizations' corporate brands is generally more important than that of specific product brands. For this reason, many service organizations are keen to link themselves to good social causes. The Tesco supermarket group's support for unleaded petrol and recycling schemes helped to give it a distinctive positioning as an environmentally friendly store during the late 1980s. The opposite—linking a corporate brand to a bad cause—can have long-term harmful effects on an organization—for example, the association of Barclays Bank with an oppressive government in South Africa during the 1970s.

Some marketers—for example, Anderson (1982)—argue that marketing itself cannot claim to be a discipline if it is unwilling to investigate systematically issues of social welfare impacts and the impacts of market-based distribution systems. Others such as Arbratt and Sacks (1988) point out that there is not necessarily any incompatibility between traditional marketing objectives and societal objectives, as the societal marketing concept does not involve a company in foregoing its long-term profitability and survival objectives. Critics of the societal marketing concept—for example Arndt (1977)—argue that most external benefits provided under the guise of societal marketing are in fact rapidly internalized by their provider. Thus litter bins sponsored by a fast-food restaurant, the provision of recycling points by supermarkets and donations to animal charities are simply new ways of gaining awareness with the public using values that are currently fashionable.

2.8 FURTHER REFINEMENTS IN MARKETING THOUGHT

This chapter opened with some standard definitions of marketing, but it is useful to record here a number of developments of the marketing approach that are of particular interest in the marketing of services. These concern the way in which an organization markets itself to its staff, how sections within an organization interact with each other and the process of turning a series of discrete relationships with customers into a long-term relationship.

2.8.1 Internal marketing

Marketing has traditionally focused on the external customers of an organization. However, it is increasingly being recognized—especially within the service sector—that many of the marketing processes applied to external relationships are of equal value to internal relationships. Much effort is often placed on selling the values of an organization to its employees to ensure that they share an understanding of its purpose and the service position which it seeks to adopt with regard to its external customers. Communication techniques that are commonly applied to external customers are turned inwardly—for example, through internal staff newsletters, and educational programmes. Internal and external marketing programmes frequently overlap, as where a television advertising campaign has a secondary aim of reaffirming confidence in an organization held by its employees. The subject of internal marketing is explored in more detail in Chapter 9.

2.8.2 Network marketing

Increasing attention is being paid to the idea of treating an organization as a series of producers and consumers of services who market their output to each other within the organizational structure. Many organizations have structured themselves into matrix-type structures where one group takes responsibility for managing productive capacity while another manages relationships with the organization's customers. There is widespread evidence, recorded by Chandler (1962) and Rumelt (1974), that the adoption of the 'M' form and matrix structures within large organizations causes many internal transactions to become market mediated rather than planned. In this way, an in-house printing service within a large organization may find itself subjected to marketing disciplines when it has to compete with outside printers—either on a job-by-job basis or as part of a periodic review—for the printing work required by other departments.

The development of internal marketing networks has been particularly important within the public sector. Many public services distributed to consumers by centrally planned methods may nevertheless be market mediated at the point of production. The requirements for compulsory competitive tendering of many local authority services such as refuse collection and grounds maintenance has added to this effect. A number of authors—for example, Brooke (1985) and Hood (1991)—recognize that local authorities are becoming enabling bodies which may not meet their clients' needs directly but provide resources and leadership through a network of suppliers.

2.8.3 Relationship marketing

The importance of customer relationships is emerging as an important requirement for effective services marketing. While some services can adequately be delivered by means of a series of discrete transactions, others are more effectively provided at the opposite end of what Gronroos (1991) describes as a Marketing Strategy Continuum by means of a relationship marketing strategy. Some have argued that developing relationships has become the key focal point for marketing attention, replacing earlier preoccupation with service, and before that, with product development (Christopher et al., 1991).

It has been pointed out by many, including Berry (1983) and Jackson (1985), that the cost of establishing contact with a potential customer and making the first sale is often so great that the return on the initial sale is minimal, if not negative. For many service industries, it is only when a relationship becomes established that the customer becomes profitable to the seller.

Exchanges should not be seen in isolation as a series of discrete events but should take place in order to establish and extend a relationship. Houston and Gassenheimer (1987) argue that if attention is limited to the study of single, isolated exchanges, the heart of marketing is ignored, while Levy and Zaltman (1975, page 27) define marketing as a system where people or groups are interrelated, engaged in reaching a shared goal and have 'patterned relationships with one another'.

In establishing and maintaining customer relations, the seller gives what Gronroos (1989) describes as a set of promises. These are connected with, among other things, the nature of a service, financial solutions or the transfer of information. On the other hand, the buyer gives another set of promises concerning his or her commitment to the relationship. In many situations, there are many parties involved in a relationship. The buyer and seller may act in a network consisting of suppliers, distributors, other customers and customers' customers. Gronroos argues that for services marketing, the promise concept is as important as the exchange concept.

A number of strategies are used by service providers to develop relationships with their customers. At a relatively simple level, incentives for frequent users can help to develop short- to medium-term loyalty. In this way, many airlines reward frequent business passengers with free or reduced-price leisure tickets. At its more extensive, a relationship can develop to the point where the customer assigns considerable responsibility to the service provider for identifying the customer's needs and providing solutions. In this way, many manufacturing companies leave to specialist road-haulage companies the task of arranging delivery schedules which are most convenient for its customers, relying on the knowledge gained during previous dealings.

In some services, the relationship between customer and supplier is constrained by ethical considerations. As an example, solicitors and accountants may be able and willing to supply services that their customers request and are able to pay for, but are constrained from entering into a transaction because their professional code of conduct prohibits it. Sometimes the relationship involves a fundamental degree of trust which overrides marketing considerations. A doctor, for example, enters into relationships with patients who may have little knowledge about the nature of their problems and may not have the ability to query any diagnosis that the doctor makes. Where the precise nature of a complaint is unknown, an operation may be undertaken without prior specification of the work to be carried out. If the patient is anaesthetized, he or she is unable to exercise any degree of control over the relationship. In circumstances such as these, marketing promises must co-exist with ethical codes of practice.

An important element in the development of relationship marketing strategies lies in a company's dealings with its intermediaries. Again, the focus of attention moves away from seeing each transaction between service principal and intermediary as a discrete activity. Instead, the two seek to work to common goals through shared problem solving. Modern database technology offers many examples of how service principals have sought to add value to the total service received by the customer. The installation of an airline's software in a travel agency, for example, can help the latter to deliver a faster and more reliable service to the airline's customers than might have been the case if the agency had been left to solve processing problems by itself.

While service companies seek to develop closer relationships with their clients, this has to be seen in the context of many consumers' growing confidence to venture outside a relationship. This is illustrated in the growing tendency for private customers to change their bank accounts whenever it seems financially attractive to do so, rather than viewing a bank as an institution that can be relied upon to deliver a wide range of needs over a long period of time.

The methods used to manage relationships between producer and consumer are examined in more detail in Chapter 7.

REVIEW QUESTIONS

1. Of what use is the concept of a marketing mix for the development of marketing strategies for services?
2. Why is it important for service organizations to segment their markets?
3. Analyse the nature of the needs that may be satisfied by a household mortgage.
4. Consider what benefits have resulted to users as a result of the progressive liberalization of telephone services in the UK. Using examples, illustrate how British Telecom has adapted to its new marketing environment.
5. To what extent do you think that it is valid to talk about the societal marketing concept within the services sector?
6. What problems may be associated with an over-enthusiastic adoption of marketing within the public services sector?

THREE

STRATEGIC MARKETING PLANNING

OBJECTIVES

After reading this chapter, you should be able to understand:

- The role of marketing planning as an on-going process and the reasons for its increasing importance to service organizations
- The relationship between marketing planning and corporate planning
- Methods used to analyse an organization's current market position, its strengths and weaknesses and the opportunities and threats it faces
- The importance of defining an organization's mission and objectives
- Methods of identifying, evaluating and selecting strategic alternatives

3.1 INTRODUCTION

For market-oriented service organizations, strategic marketing planning is an on-going process. Organizations which confine their planning activity to a short period surrounding the production of the annual marketing plan cannot be described as genuinely market oriented. A number of crucial elements within the strategic marketing planning process can be identified, although the extent to which these are carried out within a formally defined marketing department— rather than at corporate level—will vary from one organization to another. Five key functions of marketing planning within this on-going process are:

1. *Analysing the current market position of the organization.* (*'Where are we now?'*) In asking where the organization is at the present time, a foundation is laid on which future decisions can be based. Such issues as the organization's current market share, the size and nature of its customer base, customer perceptions of the organization's output and its internal strengths and weaknesses in terms of production, personnel and financial resources need to be addressed in both a quantitative and a qualitative manner.
2. *Setting objectives for the organization and its marketing effort.* (*'Where do we want to be?'*) Management is about using the resources of an organization to achieve some form of objectives, which can range from basic survival through to quantified financial objectives or qualitative level of service objectives. Without clearly specified objectives, marketing management can drift aimlessly.
3. *Identifying and evaluating strategic alternatives.* (*'How can we get there?'*) The same ultimate objectives can usually be met by pursuing a number of alternative plans of action. Identifying

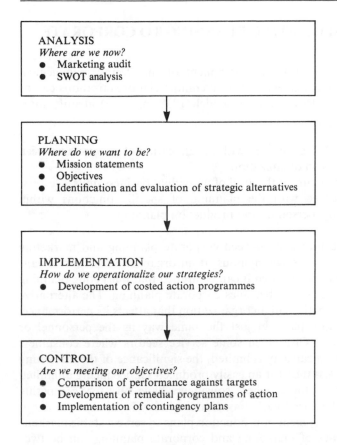

Figure 3.1 The analysis, planning, implementation and control process

the strategic alternatives open to an organization relies on interpreting data and evaluating a number of possible future scenarios. Within this evaluation, factors such as the likelihood of success, the level of downside risk and the amount of resources required to implement a strategy need to be taken into consideration.

4. *Implementing the chosen strategy. ('What will we do?')* Having chosen a strategic route by which to achieve objectives, this must be translated into an operational programme, specifying—among other things—detailed promotional and pricing plans which operationalize the promotional and pricing strategies.

5. *Monitoring and controlling ('Did we get there?')* Marketing plans are of little value if they are to be implemented only half-heartedly. An on-going part of the marketing process is therefore to monitor the implementation of the plan and to seek explanation of any deviation from plan and—where appropriate—take corrective action.

The elements of the strategic marketing management process can be summarized as analysing, planning, implementing and controlling and are shown diagramatically in Figure 3.1. This chapter concentrates attention on the planning element of this process. Although reference is made to the other elements of the process, analysis is considered more fully in Chapter 5 and implementation and control in Chapter 4.

3.2   THE CONTRIBUTION OF MARKETING PLANNING TO CORPORATE PLANNING

The process of marketing management is just one component of the overall management process within an organization. Strategic management within commercial organizations can be seen as operating at a number of levels. Hoffer and Schendel (1978, page 27) identify three distinct levels:

- Corporate strategic management which is concerned with the allocation of resources between the various business units that make up an organization
- Business strategic management which occurs at the level of individual business units
- Functional strategy which is concerned with the planning of specific functions within organizations—for example, marketing, personnel and production planning.

There can be argument about the relationship between corporate planning and marketing planning. At one extreme, the two are seen as synonymous. If an organization stands or falls primarily on its ability to satisfy customer needs, then it can be argued that marketing planning is so central to the organization's activities that it becomes corporate planning. The alternative view is that marketing is just one of the functions of an organization that affects its performance. Marketing takes its goals from corporate plans in just the same way as the personnel or production functions of the organization. Clearly, in some service sectors where consumers have relatively little choice and production capacity is limited, the significance of the marketing plan to the corporate plan is somewhat less than for an easily produced service facing unlimited competition. In the case of many public utilities where consumers have very few competing alternative services available to them, the term 'marketing planning' may be used in name but given much less significance than the development of production plans to serve a stable market.

The relationship between the processes of marketing and corporate planning can be two-way, again reflecting the importance of marketing to the total planning process. Marketing information is fed into the corporate planning process for analysis and formulation of the corporate plan in a process sometimes referred to as 'bottom-up planning'. The corporate plan is developed and functional objectives specified for marketing in a 'top-down' process.

3.2.1   Corporate strategic planning

The basic idea of corporate strategic planning is to provide a framework within which a whole range of more detailed strategic plans can be developed. Corporate planning embraces other elements of the planning process in a horizontal and vertical dimension:

- In the horizontal dimension, a corporate strategic plan brings together the plans of the specialized functions that are necessary to make the organization work. Marketing is just one function of an organization which generates its own planning process—other functional plans found in most organizations are financial, personnel and production. The components of these functional plans must recognize interdependencies if they are to be effective. For example, a bank's marketing strategic plan which anticipates a 50 per cent growth in sales of mortgages over a five-year planning period should be reflected in a strategic production plan that allows for the necessary processing capacity to be developed and a financial plan that identifies strategies for raising the required level of finance over the same time period.
- In the vertical dimension, the corporate planning process provides the framework for strategic decisions to be made at different levels of the corporate hierarchy. Objectives can be

specified in progressively more detail, from the global objectives of the corporate plan to the greater detail required to operationalize them at the level of individual operational units (or Strategic Business Units) and—in turn—for individual products.

The precise nature of the corporate planning process varies between organizations—it has been described by Henry (1971) as an essentially *ad hoc* process, pragmatically adapted by a combination of logical and irrational processes to meet the changing needs of an organization. Some organizations put a lot of detail into a corporate plan which the managers of each strategic business unit are expected to follow closely. Others may view the corporate plan as no more than a general statement of aims which strategic business unit managers achieve in a manner they consider most appropriate. A comparison of two of the major UK clearing banks—National Westminster and the TSB—shows the former taking a much more centralized attitude towards corporate planning than the latter, which during the late 1980s left much more detail to individual branch managers. Similarly, the distinction between corporate planning and marketing planning can be very imprecise. Essentially, it does not matter who undertakes marketing planning, so long as it gets done.

3.3   THE RATIONALE FOR STRATEGIC PLANNING

Strategic marketing planning is the process of ensuring a long-term good fit between the requirements of an organization's environment and the capabilities which it possesses. The process has been defined by Kotler (1991) as:

the managerial process of developing and maintaining a viable fit between an organization's objectives and resources, and its changing market opportunities. The aim of strategic planning is to shape and re-shape the company's business and products so that they combine to produce satisfactory products and growth.

The idea that organizations should need to plan strategically over the medium to long term was often not recognized in the comparatively stable markets which many service industries faced before the 1970s. Banks, for example, could survive and prosper on the basis of short-term operational planning—in Britain until the 1980s, change in banks' marketing environments was very gradual. During the 1980s the effects of deregulation of financial markets and the quickening pace of technological change forced banks to pay much more attention to the direction in which they sought to move their business. Faced with competition on a large number of fronts, they had to make choices about which areas they would use their limited financial and managerial effort to attack and which would be allowed to fade away.

The importance of strategic planning varies between organizations. In general, as the size of an organization increases, so too does the scale of risks—strategic planning can be seen as an attempt to manage the level of risk facing an organization. On the other hand, many smaller service businesses often develop strategic marketing plans unconsciously without any explicit statement of direction or formally written plan—they may specify a tactical programme for the forthcoming year, but leave longer-term strategy unstated. Even within small service businesses which appear to manage successfully by 'muddling through' without a formal strategic planning process, its introduction can focus an entrepreneur's attention on long- rather than short-term aims. Entrepreneurism and strategic planning need not be mutually exclusive processes. An alternative to the accepted principles of disciplined strategic planning is the concept of 'freewheeling opportunism' whereby opportunities are exploited as they arise and judged on their individual merits within a loosely defined overall corporate strategy.

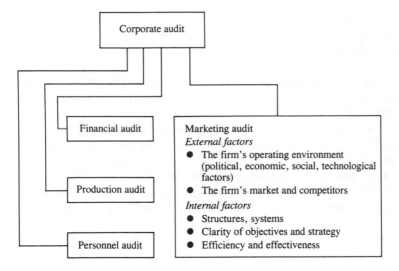

Figure 3.2   The corporate audit

Giving strategic direction to an organization involves more than analysing the needs of consumers and gearing its resources to earn good short-term profits from meeting these needs. For commercial service organizations, maintaining a balanced portfolio of activities can be just as important as earning adequate short-term profits. In this respect, a bank may be meeting a proven need by lending money to fund property purchase and earning acceptable returns from it. However, a strategic approach to portfolio management may lead it to diversify into some other activity with a counterbalancing level of cash flow and risk, turning away business that may seem attractive in the short term.

3.4   THE MARKETING PLANNING PROCESS—POSITION ANALYSIS

An organization that can clearly identify its current position and capabilities should be in a good position to begin the process of analysing future strategic alternatives. Although the more detailed subject of market analysis is considered in Chapter 5, the aim here is to identify the basic processes which allow a sound foundation for strategic planning.

3.4.1   The marketing audit

Audits have been used for some time to assess the efficiency and effectiveness of a number of functions of organizations. The financial audit is probably the most widely used, and in its widest sense is employed to assess the true level of financial resources that an organization has at its disposal. Personnel and production audits are similarly used to establish the personnel and production strengths and weaknesses of an organization, respectively, and the nature of the environments in which these functions operate. Together, these contribute towards the corporate audit—an assessment of the overall strengths and weaknesses which an organization possesses relative to its environment. The corporate audit is represented diagrammatically in Figure 3.2.

A marketing audit is a relatively new concept and although many of its elements overlap with those of the more traditional functional audits, it contributes towards the corporate audit by addressing three major issues:

- The nature of the environmental threats and opportunities facing the organization
- The strengths and weaknesses of the organization in terms of its ability to cope with threats and opportunities presented by its environment.
- The organization's current market position

The first of these essentially addresses environmental or market variables over which marketing management has little or no direct control. The second is concerned with the internal capabilities of marketing management in terms of its structures, resources and procedures. The third element is a reflection of the position that management has established in its marketing environment.

The importance of an audit has been emphasized by McDonald (1984, page 14), who defines an audit as:

... a systematical, critical and unbiased review and appraisal of the environment and of the company's operations. A marketing audit is part of the larger management audit and is concerned with the marketing environment and marketing operations.

To be effective, a marketing audit needs to be comprehensive, systematic, independent and periodic. A comprehensive audit implies that it covers all the major elements of an organization's activities, including those that are apparently performing well, rather than concentrating solely on problem areas. A systematic audit implies that the audit has a coherent structure and is followed by the development and implementation of plans that are based on the outcome of the audit. The greater the independence of a person undertaking an audit, the more useful it is likely to be through objectivity, which may be inhibited where vested interests are at stake.

The frequency with which a marketing audit is undertaken will be affected by a number of factors, the most important of which are the nature of the business, the speed of environmental change, the cyclical nature of the market in which it operates and the cost of undertaking an audit. At one extreme, Baker (1985, page 192) argues that marketing audits should be conducted on a continuous but selective basis, while at the other, Bureau (1981) has suggested that if the process is conducted more frequently than once every five years, the process itself will demoralize marketing personnel.

3.4.2 SWOT analysis

A framework widely used in marketing audits is a grid that plots internal strengths and weaknesses in one half and external opportunities and threats in the other. The terms 'opportunities' and 'threats' should not be viewed as 'absolutes', for as Johnson and Scholes (1988, page 77) point out, what might appear at first sight to be an opportunity may not be so when examined against an organization's resources and the feasibility of implementing a strategy.

A SWOT analysis summarizes the main environmental issues in the form of opportunities and threats (O&T) facing an organization. With this technique, these are specifically listed alongside the strengths and weaknesses (S&W). The latter are internal to the organization and the technique is used to put realism into the opportunities and threats. In this way, the environment may be assessed as giving rise to a number of possible opportunities, but if the organization is not capable of exploiting these because of internal weaknesses then they should perhaps be left alone. Kotler (1991) suggests that these strengths and weaknesses be grouped under marketing, financial, manufacturing, and organizational factors. The marketing audit discussed earlier in this chapter is one systematic method of assessing the strengths and weaknesses of the company.

STRENGTHS Strong financial position Good reputation with existing customers Has aircraft which can service the market	WEAKNESSES Has no allocated take-off or landing 'slots' at main airport Poor network of ticket agents Aircraft are old and expensive to operate
OPPORTUNITIES Market for business and leisure travel is growing Deregulation of air licensing allows new opportunities Costs of operating aircraft are falling	THREATS Channel Tunnel may capture a large share of market Deregulation will result in new competitors appearing Growth in air travel will lead to more congestion

Figure 3.3 SWOT analysis for a hypothetical airline considering entry to the scheduled London–Paris air-travel market

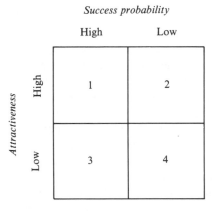

1. Attractive opportunity which fits well with company's capabilities.

2. Attractive opportunity but low probability of success, poor fit with company's capabilities.

3. High probability of success if company takes this opportunity, but not an attractive market.

4. Let us forget this one.

Figure 3.4 Opportunity matrix

The principles of a SWOT analysis are illustrated in Figure 3.3 by examining how an airline which has an established reputation as a charter carrier could use the framework in assessing whether to enter the scheduled service market between London and Paris.

3.4.3   Environmental threat and opportunity profile (ETOP)

A marketing opportunity can be defined as 'an attractive arena for company marketing action in which the company would enjoy a competitive advantage' (Kotler, 1991) and should be assessed for its attractiveness and success probability. Attractiveness can be assessed in terms of potential market size, growth rates, profit margins, competitiveness and distribution channels. Other factors may be technological requirements, degree of government interference, environmental concerns and energy needs. Set against the measure of attractiveness is the probability of success, which depends on the company's strengths and competitive advantage, including, for example, such issues as access to cash, lines of credit or capital to finance new developments. Technological and productive expertise, marketing skills, distribution channels

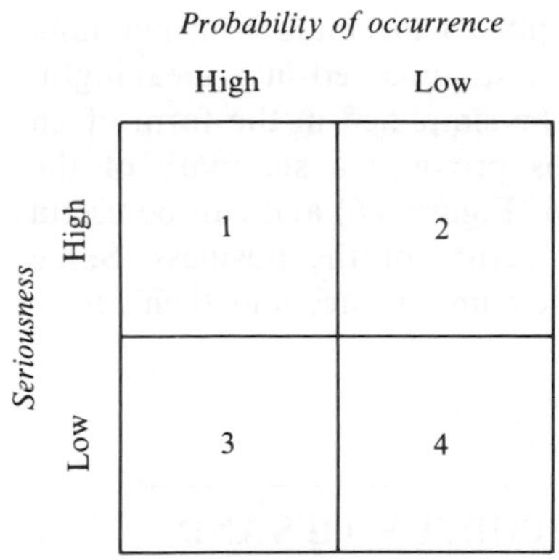

Probability of occurrence

High   Low

High 1	2
Low 3	4

Seriousness

1. A major risk (e.g. a major competitor is likely to launch a superior product). Must have a contingency plan.

2. Unlikely to occur, but company must be prepared for the consequences if it does.

3. Not a major problem if—as likely—it does occur.

4. Minor problem, unlikely to occur.

Figure 3.5   Threat matrix

Factor	Major opportunity	Minor opportunity	Neutral	Minor threat	Major threat	Probability
ECONOMIC						
Interest rates ↑15%					✓	0.8
£ falls ↓$1.00	✓					0.4
Disposable incomes do not						
rise for 5 years				✓		0.3
POLITICAL						
Change of political party – more spending on education and public transport			✓			0.9
LEGAL						
European Community restricts direct mail				✓		0.1
MARKET						
Competitor launches major TV campaign				✓		0.5

Probability scale from 0.1, very unlikely to happen, to 0.9, very likely to happen

Figure 3.6   Environmental Threat and Opportunity Profile

and managerial competence will also need to be taken into account. A simple matrix (Figure 3.4) can be constructed to show the relationship between attractiveness and success probability.

An environmental threat can be described as 'a challenge posed by an unfavourable trend or development in the environment that would lead, in the absence of purposeful marketing action, to the erosion of the company's or industry's position' (Kotler, 1991). In this case the threats should be assessed according to their seriousness and the probability of occurrence. A Threat matrix (Figure 3.5) can then be constructed.

In order for an environmental analysis to have a useful input to the marketing planning process, a wide range of information and opinions needs to be summarized in a meaningful way. The information collated from the detailed analysis can be simplified in the form of an Environmental Threat and Opportunity Profile (ETOP). This provides a summary of the environmental factors that are most critical to the organization (Figure 3.6) and can be useful in stimulating debate among senior management about the future of the business. Some analysts suggest trying to weight these factors according to their importance and then rating them for their impact on the organization.

TURBULENCE IN BROADCASTING SIGNALS OPPORTUNITIES AND THREATS

In 1991 a new opportunity arose in the UK for companies to bid for commercial television franchises granted periodically by the government. Since they were last issued in 1981 a new Broadcasting Act introduced by the government had changed the regulations for commercial television and the criteria by which bidders for the franchises were to be judged. In short, the government's intention was to create more competition in the bidding to raise revenue and to curtail broadcasting monopolies. The franchises would be given to the highest bidders subject to a minimum 'quality threshold'.

Opportunities presented by the new licensing arrangements resulted in many new consortia being created to bid for licences. Many of the new consortia members were well resourced but had no experience of broadcasting, while others had the experience but lacked the resources. An important reason for organizations seeking to join a consortium rather than bidding alone was that they had analysed their strengths and weaknesses in relation to the opportunities and threats, and concluded that a consortium offered a greater chance of success. In this way a number of new consortia were formed to bid for the breakfast television franchise, which was currently held by TV-

AM. Among these was a consortium called Daybreak whose partners included ITN, the *Daily Telegraph*, MAI (an advertising group), Carlton Communications, NBC (an American TV network) and Taylor Woodrow (a construction company). Other bidders included a consortium comprising London Weekend Television, STV (Southern Television) and Broadcast Communications (owned by *The Guardian* newspaper and Disney).

In their assessment of the new ITV franchises, bidders were aware of a number of opportunities and threats facing them. Among the threats was the fall in advertising revenue as a result of the economic recession. Over the longer term, a number of emerging threats were identified. First, the Broadcasting Act meant that when the franchise next came up for renewal, the bidding would be even more competitive. Second, the development of satellite television and the possibility of another terrestrial channel, Channel 5, being licensed by the government posed further threats to advertising revenue. Third, advertising revenues were further threatened by the possibility of the BBC being allowed to carry advertising on its channels in order to reduce its dependence on the public purse.

3.5 DEFINING CORPORATE AND MARKETING OBJECTIVES

Having identified the current position of the organization and its environment, the next stage in the planning process is to give it direction for the future. In this section, the sense of giving direction is examined at a number of levels, starting at the general level of setting corporate goals, then working through a hierarchy of aims to the formulation of specific marketing objectives.

3.5.1 Defining the corporate mission

Organizations are initially set up for a specified purpose. In the case of a private sector company, its purpose may be enshrined in very general terms in its Memorandum and Articles of Association, while for public sector bodies, an Act of Parliament may describe the broad area of responsibilities that the body is to be given. In most cases, these initial statements of purpose may be too general to be of help to managers, acting as a very loose constraint on future activities rather than as an aid to formulating strategy. As an example, the Memorandum of British Gas plc includes a statement which could be taken to include the operation of undertakers, travel agents and decorators in its purposes. Over time, the original purposes of an organization may change—changed conditions in its marketing environment or growth into new service areas may leave some confusion about its current purpose.

A corporate mission statement is a means of reminding everyone within the organization of its essential purpose. Drucker (1973) identifies a number of basic questions which management should ask when it perceives itself drifting along with no clear purpose, and which form the basis of a corporate mission statement:

- What is our business?
- Who is the customer?
- What is value to the customer?
- What will our business be?
- What should our business be?

By forcing management to focus on the essential nature of the business they are in and the nature of customer needs which they seek to satisfy, the problem of 'marketing myopia' advanced by Levitt (1960) can be avoided. Levitt argued that in order to avoid a narrow, shortsighted view of their business, managers should define their business in terms of the needs that they fulfil rather than the products they produce. In the classic example, railway operators had lost their way because they defined their service output in terms of the technology of tracked vehicles, rather than in terms of the core benefit of movement which they provided. Accountants learnt the lesson of this myopic example during the 1970s by redefining their central purpose away from a narrow preoccupation with providing 'accounting services' to a much broader mission statement which spoke of supplying 'business solutions'.

For a mission statement to be useful, it must be a relevant and up-to-date statement of core corporate values which allows geographically dispersed personnel within an organization to share a sense of opportunity, direction, significance and achievement. The mission statement has been likened to an invisible hand which guides employees to work independently yet collectively towards achieving the organization's goal. Within the marketing planning process, a clear mission statement helps to identify the nature of the market opportunities which the company should be investigating in more detail, while filtering out search activity and proposals that do not fall within its defined mission.

Statement of Purpose

We aim to be...
a world class energy company and the leading
international gas business

by...

▶ running a professional gas business providing safe,
secure and reliable supplies

▶ actively developing an international business in
exploration and production of oil and gas

▶ making strategic investments in other energy-related
projects and businesses world wide

▶ satisfying our customers' wishes for excellent quality of
service and outstanding value

▶ constantly and energetically seeking to improve quality
and productivity in all we do

▶ caring for the environment

▶ maintaining a high quality workforce with equal
opportunities for all

▶ cultivating good relations with customers, employees,
suppliers, shareholders and the communities we serve
and thereby improving returns to shareholders.

British Gas

Figure 3.7   An example of a mission statement—British Gas plc

In the services sector, where the interface between the consumer and production personnel is often critical, communication of the values contained within the mission statement assumes great importance. The statement is frequently repeated by organizations in staff newsletters and in notices at their place of work. An example of a mission statement which is widely communicated to the workforce—as well as to customers—is provided by British Gas (see Figure 3.7).

The nature of an organization's mission statement is a reflection of a number of factors:

- The organization's ownership, which can lead to significant differences between the public sector, private sector and charities
- The previous history of the organization, in particular any distinct competences which it has acquired or images it has created in the eyes of potential customers
- Environmental factors, in particular, the major opportunities and threats that are likely to face the organization in the foreseeable future

- Resources available—without resources for their accomplishment, a mission statement has little meaning.

Missions define in general terms the direction in which an organization seeks to move. They contain no quantifiable information that allows them to be operationalized. For this to happen, objectives need to be set.

3.6   SETTING CORPORATE OBJECTIVES

Having carried out a situation analysis and defined its corporate mission, the vital task of setting objectives can begin. Objectives have a number of functions within an organization:

- They add to the sense of purpose within an organization, without which there would be little focus for managers' efforts.
- They help to achieve consistency between decisions made at different points within the organization—for example, it would be inconsistent if a production manager used a production objective that was unrelated to the marketing manager's sales objective.
- Objectives are used as motivational devices and can be used in a variety of formal and informal ways to stimulate increased performance by managers.
- Objectives allow for more effective control within an organization. Unless clear objectives have been set at the outset, it is very difficult to know whether the organization has achieved what it set out to do, and to take any corrective action if its efforts seem to be going adrift during the plan period.

To have most value to marketing management, objectives should possess a number of important characteristics:

- Objectives should be quantified. In the private services sector, the most important objectives can usually be expressed in terms of profitability, sales or market share. Within some public services, these terms may have litle meaning, but objectives should nevertheless be quantifiable. For example, libraries may set objectives in terms of the number of books borrowed or museums the number of visitors.
- Objectives must specify the time period to which they relate. In the case of a new service launch, an objective may be to recover 80 per cent of costs during the first year of operation, breaking even by year 2 and achieving a 25 per cent return on capital invested by year 3.
- To be effective, objectives must be capable of realistic achievement and accepted as such by the people responsible for acting on them. If objectives are set unattainably high, the whole process of planning could be brought into disrepute by staff in an organization. Where objectives are devolved to a service manager, these should reflect factors over which the manager has some degree of control. As an example, a product manager for mortgages should have some control over the volume of funds available for lending, otherwise any restriction may make a nonsense of an objective to achieve a specified sales target.
- There must be consistency between objectives. Inconsistency may, for example, occur where a sales objectives can only be achieved by reducing selling prices, thereby making it impossible to achieve a profit objective. Furthermore, objectives must be ranked in order of priority. Managers of a restaurant chain presented with a list of five 'key objectives', such as contribution to fixed costs, total sales revenue, number of visits by customers, average spend per visit and average customer waiting time, may struggle with apparently conflicting objectives. This can be resolved by ranking them in order of importance.

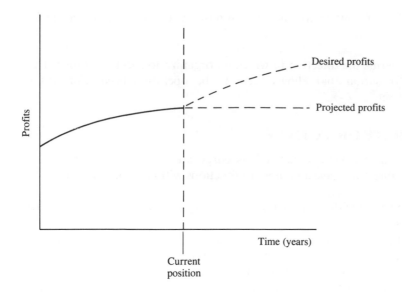

Figure 3.8 The planning gap

Organizations set a variety of objectives which are acted upon by their staff and the nature of these objectives can be classified into a number of categories:

- The ultimate goal of most private sector service providers is to produce an acceptable level of profits to its owners, hence it is profit objectives that feature prominently in the hierarchy of objectives that are communicated vertically through the planning hierarchy.
- Growth objectives may be important to organizations operating in rapidly expanding market sectors where a slow rate of growth effectively means that the organization is falling behind its competitors. In some industries, growth may be an essential objective in order to achieve a critical mass at which significant economies of scale occur.
- Technical objectives are set by organizations where technology is an important element in gaining competitive advantage over competitors.
- Quality of service objectives are frequently set for line managers within the private services sector—for example, one of many objectives set for branch bank managers relates to the length of waiting time for their customers. Quality of service objectives often assume overriding importance for public services where financial objectives act more as constraints. Time taken to process licence applications by the DVLA and the length of waiting lists for a health authority are typical bases for setting quality objectives.
- Sales and market share objectives are set by most private sector organizations. At the corporate level, it can be argued that these represent strategies rather than objectives—a specified profit objective could be achieved either by a low-volume, high-price strategy, or by an objective which seeks a greater market share but at the expense of lower prices. However, once the strategy is determined at corporate level, this is subsequently translated into specific objectives for line managers.

As an example of the diversity of objectives set by firms, a study of 28 professional services firms by Moutinho (1989) found that most had defined their primary goals in terms of sales volume (fee income) and profitability. Following these criteria, in order of use were the firm's image goals, return on investment and market share.

Having studied its operating environment, an organization will come to a view as to what objectives it should set itself for the planning period. A common starting point for goal setting is to look at previous performance and project past trends forwards to see what the organization would be capable of achieving if all other factors were held constant. Where the actual objectives set are greater than the position projected from previous trends, the result is what Ackoff (1970) terms a 'planning gap', illustrated in Figure 3.8. Where a planning gap exists, the aim of the planning process is to close the gap. This can be done by reducing downward the original objective to a level that is more realistic, given the historical pattern, or alternatively, action can be taken to accelerate the trend rate from its historical pattern to a higher level by means of marketing strategy. In practice, the planning gap is reduced by a combination of revising objectives and amending marketing strategies. In the case of totally new service offerings, it can be difficult to identify the historical trend line.

3.7   IDENTIFYING STRATEGIC ALTERNATIVES

The relationship between the corporate planning and marketing planning processes is neither clear-cut nor uni-directional. It was noted earlier that the importance of the marketing plan to the corporate plan varies from one organization to another. Furthermore, the process of planning is iterative. Corporate plans require information to be fed from the functional areas of an organization, synthesized into a corporate plan and fed back to these functional areas in the form of specific objectives. The process of finalizing the corporate plan could involve a number of iterations until optimization is achieved between all areas.

Having established the objectives to which it is to work, marketing management can set about the task of developing plans to achieve these objectives. Plans are produced at three levels—strategic, tactical and contingency.

3.7.1   Strategic, tactical and contingency planning

The strategic element of a marketing plan focuses on the overriding direction that an organization's efforts will take in order to meet its objectives. The tactical element is more concerned with plans for implementing the detail of the strategic plan. The division between the strategic and tactical elements of a marketing plan can sometimes be difficult to define. Typically, a strategic marketing plan is concerned with mapping out direction over a five-year planning period, whereas a tactical marketing plan relates to implementation during the next twelve months. Naturally, many service industries view their strategic planning periods somewhat differently. The marketing of large-scale infrastructure projects, such as airports or underground railways, requires a much longer strategic planning period to allow for the time delays in developing new capacity and for the fact that when capacity does become available, it will have a very long life with few alternative uses. The time taken to build a new airport terminal from the proposal stage to full opening is typically in the order of 5–10 years. Not only does the technology of airports require a long strategic planning period, the nature of the competitive environment allows an airport operator to take a longer-term view, with little likelihood of unexpected direct competitors coming onto the scene during its planning period. On the other hand, some service industries operate to much shorter strategic planning periods where new productive capacity can be produced quickly and where the environment is turbulent. An office-cleaning contractor using largely casual labour and simple technology will need to respond rapidly to changes in its environment, such as the loss of government contracts or the emergence of lower-cost competition. The organization's strategic marketing plan will probably give only a very general statement of direction beyond a two- or three-year planning period.

A third element of the marketing plan involves the development of contingency plans. These seek to identify scenarios where the assumptions of the position analysis on which strategic decisions were based turn out to be false. For example, the planning of a new airport may have assumed that fuel prices would rise by no more than 10 per cent during the plan period. A contingency plan would be useful to provide an alternative strategic route if, halfway during the plan period, fuel prices suddenly doubled and looked like remaining at the higher level for the foreseeable future, causing a fall in the total market for air travel. A contingency plan would identify options for the airport to react to such events, such as increasing its promotional expenditure to preserve its share of a diminishing market, or identifying alternative sources of revenue—for example the development of industrial estates and business centres on airport land—that are not directly related to the level of demand for air travel.

3.8 ANALYSIS OF TRENDS

Strategy formulation begins with an analysis of an organization's current position and objectives (discussed earlier), and builds on this by identifying trends that will influence the choice of a strategy. A strategy may prove ineffective if it is based on a misunderstanding of trends in underlying internal and external factors. For this purpose, a number of analytic frameworks are available and the choice of framework will depend upon the following factors:

- The level of turbulence in the marketing environment will vary between firms operating in different markets. For example, the marketing environment of an undertaker has been—and will probably continue to be—less turbulent than that of a commercial radio station. An extrapolation of recent trends may be adequate for the former but the latter must seek to understand a diverse range of changing forces if it is to predict accurately the likely future nature of its operating environment.
- The cost associated with an inaccurate forecast will reflect the capital commitment to a project. A window cleaner with only limited investment and transferable skills can afford to pay only limited attention to understanding his or her environment. On the other hand, the cost of developing a new rapid-transit system will call for relatively sophisticated techniques if expensive failure is to be avoided.
- More sophisticated analytic techniques are needed for long-term projects where there is a long time lag between the planning of the project and the time when it begins to yield its stream of service output. The problem of inaccurate forecasting will be even more acute where an asset has a long lifespan with few alternative uses.
- Qualitative and quantitative techniques may be used as appropriate. In looking at the future, facts are hard to come by. What matters is that senior management is in a position to make better-informed judgements about the future in order to aid strategic marketing planning.

3.8.1 Trend extrapolation

At its simplest, a firm identifies a historic and consistent long-term change in demand for a product over time and seeks to explain this in terms of change in some underlying variables. Marketing planning then tries to predict changes in these underlying variables and therefore—on the basis of the long-term relationship between variables—the likely future size and nature of a market.

While multiple correlation techniques can be used to identify the significance of historical relationships between a number of variables, extrapolation methods suffer from a number of shortcomings. First, one variable is seldom adequate to predict future demand for a product, yet it can be difficult to identify the full set of variables that have an influence. Second, there can be no certainty that the trends identified will continue in the future. Trend extrapolation takes no account of discontinuous environmental change, as was brought about by the sudden increase in oil prices in 1973 and the effects this had on demand for air travel. Third, trend extrapolation is of diminishing value as the length of time which it is used to forecast increases—the longer the time horizon, the more chance there is of historic relationships changing and new variables emerging. Fourth, it can be difficult to gather information on which to base an analysis of trends. Indeed, a large part of the problem in designing a marketing information system is in identifying the type of information that may be of relevance at some time in the future.

At best, trend extrapolation can be used where planning horizons are short, the number of underlying variables relatively limited and the risk level relatively low.

3.8.2 Expert opinion

Trend analysis is commonly used to predict demand where the state of the underlying variables can be forecast with some accuracy. In practice, it can be very difficult to predict what will happen to these variables. One solution is to consult expert opinion to obtain the best possible forecast.

In Diffenbach's (1983) study of US corporations, 86 per cent of all firms said they used expert opinion as an input to their planning process. Expert opinion can vary in the level of its speciality, from an economist being consulted for a general forecast about the state of the national economy to industry-specific experts. Expert opinion may be unstructured and come from a few individuals inside the organization, or from external advisors or consultants. Senior managers in organizations of any significant size tend to keep in touch with developments by a number of means. Paid and unpaid advisors may be used to keep abreast of a whole range of issues such as technological developments, the environment, government thinking and intended legislation. Large companies may employ MPs or MEPs (European Members of Parliament) as advisors as well as retired civil servants. Consultancy firms may be employed to brief the company on specific issues or monitor the environment on a more general basis.

Relying on individuals may give an incomplete or distorted picture of the future. There are, however, more structured methods of gaining expert opinion, one of the best known being the Delphi method. This involves a number of experts, usually from outside the organization, who preferably do not know each other and who do not meet or confer during the process. A scenario or number of scenarios about the future are drawn up by the company, and posted out to the experts. Comments are returned and the scenario(s) modified according to the comments received. The process is run through a number of times with the scenarios being amended on each occasion. Eventually a consensus of the most likely scenario is arrived at. It is believed that this is more accurate than relying on any one individual, because it involves the collected wisdom of a number of experts who have not been influenced by dominant personalities.

3.8.3 Scenario building

Scenario building is an attempt to paint a picture of the future by building a small number of alternative scenarios based on differing assumptions. This qualitative approach is a means of

Wild cards \ Possible events	OPEC force price of oil to $40 per barrel	OPEC cartel collapses: oil drops to $12 per barrel	Economic downturn becomes a slump and lasts for 5 years	Government introduces heavy fossil-fuel taxes	
New hydrogen-powered engine cuts costs and pollution					
Development of 'virtual reality' allows people to gain experience of travel without actually travelling					
Possible link between flying and cancer causes fear of flying					
New wave of aircraft terrorism					

Figure 3.9 Cross-impact analysis

handling environmental issues which are hard to quantify because they are less structured, more uncertain and may involve very complex relationships.

In the real world, many unpredictable environmental factors can interact with each other, resulting in a seemingly endless permutation of scenarios. One method of analysing the relationship between environental factors is a Cross Impact Analysis, which presents a framework within which the combined effects of changes in a number of factors can be assessed. A number of permutations are shown in Figure 3.9, where the interaction of the distinct possibility of oil prices rising to $40 per barrel with the 'wild card' event of cancer being linked to flying can be noted. For an airline, a development option if this scenario came true might be to rapidly downsize its passenger-carrying capacity and to concentrate on business and freight traffic.

The use of scenarios can allow a company to come to a view as to which is the most likely outcome, and plan accordingly, while still being able to develop contingency plans that could be rapidly implemented if any of the alternative foreseen scenarios came true.

3.9 STRATEGY FORMULATION

Having analysed its business environment and formed a view of the future, organizations must then identify the strategic alternatives that would allow them to achieve their objectives. From these alternatives, a strategy will be selected and implemented.

Competitors within an industry may each pursue very different strategies, but all may be capable of achievement, given that each organization may be pursuing quite different objectives, and may possess differing strengths and weaknesses. Analysts have developed numerous methodologies for classifying the diversity of marketing strategies. While there is no definitive basis for categorizing the strategic alternatives open to an organization, three focal points for strategy development will be considered here in detail:

- Strategies that focus on gaining competitive advantage
- Strategies that focus on growth options
- Strategies that focus on the development of portfolios.

This does not represent a strategy typology but merely a useful classification device for considering the literature. In practice, strategy development will bear some relation to each of these three focal points.

3.10 STRATEGIES FOR COMPETITIVE ADVANTAGE

Firms must be aware of who their competitors are and of their relative strengths and weaknesses. In all competitive markets, the strategic decisions made by an organization are frequently a response to actions—or possible future actions—by competing organizations. One method of identifying and selecting strategies is to identify those activities for which an organization has a competitive advantage over its competitors. Porter (1980) has reduced competitive advantage-based strategies to three generic types:

- *Overall cost leadership* Here, the organization puts a lot of effort into lowering its production and distribution costs so that it can win competitive advantage by charging lower prices. Organizations pursuing this strategy need to be efficient at production. Cost leadership can result from being able to achieve economies of scale. In services which use high technology, or which require highly trained labour skills, a learning curve effect may be apparent (also called a cost experience curve). By operating at a larger scale than its competitors, a firm can benefit more from the learning curve and thereby achieve lower unit costs. While this may be true of some service industries, others face only a very low critical output at which significant economies of scale occur—solicitors and hairdressing, for example. For organizations in these sectors, cost leadership would be a difficult strategy as many rival firms would also be able to achieve maximum cost efficiency. A cost leadership strategy is more likely to be effective where a high level of output relative to market size is necessary in order to achieve economies of scale, as is the case with the operation of a national car breakdown and recovery service which requires a high minimum level of investment in infrastructure. This prevents small local operators competing on the basis of lower overhead costs, leaving the major competitors to cut costs and hence offer any given level of service at a lower price.

- *Differentiation* Organizations seek to achieve superior performance of a service, adding value to the offering which is reflected in the higher price a customer is prepared to pay. One way in which firms seek to gain advantage over their competitors is by offering greater quality relative to price than their competitors. Added value can also be provided by offering completely new services which are not yet available from competitors, by modifying existing services or by making them more easily available in order to give them a competitive advantage. In this way, a bank could seek superior performance in areas such as the greatest number of branches, the highest rates of interest on savings accounts, the greatest number of cash machines or the most convenient home-banking service. An organization can realistically aim to be leader in one of these areas, but not in all at the same time. It therefore develops those strengths which will give it a differential performance advantage in one of these benefit areas. A bank that has the most comprehensive branch network may build upon this by seeking to ensure that it is open at times when customers wish to visit it, that there is no excessive waiting time and that it presents a bright and inviting image to customers. A problem of a differentiation strategy for services is that a service can be easily copied and a company seeking to differentiate by innovation may soon find its innovatory service copied by competitors.
- *Focus* An organization may focus on one or more small market segments rather than aiming for the whole market. It becomes familiar with the needs of these segments and gains competitive advantage by cost leadership or differentiation within its chosen segment, or both. A cost focus strategy requires an organization to segment its market and to specialize in products for that market. By concentrating on a narrow geographical segment, or producing specialized services for a very small segment, the organization can gain economies of scale in production. In this way a holiday tour operator could focus on disabled travellers living in south-east England. By building up volume of specialized holidays, it may achieve operating economies—for example, the ability to spread the capital cost of specialized vehicles over a large number of customers. By focusing on the south-east market, it can reduce the costs that may result from attempting to arrange transport connections from geographically remote market segments. A quality differentiation strategy entails selecting a market segment and competing on the basis of the differential quality offering of a service aimed at that segment.

  A focus strategy may be appropriate for a company seeking to enter a market for the first time. Mortgage lenders entering a new national market may focus on small segments by providing specialized products such as foreign currency mortgages or special mortgages for second holiday homes.

  Despite the advantages of a focus strategy described above, there are also dangers. The segments which form the focus may be too small to be economical in themselves. Moreover, an overreliance on narrow segments could leave an organization dangerously exposed if these segments go into decline. Overseas financial institutions who focused on specialized segments of the UK mortgage market faced great difficulty when the market went into decline from 1988 onwards and many of them were forced to abandon the UK market completely.

For firms pursuing a similar strategy aimed at similar market segments, Porter contends that the one which pursues that strategy most effectively will meet its objectives most effectively. Thus, of all the car hire companies pursuing a cost leadership strategy, the one which actually achieves the lowest level of costs will be the most successful. Firms which do not pursue a clear strategy are the least effective. Although they try to succeed in all three strategic alternatives, they end up showing no cost leadership, no differential advantage and no clear focus on one customer group.

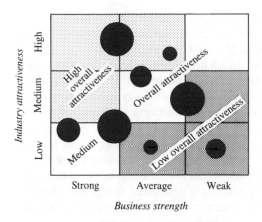

Figure 3.10 Market attractiveness—competitive position portfolio classification and strategies

3.10.1 Competitive advantage grids

Organizations seek to match their own internal strengths with the opportunities available in their environment. A number of matrix type approaches have been used to show the relationship between these two factors. One which is commonly used for identifying strategies is the General Electric (GE) Market Attractiveness—Competitive Position Classification (Figure 3.10). The grid comprises two dimensions—market attractiveness and competitive position. These are plotted in Figure 3.10 where each of these scales is divided into three classifications, resulting in a matrix of nine cells. Clearly, the best match is obtained in the top left-hand cell (a highly attractive market and a strong competitive position). Neither a strong company in an unattractive market nor a weak company in an attractive one will have the potential success as those in this category. As a portfolio model (see below) the grid can be used to analyse the current offering of a business. As a basis for strategy formulation, it focuses attention on finding strategies that match an organization's internal strengths and weaknesses with the opportunities and threats presented by its operating environment.

The key to making this model useful in formulating marketing strategy is to measure the two dimensions of the grid. Marketing attractiveness may typically include such factors as the size of a market, its projected growth rate and earnings performance. Competitive advantage could comprise brand strength, experience in a market and the availability of financial and human resources to serve that market. In developing an index, weights must be attached to each of these components and sometimes a subjective assessment made of each component. Ownership of a strong brand may be an essential element of competitive advantage for a firm in the package holiday business and would therefore be given a relatively high weighting, although the task of assessing how strong a brand is remains largely subjective.

While it is a simple conceptual framework for strategy formulation, this type of grid has a number of problems in application, especially within the services sector, in addition to the measurement problems described above.

First, it can be difficult to define what constitutes a market. For all products, it can be difficult to identify which near-competitors should be considered to be part of the market under analysis. With services, this becomes a problem where service availability is defined in geographical terms. Thus the market for a proposed new solicitor's practice may look attractive when defined solely in terms of a small market town which is being studied. However, if it is accepted that clients are prepared to travel some distance to see a solicitor, the market can only sensibly be assessed by including an analysis of the market for solicitors' services in the surrounding region, the boundaries of which are difficult to define.

Second, market attractiveness is a dynamic measure and what is important is how attractive a market will appear at the time when a proposed strategy is implemented. If a market seems attractive to one organization, then it probably appears equally so to others, who may possess equal competitive advantage in addressing the market. If all such firms decide to enter the market, oversupply results, profit margins become squeezed and the market becomes relatively unattractive. Services that are easy to copy can be designed and introduced to the market relatively quickly and can prove such models to be highly unstable at formulating strategy. An example is the UK video-rental market, which in the mid-1980s looked highly attractive, given the rapid growth in ownership of videocassette recorders and good margins earned by those operators in the market. This was the signal for many companies to enter the market, with some chains such as Ritz and Blockbuster being built up very rapidly. The result was that by 1990, the market—whose growth rate had slowed down—had become very unattractive, with poor returns and a number of business failures.

3.10.2 Competitive response models

In competitive markets, an organization cannot sensibly formulate strategic alternatives without reference to the strategies of its competitors. Two key issues need to be addressed:

- The actions competitors may take, the effects they will have on a firm's business and the methods by which the firm might respond to this reaction
- The responses competitors may have in reply to the firm's own strategy.

Porter identifies a number of competitor responses which can be classified into three broad categories:

- Neutral moves are those made by competitors which are not seen to be threatening, at least at the time. There is a danger that such moves can conceal the true intention of the competitor. A road haulier may seem to pose no threat by acquiring a depot some distance from its base, but this could be the first step in tackling a market that demands national coverage.
- Offensive moves are likely to improve an organization's position and therefore may bring about a response from competitors. Whether such moves prove to be successful depends upon how accurately an organization predicts the level and nature of retaliation.
- Defensive moves are designed to protect an organization's position or to prevent future conflict.

Kotler (1991) identifies four common competitors' likely response profiles:

1. The 'laid back' competitor does not react quickly to a competitor's move. This could be because it feels that their customers are loyal, or they are slow in noticing the competition, lack the funds to respond, or they may be harvesting a product and moving out of that particular market.
2. The 'selective' competitor reacts to certain types of competition, but not to others. It may respond to price cuts but not to an increase in advertising expenditure. Identifying strategic response strategies requires identification of the key factors to which a competitor is likely to respond.

PRODUCTS

	Existing	New
Existing	**MARKET-PENETRATION STRATEGY** Achieve higher market share among present segment of leisure users	**PRODUCT-DEVELOPMENT STRATEGY** Develop health club aimed at present clientele
New	**MARKET-DEVELOPMENT STRATEGY** Target business customers	**DIVERSIFICATION** Develop a fast-food restaurant in a nearby town

MARKETS

Figure 3.11 An application of Ansoff's growth matrix to a hotel operator

3. The 'tiger' competitor reacts swiftly and strongly to any assault on its market, giving a signal to those who threaten it that it will fight to the finish.
4. The 'stochastic' competitor reacts in a seemingly random manner, making it difficult to predict its reaction on the basis of its history or economic position, or anything else.

A logical development of competitor response models is found in game theory. Since its development by Von Neumann and Morganstern in 1944, game theory has found a number of applications in the field of marketing strategy. It has been found, for instance, by Karnani (1984) to be useful in explaining the behaviour of mature oligopolistic markets where market share is only gained at the expense of another participant. The key requirements for game theory to work are a small number of players, conflict, interdependence, relatively high market share and a highly interactive competitive environment. Some of the assumptions of game theory have resulted in its usefulness as a tool for predicting behaviour being challenged. It assumes rational reactions by competitors, while in reality many strategic decisions are highly irrational, as where an entrepreneur pursues growth strategies which are not economically sound but which may boost his or her ego. Game theory also assumes that there is perfect and complete information about the market in question. With very few exceptions (for example, civil aviation, banking), information is in fact likely to be very selective.

3.11 GROWTH STRATEGIES

Most private sector service organizations pursue growth in one form or another, whether this is an explicit aim of the organization or an implicit one of its managers. The thrust for growth can be channelled into one of a number of directions and it is therefore useful to develop frameworks for analysing the growth strategies open to organizations.

3.11.1 Product–market growth strategies

An organization's growth can conceptually be analysed in terms of two key development dimensions—markets and products. This conceptualization forms the basis of the Product/Market Expansion Grid proposed by Ansoff (1957). Products and markets are each analysed in terms of their degree of novelty to an organization and growth strategies identified in terms of these two dimensions. In this way, four possible growth strategies can be identified. An illustration of the framework, with reference to the specific options open to a seaside holiday hotel, is given in Figure 3.11.

The four growth options are associated with differing sets of problems and opportunities for organizations. These relate to the level of resources required to implement a particular strategy and the level of risk associated with each. It follows, therefore, that what might be a feasible growth strategy for one organization may not be for another. The characteristics of the four strategies are as follows:

1. *Market-penetration strategies* This type of strategy focuses growth on the existing product range by encouraging higher levels of take-up of a service among the existing target markets. In this way a specialist tour operator in a growing sector of the holiday market could—all other things being equal—grow naturally simply by maintaining its current marketing strategy. If it wanted to accelerate this growth, it could do this first, by seeking to sell more holidays to its existing customer base and second, by attracting customers from its direct competitors. If the market was in fact in decline, the company could only grow by attracting customers from its competitors through more aggressive marketing policies. This strategy offers the least level of risk to an organization—it is familiar with both its products and its customers.

2. *Market-development strategies* This type of strategy builds upon the existing product ranges that an organization has established but seeks to find new groups of customers for them. In this way a specialist regional ski tour operator which had saturated its current market might seek to expand its sales to new geographical regions or to attract custom from groups beyond its current age/income groups. While the organization may be familiar with the operational aspects of the service it is providing, it faces risks resulting from possibly poor knowledge of different buyer behaviour patterns in the markets it seeks to enter. As an example of the potential problems associated with this strategy, many UK retailers have sought to offer their UK shop formats in overseas markets only to find that those features which attracted customers in the UK failed to do so in other countries.

3. *Product-development strategies* As an alternative to selling existing products into new markets, an organization may choose to develop new products for its existing ones. A ski tour operator may have built up a good understanding of the holiday needs of a particular market segment—perhaps an 18–35-year-old affluent south-eastern segment—and seeks to offer a wider range of services to them than simply skiing holidays. It may offer summer activity holidays in addition. While the company minimizes the risk associated with the uncertainty of new markets, it faces risk resulting from lack of knowledge of its new product area. Often a feature of this growth strategy is collaboration with a product specialist who helps the organization to produce the service, leaving it free to market it to its customers. A department store wishing to add a coffee shop to its service offering may not have the skills and resources within its organization to run such a facility effectively, but may subcontract an outside catering specialist. Sometimes growth into new service areas can be most effectively brought about by means of a joint venture. The retailer J. Sainsbury had, for example, sought to add household goods and DIY materials to its existing range of grocery supermarkets. To achieve an acceptable level of product knowledge—and a critical mass—it joined with British Home Stores to form SavaCentres to sell household goods and with the Belgian retailer BM SA to set up a chain of Homebase DIY stores, all appealing to broadly the same profile of customer as its grocery stores.

4. *Diversification strategies* Here, an organization expands by developing new products for

new markets. Diversification can take a number of forms. The company could stay within the same general product/market area but diversify into a new point of the distribution chain. For example, an airline which sets up its own travel agency moves into a type of service provision that is new to the organization, as well as dealing directly with a segment of the market with which it probably had previously few sales transactions. Alternatively, the airline might diversify into completely unrelated service areas aimed at completely different groups of customers—by purchasing a golf course or car dealership, for example. Because the company is moving into unknown markets and product areas, this form of growth can be quite risky. Diversification may, however, help to manage the long-term risk of the organization by reducing dependency on a narrow product/market area.

In practice, most growth is a combination of product development and market development. In very competitive markets, a service supplier would probably have to slighly adapt its product if it was to become attractive to a new market segment. For the leisure hotel seeking to capture new business customers, it may not be enough simply to promote existing facilities. In order to meet business peoples' needs, it may have to refurbish facilities to make them more acceptable to business customers and offer new services—for example, the facility for visitors to pay by account.

3.11.2   Organic growth versus growth by acquisition

There are two basic means by which an organization can grow—through organic growth and by acquisition, although many organizations grow by a combination of the two processes. The manner of growth has important marketing implications—for instance, in the speed with which an organization is able to expand into new market opportunities. The basis of the two types of growth is analysed below.

Organic growth   Organic growth is considered to be the more 'natural' pattern of growth for an organization. An initial investment results in profits, an established customer base and a well-established technical, personnel and financial structure. This provides a foundation for future growth. In this sense, success breeds success, for the rate of the organization's growth is influenced by the extent to which it has succeeded in building up internally the means for future expansion.

In terms of marketing, an organization may grow organically by tackling one segment at a time, using the resources, knowledge and market awareness it has gained in order to deal with further segments. Many retail chains have grown organically by developing one region before moving on to another. Sainsbury grew organically from its southern base towards the northern regions, while Asda grew organically during the 1970s and early 1980s from its northern base towards the south. Other organizations have grown organically by aiming a basically similar product at new segments of the market—as Thomson Holidays has done in developing slightly differentiated holidays aimed at the markets for youth and the elderly.

There is evidence that service firms may find organic growth difficult where new market opportunities suddenly arise. Within the financial services sector, a study by Ennew *et al.* (1992) found that many of the assets of companies—such as specialized staff and distribution networks—were quite specific to their existing markets and could not easily be adapted to exploit new markets. Growth by acquisition was in many cases considered to be a better method of expansion.

Growth by acquisition   The rate of organic growth is constrained by a number of factors, including the rate at which a firm's market is itself growing. An organization seeking to grow organically in a slowly developing sector such as household insurance will find organic growth more difficult than one serving a rapidly growing sector such as telecommunications. Also, companies with relatively high capital requirements will find organic growth relatively slow.

Growth by acquisition may appear attractive to organizations where organic growth is difficult. In some cases it may be almost essential in order to achieve a critical mass that is necessary for survival. The DIY retail sector in the UK is one where chains have needed to achieve a critical mass in order to pass on lower prices resulting from economies in buying, distribution and promotion. Small chains have not been able to grow organically at a sufficient rate to achieve this size, resulting in their take-over or merger to form larger chains. The rapid growth of the Texas DIY chain was partly due to its acquisition of a number of smaller chains, such as Unit Sales.

Growth by acquisition may occur where an organization sees its existing market sector contracting and seeks to diversify into other areas. The time and risk associated with starting a new venture in an alien market sector may be considered too great. Acquiring an established business could be less risky, allowing access to an established client base and technical skills.

Growth by acquisition can take a number of forms. The simplest is the agreed take-over where one firm agrees to purchase the majority of the share capital of another. Payment can be in the form of cash or shares in the acquiring company, or some combination of the two. A take-over can be mutually beneficial where one company has a sound customer base but lacks the financial resources to achieve a critical mass while the other has the finance but needs a larger customer base. Many take-overs occur where the founder of a business is seeking to retire and to liquidate the value of the business.

A major problem for firms seeking to grow within the service sector by acquisition lies in the fact that often the main assets being acquired are the skills and knowledge of the organization's employees. It has been pointed out by Thomas (1978) that, unlike physical assets, key personnel may disappear following the acquisition, reducing the earning ability of the business. Worse still, key staff could defect to the acquiring company's competitors. There is evidence that much of the investment of financial institutions in acquiring estate agencies during the late 1980s was lost when key personnel left with their list of contacts to set up rival agencies.

3.12 PORTFOLIO PLANNING

Service providers operating in a market environment face increasingly turbulent patterns of demand. For a company to put all its efforts into supplying a very limited range of services to a narrow market segment is potentially dangerous. Overreliance on this one segment can make the survival of the organization dependent upon the fortunes of this segment and its liking for its product. In any event, the fact that most markets change to some extent over time would imply that its products will eventually move out of line with customers' requirements. For these reasons, organizations seek to manage their growth in a manner that maintains a portfolio of activities.

Risk spreading is an important element of portfolio management that goes beyond marketing planning. Some service providers deliberately provide a range of services which—quite apart from their potential for cross-selling—act in contrasting manners during the business cycle. For this reason, accountancy firms have become potentially more stable units as they have amalgamated, by allowing pro-cyclical activities such as management buy-out expertise and venture capital investment to be counterbalanced by contra-cyclical activities such as insolvency work. Service organizations often take on a base load of relatively unattractive but predictable work to counterbalance highly cyclical work. Solicitors may undertake criminal defence work to cushion them against overreliance on relatively lucrative but cyclical property conveyancing. Sometimes, statutory requirements may require a balanced portfolio of output—the Bank of

England's regulation of the UK banking system, for example, imposes constraints on banks' freedom to be market-led in the pattern of their lending decisions.

3.12.1 Portfolio analysis—the BCG matrix

One commonly used framework for analysing business portfolios is the Boston Consulting Group's (BCG) Market Share/Growth Matrix. Although it has been most commonly used to analyse portfolios of manufactured goods, the original concept derives from financial services portfolios (see Morrison and Wensley, 1991). The framework was originally developed as a means of bringing about a more rational basis for allocating funds, focusing on business generation and funds allocation in response to the challenges of a dynamic competitive environment. Its rationale was that growth decisons should not be taken in a narrow piecemeal fashion, but should consider the implications for the business as a whole.

Two dimensions for classifying an organization's portfolio of producers are used – relative market share and the market growth rate for the product. Market share – relative to that of its competitors – is considered to be indicative of the extent to which cash can be generated. Also, by selling more than its competitors, companies can gain from economies of scale. It is therefore likely that if prices are the same, the company with the largest market share will be generating the most profit. Market growth rate is a measure of a product's cash usage. In a fast-growing market, products tend to be high users of cash, necessary to support the purchase of new equipment, development of new outlets and high promotion costs.

An organization's products are classified according to the stage they have reached in their lifecycle. During the early stages of their lives, products tend to be net users of cash, incurring high development and launch costs but bringing in relatively little revenue. During the growth period, further expenditure in new capacity may be needed to cope with increased demand. At this stage, competitors start to appear, resulting in high promotion costs. It is only when a product reaches later stages of its growth or during maturity that it becomes a net cash producer. At this point, little new money is spent on equipment and the firm benefits from a high level of sales and economies of scale.

In the Boston Matrix, Relative Market Share is shown moving from high to low on the horizontal axis while Market Growth Rate moves from high to low on the vertical one. The matrix denotes four categories of products:

- 'Stars' are products with a high market share and high market growth. They are probably quite a new product in a market that is growing fast. They are also probably generating as much cash as they are using.
- The 'Problem Child' denotes a product which has a low market share but high market growth. This could be a product that has not yet reached a dominant position in its market. Alternatively, it could be a product that once had a dominant position but is now declining. As there is high market growth, it is a net cash user.
- The 'Cash Cow' has a high market share but low market growth. Here there is reasonable stability with a lot of cash being generated but little being used.
- The 'Dog' has a low market share with low market growth. It has no real future and is a drain on cash, although there may still be reasons for including it in the portfolio (product-deletion decisions are considered in more detail in Chapter 6).

Attempts have been made to apply this approach to services. Newbould (1982) has applied the Boston Matrix to Higher Education programmes to prescribe strategic policies for US universities (see Figure 3.12). He believes that this type of analysis can also be applied to

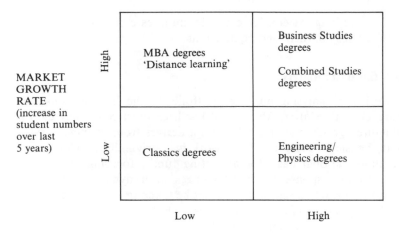

MARKET
GROWTH
RATE
(increase in
student numbers
over last
5 years)

MARKET-SHARE DOMINANCE
(ratio of student numbers of university being analysed
to numbers of largest competing university)

Figure 3.12 Portfolio analysis of a university's course offering (modified from Newbould, 1982)

particular subject disciplines and considers that each programme can be analysed in terms of the alternatives broadly outlined for it by its position in the matrix.

Having identified where the different elements of a firm's portfolio fit into the matrix, effective portfolio management is about using any surplus cash from the cash cows to invest in stars. Additionally, some surplus cash should be invested in a selected number of problem children which may prove to be the stars of the future. Similarly, investing in stars will lead to the development of future cash cows. A balanced portfolio comprises a large number of new products from which major cash generators should emerge, sufficient mature products to generate cash to finance future growth products and a sensible approach to deletion of products which have become a cash drain on the company.

Although applications of portfolio planning approaches do seem appealing, marketers need to temper their enthusiasm by considering their potential pitfalls:

- First, portfolio planning has more dimensions than simply market share/market growth rate.
- Second, there are conceptual and practical problems of defining products and markets. Service offerings can comprise a number of interdependent offerings where one part may be a star while another is a dog. While telephone banking may be a star, a bank's current account business to which it is linked may be becoming a dog, showing no market growth and a falling market share in the face of competition from building societies. It can also be difficult to distinguish one service from another as it is often possible to produce slight variations of services very easily. Should a current account which offers a free overdraft facility but makes an annual charge be considered a different product from one that has neither? It is also difficult to define just what constitutes a market in the case of services. For locally produced and consumed services such as those of a painter and decorator, the idea of a national market may have no meaning. The only one that matters is the achievable local market, which is much more difficult to define.
- Third, the underlying assumptions of the BCG matrix can be challenged. While a high market share is often associated with relatively high returns on capital, there are many cases where this does not hold. Travel agents in the UK can earn good returns either by being very

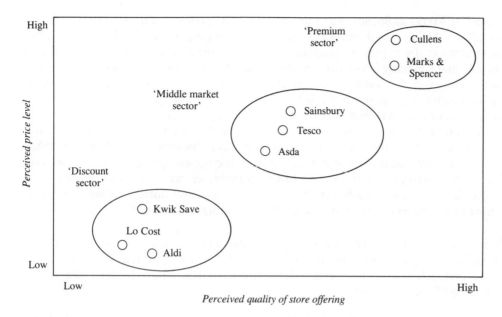

High

Perceived price level

Low

'Premium
sector'

○ Cullens

○ Marks &
Spencer

'Middle market
sector'

○ Sainsbury

○ Tesco

○ Asda

'Discount
sector'

○ Kwik Save

Lo Cost
○

○ Aldi

Low   High

Perceived quality of store offering

Figure 3.13   A simplified product-positioning map for UK supermarkets

large and achieving economies of scale in buying and promotion or by remaining small, reducing their overheads and obtaining a high level of customer loyalty.

• Another major criticism levelled at the approach is that it is based on a large number of assumptions which may not in fact be realistic—the direct link between market share and cash flow, for example.

3.13   POSITIONING STRATEGY

Positioning strategy is used by an organization in an attempt to distinguish its offerings from those of its competitors in order to give it a competitive advantage within a market. Positioning puts a firm in a subsegment of its chosen market. Thus a firm which adopts a product positioning based on 'high reliability/high cost' will appeal to a subsegment which has a desire for reliability and a willingness to pay for it. For some marketers (for example, Ries and Trout, 1981) positioning is essentially a communications issue where the nature of a service is given and the objective is to manipulate consumer perceptions of it. Others, such as Lovelock (1984), point out that positioning is more than merely promotion but involves considerations of pricing, distribution and the nature of the service offer itself, the core around which all positioning strategies revolve.

Organizations must examine their opportunities and take a position within a marketplace. A position can be defined by reference to a number of scales. Service quality and price are two very basic dimensions of positioning strategy which are relevant to service industries. Figure 3.13 shows these two scales applied to UK supermarket retailing in which both the price and quality scales are conceptualized as running from high to low. Quality in this case can be considered as a composite of range, speed of service, quality of personnel, quality of the shopping environment, etc. Price can be a general indication of price levels charged relative to competitors. The position of a number of UK grocery retailers is shown on the grid. This shows clearly that most supermarkets lie on a diagonal line between the high quality/high price position adopted by Marks & Spencer and the low price/low quality position adopted by Kwik Save. Points along this diagonal represent feasible positioning strategies for supermarket operators. A strategy in the upper-left quadrant (high price/low quality) can be described as a 'cowboy' strategy and generally is not sustainable, although it may be an attractive position in some instances—for example, some tourism-related activities where tourists are unlikely to return to the area again. A position in the lower-right strategy (high quality/low price) would indicate that an organization is failing to achieve a fair exchange of value.

An analysis of competitors relative to market size can indicate the attractiveness of alternative positioning strategies. An analysis of UK grocery retailers towards the end of the 1980s indicated that while there was an abundance of stores in the upper-right quadrant, there were relatively few in the lower-left one in relation to the numbers of people who would represent attractive target markets for stores adopting this position. The result during the late 1980s was the development of a number of low-cost/low-quality operators such as Aldi and Netto to take this position.

Although price and quality were used in the example above, these are too simplistic in themselves as criteria for positioning. Wind (1982 pages 79–81) has suggested six generic scales along which all products can be positioned. These are examined below by reference to the possible positioning of a leisure centre:

- *Positioning based on specific product features* For example, a leisure centre can promote the fact that it has the largest swimming pool in the area or the most advanced solarium.
- *Positioning on benefits or needs satisfied* The leisure centre could position itself somewhere between meeting pure physical recreation needs and pure social needs. In practice, positioning will combine the two sets of needs—for example, by giving up gym space to allow the construction of a bar.
- *Positioning on the basis of usage occasions* The centre could be positioned primarily for the occasional visitor, or the service offering could be adapted to aim at the more serious user who wishes to undertake a long-term programme of leisure activities.
- *Positioning for user category* A choice could be made between a position aimed at satisfying the needs of individual users and one aimed at meeting the needs of institutional users such as sports clubs and schools.
- *Positioning against another product* The leisure centre could promote the fact that it has more facilities than its neighbouring competition.
- *Positioning by product class* Management could position the centre as an educational facility rather than a centre of leisure, thus positioning it in a different product class.

Selecting a position for a service involves three basic steps;

- Identifying the organization's strengths and the opportunities of the marketplace to be exploited. An organization already established in a particular product position will normally have the advantage of customer familiarity to support any new service launch. A holiday tour operator which has positioned itself as a high-quality/high-price one can use this as a strength to persuade customers to pay relatively high prices for a new range of value-added holidays. Sometimes a weakness can be turned into a strength for positioning purposes—the Avis car-rental chain stresses that by being the number two operator, it has to try harder. Against internal strengths must be considered the attractiveness of a subsegment. For the tour operator seeking to build upon its strong reputation for offering high-quality/high-cost holidays, an analysis of the market may reveal greater opportunities in a segment which seeks a basic budget range of holidays. Should the organization decide to enter this market, it must avoid tarnishing its established brand values by association with a lower-quality product. One solution is to adopt a separate identity for a new service which assumes a different position. The UK retail group Sears, for example, developed the 'Your Price' identity to position a new chain of low-price/basic-quality clothes' stores away from its more mid-market chain of Fosters stores.

- Evaluating the position possibilities and selecting the most appropriate. An organization may discover a number of potential positions but many may have to be discarded if they result in uneconomically small market segments, or are too costly to develop. Other positions may be rejected as being inconsistent with an organization's image. Selection of the remaining possibilities should be on the basis of the organization's greatest differential advantage in areas that are most valued by target customers.

- Developing the marketing mix and establishing in the eyes of target customers the position that has been adopted. Organizations must develop programmes to implement and promote the position they have adopted. In this way an airline which positions itself as providing superior in-flight cabin crew services must develop a programme for recruiting, training, motivating and retaining appropriate crews who can deliver the desired service. It must also develop a creative platform for its promotional programme which makes clear in the minds of target customers just what a brand stands for. Positioning for a service industry differs from a manufacturing industry in that the method of producing the service is an important element of the positioning process.

Services can be positioned either on a stand-alone basis or as part of a service organization's total service range—in effect, the service organization adopts a position, rather than the individual service. The fact that consumer decision processes are likely to evaluate the service producer at least as much as a particular service makes this approach to position analysis attractive. Shostack (1987) suggests that within a range of services provided by an organization (or 'service family'), a marketer can consider positioning strategies based on structural complexity and structural diversity. Structural complexity refers to the number of steps that make up a service-production process and diversity the extent to which service output is variable. In this way, a doctor's service is highly complex in terms of the number of processes involved in a consultation or operation. It is also highly variable, for service outcomes can be diverse in terms of both planned and unplanned deviations in outcomes. Some processes can be high in complexity but low in diversity. Hotels, for example, offer a wide range of processes but are able to establish relatively low levels of diversity. An example of a service that is low in complexity but high in diversity is provided by a singer.

Positioning is seen by Shostack as a process of deciding how the service provider wishes to position its total range of services in relation to its customers—complexity and diversity are two key dimensions by which an organization can be positioned. Positioning decisions have implications for the overall image of the provider, and hence of individual services within its range. As an example, a dentist could take a more divergent position by adding general counselling on health matters or reduce it by undertaking only diagnostic work. Complexity could be increased by adding retailing of supplies or reduced by offering only a limited range of dental treatments. Some of these options are shown diagrammatically in Figure 3.14. The position adopted by an organization will be influenced by its strengths and weaknesses relative to the market that it seeks to address. A large dental practice may be better placed to position itself as a provider of complex services, but would need to ensure that diversity in outcomes was minimized in order not to affect its image adversely. A small dentist may find the most appropriate service position to be the provision of relatively simple services with divergent outcomes.

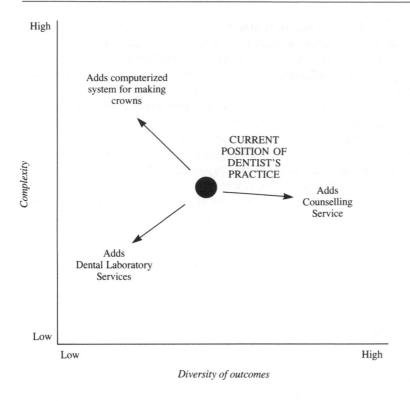

Figure 3.14 Service-positioning strategies based on service structure (based on Shostack, 1987)

Many service organisations have found a low-complexity/low-diversity position to offer great opportunities for exploiting niche markets. In this way, solicitors have set up as specialist will-writing businesses, offering one product line with little scope for variability. By developing expertise and reducing overheads, such companies can satisfy customers who do not have the need for the more complex but also more divergent services of full service solicitors.

3.13.1 Repositioning

Over time, organizations may seek to reposition their service offering. This could come about for a number of reasons:

- The original positioning strategy was inappropriate. Over-estimation of an organization's competitive advantage or of the size of the subsegment to which the positioning was intended to appeal could force a re-evaluation of positioning strategy.
- Where the nature of customer demand has changed. For example, it is argued that UK customers' attitudes towards package holidays changed during the late 1980s away from a stress on low price towards a position where consistent standards became of greater concern. Many tour operators accordingly repositioned their offering to provide higher standards at higher prices.
- Service providers seek to build upon their growing strengths to reposition towards meeting the needs of more profitable sub-segments. In many service industries, organizations start

life as simple, no-frills, low-price operations, subsequently gaining a favourable image which they use to 'trade up' to relatively high-quality/high-price positions. This phenomenon is well established in the field of retailing in which McNair (1958) identified what has become known as the 'Wheel of Retailing'. This contends that retail businesses start life as cut-price, low-cost, narrow-margin operations which subsequently 'trade up' with improvements in display, more prestigious premises, increased advertising, delivery and the provision of many other customer services that serve to drive up expenses, prices and margins. Eventually, retailers mature as high-cost, conservative and 'top-heavy' institutions with a sales policy based on quality goods and services rather than price appeal. This, in turn, opens the way for the next generation of low-cost innovatory retailers to find a position that maturing firms have vacated.

REVIEW QUESTIONS

1. What can marketing planning contribute towards corporate planning within the services sector?
2. Giving examples, in what ways does the setting of marketing objectives differ between the private and public services sectors?
3. Using a service organization with which you are familiar, carry out a SWOT analysis on the current position of the organization.
4. Examine the strategic alternatives open to a restaurant chain seeking to expand and suggest a framework within which strategic alternatives may be evaluated.
5. What is the value of contingency planning within the service sector? Identify one sector where the production of contingency plans is likely to be important, and the factors which need to be taken into account.
6. What factors should be taken into consideration by a travel agency in seeking to position its chain of outlets?

FOUR

MANAGING THE MARKETING EFFORT

OBJECTIVES

After reading this chapter, you should be able to understand:

- Methods by which marketing departments are structured and the relationship between structure and effectiveness in achieving corporate and marketing objectives
- The importance within the service sector of the interrelationships between marketing management and management of other functional areas
- Methods of introducing market-oriented management cultures within service organizations, especially public sector service ones
- The importance of marketing information as a resource to be managed
- Methods of monitoring and controlling marketing performance

4.1 INTRODUCTION

If strategic marketing planning is to have value to an organization, the strategies adopted must be effectively implemented. This chapter examines a number of issues central to the effective management of the marketing effort within service organizations. First, the organizational structures within which marketing planning and implementation takes place are considered—the development of appropriate structures and procedures can help or hinder the task of implementing a marketing orientation. Second, information is a vital input to the marketing management process and its role within the management process is studied. Finally, issues of monitoring and controlling the implementation of marketing programmes are addressed.

4.2 MARKETING MANAGEMENT FRAMEWORKS

It was suggested in Chapter 3 that the existence of a marketing department in an organization may in fact be a barrier to the development of a true customer-centred marketing orientation. By placing all marketing activity in a marketing department, non-marketing staff may consider themselves to be absolved of responsibility for the development of customer relationships. In service industries where production personnel are in frequent contact with the consumers of their service, a narrow definition of marketing responsibility can be potentially very harmful. On the other hand, a marketing department is usually required in order to co-ordinate and implement those functions which cannot sensibly be delegated to operational personnel—advertising, sales management and pricing decisions, for example. The importance that a

Figure 4.1   Functional organization of a marketing department

marketing department assumes within any organization is partly a reflection of the nature of its operating environment. An organization operating in a fiercely competitive environment would typically attach great importance to its marketing department as a means of producing a focused marketing mix strategy by which it can gain competitive advantage over its competitors. In contrast, an organization operating in a relatively stable environment is more likely to allow strategic decisions to be taken by personnel who are not marketing strategists. For example, pricing decisions may be made by accountants with less need to understand the marketing implications of price decisions.

This chapter initially analyses the role of the marketing department within service organizations (where such a department exists) and examines how this can be organized most effectively, not only to allow for the effective implementation of marketing strategy but also to facilitate strategic marketing decisions. An analysis is then made of the important relationships between the marketing function of an organization and its other specialist functions such as production, personnel and finance. The important issue here is how these can be made mutually supportive in meeting customers' needs.

4.3   THE INTERNAL ORGANIZATION OF A MARKETING DEPARTMENT

Responsibilities given to marketing departments within service organizations vary from one company to another, reflecting the competitive nature of their business environments and also their traditions and organizational inertia. Within marketing departments, four basic approaches to allocating these responsibilities are identified here, although in practice, most marketing departments show more than one approach to structure or combine them in 'matrix' type structures. The four approaches allocate marketing responsibilities by:

- Functions performed
- Geographical area covered
- Products or groups of products managed
- Market segments managed

4.3.1   Functional organization

A traditional and common basis of organizing a marketing department is to divide responsibilities into identifiable marketing functions (Figure 4.1). Typically, these may be advertising, sales, research and development, marketing research, customer services, etc. The precise division of the functional responsibilities will depend upon the nature of an organization. Buying and merchandising are likely to be an important feature in a retailing organization, while research and development will assume greater importance for a technology-based service such as telecommunications.

The main advantage of a functional organization lies in its administrative simplicity. Against this, there can be a tendency for policy responsibility on specific services or markets to become lost between numerous functional specialists. There is also the possibility of destructive rivalry between functional specialists for their share of marketing budgets—for example, rivalry between an advertising manager and a sales manager for a larger share of the promotional budget.

4.3.2 Geographical organization

Organizations providing a service nationwide frequently arrange many marketing functions on a geographical basis. This applies particularly to the sales function, although it could also include geographically designated responsibilities for service development (for example, opening new outlets) and some local responsibility for promotion. For service organizations operating at an international level there is usually some geographical basis in the manner in which marketing activities are organized in individual national markets.

4.3.3 Product-management organization (or) 'M' form or multi-divisional form

Multi-output organizations frequently appoint a product manager to manage a particular service or group of services. This form does not replace the functional organization, but provides an additional layer of management which coordinates the functions' activities. The product manager's role includes a number of key tasks:

- Developing a long-range and competitive strategy for a product or group of products
- Preparing a budgeted annual plan
- Working with internal and external functional specialists to develop and implement marketing programmes—for example, in relation to advertising and sales promotion
- Monitoring the product's performance and changes occurring in its business environment
- Identifying new opportunities and initiating product improvements to meet changing market needs

A product–management organization structure offers a number of advantages for service providers (Figure 4.2):

- The product offering benefits from an integrated cost-effective approach to planning. This particularly benefits minor products which might otherwise be neglected.
- The product manager can in theory react more quickly to changes in the product's marketing environment than would be the case if no-one had specific responsibility for the product. Within a bank, a mortgage manager is able to devote much time and expertise to monitoring trends in the mortgage market and can become a focal point for initiating and seeing through change when this is required because of environmental change.
- Control within this type of organization can be exercised by linking divisional managers' salaries to performance (see, for example, Demski and Baiman, 1980).

Against this, product-management structures are associated with a number of problems:

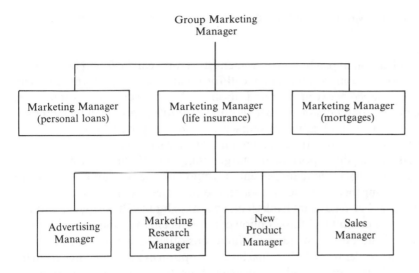

Figure 4.2 Product-management organization

- The most serious occurs in the common situation where product managers are given a lot of responsibility for ensuring that objectives are met but relatively little control over resource inputs that they have at their disposal. Product managers typically must rely on persuasion to obtain the cooperation of advertising, sales and other functional specialist departments. Sometimes this can result in conflict—for example, where a product manager seeks to position his or her service in one direction while the advertising manager seeks to position it in another in order to meet broader promotional objectives.
- Confusion can arise in the minds of staff within an organization as to whom they are accountable for their day-to-day actions. Staff involved in selling insurance policies in a branch bank may become confused by possibly conflicting messages from an operations manager and a product-marketing manager.
- A problem that is particularly relevant to many service industries lies in product-marketing managers' tendency to be in their jobs for only a few years before moving on to another position. The knowledge gained of markets and the confidence of key customers is therefore partially lost and must be rebuilt by the successors.
- Product-marketing management structures lead to larger numbers of people being employed, resulting in a higher cost structure which may put the organization at a competitive disadvantage in price-sensitive markets.
- Research has suggested that the existence of optimal product management structures is rare (Hill and Pickering, 1986) and that it is typically associated with an unwillingness of senior management to delegate authority to product managers. Furthermore, research in the service industries (for example, Channon, 1978; Ingham, 1991) suggests that the interdependencies of many service industries makes product management structures difficult to implement and control. Research by the latter into the UK insurance industry found a high level of intra-organization transactions and a lack of profit-centre status enjoyed by divisions, associated with inappropriate internal transfer pricing and poor incentive and control systems. While this type of structure may be appropriate for a diversified conglomerate, it was shown to be inappropriate for insurance businesses where many functions are closely interdependent, allowing very little freedom of action for individual product managers. Within the insurance

industry, a hybrid structure was observed which reflected the need for some degree of centralization.

Finally, an interesting application of product-management structures can be found in a number of service industries where ethical considerations may call for separation of functions. This can occur where a relationship developed between an organization and a customer in one product area can result in unethical marketing practices in another. A good example is provided by merchant banks offering portfolio management and capital-raising services. In a proposed take-over bid, it is often necessary for those involved in raising the capital required by a client to work very discreetly for fear of prematurely raising the share price of the target company. If this information was available to those staff working in portfolio management, it would give them an unfair advantage over the market generally, allowing them to build up a shareholding in the target company ahead of the announcement of a take-over bid. Merchant banks have sought to build 'Chinese walls' around their operations where this risk is present and the adoption of a product management structure can allow this potential conflict of interests to be reduced. Numerous other service industries can be identified where similar ethical problems can be lessened by the adoption of a product management structure. Accountants selling both auditing and management consultancy services to a company may be tempted to gain business in the latter area at the expense of integrity in the former.

4.3.4　Market-management organization

Many organizations provide services for a diverse range of customers who have widely varying needs. As an example, a cross-Channel ferry operator provides basically a similar service of transport for the private car driver, the coach operator and the freight operator, among others. However, the specific needs of each group of users vary significantly—a coach operator and a road haulier are likely to differ in the importance they attach to service attributes such as flexibility, ease of reservations, the type of accommodation provided, etc. In such situations, market managers can be appointed to oversee the development of particular markets, in much the same way as a product manager oversees particular products. Instead of being given specific financial targets for their products, market managers are usually set growth or market share targets. The main advantage of this form of organization is that it allows marketing activity to be focused on meeting the needs of distinct and identified groups of customers—something which should be at the heart of all truly marketing-oriented organizations. It is also likely that innovative services are more likely to emerge within this structure than where an organization's response is confined within traditional product management boundaries. For example, a ferry operator's market manager specifically responsible for developing coach-tour traffic may be in an advantageous position to develop innovative group package holidays aimed at coach operators. Market-management structures are also generally more conducive to the important task of developing relationships with customers, especially for business-to-business services. Where an organization has a number of very important customers, it is common to find the appointment of key account managers to handle relationships with those clients.

Many of the disadvantages of the product-management organization are also shared by market-based structures. Again there can be a conflict between responsibility and authority and this form of structure can also become expensive to operate.

4.3.5　Matrix organization

Organizations which produce many different products for many different markets may experience difficulties if they adopt a purely product- or market-based structure. If a product

Market managers

	Small businesses	Large businesses	Personal customers
Insurance			
Stockbroking			
Lending			

Product managers

Figure 4.3   Matrix organization structure applied to a financial services organization

management structure is used, product managers would require detailed knowledge of very diverse markets. Similarly, in a market-management structure, market managers would require detailed knowledge of possibly very diverse product ranges. An alternative is to introduce a matrix type of organization which combines market managers with product managers (see Figure 4.3). Product managers concentrate on developing new products and promoting their own particular product, while market managers focus on meeting consumer needs without any preference for a particular product. An example of matrix structures can be found in many vehicle distributors, where market managers are appointed to identify and formulate a market strategy in respect of the distinct needs of private and business customers, etc., as well as being appointed to manage relationships with key customers. Market managers work alongside product managers who produce specialized activities such as servicing, bodywork repairs and vehicle hire which are made available to final customers through the market managers.

The most important advantages of matrix structures are that they can allow organizations to respond rapidly to environmental change—short-term project teams can be assembled and disbanded at short notice to meet changed needs. Project teams can bring together a wide variety of disciplines and can be used to evaluate new services before full-scale development is undertaken. A bank exploring the possibility of developing a banking system linked to personal customers' home computers might establish a team drawn from staff involved in personal account marketing and staff responsible for technology-based research and development. The former may include market researchers and the latter computer development engineers. Matrix structures need not necessarily be confined within the boundaries of a traditional marketing department—indeed, matrix organizations would normally embrace all of an organization's functions. In this wider context, the flexibility of matrix structures can be increased by bringing temporary workers into the structure on a contract basis as and when needed. During the 1990s there has been a trend for many service organizations to lay off significant numbers of workers—including management—and to buy them back when needed. As well as cutting fixed costs, such 'modular' organizations have the potential to respond very rapidly to environmental change.

Where matrix structures exist, great motivation can be present in effectively managed teams. Against this, matrix type structures can be associated with problems. Most serious is the confused lines of authority that may result. Staff may not be clear about to which superior he or she is responsible for a particular aspect of their duties, resulting in possible stress and demotivation. Where a matrix structure is introduced into an organization with a history and culture of functional specialization it can be very difficult to implement effectively. Staff may be reluctant to act outside a role which they have traditionally defined narrowly and guarded jealously. Finally, matrix structures invariably result in more managers being employed within an organization. At best, this can result in a costly addition to the salary bill. At worst, the existence of additional managers can also actually slow down decision-making processes where the managers show a reluctance to act outside a narrow functional role.

The great diversity of organizational structures highlights the fact that there is not one unique structure which is appropriate to all firms, even within the same service sector. Overall, the organization of a marketing department must allow for a flexible and adaptable response to customers' needs within a changing environment, while aiming to reduce the level of confusion, ambiguity and cost inherent in some structures.

PULLING OUT ALL THE STOPS AT BRITISH TELECOM

During the 1980s, British Telecom (BT) was transformed from a bureaucratic, unresponsive public sector organization to a private company which faced real competition in some of its many markets. One of the most hotly contested was the multi-line business user market. The management structures which may have allowed survival in a centrally planned environment were no longer capable of gaining advantage over aggressive newcomers such as Mercury Telecommunications.

Customers' complaints about BT reflected badly on the way in which customer relationships were managed. Business users found themselves with no one single point of first contact within the organization. Instead, they were forced to try numerous avenues within the seemingly monolithic organization before even a simple problem could be resolved. In a similar manner, there was a very poor management framework for overseeing each of the many specialized services which BT provides. When the premium-rate information service business developed in the mid-1980s, the development and launch for the whole business nationwide was handled on a part-time basis by a manager with very poor administrative

back-up. The product appeared to lack any focus of attention in much the same way as individual customers.

Towards the end of the 1980s, a revolution had occurred within BT in the way it managed its service to business clients. A key element of the change was the appointment of named account managers to handle the whole relationship between BT and those clients. Account managers were appointed and given intensive customer-care training, allowing them to take on the role of a consultant to clients, analysing their needs and jointly arriving at possible solutions. The dedication of named account managers to individual customers allowed them to build up on-going trust and relationships, something which was not possible previously, when BT/customer interaction was based on a succession of sales staff selling often-unrelated services in isolation from each other.

By the end of 1991, half of all BT's business customers had been assigned an account manager, with a target for every business customer to have one by April 1993. Their backgrounds reflected a desire by BT to bring about a cultural change from that which existed when it had a relatively cosy monopoly of business customers. More than half of the account managers were external recruits from organizations such as IBM, DEC and Unisys, where the corporate culture emphasized the need to focus on competitively meeting customer needs through excellence. New methods of monitoring and controlling account managers were introduced with regular surveys of a sample of 2500 business customers. In September 1991, two-thirds of respondents described their account managers as either very or reasonably impressive—a figure which had gone up by one-third since 1988.

In addition to account managers managing individual customers' business, product managers were also appointed to oversee the management of individual services. This has proved to be particularly valuable for new business services launched into competitive markets. The premium information services now have their own manager, and managers have been appointed where new business opportunities have appeared—for example, the creation of a 'Golden Number' service to provide business customers with easily memorizable telephone numbers.

4.4 THE RELATIONSHIP BETWEEN MARKETING AND OTHER ORGANIZATIONAL FUNCTIONS

The importance attached to an organization's marketing activities is influenced by the nature of the environment in which it operates. It was noted in Chapter 2 that the business environment could favour a production or a sales orientation rather than a marketing one. In a truly production-oriented firm, a marketing department has little role to play, other than merely processing orders. In this way the gas and electricity boards in the UK before privatization faced relatively stable markets with little effective competition. Marketing assumed less importance than the exploration of new energy sources and more efficient methods of distribution. Even with the advent of privatization, the majority of the new companies' markets remained stable, with marketing assuming most significance in those areas of activity, such as showroom sales of gas and electricity equipment, which faced effective competition.

In a truly marketing-oriented service organization, marketing responsibilities cannot be confined to something called a marketing department. In the words of Drucker (1973):

Marketing is so basic that it cannot be considered to be a separate function. It is the whole business seen from the point of view of its final result, that is, from the customer's point of view.

In marketing-oriented organizations the customer is at the centre of all activities. He or she is the concern not simply of the marketing department but also of all the production and administrative personnel whose actions may directly or indirectly impinge upon the customer's enjoyment of the service. In a typical service organization, the activities of a number of functional departments impinge on the service outcome received by customers:

- Personnel plans can have a crucial bearing on marketing plans. The selection, training, motivation and control of staff cannot be considered in isolation from marketing objectives and strategies. Possible conflict between the personnel and marketing functions may arise where—for example—marketing demands highly trained and motivated front-line staff, but the personnel function pursues a policy which places cost reduction above all else.
- Production managers may have a different outlook compared to marketing managers. A

marketing manager may seek to respond as closely as possible to customers' needs, only to find opposition from production managers, who argue that a service of the required standard cannot be achieved. A marketing manager of British Rail may seek to segment markets with fares tailored to meet the needs of small groups of customers, only to encounter hostility from operations managers who are responsible for actually issuing and checking travel tickets on a day-to-day basis and who may have misgivings about the confusion that finely segmented fares might cause.

- The actions of finance managers frequently have a direct or indirect impact on marketing plans. Ultimately, finance managers assume responsibility for the allocation of funds that are needed to implement a marketing plan. At a more operational level, finance managers' actions in respect of the level of credit offered to customers, or towards stockholdings where these are an important element of the service offering can also significantly affect the quality of service and the volume of customers which the organization is able to serve.

Marketing requires all these departments to 'think customer' and to work together to satisfy customer needs and expectations. There is a debate as to what authority the traditional marketing department should have in bringing about this customer orientation. In a truly marketing-oriented service company, marketing is an implicit part of everyone's job. In such a scenario, marketing becomes responsible for a narrow range of specialist functions such as advertising and marketing research. Responsibility for the relationship between the organization and its customers is spread more diffusely throughout the organization. Gummesson (1991) uses the term 'part-time marketer' to describe staff working in service organizations who may not have any direct line-management responsibility for marketing, but whose activities may indirectly impinge on the quality of service received by customers.

Some measure of the importance of the multiplicity of contacts between the organization and its customers can be found by counting the total number of interactions customers have with a particular organization's employees—both marketing and non-marketing. These are sometimes referred to as 'moments of truth', and in a study of Scandinavian Airline Systems, Carlzon (1987) estimated these to be in the order of 50 million per annum.

It can be argued that the introduction of a traditional marketing department as described above to a service organization can bring problems as well as benefits. In a survey of 219 executives representing public and private sector services organizations in Sweden, Gronroos (1982b) tested the idea that a separate marketing department may widen the gap between marketing and operations staff. This idea was put to a sample drawn from marketing as well as other functional positions using a Likert-type scale with five points ranging from agreeing strongly to disagreeing strongly. The results indicated that respondents in a wide range of service organizations considered there to be dangers in the creation of a marketing department. An average of 66 per cent agreed with the notion, with higher than average agreement being found among non-marketing executives, and those working in the hotel, restaurant, professional services and insurance sectors.

4.5 IMPROVING ORGANIZATIONAL EFFECTIVENESS FOR MARKETING

Numerous studies have sought to identify those factors within organizations which result in an organization being able to address its markets most effectively. The McKinsey 7S framework developed by Peters and Waterman (1982) identified seven essential elements for a successful business, based on a study of the most successful American companies. The elements are broken down into the hardware (Strategy, Structure and Systems) and the software (Skills, Staff, Styles and Shared values). Formalized strategies, structures and systems on their own were not considered to be sufficient to bring about success. These could be operationalized only with appropriate intangible actions.

At a strategic level, a number of methods can be used to develop a more responsive marketing orientation within an organization:

- The appointment of senior management who have a good understanding of the philosophies and practices of marketing.
- The introduction of in-house educational programmes which aim to train non-marketing management to empathize with customers' expectations.
- The introduction of outside consultants who can apply their previous experience of introducing a marketing culture to an organization from an impartial perspective.
- A commonly used method of making management think in marketing terms is to install a formal market-oriented planning system. This can have the effect of forcing managers to work through a list of market-related headings, such as an analysis of the competitive environment and identification of market opportunities when developing their annual plans.

Organizational culture is often raised as a factor which may contribute significantly to effective marketing management. It has been described by Jelinek *et al.* (1983) as 'some underlying structure of meaning that persists over time, constraining people's perception, interpretation and behaviour'. Numerous recent comparative studies of the performance of European-, American- and Japanese-managed organizations have introduced the concept of culture as a possible explanation for differences in competitive effectiveness where few differences in the structural characteristics of organisations are evident (Pascale and Athos, 1981). Within many parts of the service sector, it has proved difficult to alter cultural attitudes when the nature of an organization's operating environment has significantly changed, rendering the established culture a liability in terms of strategic marketing management. As an example, the cultural values of UK clearing banks have continued to be dominated by prudence and caution when in some product areas such as insurance sales a more aggressive approach to marketing management is called for.

In addition to the dominant culture of an organization, it is often possible to identify different subcultures within the same organization. Handy (1989) argues that organizations tend to have elements of different cultures appropriate to the structure and circumstances of different operating units within their structure. He identifies four types of culture:

- The power culture is found mainly in smaller organizations where power and influence stem from a single central source, through whom all decisions, communication and control are channelled. Because there is no rigid structure within the organization, it is theoretically capable of adapting to change very rapidly, although its actual success in adapting is dependent on the abilities of the central power source.
- The role culture is characterized by a formal, functional organization structure in which there is relatively little freedom and creativity in decision making. Such organizations are more likely to be production oriented and can have difficulty responding to new market opportunities.
- The task culture is concerned primarily with getting a given task done. Importance is therefore attached to those individuals who have the skill or knowledge to accomplish a particular task. Organizations with a task-oriented culture are potentially very flexible, changing constantly as new tasks arise. Innovation and creativity are highly prized for their own sakes.
- The person culture is characterized by organizations which are centred around serving the

interests of individuals within it. It is a relatively rare form of culture in any market-mediated environment, but can characterize, for example, campaigning pressure groups.

There has been debate on the relationship between marketing strategy and the organizational structure within which such strategy is developed and implemented. The traditional view is that structures adapt to fit the chosen strategy, although more recent thought has focused on the idea that strategy is very much dependent upon the structure adopted by an organization. An approach suggested by Giles (1988) is a 'structured iterative marketing planning process', which works by creating a cross-functional team of managers for the purpose of designing a marketing plan for a market or market segment selected by top management for attention. The resulting plan is likely to represent a high degree of commitment and ownership by those involved in creating it. The attraction of this type of approach is that it challenges managers to design better ways of addressing their markets by allowing things to be said which, in a conventional planning process, may be politically unacceptable. The marketing problem defines the agenda, rather than having it determined by the structure and political ideology of the organization. The process is designed to bring about marketing-led strategic change within the organization (Piercy, 1990).

4.6 INTRODUCING STRATEGIC MARKETING MANAGEMENT WITHIN THE PUBLIC SECTOR

Marketing management is increasingly being introduced to the public sector. However, attempts to introduce marketing management structures must recognize the great diversity of public sector marketing tasks. While some parts of the public sector function in competitive markets just like any private sector organization, others provide very complex services which, by their nature, can only be distributed by centrally planned allocation. To assess the appropriateness of marketing management structures within the public sector, public services can be classified using a framework analysing two aspects of the service in question:

1. The complexity of the service provided
2. The nature of the environment in which the service is provided

Public services can be described as complex where they involve diverse interdepartmental relationships in production. The operation of a youth service may involve considerable liaison between the educational and social services, the police and the recreation sections of local authorities. At the other end of the scale, services can be described as simple where a relatively narrow range of functional specialists are involved in their production. The operation of a local authority parks department, for example, is less likely to involve much liaison with specialists from other departments.

The second dimension of this analysis concerns the nature of the operating environment of a service. This can range from a totally planned environment where externalities (and often legislation) make market-mediated exchanges very difficult to achieve (for example, land-use planning and emergency services) to a market-mediated one which, for practical purposes, is indistinguishable from that facing a private sector company. These two scales are shown in Figure 4.4, where four quadrants are identified with reference to local authority services:

- The most straightforward task for marketing management is found in quadrant II (a simple service in a market-mediated environment), where marketing has gained a ready acceptance. Local authority bus services and airports can easily be isolated into separate operating units

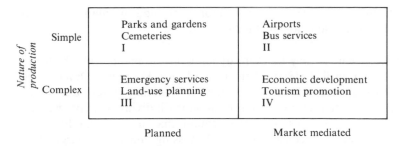

Nature of operating environment

Figure 4.4   A classification of local authority services

and can develop their own marketing culture to respond to the challenges of their environment. The task of marketing management is essentially similar to that of a private sector organization.

- In quadrant III (a complex service in a planned environment) marketing philosophies can have little meaning where the presence of externalities require significant centralized methods of distributing costs and benefits. Here, strategic decisions are based on social/political criteria and any attempt to introduce marketing management can only allow for some relatively superficial marketing practices (such as client-care programmes).

- In quadrant I (simple services in a planned environment), services have often been simplified further with a distinction made between those parts of the service which yield too many externalities to allow market-mediated distribution and those parts where such a system of distribution is considered desirable. As an example, some activities of a museum—such as assessing the scholarly significance of an object—cannot sensibly be left to market forces, whereas other activities (for example, refreshment facilities) are capable of competing with other private and public sector facilities. In this quadrant, there is frequently ambiguity over the expectations of marketing management.

- In quadrant IV marketing management within the public sector faces its most difficult challenge. These are complex services that involve many sections of an authority in their production, and which are subject to a market-mediated environment. The authority must develop an authority-wide marketing culture, or risk losing clients to other competing organizations. Examples include the tourism marketing and economic development functions of local authorities.

A growing feature of the public sector is the emergence of single-service, 'arm's length' agencies which have been given duties previously carried out within government itself. The number of such companies grew rapidly during the 1980s and a number of reasons can be identified for their creation:

- A desire to bridge the cultural gap that exists between the bureaucracy of large public sector structures and the potential dynamism of small semi-autonomous quasi-private sector organizations.

- With many private and public sector organizations responsible for marketing overlapping services, it may be possible to reduce duplication by pooling these efforts in a semi-autonomous organization.

- By creating a semi-autonomous body at arm's length it is sometimes possible for the body to gain access to additional funds from the private sector (although in many cases the government continues to set an external financing limit).

While these new single-service agencies may be more dynamic in the manner in which they address their users, Barnes and Campbell (1988), in their study of local Economic Development Companies, contrast the benefits of escape from a bureaucratic planning culture against the potential problems associated with a market-based culture in which individuals may lose sight of the organization's original values. In this way, they found that many local Economic Development Companies had become more conservative by dismissing financially marginal but socially valuable projects.

MARKETING INWARD TOURISM—AN ORGANIZATIONAL CHALLENGE FOR LOCAL AUTHORITIES

Because of its importance in local economic regeneration, many local authorities in the UK have developed strategies to attract tourists to their areas. This has been associated with a steady increase in budgets allocated for tourism marketing—for the year 1990/91, total local authority expenditure on tourism promotion in England was £51.2 million (Chartered Institute of Public Finance and Accountancy, 1991).

The tourism product being marketed by local authorities is a combination of elements from both the private and the public sectors—the former responsible for tourist attractions operating to narrow commercial criteria, while the latter has responsibility for infrastructure and planning policies that affect tourism. In view of the external benefits inherent in area-tourism promotion, the local authority also plays a large role in promoting the benefits of its area.

Tourism marketing management poses a number of problems for local authorities. Many of the facilities that impinge on tourists' enjoyment of an area—such as car parking, cleanliness, planning and conservation policies—have traditionally operated in a bureaucratic planning culture rather than a marketing one. In marketing an area, local authorities are constrained by bureaucratic culture and political pressure to meet the needs of local residents as well as those of potential visitors. But against this, the visitors whom the local authority is seeking to attract are becoming increasingly selective in the face of competition from many areas. In short, local authorities have had to become very customer-centred.

In an attempt to combine the need for centrally administered marketing of an area with the dynamism of the private sector, local collaborative marketing ventures have become common in this field. During the latter part of the 1980s a new type of single-service arm's-length agency—the Tourism Development Action Programme (TDAP)—has been created in a number of tourism-seeking areas with a view to overcoming some of the problems identified above.

TDAPs are an initiative of the English Tourist Board and involve a partnership between private and public sector organizations. The partners typically comprise District and County Councils, Urban Development Corporations, local landowners, hotel owners and operators of tourism attractions. Partners contribute funds to support items of expenditure which in their own right may not yield a return but result in more tourist spending across the area as a whole. Most of the later TDAPs have been incorporated as formal limited companies, providing an organizational structure which is separately accountable and is attractive to private sector partners. The first TDAP was established in Bristol in 1984. By January 1992, 26 TDAPs had been created, of which eight had completed their initial 3-year term and have continued in some modified form (Bramwell and Groom, 1989).

The dynamism and private sector culture of these organizations have allowed strategic marketing decisions and action programmes to be developed. The TDAP marketing management culture has also been found to filter back to the local authority in the way in which it provides public sector facilities to satisfy tourists' needs (Palmer, 1993). Examples of successful collaboration include the development of conference centres which bring together private sector conference and hotel developers, transport operators and local authorities. The last can achieve diverse objectives (such as creating employment or eliminating eyesores) more effectively by delivering its services—such as signposting, car-park provision and land-use planning—within the framework of a marketing strategy developed jointly with the private sector.

4.7   MANAGING MARKETING INFORMATION

Marketing management requires a constant flow of information for two principal purposes;

- To provide information as an input to the marketing planning process—for example, on developments in the organization's marketing environment
- To monitor the implementation of marketing programmes and allow corrective action to be taken if performance diverges from target.

The use of information has been identified as a source of a firm's marketing orientation (Kohli and Jaworski, 1990) which allows it to obtain a sustainable competitive advantage (Porter and Millar, 1985). Piercy (1985) has argued that processing information should be regarded as the fifth 'P' of the Marketing Mix. Information represents a bridge between the organization and its environment and is the means by which a picture of the changing environment is built up within the organization. Marketing management is responsible for turning information into specific marketing plans.

As information collection, processing, transmission and storage technologies improve, information is becoming more accessible not only to one particular organization but also to its competitors. Attention is therefore moving away from how information is collected and towards whom is best able to make use of it. It is too simple to say that marketing managers commission data collection by technical experts and make decisions on the basis of these data. There has been recent research interest in the relationship between market researchers and marketing managers, focusing on the role of trust between the two and how its presence helps to reduce risk (Moorman et al., 1992).

The concept of trust is reflected in the requirement that the collection of marketing research should be driven by meeting decision makers' needs, rather than those of people producing information. Clear aims must be set, which may include the need for information on the size and characteristics of markets, customer attitudes and awareness of brand names, the effectiveness of the firm's pricing and distribution policies, to name but a few. Aims should specify the

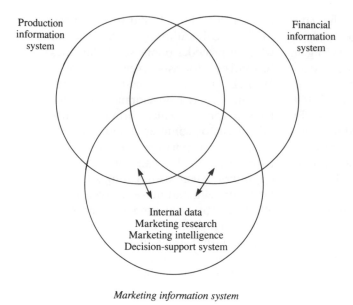

Marketing information system

Figure 4.5   A systems approach to managing information

frequency with which information is to be collected, the speed with which it is to be transmitted, the level of accuracy required, to whom it is to be given and who is responsible for acting on it.

Marketing research allows management to improve its strategic planning, tactical implementation of programmes and monitoring and control. A practical problem for marketing planning is that information is typically much more difficult to obtain to meet strategic planning needs than it is to meet operational and control ones. There can be a danger of marketing managers focusing too heavily on information that is easily available at the expense of that which is needed.

The complexity of the task of gathering information about the marketing environment will vary between individual firms. Ansoff (1984) attributes this variation to two principal factors. First, firms will perceive varying levels of uncertainty in their environment as measured by the rate of environmental change. Second, the complexity of the task is affected by the range of activities in which a company is either involved, or is likely to be in the future.

Many analyses of organizations' information collection and dissemination activities take a systems perspective. The collection of marketing information can be seen as one subsystem of a much larger management information system. Others typically include production, financial and personnel systems. In a well-designed management information system, the barriers between these systems should be conceptual rather than real. For example, sales information is of value to all these subsystems to a greater or lesser extent (see Figure 4.5).

Insofar as a marketing information subsystem can be identified, it can be seen conceptually as comprising four principal components, although in practice, they are operationally interrelated:

- Much information is generated within organizations, particularly in respect of operational and control functions. By carefully arranging its collection and dissemination, internal data can provide a constant and up-to-date flow of information at relatively little cost, useful for both planning and control functions. Its use is considered in more detail in Chapter 5.

- Marketing research is that part of the system concerned with the structured collection of marketing information. This can provide both routine information about marketing effectiveness—such as brand-awareness levels or delivery performance—and one-off studies, such as changing attitudes towards diet or the pattern of income distribution. The detailed practices of marketing research are considered in more detail in Chapter 5.

- Marketing intelligence comprises the procedures and sources used by marketing management to obtain pertinent information about developments in its marketing environment. It complements a marketing research system, for whereas the latter tends to focus on structured and largely quantifiable data—collection procedures, intelligence gathering concentrates on picking up relatively intangible ideas and trends. Marketing management can gather this intelligence from a number of sources, such as newspapers, specialized cuttings services, employees who are in regular contact with market developments, intermediaries and suppliers to the company, as well as specialized consultants.

- Marketing decision support systems comprise a set of models which allow forecasts to be made. Information is both an input to such models—in that data are needed to calibrate a model—and an output, in that models provide information on which decisions can be based. Models are frequently used in service-outlet decisions (see Chapter 10), where historical data may have established a relationship between one variable (for example, the level of sales achieved by a particular service outlet) and other variables (pedestrian traffic in a street). Predicting the sales level of a proposed new outlet then becomes a matter of measuring pedestrian traffic at a proposed site, feeding this information into the model and calculating the predicted sales level.

The effectiveness of marketing information systems will be determined by a number of factors:

1. *An accurate definition of the information needs of the organization* Needs can themselves be difficult to identify and it can be a great problem to locate the boundaries of the firm's environments and to separate relevance from irrelevance. This is a particular problem for large multi-product firms. The mission statement of an organization may give some indication of the boundaries for its environmental search. The TSB Bank, for example, has a mission statement which includes an aim for it to be the dominant provider of financial services in the UK. The information needs therefore include anything related to the broader environment of financial services rather than the narrower field of banking.

2. *The extensiveness of the search for information* A balance has to be struck between the need for information and the cost of collecting it. The most critical elements of the marketing environment must be identified and the cost of collecting relevant information weighed against that which would result from an inaccurate forecast.

3. *Speed of communication* The marketing information system will only be effective if information is communicated quickly and to the appropriate people. Deciding what information to withhold from an individual and the concise reporting of relevant information can be as important as deciding what to include if information overload is to be avoided.

4.8   CONTROLLING THE MARKETING MANAGEMENT PROCESS

Having developed strategic marketing plans and programmes of action to implement those strategies, it is essential that marketing management ensures that these are being implemented in a way that allows objectives to be met. Marketing management control systems should exist and their general purpose has been described by Anthony (1988, page 7):

The management control function includes making the plans which are necessary to ensure that strategies are implemented. Management control is the process by which managers influence other members of the organisation to implement the organisation's strategies.

Control can take place at various levels within the marketing planning process, from the strategic to the operational level. Successful control mechanisms have three components:

- The setting of targets or standards of expected performance
- The measurement and evaluation of actual performance
- Taking corrective action where necessary

4.8.1   Setting targets

Corporate objectives specified earlier in the planning process provide a foundation from which all subsequent targets are derived. In general, the greater the level of disaggregation of targets, the greater the degree of control that will be possible. To be effective in a control process, targets should be specified which:

- Give individual managers a clear indication of the standards of performance expected of them.
- Distinguish between controllable variables that can be managed by an individual manager and those that are uncontrollable and should therefore be excluded from their standards for performance.
- Allocate targets to the right person. Ultimately, all costs and revenues are someone's responsibility and should be monitored and controlled at the appropriate point within an organization. Even a relatively fixed and uncontrollable element such as rent can become controllable by senior management over the longer term.
- Show which targets are to take priority. In any event, targets should not be mutually incompatible.
- Are sufficiently flexible to allow for changes in the organization's environment that were not foreseen at the time the targets were set.

Conflict can arise in the process of setting targets where trade-offs are necessary between short- and long-term targets. Very often, in order to improve short-term goal attainment, control action may be taken at the expense of long-term targets. Similarly, controls in respect of long-term objectives may call for short-term sacrifices. Managers are very often under pressure to achieve good short-term results, on the basis of which they may gain promotion. This can continue up the management hierarchy, with managers being rewarded for meeting short-term targets, even if these may damage the long-term prospects of their organization.

For control purposes, quantitative targets are generally preferred to qualitative ones. Many apparently qualitative targets, such as customer satisfaction and attentiveness of front-line service personnel, can often be reduced to quantifiable indices—for example, by setting targets for the number of complaints received, or the percentage of customers booking a repeat service, or by using an analytic technique such as SERVQUAL (see Chapter 8). There is a danger, however, in setting purely quantified targets, as these will almost, of necessity, be a series of relatively simple indicators. Staff seeking to achieve these targets may concentrate their attention on meeting them, possibly at the expense of other more important qualitative aspects of their performance. A telephone-enquiry office set with a target of answering a specified number of calls per hour may lose sight of the quality of information given during the call if its attention is primarily focused on responding within a target time. There is also an argument that a more realistic appraisal system for senior marketing management might be to examine the quality of the decisions that a manager made during the previous period, taking account of the fact that the operating environment posed numerous problems and opportunities which may not have been apparent at the time that targets were initially set.

4.8.2 Measuring and evaluating performance

A marketing-information system assumes an important role for measuring and evaluating performance. Typical information which may be collected and used for control purposes includes:

- Financial targets—sales turnover/contribution/profit margin disaggregated by product/business unit
- Market analysis—market-share performance
- Effectiveness of communication—productivity of sales personnel, effectiveness of advertising or sales promotion
- Pricing—level of discounts given, price position
- Personnel—level of skills achieved by workforce, survey of customer comments on staff performance

Where performance is below target, the reasons may not be immediately obvious. A comprehensive marketing-information system can allow an organization to analyse variance. A uniform fall in sales performance across the organization, combined with intelligence gained about the state of the market, would suggest that remedial action aimed at improving the sales performance of individual sales personnel may not be as effective as a reassessment of targets or strategies in the light of the changed sales environment.

Efficiency and effectiveness are two fundamental ways of measuring performance. Efficiency can be defined in terms of an organization's success in turning inputs into outputs, while effectiveness is the level of success in producing a desired result. An efficient business cannot succeed if it is efficient at doing the wrong things—i.e. it is ineffective.

Where an organization competes in a market on the basis of its cost leadership, efficiency may be a key measure for evaluating management performance. Within the service sector, important efficiency measures can include the number of services performed per employee, value of sales achieved per salesperson, the cost of advertising per thousand valued impressions and the level of utilization of assets (for example, load factors on aircraft).

Organizational effectiveness can be measured using the goal model or systems resource approaches. The former is expressed in terms of the extent to which specified goals are surpassed. For example, a library that exceeded its goal of increasing the number of visits during the week of a national libraries campaign may be considered to be effective in meeting this particular goal. Whether its policy has been effective overall will depend upon the extent to which this represented an important goal. The library may have been effective at increasing the number of visits but ineffective in a higher-order goal of increasing the number of books borrowed during the year. The systems resource approach defines effectiveness as the degree to which an organization is successful in acquiring and utilizing scarce resources. More effective organizations survive because they can maintain a greater intake of resources than is required to produce their output. A library may be effective in obtaining visitors but ineffective in securing an adequate and up-to-date supply of books or sponsorship for events held in the library.

4.8.3 Exercising control

A good planning and control system can generate a lot of information. The key to effective control is to give the right information to the right people at the right time. Providing too much can be costly in terms of the effort required to assemble and disseminate it and can also reduce effective control where the valuable information is hidden among information of secondary importance. Also, the level of reporting will be determined by the level of tolerance allowed for compliance to target. An analysis of variance from target should indicate if the variance is within or beyond the control of the person responsible for meeting the target. If it is beyond their control, the issue should become one of revising the target so that it becomes achievable once more. If the variance is the result of factors that are subject to a manager's control, a number of measures can be taken to try to revise behaviour:

- Bureaucratic control can be used where instructions are sent to subordinates, failing which, disciplinary action is taken.
- Incentive schemes can be used as a control mechanism. Incentives are often linked directly to performance—performance bonuses and sales commission, for example.
- The allocation of resources (including personnel) offers an important form of organizational control as this has the effect of facilitating some actions and inhibiting others.
- Informal controls can be exercised at a number of levels. Jaworski (1988), for example, identifies three levels of informal control—self-control, social control and cultural control. The first is essentially based on a system of incentives that may be financial or psychological (for example passing on customer comments about serving staffs' performance). Social control is applied within small groups where violation of a group norm causes other group members to put subtle pressure on the deviating member to perform to standard. Cultural control results from a process of internalizing the cultural norms within each individual so that he or she can be expected to behave in accordance with the norms. In some organizations the cultural norm may be that 'the customer is always right' and through cultural control, individuals will always attach great importance to this value.

BRINGING CONTROL TO BRITISH RAIL

British Rail provides a highly complex service to diverse groups of users. Complexity results from the interdependency of many aspects of its operations—tracks and terminals are frequently shared by a diverse range of services, resulting in a high level of fixed costs which have to be allocated on some basis. Among the customer groups for whom British Rail caters are casual long-distance leisure passengers, regular short-distance commuters, parcel users and high-volume freight users. Since nationalization in 1948, British Rail has been organized on a geographical basis. The Western, South-ern, Eastern, London Midland and Scottish Regions were essentially responsible for producing and marketing all rail services in their regions. Within each of these, controlling performance proved to be a very difficult task as a high proportion of costs and revenue was shared between different categories of user.

During the early 1980s, British Rail sought to restructure its operations to achieve a greater level of control. The first stage was to create a matrix type of organization structure which allocated responsibility for marketing British Rail's services to managers with responsibility for a number of identifiable customer groups. Five 'sectors'—InterCity, Network SouthEast, Regional Railways, Railfreight and Parcels—were created and their management given clear and narrow objectives. Each of these managers was responsible for negotiating the supply of operational resources from the regions, which remained part of the structure. As with most matrix type organizations, control problems soon became apparent as the sector marketing managers had very little control over the resources which were provided by the regions. Poor reliability by the InterCity manager could always be blamed on inadequate signalling facilities provided by the regional operating structure.

In a far-reaching move in April 1991, British Rail announced that it was to devolve a significant level of decision making to profit-centre managers. By April 1992, the five regions had been abolished and replaced by 20 profit centres, leaving the British Railways Board to retain responsibility for strategic matters such as investment programmes, financial targets and safety. The 20 profit centres are now each run by a director and own all the rolling stock, track and signalling used. Network SouthEast, which provides rail services in London and the south-east region, was divided into nine semi-autonomous divisions, some of which are quite substantial businesses in their own right. The largest—SouthWest, which covers all services from Waterloo—had an income in 1990 of £252 million, covered 800 route miles and employed 8000 staff, while the smallest—London, Tilbury and Southend—had an income of £65 million, covering 70 route miles with a staff of 1500. InterCity was divided into five route divisions and Regional Railways into five subdivisions.

In an effort to make each profit centre more cost-conscious, charges are levied on trains from one profit centre using the facilities of another. Directors of each profit centre know exactly what they are responsible for and have complete accountability for their operations.

REVIEW QUESTIONS

1. What are the marketing problems and opportunities of a product-management structure for an insurance company?
2. What is meant by a matrix organization structure? Suggest service industries for which this type of structure might be appropriate and discuss its possible strengths and weaknesses.
3. Do you agree with the idea that a marketing department can actually be a barrier to the successful development of a marketing orientation within service organizations? Give examples.
4. What are the main differences in implementing a market-oriented management structure within the public as opposed to the private service sector?
5. In what ways is marketing information such a valuable resource to service organizations?
6. Suggest steps that could be taken by a telecommunications company to make its marketing management more responsive to customers' needs.

FIVE

ANALYSING AND RESEARCHING SERVICES MARKETS

OBJECTIVES

After reading this chapter, you should be able to understand:

- The relationship of marketing research to an organization's broader marketing information system
- The purposes for which marketing research is undertaken by service organizations and the reasons for its increasing importance
- Methods used to collect and analyse marketing research data
- The role of marketing research in segmenting services markets
- Insights into the complex processes of service buying behaviour provided by marketing research

5.1 INTRODUCTION

Marketing information has to be seen in the context of the interfunctional dynamics of an organization. A timely supply of appropriate information provides feedback on an organization's performance, allowing actual performance to be compared with target. On the basis of such information, control measures can be applied which seek—where necessary—to put the organization back on its original targets. Organizations also learn from the past in order to better understand the future. For making longer-term planning decisions, historical information is supplemented by a variety of continuous and *ad hoc* studies, all designed to allow better-informed decisions to be made. Marketing research cannot in itself produce decisions—it merely provides information which must be interpreted by marketing managers. As an interfunctional integrator, marketing information draws data from all functional areas of an organization, who in turn use the information to perform their functions more effectively. Research involving employees, both as sources of information and recipients of research findings, assumes importance as an integrating device.

Above all else, marketing research is a means of keeping in touch with customers. Central to this is an understanding of the processes which customers use in evaluating services, before purchase, during the service process and after consumption. Quality is frequently cited as a factor on which customers base their choice of service, but its measurement poses a number of conceptual and practical problems. These are considered in more detail in Chapter 8.

This chapter opens by considering marketing information in the context of organizations and their environment, before describing the role of marketing research within marketing

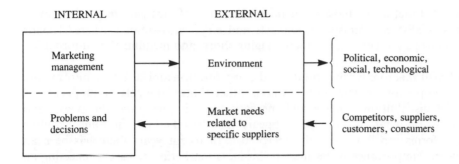

Figure 5.1   The flow of marketing research information (adapted from Chisnall, 1986)

information systems. Following this, an outline of the marketing research process will be set in the context of the services sector with a detailed analysis of its aims and techniques. Finally, a number of models that have been developed to understand buyer behaviour processes are discussed.

5.2   MARKETING INFORMATION IN CONTEXT

Marketing research can be seen as a two-way flow of information between an organization and its environment: The importance of the two-way nature of the information flow has been emphasized by Chisnall (1986) and the principal features of this flow are illustrated in Figure 5.1. Although research into organizations' operating environment focuses on identifying the needs of actual and potential customers and consumers, this has to be placed within the context of research into wider political, economic, social and technological developments.

An example of this two-way flow of information and influence between an organization's management and its environments is seen in the rapid development of communications and information technology. Recent technological innovations—for example, Electronic Point of Sale (EPOS) systems—have enabled service companies to greatly enhance the quality of their core services in terms of speed, accuracy and consistency. In turn, the resulting increase in operational efficiency, combined with the additional information which it is now possible to generate, has allowed service organizations to improve other areas of their service offering—such as sales after-care—as a means of gaining competitive advantages. At the same time, the increasing ease with which data can be collected and disseminated has made it easier for services companies to manage service quality by setting quantifiable objectives that can be effectively monitored.

New technologies are, of course, only one aspect of an organization's marketing environment which need to be understood and evaluated. Organizations must also understand the effects of other environmental factors such as the state of the local or national economy. Without this broader environmental information, routine pieces of marketing research information—such as the market share held by a company's brands over the past year—cannot be interpreted meaningfully. Such environmental factors can arguably be more important for services than for manufacturing industries; most obviously for financial services, but also in sectors such as leisure and travel, where consumers' expenditure reflects national economic performance more closely than is the case for many fast-moving consumer goods.

It must be said, however, that although the tracking of macro-environmental trends can be of great strategic importance to service organizations, it constitutes a relatively limited part of the marketing research function in most companies. The task of strategic research is more likely to be left to specialist economists, sociologists and engineers—among others—leaving marketing research managers to concentrate on managing short- and medium-term information needs.

As well as these broad macro-environmental trends, organizations must gather information about their immediate operating environment. Among other things, the role of suppliers and buyers, the nature of distribution systems and, perhaps most importantly, the power and influence of competitors (in whatever guise they appear) must be taken into account if routine marketing research information is to be fully interpreted. In recent years there has been an extension in the role and importance of business-to-business marketing research, reflecting an increased recognition by managers of the effects on their operations of increasingly rapid changes in their immediate marketing environment. Business-to-business research is no longer limited to organizations within the traditional manufacturing sector, while the development and growth of competitive intelligence (which now has its own professional society within the UK), as part of the marketing intelligence operation, reflects a growing concern with competitive activity in a wider context than simply competitive brand shares.

5.3 MARKETING INFORMATION SYSTEMS AND THE ROLE OF MARKETING RESEARCH

The need for some form of Marketing Information System (MIS) and its role within marketing management was discussed in Chapter 4. Here, the nature of the MIS is examined in more detail.

Kotler (1991, page 96) defines a MIS as a system that 'consists of people, equipment and procedures to gather, sort, analyse, evaluate and distribute needed, timely and accurate information to marketing decision-makers'. A perfect MIS would gather all possible external information described in Figure 5.1, along with internal information generated within the organization, filtering out that which is not relevant to particular problems and decisions, and present the relevant information in a logical and easily digestible format.

Marketing Information Systems are continuing and interactive structures, implying that although they may be formally managed by a specialist cluster of people using specialized equipment and procedures, interaction with data users and data generators is crucial. Parasuraman (1991) has proposed a model which identifies the relationship between the key sources and operations of such systems, though the extent to which they are formalized depends largely on the size and nature of an organization. The importance of trust and good working relationships between the various parties involved in a MIS has been emphasized by Deshpande and Zaltman (1984).

It is impossible to define with accuracy the exact functions of marketing research within MISs, as organizations differ so widely in size and structure. However, in Figure 5.2 an attempt has been made to show by means of shaded boxes the areas inside which the marketing research function normally operates.

Information sources can be divided into those that are available internally within an organization and those collected from external data sources. It is in the area of internal data collection that the line between marketing research and other MIS functions is most difficult to define in a neat textbook fashion. Much depends on the size, scope and structure of the MIS itself. In many large organizations the collation of regularly generated information, such as costs and sales figures, will not be central to the research activity. However, marketing research may well generate new information from within the organization—for example, by collecting data on a more *ad hoc* basis from key groups such as management, the salesforce and front-line service personnel.

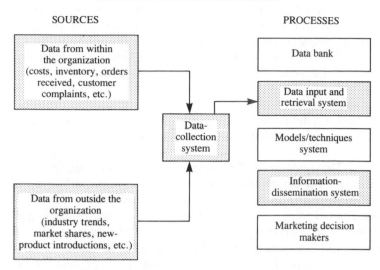

MARKETING INFORMATION SYSTEM

SOURCES   PROCESSES

Figure 5.2   The role of marketing reseach within the sources and processes of a marketing information system (adapted from Parasuraman, 1991)

In practice, the main focus for marketing research activity within most service organizations is external data collection, referring to what Chisnall (1986) calls market needs related to specific supplies (see Figure 5.1). In so far as such data must be analysed and disseminated, market researchers become involved in data input and retrieval, and information-dissemination systems. In smaller organizations it is possible that the research function will also incorporate the setting-up and operation of data banks and the development of models and systems which incorporate information gathered by researchers.

Two main purposes of marketing research can be identified. First, it provides management with market and product-specific information, which allows it to minimize the degree of uncertainty in planning its marketing effort. This risk-minimization function can apply to the whole of the marketing operation, or to any of its constituent parts, such as advertising. It has been pointed out by Crimp (1990), however, that relatively few market researchers are involved in strategic organizational decisions—instead, they perform an essentially operative role. Second, marketing research has a control function, allowing management to monitor the performance of its plans once they have been implemented. Because information in both cases comes, directly or indirectly, from the marketplace, it is often considered—by researchers at least—to form the key element of a Marketing Information System.

5.4   MAJOR RESEARCH USES IN SERVICES MARKETING

Any distinction between services and goods marketing research is becoming increasingly blurred as manufacturers also concentrate on the service and other intangible elements of their offering. One sign of this is the recent considerable increase in research by manufacturers into their corporate image. While manufacturing companies such as ICI develop and monitor corporate image programmes (World Class) alongside product-branding symbols (the Dulux dog), services companies seek ways in which they can overcome problems of identification and brand loyalty towards intangibles by developing strong, often anthropomorphic symbols (non-human symbols with which humans nevertheless identify) to help differentiate themselves from competitors. Examples of this can be seen in the associated symbols of UK banks for example, the resurrection by Lloyds Bank of the Black Horse in 1984 and the Midland Bank's Griffin. In this context the fairly recent development of substantial demand for marketing research from services companies, given that the sector depends on customer definitions of their offerings, is ironic.

There is little doubt about the importance of marketing research to service organizations. Christopher Lovelock (1991) identifies a number of factors that tend to characterize successful service businesses. Among these, two are particularly pertinent to this chapter:

- *Capturing and using customer data* The significance of information for the planning of marketing activities has already been stated. The consequent implications for services marketers are therefore apparent and some of their specific needs in this area are outlined below.
- *Soliciting feedback from customers and employees* It has already been stated that the gathering of information from customers is vital to marketing success in general. However, in service industries it is particularly important as customers do not have a tangible product to assess according to some predetermined criteria that they have set out. A large number of predominantly intangible variables contribute to overall satisfaction and may influence the way that each experience is perceived. Therefore the constant or intermittent interaction between customers and the service provider, which occurs as a stream of service encounters, must be evaluated as an on-going process in order to ascertain the degree of customer satisfaction, which may fluctuate from one encounter to another. Some aspects of a service may be perceived as good on one occasion and bad on another, for instance, a customer may be satisfied with the time spent queuing at a post office one week and dissatisfied the next. Loyalty comes from developing a good long-term relationship with customers and feedback should be solicited on a regular basis in order to determine the level of satisfaction that is being achieved. There needs to be some means by which the post office knows when a customer is dissatisfied and the reasons why.

The variability of services makes research into them very different compared to manufactured goods which may be used repeatedly without any variance. In addition, goods marketing does not normally involve any face-to-face interaction with production staff, unlike services, where employees usually perform the service on, or in conjunction with, the customer. The crucial importance of staff in making the service offer a satisfactory one increases the necessity to examine their perceptions. Because employees can contribute so much to service quality it is important to consider their views about how well a service is being received by customers and how it may be improved. After all, it is the front-line staff within an organization who have regular and close contact with the users of a service, so the information that they provide can be of enormous value.

Furthermore, the concept of internal marketing which is vital to the provision of a quality service requires that organizations should undertake employee research because employees can be seen as internal recipients of marketing efforts. A successful services company should be just as proficient at managing the management/staff interface as it is at the staff/customer one. Evidence of this is provided by Tim Melville-Ross (1989), Chief Executive of the Nationwide Anglia Building Society, who has pointed out the need to involve staff in service quality programmes. He proposes that in order to be truly effective, organizations should address the service given to internal customers—feedback from these customers should be treated as an important aspect of services marketing research.

Current practice in services marketing research reflects the growing emphasis put upon the maintenance of quality standards of service. In very simple terms, the essence of service quality is understanding what customers want and ensuring that they are provided with it on a continuous basis. It is therefore of the utmost importance that service organizations understand their customers' requirements, i.e. what motivates them to use the service provided. The critical factor in measuring service quality is to identify the variance between what customers get as opposed to what they want. This is a highly subjective matter, and requires careful qualitative analysis of customers' expectations of the service and their perceptions of service delivery.

The marketing research process can be taken a stage further to identify segments of the population in terms of their similarity of service expectations. Studies that indicate different sets of customers who have a common buying behaviour can be of great strategic value. Using the principle of benefit segmentation, it is possible to identify the differing requirements of groups of customers in terms of the components of service quality that they perceive as important, and target them with appropriately designed service offerings.

Service quality measurement is considered to be of such fundamental importance to services marketing that a separate chapter (Chapter 8) is devoted to discussing approaches to conceptualizing and measuring service quality. Quality issues in fact lie behind the motivation for much of the marketing research which is carried out within the service sector. Some of the more important uses are listed below:

- *Research into customer needs* Research is undertaken to learn what underlying needs individuals seek to satisfy when they buy services. Identifying needs that are currently unmet by service offerings spurs new service development.
- *Research into customer expectations* A variety of qualitative techniques are used to study the standards of service which customers expect when consuming a service—for example, with respect to delays, friendliness of staff, etc.
- *Customer-perception studies* The most important definition of service quality is what the customer considers the quality level to be. Perception studies can be undertaken before purchase of a service to test the extent to which external factors may have influenced the way an individual perceives an organization or its specific offerings. Such studies can also be undertaken during or after consumption to test the perceived level of quality delivery.
- *Monitoring of service delivery* In addition to surveys of customers' perceptions of service delivery, organizations usually measure the technical aspects of service delivery. The reliability of a train service and waiting time at a bank are examples of technical quality that can be measured by observation without interaction with customers. 'Mystery Shopper' surveys are gaining popularity as a technique for observing service delivery processes.
- *Customer surveys Ad hoc* or regular programmes of survey research carried out among customers provide information about their perceptions and expectations. These can have the dual functions of providing the service organization with much-needed information as well as a public relations tool by allowing customers to feel that they have made their feelings known in a way that may allow them to be acted upon.
- *Similar industry studies* Many service industries can learn from research undertaken in what at first appear to be totally unrelated industries. By learning about operating practices and customer reactions to their service offering, marketing managers in one sector such as shipping can discover much from studies carried out within, for example, the hotel sector.
- *Research into service intermediaries* Agents, dealers and other intermediaries are close to consumers and therefore form a valuable conduit for gathering marketing research. In addition, intermediaries are customers of service principals, therefore research is undertaken to establish—among other things—their perceptions of the standard of service that they are receiving from the service principal.
- *Key client studies* Most organizations see some customers as being more important than

others, on account of the volume and/or the profitability of the custom they generate. Where a company derives the majority of its income from one customer, it may make a particular effort to ensure that this customer is totally satisfied with its standards of service and prices. The loss of the business as a result of shortcomings of which it is unaware could otherwise be catastrophic. In some cases, the relationship with key customers may be of such mutual importance that each partner may spend considerable time jointly researching shared problems. For example, an airport operator with two or three key airline customers may jointly develop a programme of research to judge passengers' perception of the total experience they have as they pass through the airport. Sometimes, key clients with whom a sound relationship has been built up can be used as a basis for researching new service ideas before they are released more widely.

- *Customer panels* As a means of keeping in regular contact with current and potential customers, panels are often used. These can provide valuable information about proposed new service launches, as well as monitoring perceptions of current service delivery.

- *Transaction analysis* Many organizations track the progress of services provided to clients, both during and after delivery. This can give valuable information about customer perceptions of service quality compared to their expectations. It can also be used internally to monitor the attainment of performance targets.

- *Analysis of complaints* Service organizations often see complaints as a positive source of information from customers, for if complaints are communicated to management it is in a better position to prevent future repeats of the factors that gave rise to the complaints than would be the case if aggrieved customers remained silent and quietly took their custom elsewhere. For this reason, many service organizations try to make it easy for their customers to communicate grievances to them, and carefully analyse their responses.

- *Employee research* As part of a programme of internal marketing, research into employees is often undertaken by service organizations. This can focus on employees as internal customers of services within an internal market as well as their thoughts on the methods of service provision. Employee suggestion schemes form an important part of research into employees.

COUNCIL USES MARKETING RESEARCH TO PUT ITS HOUSE IN ORDER

In 1988 the market research organization MORI undertook a piece of consumer research on behalf of Warwick District Council—the Tenant Satisfaction Survey. Although the Council's Housing Officers thought that they provided a first-class housing service, the newly appointed Chief Housing Officer—inspired by the concept of customer care and the new housing legislation—wanted to test this out by conducting independent research of the Council's users.

Undertaking research was considered to present valuable opportunities both as an input to the policy-making process and as a means of assessing the effectiveness of policy implementation. The latter was to be achieved through a follow-up survey two years later, when policy changes had been completed.

MORI, who were experienced in undertaking consumer projects on behalf of councils, were attracted by this survey. It offered the agency one of the few opportunities to use a pure, unclustered random sample. As the Council has a database of all its properties, it was possible to list them in geographical order and draw a straightforward one-in-ten sample across the regions used by the Housing Department. The only variation from a purely random selection involved slight over-sampling in rural areas to make the sample more robust. MORI drew a sample of 1221 names from the tenant list and interviewers were sent out to conduct personal in-house interviews with the person in each household who had most dealings with the Department. The level of cooperation and the consequent response rate was very good—906 respondents in total, or a contact rate of 74.2 per cent.

The results of the survey were pleasing for the Council—the tenants were quite flattering about many aspects of the housing service. Overall, two-thirds of tenants were satisfied with the service provided and in a comparative analysis, Warwick District Council received a higher rating than any other authority that MORI had previously studied. However, from an analysis of the data, the Council was able to identify some areas where policy measures were required. These included communications with tenants, efficiency of heating, speed and quality of repairs, consultation on proposed improvements and awareness of the legislation on Tenants' Choice.

The resultant policy outcome was the implementation of an action plan which included:

- The introduction of a feedback instrument (a [Dis]Satisfaction card) for monitoring the repairs service. Tenants were unhappy with the speed and quality of the repairs service.
- A series of meetings was arranged on Tenants' Choice legislation to counteract the low level of awareness of the implications of the Housing Act 1988.
- Tenant consultation was to be improved. There was also concern about the limited amount of informa-

tion provided by the Council.
- A budget was given to the Department for the creation of a Tenants' Handbook and Newsletter in response to the criticism of council communications.
- The recruitment of an additional receptionist at the Housing Office and refurbishing of the waiting areas. A concern had been expressed about the speed with which enquiries were handled at the Office.

After this series of actions by the Council the survey was repeated in order to evaluate customers' reactions to the changes. The programme of initiatives was generally well received and satisfaction remained high. In particular, the new communications policy met with approval and more customers now felt that they were being kept well informed. The overall shift in emphasis towards customer care was seen to be a great improvement in the Council's marketing.

This study did not involve intricate research methods—it used classic random sampling techniques and a classic pre/post-test methodology—but it was favourably received by the client and proved to be very effective. The research programme worked because the client had a clear idea about what it wanted to find out, which enabled the agency to focus on the key issues. It illustrates how rigorous research techniques, combined with an understanding of the market being surveyed and clear guidance from the client, will result in cost-effective, actionable research.

Adapted from Dyas, D. and Burns, T., 'Towards an Action Plan', published in Martin, D. and Goodyear, J. (Eds) (1991), *Research Works*, AMSO/NTC Publications.

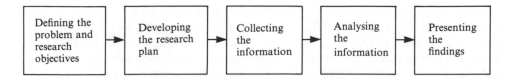

Figure 5.3 The marketing research process

5.5 THE MARKETING RESEARCH INDUSTRY AND ITS PROCESSES

Most discussions of marketing research activity include a definition, and this chapter is no exception. The Market Research Society of Great Britain defines the process as 'the means used by those who provide goods and services to keep themselves in touch with the needs and wants of those who use those goods and services'.

Within the context of services industries, this definition could be extended to include the means by which management keeps in touch with the motivation and behaviour of its staff. In either case, the key phrase, which encompasses all marketing research activity and which differentiates it from the wider scope of marketing information systems, is *keeping in touch*. Data collected should be as up-to-date and relevant to the problem as time and cost constraints allow.

Kotler (1991) describes the stages of the marketing research process in a much simpler, linear format than that offered above, beginning with the definition of the research problem and ending with the presentation of the findings (see Figure 5.3).

It can be seen that this process follows the same basic pattern as for other forms of research activity, such as scientific or academic research. To be useful, keeping in touch needs to be conducted objectively and accurately. Casual, unstructured research is, at best, wasteful and, at worst, misleading.

Market research is itself a service industry, with its own functions and specialisms. In order to explain the way in which the process illustrated in Figure 5.3 works, it may be useful to briefly describe the structure of the industry. Essentially, market researchers fall into two groups:

- Those employed by service companies themselves—for example, banks, holiday operators and social services (often referred to as 'client' companies). These researchers provide information for internal use and generally have specific product and market knowledge of their sector.
- A second group of researchers are employed by marketing research organizations whose specific purpose is the supply of information to other users. These supply companies are often referred to as 'agencies', something of a misnomer as they are paid on a fee rather than a commission basis. Staff employed by these companies can generally achieve a high level of expertise in particular research techniques, some of which are described below.

The research process allows for the expertise of both groups to be incorporated at different stages. Client company researchers define a research problem, after discussion with marketing and other management. This is usually communicated to potential suppliers in the form of a research brief. The objectives of the study are set by matching management information needs with what can realistically be obtained from the marketplace, particularly in the light of time and budgetary constraints, and may well be defined after initial discussions with possible suppliers.

The area in which marketing research agencies dominates is that of information collection. The degree to which the client company will be involved in developing the research plan and analysing and presenting the findings varies; to a large extent this depends on the size and expertise of its research department. Before deciding on the final plan, however, most client companies approach several possible suppliers and ask for their suggestions in the form of a research proposal.

The research problem almost always results from a gap in the market information already available to management. For example, a company may have comprehensive and up-to-date information on the market for its current products, but may wish to discover what—if any—market needs remain unsatisfied, in order to develop new products.

The purposes of marketing research are varied—some of the principal ones are:

- Defining market characteristics (for example, defining the services required by package-holiday purchasers who use travel agents)
- Describing market characteristics (for example, a client may wish to have described to them merely the behaviour of families with children when purchasing package holidays)
- Measuring market characteristics (as where a client tour operating company wishes to establish the package-holiday market shares of major UK travel agents)
- Analysing market characteristics—a more thorough investigation of the above information (for example, an analysis of holiday-buying behaviour according to the age, income or lifestyle of different segments of the population).

The research techniques suggested in the research plan, or proposal, will depend on which of these purposes the research is being undertaken for as well as the sources of information available.

In addition to these essentially forward-looking planning uses for marketing information, it also has valuable control functions within organizations. While information used for internal control (for example, monitoring sales turnover and advertising budgets) is mainly collected from within an organization, externally gathered information can also be used for control purposes. In this way, total market size data can be used for control purposes in respect of an organization's market share objective.

5.6 SOURCES OF INFORMATION

Data sources are traditionally divided into two categories according to the methods by which they were collected. These are known as secondary and primary data sources—often referred to as desk and field research, respectively. Most organizations would approach a research exercise by examining the available sources of secondary data.

Secondary data refers to information which in some sense is second-hand to the current research project. Data could be second-hand because they have already been collected internally by the organization, albeit for a different primary purpose. Alternatively, the information could be acquired second-hand from external data sources.

Internal information, on products, costings, sales, etc., may be accessed through an organization's MIS. Where such a system does not exist formally, the information may still be available in relevant departmental records, although it would probably need to be reworked into a form that market researchers can use. Despite modern data-processing technology, the task of

Table 5.1 Some examples of secondary services marketing research

National media – e.g. *Financial Times* industry surveys
Trade, technical and professional media – e.g. *Travel Trade Gazette, Banking World*
Government departments and official publications – e.g. *General Household Survey, Transport Statistics*
Local and national chambers of commerce and trade
Professional and trade associations – e.g. British Tourist Authority, Law Society
Yearbooks and directories
Subscription services, providing periodic sector reports on market intelligence and financial analyses, such as Mintel, MEAL, Keynote

ploughing manually through stacks of back-invoices in order to quantify annual sales by product and customer is still not unknown.

There are numerous external sources of secondary data, in both document and electronic format. These cover government statistics, trade associations and specialist research reports. A good starting point for a review of these is still the business section of the nearest city library. Some examples of secondary data sources are shown in Table 5.1.

Traditionally, it has been much easier to find external secondary information on goods than services. However, there has been a considerable increase in services marketing intelligence reports in recent years. In addition, a number of research agencies operate retail audits which generate trend data, distributed on a syndicated basis. Traditionally, these sources have been geared towards fast-moving consumer goods, and, as such, provide invaluable feedback for retailers. Data are also often obtainable from special-interest panels—for example, information on attitudes towards insurance is obtainable from a regular motorists' panel.

It is also worth checking on whether other organizations, possibly even competitors, have conducted similar studies to the one which is proposed. Arlington Management Services, in association with the Department of Trade, produce a regularly updated publication called *MarketSearch*, an international directory of published market research. Although this information will not be as up to date or relevant as that obtained by commissioning a new survey, it will normally be available at a fraction of the cost.

While secondary, or desk, research, as the name implies, is not the most exciting activity in the world, it is eminently worth while, although the research objectives may not be achieved by this method alone. It can, however, be conducted by company employees, and provides a useful starting point for further investigation. Undertaking unnecessary primary research that is available through secondary sources is an expensive and time-consuming exercise.

Primary, or 'field', research is concerned with generating new information direct from the target population. The phrase 'keeping in touch' was highlighted earlier, and marketing research professionals spend most of their time designing and implementing such studies, on either an *ad hoc* (one-off) or a continuous (monitoring) basis. Primary research in the service sector has expanded rapidly since the early 1980s. Part of the reason for this may be the lack of previously published data.

5.7 RESEARCH METHODS

One important decision that needs to be made when developing a primary research plan is whether to conduct a qualitative or a quantitative survey.

5.7.1   Qualitative research

Qualitative research is the exploration and interpretation of the perceptions and behaviour of small samples of target consumers, and the study of the motivators involved in purchasing choices. It is highly focused, exploring, for example, the relationship between respondents' motives and their behaviour in depth. The techniques used to encourage respondents to speak and behave honestly and unselfconsciously are derived from the social sciences, particularly psychology.

When definitions and descriptions are needed—in other words, when no-one knows exactly where to start—qualitative research is at its most useful. It can define the parameters for future studies, and identify key criteria among consumers which can then be measured by quantitative research. In the services sector, where the central focus of the organization's offering is rarely physical, qualitative research is particularly important. There are almost as many definitions of what constitutes a service, it seems, as there are services themselves. Gronroos (1990c), alone, lists eleven, and then adds his own. The search for a watertight definition involves a great deal of mental gymnastics. Therefore the chances of an individual service organization—be it a bank, a restaurant or a health authority—being able to define the nature of its own particular service repertoire to the market are slim.

Where the researcher has no idea what elements of a service offering are of importance to the customer, and therefore warrant investigation, a good starting point is to ask the customers what they consider to be important. It is important, however, that they are asked in as objective and sympathetic a form as possible. Qualitative research plans generally incorporate a discussion outline for those collecting the information, but are essentially unstructured and respondent-led.

5.7.2   Quantitative research

Quantitative research is used to measure consumer attitudes and choices where the nature of the research has been defined and described. These studies are designed to gather information from statistically representative samples of the target population. In order to achieve total accuracy it would be necessary to take a complete census of everyone in the target group. The scale and cost of the UK census, however, illustrates the impracticality of this in most cases. Therefore, samples of respondents are selected for interview, the sample size being related to the size of the total population and degree of statistical reliability required, balanced against time and cost constraints. However, in order to achieve margins of error small enough to make the final measurements useful, quantitative research, as its name implies, is usually conducted among several hundred (sometimes thousands) of respondents. For this reason, information is generally obtained using standardized structured questionnaires.

In order to achieve statistical reliability, the total sample needs to be selected so that it is representative of the market being investigated. The main planning choice here is between probability (random) and quota samples.

In a random sample all members of the total population being investigated have a known chance of being included. The most-used method of manual random selection involves a table of random numbers. Units of the population are matched with these numbers to construct the total sample. There are an increasing number of databases available which generate random samples, such as the *Yellow Pages* database, but the simplest way to find out how this works is to choose a total population (such as a list of the students taking a marketing course). Using a random numbers table (reproduced in all standard statistics textbooks), a method of selecting the numbers is chosen (horizontal or vertical lines, for example), and the list is counted down, highlighting those student names which correspond to each number.

Random sampling is a useful method of selection where the total population size is small, such as for an internal survey within an organization, or where little is known about the structure of the target group. However, it is an expensive and time-consuming method of selecting samples from large populations. In market research, therefore, quota samples tend to be used whenever possible.

Quota samples work by dividing the population into subgroups and selecting a sample that reflects the relative importance of each of these groups within the population. The structure of the population to be studied can be established by reference to external sources (especially a national census) or it may be possible to extract particular market characteristics from secondary research sources, such as internal client lists and published market sector reports. A quota frame is then devised, which reflects this structure. As an example, a bank may wish to undertake a survey among couples with joint current accounts. Previous research might show that the proportion of joint account holders who are in the upper ABC1 social groups is 65 per cent and therefore in a total sample of 1000 joint account holders the number of representatives of such couples who are in the ABC1 social groups would be 650. These can be cross-matched with other variables such as age to produce the quota frame.

In qualitative research, total sample sizes are usually dozens rather than hundreds, yet total populations may extend to hundreds of thousands. Here, the sample cannot hope to be statistically representative. Nevertheless, samples are still constructed in this way to reflect the nature of the market being investigated.

5.7.3   Data collection

Data can be collected either indirectly by observation or through direct interaction with the person being researched. Observational techniques claim objectivity, being more free of respondent bias, but are limited to descriptions of behaviour. They find a number of uses within the services sector, for both planning and control purposes. Examples of the former include site-location decisions which are often based on observation of pedestrian or vehicle flows past a site, as well as the routine monitoring of competitor price levels. An example of a control function of observation techniques is seen in the increasing use of 'Mystery Shopper' surveys to monitor performance standards.

However, most surveys need to examine attitudes and past as well as present behaviour. A survey would also normally require some personal or historical information about respondents, for sampling and segmentation purposes. Questioning is therefore the more generally used method of survey research. Questions can be asked face to face, by telephone or distributed for self-completion. In qualitative research, the open-ended nature of the questions, and the need to establish respondent confidence, precludes the use of telephone and self-completion interviews. Face-to-face (or personal) depth interviews are used particularly in business-to-business research, where confidentiality is especially important, and it is usually most convenient for respondents to be interviewed at their place of work.

In consumer markets, however, group discussions are most often used. Groups normally consist of about eight people, plus a trained moderator—often a psychologist—who leads the discussion. Respondents are recruited by interviewers, who use recruitment questionnaires to ensure that those invited to attend reflect the demography of the target market, and to filter out unsuitable respondents. In national markets, groups are arranged at central points throughout the country, the number of groups in each region once more reflecting the regional breakdown of the target population.

Where quantitative research is conducted personally or by telephone, each interviewer is allocated a certain number of interviews, to be selected according to random sampling or quota instructions. While considerably cheaper than personal interviews, the refusal rate for telephone surveys can be up to three times higher than for personal interviews. It is not advised for surveying lower social groups where telephone ownership is lowest. The increased use of computer-assisted information collection for telephone (CATI) and personal interviews (CAPI) has speeded up the whole survey process considerably, with responses being processed as they are received. Immediately prior to the 1992 UK General Election these systems were instrumental in the next-day publication of survey results from total sample sizes extending into thousands.

In the case of self-completion surveys, respondents obviously self-select, so no matter how carefully the original sample to be contacted is chosen, the possibility of bias is highest. Furthermore, the response rate may be as low as 10 per cent, particularly where a postal survey is used. However, some service sector companies, particularly airlines and hotels, have used self-completion questionnaires for a number of years to obtain customer feedback. This form of survey is prevalent in data collection in the area of customer satisfaction. For example, British Gas, Lloyds Bank and the Royal Mail regularly use this method of research.

It was noted earlier that the collection of market information is the part of the research process most dominated by research agencies rather than client companies. There are two main reasons for this. The first is that very few client companies, however large or diverse their repertoire of services, can generate sufficient research to warrant the full-time employment of armies of interviewers throughout the country. The second is that respondents are more likely to give honest answers to third parties than when replying directly to representatives of the organization providing the service being discussed.

This element of honesty, or objectivity, is particularly important in the service sector, where respondents' perceptions of the core service cannot be separated and measured independently of the image of the supplying organization and its employees. For example, in testing a drinks product, such as tea or beer, it is possible to isolate reactions to the core product by presenting it to respondents in blind format, i.e. in a plain (usually white) container with no clue as to the brand or manufacturing company. The respondent is then asked to rate the product along a number of key dimensions—for example, strength–weakness or light–dark colour. The extent to which perceptions are influenced by these brand or company connotations can be measured by presenting an identically constructed sample with the same product, fully branded and packaged, and measuring the differences in response along the same dimensions.

It is not always possible to effect this kind of neat separation when researching services—respondents cannot rate the level of satisfaction provided by a financial service, for example, unless they have actually experienced it. Furthermore, interviewees' responses to proposed new services cannot be isolated from their perceptions of the service provider—an insurance policy cannot be seen in isolation from the reputation of the insurance company which will be responsible for delivering the service. Indeed, some providers of services marketing research argue that attempting such a separation is undesirable. For example, it is argued by Mesure (1992) that:

General market research is usually about anonymity and confidentiality. But we believe in telling interviewers the name of the client because it produces a higher and more forthright level of response . . . it is essential to look at all aspects of the company/customer relationship—attitudinal and perceptual, as well as factual and transactional (Derek Mcsure, Managing Director, BMRB Customer Satisfaction).

5.7.4 Information analysis

The analysis of qualitative research information seeks to identify relationships between respondent motives and their behaviour. Depth interviews and group discussions are always recorded, and the transcripts from these provide the basis on which the researcher identifies common themes and semantics from which to draw conclusions. Such analysis relies heavily on respondent quotations lifted directly from the transcripts to support these conclusions. There are a few analysis packages which cluster quotations by key words or phrases, but they are by no means perfect and the process is a lengthy one. To date, computer analysis has had little impact on qualitative research.

The highly structured nature of quantitative research questionnaires, on the other hand, provides the opportunity for exhaustive analysis and interpretation. Responses can be split demographically, by usage patterns and frequency, and by lifecycle and lifestyle characteristics, so that the attitudes and behaviour of different market segments can be examined separately. In addition, statistical testing can identify significant differences between segments, and discern relationships between attitudes to particular services and consequent purchasing behaviour.

POST OFFICE USES CUSTOMER RESEARCH TO DELIVER FIRST-CLASS MAIL

The Royal Mail has for a long time been the subject of disparaging remarks and jokes made by customers at its expense. Stories of letters taking months or even years to be delivered just a few miles live on in popular mythology. However, the incidence of such comments has became much less because of measures recently embarked upon by the business.

The introduction of the Customer First initiative as part of a Total Quality Management process was the result of two factors which the Royal Mail felt would have a significant impact on its future operations. First, it recognized that it faced much stiffer competition from other media such as fax, telephone, telex, couriers and electronic mail. Second, it identified that its long-erm prosperity was dependent upon offering its customers a quality service.

In 1988 the business relied on a monitoring system which was based on internal measures of the time it took for letters to travel from the sorting office to the point at which they are ready to be delivered. This process was seen to be lacking in independence and did not take account of any final delivery problems. The Royal Mail therefore brought in the marketing research agency Research International, and together they developed a system for the continuous and impartial evaluation of service levels. It improves on the previous internal system by focusing on the variables that customers perceive as being important.

Both the End-to-End (E2E) programme (which measures the time taken from pillar box to doormat) and the Customer Perception Index (CPI) (which measures performance on a range of other quality issues) are based on the systematic collection of data. However, there needed to be some way of deciding what data should be included in the exercise.

In an attempt to understand the highly complex issue of quality, and hence what parameters to include in the on-going programme, a preliminary study was made of what customers (both personal and corporate) actually expected from the postal service. A two-stage programme of research was undertaken. The initial stage, which involved group discussions with a cross-section of customers, was designed to identify the key quality issues. The second stage developed from this and involved a large, nationally representative survey of business and personal customers, and was designed to measure the relative importance of these issues.

From the findings of the research it was possible to identify a number of hard and soft components of service quality which were considered to be important. The former, such as delivery time and the condition of the letter, would be monitored by the E2E programme. The latter, such as the extent to which the Royal Mail shows a caring attitude, trustworthiness and reliability, would be built into the national image studies (CPI).

The E2E survey operates throughout the country on a quarterly basis and results are circulated to customers. The CPI involves over 300 000 self-completion questionnaires being dispatched to customers every year.

The main challenge of Customer First lay not in getting a sophisticated research process right but in gaining acceptance across the 64 districts and their staff. In order to facilitate this and ensure the success of the Royal Mail's initiative to satisfy its external customers, the business is now actively involved in internal marketing. The value of the measurement process as a motivating tool has been recognized. To achieve this, a small team has been assembled to communicate the findings of the survey to staff at all levels of the organization. Their task is to answer queries about the process, discuss best practice and provide a practical consulting input to local quality initiatives.

Adapted from 'Royal Mail' by Diana Brown and Roger Banks, published in *Survey*, Spring 1991, and Royal Mail customer literature.

5.8 MARKET SEGMENTATION AND MARKETING RESEARCH

Segmentation is the process of dividing a market into smaller and more homogeneous segments which are then targeted with different, appropriately designed product offers. It is a fundamental principle of marketing and its advantages are well documented, as are the conditions necessary for its successful implementation. In the service industries there is a clear understanding of the benefits that may accrue from successful market segmentation and it is therefore used extensively throughout the sector. Many service organizations are at the forefront of the development of segmentation methods within the UK, with banks, building societies, insurance companies, the travel and hospitality sectors, among others, having well-defined approaches to the segmentation of their markets according to customer type.

Among the greatest exponents of segmentation are the High Street retailers. As an example, the Burton Group covers the fashion clothing market with a range of highly segmented brands such as Top Shop, Principles and Debenhams. Similarly, grocery retailers have a very clear understanding of who their customers are and what needs they seek to satisfy and position their stores in the marketplace accordingly (for example, contrast the market position of Sainsbury with that of Kwik Save).

If the segmentation methods used by service organizations are examined more closely, it becomes apparent that demographic variables tend to be the most widely used segmentation bases. In this respect service industries are no exception—the same tends to be true in goods marketing. Age, sex and socio-economic analysis along with geographic location provide useful information for building up a profile of users of a service. This can be used for targeting purposes in media planning, assisting in new-service development, and can contribute to pricing policy and service outlet location. Some indication of the importance of demographic bases for segmentation can be seen in the choice of magazines in which American Express advertise, the range of accounts offered by Midland Bank, the pricing practices of British Rail, and the location of Lunn Poly Holiday Shops.

Demographic segmentation has an important role to play in the use of direct mail (an important element of the marketing mix of many financial services companies), although in this case, demographic analysis is usually employed in conjunction with a geographic database which enables an organization to identify and locate potential customers with the necessary characteristics. The combination of these two types of segmentation variables is often referred to as 'geodemographics'.

In all these applications of segmentation methods there is a heavy reliance upon the availability of accurate and timely market data. Geodemographic methods of segmentation, for example, require sources of information about customer demographics and their geographical location and can involve secondary data acquisition or primary investigations undertaken on behalf of an organization. However, the degree of sophistication with which segmentation is being approached has moved forward considerably as advances in the capabilities of information technology have occurred. Two relatively recent developments should be mentioned:

- A number of firms offer a geodemographic segmentation analysis which allows the identification of small geographical pockets of households according to a combination of their demographic characteristics and their buying behaviour. These computerized data systems— the most well known being ACORN—are of considerable value in the planning of direct-mail campaigns, store location and merchandising.
- The wealth of data provided by Electronic Point of Sale systems (EPOS) means that services functioning in the retail arena may have access to a most powerful research tool. The applications are numerous but in this instance it is clear that such a database could enable a firm to identify who its customers are, what they buy, how often, etc., which can facilitate a whole range of marketing planning activities.

Clearly, as further advances in information technology are made and competitive pressures among service marketers intensify, an even greater sophistication in the way that markets are segmented will be invoked.

5.8.1   Segmentation studies

For most practical marketing purposes, service organizations tend to rely upon demographic and geographic data. Yet there is a real conflict between the theoretical and practical aspects of market segmentation. In practice, the established bases are employed, at least in part, because the data are readily available in this format and targeting is therefore reasonably straightforward. However, although they do have this practical value they do not really explain why there are differences in the behaviour of consumers.

There are therefore a number of other approaches to segmentation which are more theoretically sound, such as psychographics (based upon personality, attitudes, opinions and interests) and self-concept (how customers perceive themselves). Such approaches rely upon attitude-measurement techniques including Likert scales and semantic differentials in order to elicit the necessary information from customers. These segmentation bases do provide a useful supplementary set of tools for the subdivision of markets in practice, but they do, however, have to be used in conjunction with demographic profiles for targeting purposes (see Moutinho and Evans, 1992).

An alternative qualitative approach to identifying clusters of customers is based on the analysis of the components of a particular service offering. This is effectively a benefit-based technique for distinguishing market segments. A quantitative methodology for undertaking such analysis called cluster analysis is commonly applied after the qualitative stage of a study (see Lunn 1986). The segments derived from this type of investigation, based upon a combination of factors, may then be targeted by a service firm with specific product offers that have been designed in accordance with the requirements of the segments.

For service organizations to be able to sub-divide markets in a meaningful way they need to have a thorough understanding of their market—i.e. its location and the characteristics of their customers and the reasons why they buy. It follows that for market segmentation to be successful it is necessary for it to be built upon a strong programme of marketing research and analysis.

SUPERMARKETS GET READY FOR A NEW GENERATION OF YABs

The grocery retail industry in the UK is dominated by a small number of very large supermarket chains operating from large superstores, with the names of Sainsbury, Tesco, Asda, Gateway and Kwik Save being familiar to most shoppers. The high degree of concentration within the sector has not, however, influenced competition in any negative way as far as customers are concerned. The range of food and household items on sale has never been so varied and prices are very keen as the major players strive to capture further market share. However, consumer loyalty can never be guaranteed and an insight into the service requirements of shoppers may help the retailers to retain their relationship with customers.

A study undertaken by the Henley Centre for Forecasting on behalf of one of the large multiples illustrates how research on the future of the market can form a basis for strategic change. In this instance the research was concerned with predicting patterns of shopping behaviour in the mid-1990s and particularly with establishing a set of market segments based on behaviour patterns. The outcome of the Henley Centre's investigation was the identification of a number of different types of shopper based on a multi-variable approach which took account of demographic factors such as age, sex and income as well as lifestyle, personality and, finally, attitude to the shopping experience. As with so many of these studies, the resultant new breeds of shopper have been labelled with glib titles.

The Harried Hurrier will be the most important type of new shopper. These are typically burdened with squabbling children and crippled by a severe lack of time. Hurriers are averse to anything that eats into their precious minutes such as having too much choice, which makes them impatient. Another large group but spending less money will be the middle-aged Young-at-Heart who, in contrast to the first group have time on their hands and like to try new products. An important and growing species of grocery shopper is the Young, Affluent and Busy (or YABs) for whom money is not a major constraint in their quest for convenience and more interesting products, but they do have a low boredom threshold. Two other types who are expected to grow in importance are the Fastidious, who are attracted by in-store hygiene and tidiness, and the mainly male Begrudgers, who shop only out of obligation to others. At the same time, the Perfect Wife and Mother who is concerned with the balanced diet would appear to be on her way out. She is likely to be more than compensated for by the Obsessive Fad-Followers whose choice of food tends to be dominated by brand image and current trends.

It is expected that the new breeds will act as a catalyst for a shopping revolution. Although the already-established need for convenience will still predominate, retail analysts anticipate some significant changes such as in store traffic-routing systems, one-way layouts and themed food centres by nationality. There would appear to be a considerable amount to be gained from transforming the sometimes stressful encounter with the superstore into a pleasurable leisure activity.

However, balancing the needs of all these groups may prove to be a difficult task which may lead to greater specialization within the sector. For example, it is not impossible to imagine chains of speciality food retailers that act as menu stores offering the YABs the alternative of buying different dinner-party food on different days, switching the emphasis from French to Italian to Indian recipes.

(Adapted from 'Keeping 'em Rolling in the Aisles', *Marketing Week*, 11 August 1989.)

5.9 RESEARCHING BUYER BEHAVIOUR

A very important purpose of marketing research is to gain an insight into the processes and critical factors involved in customers' purchase decisions. It is important for service organizations to develop a thorough understanding of a number of aspects of their customers' buying processes, in particular:

- Who is involved in making the purchase decision
- How long the process of making a decision takes
- What is the set of competing services from which consumers make their choice
- The relative importance attached by decision makers to each of the elements of the service offer
- The sources of information that are used in evaluating competing service offers

The basic processes involved in purchase decisions are illustrated in Figure 5.4. Simple models of buyer behaviour usually see underlying need triggering a search for need-satisfying solutions. When possible solutions have been identified, these are evaluated according to some criteria. The final purchase decision is seen as a product of the interaction between the final decision maker and a range of influencers. Finally, after purchase and consumption, consumers develop feelings about their purchases which influence future decisions. In reality, service purchase decision processes can be complex iterative processes, involving large numbers of influencers and diverse decision criteria. Needs can themselves be difficult to understand and should be distinguished from expectations. The intangible nature of services and the general inability of people to check the quality or nature of a service until after it has been consumed adds to the importance of understanding the sources of information which are used in the process of evaluation.

5.9.1 Researching the decision-making unit (DMU)

Few service purchase decisions are made by an individual in total isolation. Usually other people are involved in some role and have a bearing on the final purchase decision. It is important to recognize the key players in this process so that the service format can be configured to meet these peoples' needs, and that promotional messages can be adapted and

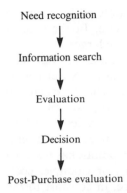

Need recognition

Information search

Evaluation

Decision

Post-Purchase evaluation

Figure 5.4   Simplified stages in the buyer-decision process

directed at the key individuals involved in the purchase decision. A number of roles can be identified among people involved in the decision process:

- Influencers are people or groups of people to whom the decision maker refers in the process of making a decision. Reference groups can be primary in the form of friends, acquaintances and work colleagues, or secondary in the form of remote personalities with whom there is no two-way interaction. Where research indicates that the primary reference group exerts a major influence on purchase decisions, this could indicate the need to take measures that will facilitate word-of-mouth communication—for example, giving established customers rewards in return for the introduction of new customers. An analysis of secondary reference groups used by consumers in the decision process can be used in a number of ways. It will indicate possible personalities to be approached who may be used to endorse a product in the company's advertising. It will also suggest which opinion leaders an organization should target as part of its communication programme in order to achieve the maximum 'trickle-down' effect. The media can be included within this secondary reference group—what a newspaper writes in its columns can have an important influence on purchase decisions.
- Gatekeepers are most commonly found among commercial buyers. Their main effect is to act as a filter on the range of services which enter the decision choice set. Gatekeepers can take a number of forms—a secretary barring calls from sales representatives to the decision maker has the effect of screening out a number of possible choices. In many organizations it can be difficult to establish just who is acting as a gatekeeper—identifying a marketing strategy which gains acceptance by the gatekeeper or bypasses them completely is therefore made difficult. In larger organizations, and the public sector in particular, a select list of suppliers who are invited to submit tenders for work may exist. Without being on this list, a provider of services is unable to enter the decision set.
Although gatekeepers are most commonly associated with the purchase of industrial services, they can also have application to consumer purchases. For many household services, an early part of the decision process may be the collection of brochures or telephoning to invite quotations for a service. While the final decision may be the subject of joint discussion and action, the initial stage of collecting the decision set is more likely to be left to one person. In this way, a housewife picking up holiday brochures acts as a gatekeeper, restricting subsequent choice to the holidays of those companies whose brochures appealed to her.
- In some cases, ordering a service may be reduced to a routine task and delegated to an individual. In industrial services, low-budget items which are not novel may be left to the

discretion of a buyer. In this way, casual window cleaning may be contracted by a buying clerk within the organization without immediate reference to anyone else. In the case of modified rebuys, or novel purchases, the decision-making unit is likely to be larger.

- The users of a service may not be the people responsible for making the actual purchase decision—this is particularly the case with many industrial service purchases. Nevertheless, research should be undertaken to reveal the extent to which users are important elements in the decision process. In the case of the business air-travel market, for example, it is important to understand the pressure that the actual traveller can exert on choice of airline, as opposed to the influence of a company buyer (who may have arranged a long-term contract with one particular airline), a gatekeeper (who may discard promotional material relating to new airlines) or other influencers within the organization (for example, cost-centre managers who may be more concerned with the cost of a service, in contrast to the user's overriding concern with its quality).
- The decision makers are the persons (or groups of individuals) who make the final decision to purchase, whether they execute the purchase themselves or instruct others to do so. With many family-based consumer services it can be difficult to identify just who within the family carries most weight in making the final decision. Research into services that are purchased jointly has suggested that in the case of package holidays, wives dominate in making the final decision, whereas with joint mortgages it is the husband who dominates. Within any particular service sector, an analysis of how a decision is made can only be achieved realistically by means of qualitative in-depth research. In the case of decisions made by commercial buyers, the task of identifying the individuals responsible for making a final decision—and their level within the organizational hierarchy—becomes even more difficult.

5.9.2 Researching the choice set

Most buyers of services do not act with total rationality—to do so would imply identifying all possible sources of supply and applying a logical evaluatory criterion to each. Although there is some evidence that organizational buyers may act with somewhat more rationality than private ones, they are still likely to show great scope for irrationality in decision making. A company buyer may prefer the simple and relatively risk-free approach of staying with the services with which he or she is familiar, rather than seeking to review all possible choices periodically. In fact, choice is made from a select set of possibilities, and these consumer choice sets can be classified according to their selectivity:

- The total set comprises all services that are capable of satisfying a given need.
- The awareness set comprises all those services of which the consumer is aware (the unaware set is the opposite of the awareness set).
- The consideration set includes those items within the awareness set which the consumer considers buying.
- The choice set is the group of services from which a final decision is ultimately made.
- Along the way to defining the choice set, some services would have been rejected as they are perceived to be unavailable, unaffordable, unsuitable, etc. These comprise the infeasible set.

Research should seek to establish the choice set against which a company's service is being compared, and on this basis the marketing programme can be adapted in order to achieve competitive advantage against other members of the choice set. In the case of a proposed new service, research may be undertaken to establish the criterion which consumers use to include a particular service within their choice set.

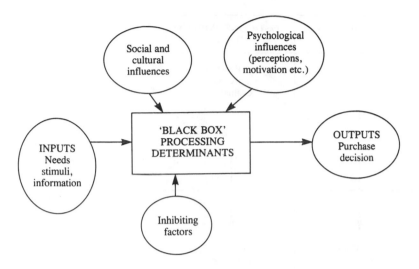

Figure 5.5 A multi-component model of consumer behaviour

5.9.3 Models of buyer behaviour

The very basic model of buyer behaviour shown in Figure 5.4 provides a useful starting point and conceptual framework for analysing buying processes. If a model is to have value to marketing managers, it should be capable of use as a predictive tool, given a set of conditions on which the model is based. For this reason, a number of researchers have sought to develop models which explain how buying decisions are made in specified situations, and from this to predict the likely consequences of changes to marketing strategy. Modelling buyer decision processes poses many problems. At one extreme, simple models such as that presented in Figure 5.4 may help in very general terms in developing marketing strategies, but are too general to be of use in any specific situation. At the other extreme, models of buyer behaviour based on narrowly defined sectors may lose much of their explanatory and predictive power if applied to another sector where assumptions on which the original model were calibrated no longer apply. In any event, most models of buyer behaviour provide normative rather than strictly quantitative explanations of buyer behaviour, and there can be no guarantee that the assumptions on which the model was originally based continue to be valid.

The earliest models of buyer behaviour focused attention on explaining the decision processes involved in goods purchases, with typical components similar to the model shown in Figure 5.5. One widely used framework which has been applied to consumer service purchase decisions is that developed by Howard and Sheth.

The model incorporates a number of elements:

- *Inputs* This element comprises information about the range of competing services that may satisfy a consumer's need. Information may be obtained from personal or published sources.
- *Behavioural determinants* Individuals bring to the purchase decision a predisposition to act in a particular way. This is influenced by the culture they live in, family and personality factors, among others.
- *Perceptual reaction* Inputs are likely to be interpreted in different ways by different individuals, based on their unique personality make-up and conditioning which results from previous purchase experiences. While one person may readily accept the advertising messages of a

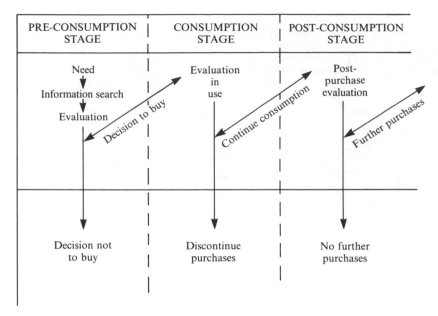

Figure 5.6 The consumption/evaluation process for services (based on Fisk, 1981)

holiday company, another may have been disappointed by that company in the past, or by holiday companies' advertising in general. They are therefore less likely to perceive such inputs as credible.

- *Processing determinants* This part of the model focuses attention on the way in which a decision is made. Important determinants include the motivation of the individual to satisfy a particular need, the individual's past experience of a particular service or organization and the weight attached to each of the factors that are used in the evaluation. For some consumers, for some services, critical product requirements may exist which must be present if a product is to be included in the decision set. At other times, consumers attach weights to each of its attributes and select the product with the highest weighted 'score'.

- *Inhibitors* A number of factors may prevent an individual moving towards making a decision to purchase a particular service, such as the ease of access to the service, its price and the terms and conditions for service delivery.

- *Outputs* The outcome of the decision process may either be to go ahead and purchase or not to buy or to defer a decision to a later date.

The Howard–Sheth model was developed as a general framework to explain both goods and services decision processes. There has been more recent recognition that this type of model does not fully address the issue of producer/seller interaction which occurs during the evaluation process. The intangibility of services and the inability of consumers to evaluate a service before consumption can also result in a much more complex process of information collection and evaluation than is the case with goods.

An example of a model which is based specifically on the service sector has been developed by Fisk (1981). The essential elements of this model are shown in Figure 5.6. The model sees the purchase process as being divided into three stages—pre-consumption, consumption and post-consumption. The pre-consumption stage comprises the range of activities that commonly take place before a purchase decision is made, beginning with the initial problem recognition, collection of information and identification of the choice set. At this stage, consumers identify what they *expect* to be the best solution. In the following consumption stage, consumers actually decide through experience what they consider to be the best choice. During this phase, expectations raised during the pre-consumption phase are compared with actual service delivery. A gap between the two results in attempts to reduce dissonance—for example, dissatisfaction resulting from failure to meet expectations may be resolved by complaining. In the post-consumption phase, the whole service encounter is evaluated and this determines whether the consumer will be motivated to continue to consume the service. Like most models, this model simplifies the buying process—for example by showing evaluation as three distinct elements, whereas in reality a service is progressively evaluated.

More specific models of buyer behaviour have been developed as a result of research into specific services sectors. Many of these have sought to rank in order of importance the factors that contribute towards the purchase decision and to identify critical factors, the absence of which will exclude a possibility from a decision set. As an example, research into restaurant choice decisions by Lewis (1981) identified five key factors used in the evaluation of a restaurant—food quality, menu variety, price, atmosphere and convenience. However, the research also found that the importance attached to each of these factors differed according to the purpose of the visit to the restaurant. The factors influencing a choice of restaurant for a celebration were quite different from those used for a general social occasion. For most categories of use, image and atmosphere appeared to be critical factors which distinguished between restaurants within the choice set. In the case of some consumers who had no independent transport, location close to the town centre was found to be a necessary factor for further consideration.

5.9.4   Consumer and organizational buyer behaviour compared

A number of reasons can be identified why the processes by which private consumers purchase services normally differ from the way in which organizations buy services:

- Two sets of needs are being met when an organization buys services—the formal needs of the organization and the needs of the individuals who make up the organization. While the former may be thought of as being the more rational, the needs which individuals seek to satisfy are influenced by their own perceptual and behavioural environment, very much in the same way as would be the case with private consumer purchases.
- More people are typically involved in organizational purchases. High-value services purchases may require evaluation and approval at a number of levels of an organization's management hierarchy. Research might indicate for particular organizations or types of organizations the level at which a final decision is made. The analysis of the Decision Making Unit (see above) may also reveal a wider range of influencers present in the decision-making process.
- Organizational purchases are more likely to be made according to formalized routines. At its simplest, this may involve delegating to a junior buyer the task of making repeat orders for services which have previously been evaluated. At the other extreme, many high-value service purchases may only be made after a formal process of bidding and evaluation has been undertaken.
- The greater number of people involved in organizational buying also often results in the whole process taking longer. A desire to minimize risk is inherent in many formal organizational motives and informally present in many individuals' motives, often resulting in lengthy feasibility studies being undertaken. In some new markets, especially overseas,

trust in service suppliers may be an important factor used by purchasers when evaluating competing suppliers, and it may take time to build up a trusting relationship before any purchase commitment is secured.

- The elements of the service offering that are considered critical in the evaluation process are likely to differ. For many services, the emphasis placed on price by many private buyers is replaced by reliability and performance characteristics by the organizational buyer. In many cases, poor performance of a service has direct financial consequences for an organization. A poor parcel-delivery service may cause merely annoyance to a private buyer but could lead to lost production output or lost sales for an organizational one.

- The need for organizational buyers' risks to be reduced and their desire to seek the active cooperation of suppliers in tackling shared problems has resulted in greater attention being paid to the development of organizational buyer–seller relationships over time, rather than seeing individual purchases in isolation. A number of studies have sought to explain these processes. For example, Hakansson (1982) argues that cooperation between buyer and seller results from social and information exchange as well as the exchange of the product itself. Exchange of these elements may become routinized over time, leading to a clear set of roles and responsibilities that each party is expected to carry out. The resulting cooperation between buyer and seller often results in adaptations which either firm may make in the elements exchanged or the process of exchange. The importance of mutual trust in the relationship between a service organization and its industrial buyers has been shown in a number of studies. Furthermore, it has been pointed out by Bowden and Scheider (1988) and Gronroos (1990b) that, as the complexity of service offerings increases, the organizational buying unit perceives a greater need for confidence and trust in its services suppliers.

5.10 CONCLUSIONS

The case has been made that there is a real need for service organizations to be deeply involved in research activity. Service providers in general have been relatively slow in their uptake of the research ethos, but many of them now find themselves at the spearhead of the industry. For many service organizations a prosperous future will flow from an acceptance of the pre-eminence of customers and their desire for service quality. A recognition of the significance of marketing research in achieving and sustaining quality can only enhance their chances of success.

However, at a time when customer charters have become widespread within the private and public services sectors, it is worth making the point that their value is solely dependent upon whether they actually take account of the requirements of customers. A commitment to quality is a much larger job than simply producing a charter, it is also a commitment of resources to a research process that systematically identifies customers' expectations and perceptions and monitors them on a continuous basis.

REVIEW QUESTIONS

1. Are there any major distinctions between the processes and practices of marketing research in services and goods markets?
2. To what extent do you agree that the intangibility of services creates a researchability problem?
3. How important is it to have a structured approach to marketing research?
4. Identify the most likely marketing research objectives for a hotel chain.

5. Are there any particular difficulties involved in the practice of segmentation policies in the service industries?
6. Explain why a thorough understanding of buyer behaviour processes may be important for a cinema chain seeking to enhance its service offer.

THE SERVICE PRODUCT

OBJECTIVES

After reading this chapter, you should be able to understand:

- The elements that constitute the service offer
- Methods by which customers evaluate service offers
- Strategic issues raised in developing the range of services offered
- Procedures for developing new services and deleting old ones

6.1 INTRODUCTION

Products form the focal point for an organization's effort in satisfying its customers' needs. The features, design, styling and ranges of the product—among other things—help the organization in gaining competitive advantage in meeting its customers' needs more effectively than its competitors. Product decisions form just one set of decisions that an organization makes in order to satisfy customers' needs. They must be related to decisions in respect of the other elements of the marketing mix in order to give a coherent market position for a service.

It was noted in Chapter 2 that the traditional marketing-mix formulation which has been applied to goods may not be appropriate for the marketing of services. However, most reformulations of the marketing mix continue to place great emphasis on product decisions, although the concept of a product and the nature of product decisions for services can be quite different compared to goods. The purpose of this chapter is to look more specifically at the service product offering and to consider conceptual frameworks for understanding the management of products in a service context.

6.2 THE SERVICE OFFER

The term 'product' is used to describe both tangible goods offerings and relatively intangible service offerings. A starting point for understanding the nature of products is to take a generic definition provided by Pride and Ferrell (1991, page 240), who define a product as:

a complexity of tangible and intangible attributes, including functional, social and psychological utilities or benefits. A product can be an idea, a service, a good or any combination of these three.

While this definition is intended to be universal in its coverage, Kotler (1991) recognizes the diversity of product offerings and proposed four categories of product offers:

- Pure tangibles
- Tangibles with accompanying services
- Major services with accompanying minor goods and services
- Pure services

The fact that most products are usually a combination of goods and services has been highlighted by Rathmell (1974), who distinguished between support goods and facilitating goods in the service offer. The former are tangible aspects of a service that aid the service provision (a textbook in education, for example), whereas facilitating goods must exist for the service to be provided in the first place (for example, a car is a prerequisite for the provision of a car-hire service). In reality, customers buy not products as such but the benefits that a product offers. The most important element of any organization's marketing mix therefore can be considered to be its 'offer', and what is being considered in this chapter is the organization's 'service offer'.

An understanding of just what constitutes the service offer from both buyers' and sellers' points of view is imperative. Sasser *et al.* (1978) see purchase bundles, or the 'service concept', as comprising three elements:

- First, physical items: these are the tangible/material elements which are the facilitating or support goods—for example, the food or drink served in a restaurant.
- Secondy, there are sensual benefits, those that can be defined by one or more of the five senses, such as the taste and aroma of a restaurant meal or the ambience of a restaurant.
- Finally, Sasser *et al.* identify the psychological benefits of a service purchase bundle. These are benefits which cannot be clearly defined and are determined by the customer subjectively. The existence of this type of benefit makes the management of the service offer very difficult.

Service offers can be distinguished from goods offers by their inseparability. The fact that a service cannot usually be separated from the person who provides it, nor from the place where it is provided, results in services being 'consumed' as soon as they are produced, and this therefore means a high degree of buyer/supplier interaction. The concept of value added in the product also takes on a new meaning. In both production and marketing the concept of value added is the difference between input and output at various levels on the supply side. Since services are not resold, Rathmell has argued that there can only be one level of value added, with the concept of input being redefined to mean only supplies consumed and the depreciation of capital goods used up in the production of a service. Finally, the effects of the organization/client interface and user participation have been seen by Eiglier and Langeard (1977) as being critical elements influencing the consumer's perception of a service product.

6.2.1 Analysis of the service offer

A number of elements within the service offer can be identified, some of which are fundamental to the nature of the product while others refine or differentiate it. For products in general, an analysis by Kotler and Andreasen (1991) distinguishes between three different levels of an individual product:

- The first level is known as the *core* product. This is defined in terms of the underlying need which a product satisfies.

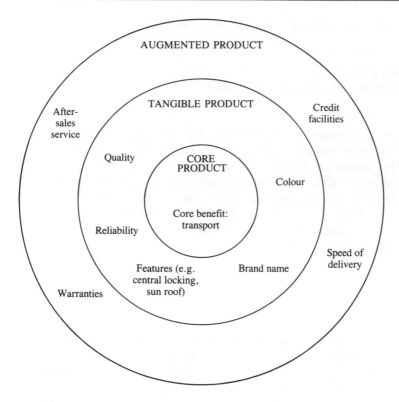

Figure 6.1 Analysis of the product offering of a car (adapted from Kotler and Andreasen, 1991)

- The second level is known as the *tangible* product level. The core product is made available to consumers in some tangible form, expressed in terms of the product's features, styling, packaging, brand name and quality level.
- The third level of product defined by Kotler and Andreasen is the augmented product. This is the tangible product plus additional services and benefits, included to satisfy additional needs of consumers and/or to further differentiate a product from its competitors. Many of these additional features tend to be services such as pre- and after-sales service, guarantees, etc.

An application of this multi-level approach to the analysis of the product offering of a car is shown in Figure 6.1.

While this analysis is held to be true of products in general, doubts have been expressed about whether it can be applied to the service offer. Is it possible to identify a core service representing the essence of a consumer's perceived need that requires satisfying? If such a core service exists, can it be made available in a form that is 'consumer friendly', and if so, what elements are included in this form? Finally, is there a level of service corresponding to the augmented product which allows a service provider to differentiate its service offer from its competitors in the same way as a car manufacturer differentiates its augmented product from that of its competitors?

A number of writers have sought to revise this basic framework to identify different levels of the service offer. Sasser *et al.* (1978) differentiate the substantive service and peripheral services.

Gronroos (1984a) distinguishes between the service concept and elements of what he calls the 'interactive marketing function'.

Most analyses of the service offer recognize that the problems of inseparability and intangibility make application of the three generic levels of product offer less meaningful to the service offer. Instead, the service offer is analysed here in terms of two components:

- The core service which represents the core benefit
- The secondary service which represents both the tangible and the augmented product levels.

6.3   THE CORE SERVICE LEVEL

Sasser *et al.* (1978) call this the *substantive* service, which is best understood as the essential function of a service. Gronroos (1984a) uses the term *service concept* to denote the core of a service offering, and states that it can be general such as offering a solution to transport problems—for example, car hire—or it can be more specific such as serving Chinese cuisine in a restaurant.

In any event, there seems to be little difference between services and material goods when considering this fundamental level of a firm's offer. All customer needs and wants are intangible—they cannot be seen or touched. The offer should be developed, produced and managed with consumers' benefit in mind in such a way that they perceive being successful in satisfying their needs and wants. The offering can be a tangible good, a service, or a combination of both.

It follows that an understanding of customers' needs and wants is vital if a service provider wishes to be successful, requiring a 'common view' or 'perceptual congruence' between itself and service users. This, in turn, requires 'soft' data of a behavioural nature which allow an understanding of the benefits a customer derives from a service. This highlights the importance of appropriate marketing research, particularly qualitative research and its attempts to measure consumers' perceptions, beliefs and attitudes. In formulating service design, Gronroos (1984a) believes that market research for services should place greater emphasis on customer perceptions of the service itself.

6.4   THE SECONDARY SERVICE LEVEL

It was noted above that the secondary level of a service offering can be seen as representing both the tangible level of a product and the augmented level. At the augmented level, service suppliers offer additional benefits to consumers that go beyond the tangible evidence. This is done to meet additional consumer wants and/or to further differentiate the product from the competition.

As there is no 'tangible' level of a service in the manner in which the term is understood in a goods context, it could be argued that it is not possible to define an augmented service. However, many of the elements normally considered to be part of the augmented product relate to *how* the product is distributed/delivered—for example, installation, delivery, credit availability and after-sales service.

The idea of intangibility implies that when a consumer decides to purchase a service there is no guarantee that he or she will be able to experience (feel, see, hear, taste or smell) the service before it is purchased. Rushton and Carson (1985) also note that in many cases, services can also be mentally intangible in that they are concepts that are difficult to grasp.

Shostack (1977) looks into the issue of intangibility in more depth. She sees services as being more than just products which are intangible:

It is wrong to imply that services are just like products except for intangibility. By such logic apples are just like oranges, except for their 'appleness'. Intangibility is not a modifier, it is a state.

Shostack's molecular model (discussed in Chapter 1) is merely her way of stating that there is a product continuum. A service dominant entity concerned primarily with intangible elements is at one extreme, and what she calls a product dominant entity consisting predominantly of tangible elements is at the other. For Shostack, the greater the weight of intangible elements in an entity, the more the divergence from the approach of goods marketing. Services knowledge and goods knowledge are not gained in the same way. Customers of physical products can 'know' their product through physical examination and/or quantitative measurement. Service reality must be defined experientially by the user and there are many versions of this reality.

For services, therefore, the secondary level of a service offer involves a combination of both tangible and intangible elements in order that the core benefit is realized by the customer. There are, however, a number of specific difficulties involved in determining the particular combination of these tangibles and intangibles. One major problem is the actual articulation of the elements, for it is far easier to articulate the tangible aspects than it is to produce and display the intangibles. In addition, the intangible elements are relatively difficult to control and therefore there is a tendency for service managers to emphasize the controllable, i.e. tangible, elements rather than the more difficult intangibles. Shostack (1977) believes that the more intangible the service, the greater the need for tangible evidence while Levitt (1981) has stressed the importance of managing tangible evidence.

Another major conceptual problem in defining the service offer is that because of inseparability of production and consumption, some elements of the secondary service level are not actually provided by the service provider but by customers themselves—for example, the student who 'reads around' a subject before attending a seminar.

Notwithstanding the above difficulties, the secondary level of the service offer can be analysed in terms of a number of elements, some of which bear comparison with those used in analysing goods offers. The principal elements are discussed below and some of these are illustrated in Figure 6.2, where an insurance product is used as an example.

6.4.1   Features

In the tangible product, features represent specific components of the product that could be added or subtracted without changing its essential characteristics. Features can be added or subtracted to the product so that an organization produces a range of products that appeal to a variety of different market segments, each with the same core needs but with each segment requiring marginally different products to satisfy slightly differing secondary needs.

In much the same way, most service offerings can be analysed in terms of differentiating features. For example, banks usually offer different types of current accounts to appeal to segments of the population with slightly differing needs. Cowell (1984) speaks of differing service forms, stating that particular bundles of tangible and intangible elements which comprise the service product represent different service forms.

6.4.2   Styling

Styling means giving the product a distinctive feel or look. Is this a possibility with a service?

It would seem at first easier to do this in relation to the tangible elements of the service offer than for the intangible ones. However, if a broader definition of style is considered to comprise an external manner, mode or approach rather than merely a physical quality, there is little

Figure 6.2   The core and secondary service elements of an insurance product

difficulty in applying this concept to the service offer. In this instance, the customer gains the 'sensual benefits' described earlier.

The inseparability of the service offer makes the relationship between customer and service provider of paramount importance, and it is through this relationship that a service manager can develop a distinctive style. For example, there is a difference between the style of a McDonald's restaurant and that of a Little Chef, although they are both in the business of selling relatively low-value, high-speed food and drink. The style of a service is a result of the combination of features, including tangible decor and the intangible manner in which front-line staff interact with customers. The overall service style can be established either before or after the target market is identified.

6.4.3   Packaging

The intangible nature of services prevents them being packaged in the traditional sense of providing physical wrapping which can both protect the product and help to develop a distinctive identity. However, the tangible elements of a service can be packaged, performing much the same function as the packaging of goods. Good packaging can make service consumption easier. For example, the design of containers can ease the handling of take-away food as well as conveying messages which distinguish the provider of the service from its competitors.

In a wider sense, service packaging can refer to the way in which tangible and intangible elements are bundled together to provide a comprehensive service offer. For example, a mortgage offer may be packaged to include building insurance and a surveyor's report, or a restaurant may include a home-delivery service in its service package.

6.4.4   Branding

The purpose of branding is to identify products as belonging to a particular organization and to enable differentiation of its products from those of its competitors. While most tangible product offerings are branded in some form, the service offering itself is less likely to be branded. Instead, it is more likely that the process of branding will focus on the service provider's corporate image. In this way, both fast-food restaurants and accountants are usually differentiated on the basis of their corporate name and reputation rather than the specific services they offer.

There are, however, instances where the service itself is branded, or there is a hierarchy of brands and sub-brands representing both corporate and service-specific identity. Often, service-specific branding has a tangible basis (for example, a 'Big Mac' offered by McDonald's) although at other times the product brand is based largely on intangibles (for example, where a bank applies specific brand names to types of account).

6.4.5   Physical evidence

While manufacturers of goods tend to introduce additional services into their augmented product, service marketers are more likely to differentiate their services from the competition by adding tangible features—for example, distinctive designs of brochures, staff uniforms and service outlets.

6.4.6   Service delivery

Just as delivery can be an important differentiator for goods, it can also be equally important for a service. According to Gronroos, service marketers should use the concept of accessibility rather than seeing service provision in terms of distribution/delivery as with goods. A number of resources affect this accessibility—for example, human resources (especially contract personnel), machines, buildings and other physical infrastructure, as well as supplementary services. These resources can be managed by a service organization to enhance the accessibility of its service to consumers. The service itself may be intangible but these resources make the delivery of the service a reality.

6.4.7   Process

Most services are concerned with the production process as much as with any final outcomes. Service design should therefore pay attention to processes and the manner in which service personnel interact with customers during this process. One approach to designing the process is to use Shostack's 'Blueprinting' (discussed in Chapter 7).

6.4.8   People

It was noted above that the people involved in the process of delivering a service can be crucial in defining that service and customers' perceptions of it. Personnel therefore become an important element of the service offering and management must define the role expectations of employees and support this with training where necessary. In addition to managing the interaction between customers and service producers' own personnel, other consumers who use or buy the service may influence the perception of the service where it is consumed in public. Many service industries therefore employ methods to control the behaviour of their customers where they are likely to influence other customers' enjoyment or image of a service.

6.4.9 Quality

The level of quality to which a service is designed is a crucial element in the total service offering. Quality is an important factor used by customers to evaluate the services of one organization in comparison to the offerings of others. In fact, customers may judge not so much the quality of an individual service offering but rather the quality of the service provider.

In goods marketing, quality can be understood as the level of performance of a product. In services marketing, quality is the perceived level of performance of a service, but measuring it can be much more difficult than for goods. Not only can it be difficult to measure quality parameters, it can also be difficult to identify to which quality factors customers attach importance. A service which may be seen by the producer as having high technical quality may in fact be perceived very differently by the consumer who has a different set of quality evaluation criteria.

The intangible nature of service quality standards is reflected in the difficulty that services companies have in designing quality standards which will be readily accepted by potential customers. Customer expectations form an important element of quality. A service that fails to meet the expectations of one customer may be considered by them to be of poor quality, while another customer receiving an identical service but who did not hold such high expectations may consider the service to be of a high quality. In this way, an irregular traveller who has won a flight on Concorde may consider all aspects of the service experience to exceed their limited expectations. On the other hand, a regular business traveller with relatively exacting expectations may rate the service as being of low quality on account of niggling problems such as the slowness of check-in facilities and the lack of attentiveness of the cabin crew.

There is increasing interest in the concept of service quality among both academics and practitioners who see superior quality levels as a way of gaining competitive advantage. For this reason, considerable research has been undertaken to understand the processes by which customers evaluate quality. A sound understanding of these processes can allow service companies to be clearer in their specification of quality levels which they incorporate into their offering, as well as allowing a clearer communication to potential customers of the service level on offer.

In general, tangible goods can be designed and produced to a predetermined standard and because such standards can generally be quantified, it is relatively easy to monitor and maintain them. With intangible services, the difficulties associated with quantification of standards makes it much more difficult for an organization to monitor and maintain a consistently high standard of service. Furthermore, the intangibility and inseparability of most services results in a series of unique buyer/seller exchanges with no two services being provided in exactly the same way. It is in an attempt to reduce the problems of uniqueness that many service providers have sought to 'industrialize' their output by offering a limited range of machine-assisted services with lower variability in output.

Because of the importance of quality in the total service offering, the subject of defining, measuring, planning, implementing and monitoring quality standards is considered in more detail in Chapter 8.

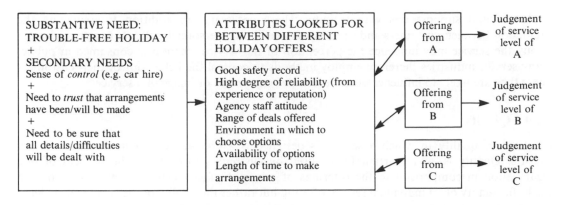

Figure 6.3   Consumer judgement of the total service offering

6.5   CUSTOMER PERCEPTION OF SERVICE ATTRIBUTES

It is important for service organizations to understand the processes by which customers evaluate the total service offering. Sasser *et al.* (1978) suggest that customers initially assess the core service for its ability to satisfy their substantive need for a service, such as a basic requirement for transport. There are, however, other secondary needs such as the need for a sense of control, trust, self-fulfilment and status which are translated into a number of sought service attributes. Sasser *et al.* (1978) have called these attributes *security* (safety of the customer and/or his or her property), *consistency* (reliability), *attitude*, *completeness* (extent of service range), *condition* (environment), *availability* and *timing* (length of time required for and pace of performance of the service). Service providers compete by producing service offerings that contain a permutation of these attributes that meet customers' secondary needs better than their competitors.

An indication of the relationship between core and secondary service levels and their relationship to customer product-evaluation processes is shown in Figure 6.3.

Faced with an array of service attributes, some understanding of the processes by which customers evaluate each bundle of attributes is desirable. Sasser *et al.* identify three possible ways that these judgements can be made:

- First, a consumer may make a judgement based on an overpowering attribute which, for that particular individual, is of great importance in a given situation.
- Second, judgement may be made on the basis of minimum levels of certain attributes but final judgement is based on the existence of a single specific attribute.
- Third, the consumer may decide upon alternatives using a weighted average of attributes.

A major difficulty with this approach, however, is that customers are often not consciously aware of what their needs are. Rathmell (1974) states that in some respects, the service product is an *idea*, and as such, the need for a service is often unrecognized by the buyer until he or she becomes aware of its availability. Even if consumers are aware of their needs, they often have difficulty in expressing their desires to service providers. In addition, customers' needs are unlikely to remain constant as individual customers and their marketing environment change.

Although the understanding of customer service requirements can be a difficult task, it is essential that service firms do not fall into the trap of being production oriented. Customer orientation has been redefined as the 'consumer benefit concept' by Bateson (1977), who argues that a service offering cannot be defined without this consumer benefit concept being considered.

6.6 SERVICE PRODUCT STRATEGIES

Few service organizations can survive by offering just one specialized service. Instead, a mix is usually provided. This section considers the issues involved in managing a product mix.

To begin, the service range offered by an organization can be disaggregated for analysis. The most basic unit of output is often referred to as an item—this is a specific version of a product. Such an item would normally be part of a product line which is a group of related product items. The product mix is the combination of products that an organization offers to customers. A distinction can also be made between the depth of a product mix and its width. Product depth refers to the number of different products in a product line, product width to the number of product lines offered by an organization.

In a services context, an example of an individual service item offered by a bank is a young person's card-based savings account. This, in turn, will form part of a line of savings accounts, and the depth of this line may be indicated by the presence of a wide range of savings accounts to meet the needs of customers who require ease of access, high interest, flexibility, etc. Savings accounts represent just one line of service offering for most banks—other lines would typically include personal loans, mortgages, credit cards, etc.

Decisions about an organization's product mix are of strategic importance. In order to remain competitive in the face of declining demand for its principal service line, a service company may need to widen its product mix. For example, the increasing diversity in food tastes has forced many specialized fast-food outlets to widen their range and traditional fish and chip shops have often had to introduce new lines such as kebabs or home-delivery services. On the other hand, decisions may need to be made to delete services from the mix where consumer tastes have changed or competitive pressures have made the continuing provision of a service uneconomic. Product-mix extension and deletion decisions are continually made so that organizations can provide services more effectively (supplying the right services in response to consumers' changing needs) and more efficiently (providing those services for which the organization is able to make most efficient use of its resources).

For any service organization, its service offering will be constrained by the capabilities, facilities and resources at its disposal. It is therefore important for service firms to constantly examine their capabilities and their objectives to ensure that the range of services provided meets the needs of the consumer as well as that of the organization. The process of ensuring that the right services are being provided in order to meet strategic objectives is often referred to as a service product audit. Key questions for an audit are:

- What benefits do customers seek from the service?
- What is the current and continuing availability of the resources required to provide the service?
- What skills and technical know-how are required?
- What benefits are offered over and above those of the competition?
- Are competitors' advantages causing the organization to lose revenue?
- Does each service provided still earn sufficient financial return?
- Do services meet the targets which justify continued funding?

The answers to these and other related questions form the basis of service-mix development strategy.

6.6.1 Developing the product mix

Marketing strategy was considered in detail in Chapter 3, where Ansoff's Product Market Expansion matrix was introduced as a framework for analysing growth options. The matrix sees development decisions as being based on the newness of markets and products. Four main service product strategies are available to a service firm:

- *Market penetration* An organization continues to supply its existing services to its existing customer segments, but seeks to increase sales from them. This may be achieved by increasing their total consumption of that type of service, or by taking consumers from competitors.
- *Market extension* New types of consumers are found for existing services. For example, a restaurant chain established in the UK may extend its operations to a new overseas market, or higher education institutions may promote their courses to new groups of mature students.
- *Service development* New or modified services are developed to sell to the current market— for example, a bank may offer a new type of charge card aimed at its current customer base.
- *Diversification* New services are offered to new markets—for example, a traditional package-holiday operator offering a conference-organizing service.

Each of these strategies involves differing levels of risk. A market-penetration strategy normally presents the lowest risk to a firm, as it is likely to be dealing with both services and consumers with which it is familiar. Both service-development and market-extension strategies involve greater degrees of risk as the organization is dealing with something new in each situation. However, the degree of risk depends on the organization's particular strengths *vis-à-vis* its competitors and on the potential opportunities available. Diversification normally creates the greatest risk of all, involving an organization with both new services and new markets.

Wilson (1972) takes Ansoff's approach a little further and considers the implications of each of these options for the service firm's resources:

- *Option 1* Attempting to sell more of its existing range of services to existing customers means that greater use of existing resources and facilities is required. Market position is also considered by Wilson as an important resource here.
- *Option 2* Attempting to sell existing services to new customers requires the use of existing resources and facilities. There are, however, no market-based resources available as the firm is entering a new market.
- *Option 3* Attempting to sell new services to existing customers means that a firm can use market resources but there is likely to be a lack of existing capability or resources to produce the new service.
- *Option 4* Attempting to sell new services in new markets makes it less likely that there are any existing resources available.

Because services go through some form of lifecycle (see below) it is essential that an organization has a strategy to maintain a balance in its portfolio of service offerings. Designing the best service product portfolio involves answering a number of important questions:

- What services should be included in the mix?
- What is the optimum range of services on offer?
- What is the most profitable mix?
- How should the mix be positioned in relation to the competition?

In order to be able to manage successfully a portfolio of services, it is important that a firm constantly monitors the performance of its services through the use of a marketing information system.

PRODUCT—DEVELOPMENT STRATEGIES BRING PROBLEMS FOR BUILDING SOCIETIES

The marketing environment of UK financial service organizations was very turbulent during the latter part of the 1980s, resulting in many organizations developing product strategies that they were later to regret. Prior to 1986, the product strategies of building societies were significantly influenced by the various Building Societies Acts. Legislation recognized that building societies had essentially been set up by members for the benefit of fellow-members—they were a means of circulating funds from individual members who wished to invest their savings securely to those members who wished to borrow to finance house purchase. The system was regulated to ensure that building societies lent their funds only for low-risk investments and were not dependent on large investors, who could withdraw their funds at short notice. In times of capital shortages, building societies assumed an almost social responsibility for rationing scarce mortgages between competing borrowers.

The Building Societies Act 1986 came amid a general air of deregulation in financial markets. The Act allowed building societies for the first time to offer services which they had previously been prevented from supplying—for example, current bank accounts. Deregulation came at a time when the commercial banks were becoming successful at offering mortgages—the core of building societies' business. Faced with such competition, most building societies launched new product lines, often in association with other financial services companies. As well as cheque accounts, the larger societies introduced their own credit cards, insurance policies, pension schemes and personal unsecured loans. The Abbey National—which had taken advantage of the legislation to convert itself from building society to public limited company status—was able to pursue an even greater product-diversification policy. It invested heavily in a new chain of 'Cornerstone' estate agents and set up a European subsidiary to offer UK-style mortgages abroad. Smaller societies tended to deepen their existing product lines rather than add new ones. Societies such as the Heart of England, Leamington Spa and Town and Country offered a range of mortgages by which borrowers were able to borrow a very high percentage—if not all—of the value of a property against which the mortgage was secured.

By the time that the recession of the early 1990s had set in, the building societies' product-diversification policies were being questioned. Some of the bolder diversifications turned into millstones round the neck of their owners—by 1992, Abbey National's estate agencies and European operations were making heavy losses. Assumptions that building societies had made about customer loyalty and the possibilities for cross-selling of products seemed to have misjudged the ability of consumers to shop around for the best deal.

Nor was deepening a product line necessarily a safe way of expanding. Many of the smaller societies which had offered increasingly complex and risky mortgages ran into financial difficulties.

During 1991, the Leamington Spa society had to be rescued by the Bradford and Bingley Building Society when a large number of its borrowers became unable to repay their mortgages, which in many cases exceeded the value of the secured property.

6.6.2 Product/service lifecycle concept

The product/service lifecycle graphically indicates the sales of a product or service over its lifetime. The concept is based on the premise that total sales and profitability of a product fluctuates according to some pattern during the product's life. A product lifecycle is shown in Figure 6.4 where sales and profitability are plotted on the vertical axis against time on the horizontal axis. Such a concept has been used for individual product items, product classes and, in fact, whole industries (see, for example, Porter, 1980).

It can be seen from the figure that a product's life can typically be divided into five phases:

Phase 1: Introduction New products are generally costly to produce and launch and may have teething problems. People may be wary of trying something new, especially a new service whose intangibility prevents prior evaluation. Sales therefore tend to be slow and are restricted to those who like trying out new products or who believe they can gain status or benefit by having it.

Phase 2: Growth By this time, the product has been tested and any teething problems have been resolved. The product is now more reliable and more readily available. People now start to see the benefits that can be gained by using the product. Sales start to increase greatly and this is a signal for competitors to start entering the market.

Phase 3: Maturity Almost everyone who wants to acquire the product has now done so, although some people may now be updating the product having purchased earlier in the lifecycle. The number of competitors in the market has risen.

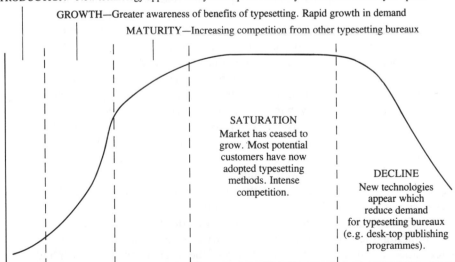

Figure 6.4 A hypothetical product lifecycle for typesetting bureaux

Phase 4: Saturation Here there are too many competitors and no further growth in the market. Competitors tend to compete with each other on the basis of price.

Phase 5: Decline With falling demand and new substitute products appearing, organizations drop out of the market.

The usefulness of the lifecycle concept lies in the recognition that marketing activity for a service is closely related to the stage in the lifecycle that a service has reached. In this way, promotional planning is closely related to the lifecycle, with emphasis typically placed in the launch phase on raising awareness through public relations activity, building on this through the growth phase with advertising, resorting to sales promotion incentives as the market matures and becomes more competitive, and finally possibly allowing promotional activity to fall as the service is allowed to go into decline. In a similar way, distribution and pricing decisions can often be related to the stage which a service has reached in its lifecycle.

Of course, the product lifecycle presented above is a conceptual abstraction. Different products move through the lifecycle at different paces. Some products have been in the maturity/saturation stage for many years (for example, current bank accounts) whereas others disappear very soon after introduction (some trendy clothes' retailers). Empirical evidence also seems to imply a variety of lifecycle modifications and mutations. Hise (1977), for example, describes some of the more likely mutations, five of which are shown in Figure 6.5.

In the first example, the product has achieved a reasonably high sales level early on, but there has been a failure to increase sales any further, although there is no sign of maturity or decline. In the second example, the product constantly increases its sales volume in each period of time—new customers are gained and present ones increase their purchase of the product. Example three, however, displays the complete opposite, with the product having started from a strong position, but now experiencing falling sales, probably due to better competition entering the market. The fourth diagram displays how in certain instances a product entering decline can be saved from the depths of decline. This could have occurred through product reformulation or some form of sales promotion. Alternatively, it could have been brought about by some external factor, such as a change in customers' tastes. Whatever the cause, the product now displays a new lease of life. Having developed a second cycle, however, decline is on the way again, although at a higher level of sales than existed previously. The final diagram displays once again the saving of a product at the decline stage. Unlike the fourth situation, however, the new cycle is at a lower level of sales than originally.

While the above comments are probably true of tangible goods, to what extent is it possible to talk about a specific services lifecycle?

Hise (1977) notes that studies have reinforced the existence of lifecycles among services. He claims that transatlantic air transportation has progressed through the standard lifecycle. In the introductory stage (from the end of the Second World War until the late 1950s), air transport incurred large development costs, was expensive and unreliable to operate and appealed to small market segments—the market continued to be dominated by shipping companies. The growth stage came when jet aircraft came into service, improving the quality of air travel and lowering its price, making it much more competitive and accessible to additional segments. The maturity stage, Hise believes, started in the 1970s and has continued since. This phase has been marked by a slowing of the growth rate and price competition among the increased number of operators.

Rathmell (1974) also sees services as having lifecycles similar to those of goods, believing that services such as telecommunications, health-maintenance delivery systems, leasing and forms of outdoor communications are all in the growth stage of the lifecycle. Watch repairing,

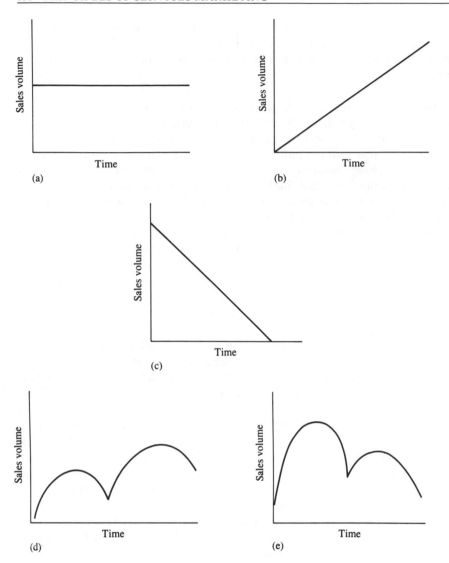

Figure 6.5 Alternative product lifecycles

domestic services and unisex higher education institutions could be considered to be moving through maturity to decline.

Instead of speaking of the lifecycle of a product, the inseparability of services may make it more appropriate to discuss the lifecycle of service providers. Sasser *et al.* (1978) identify a number of stages in the lifecycle of service organizations:

- *Stage 1—Entrepreneurial* In this stage, an individual identifies a market need and offers a service to a small number of people, usually operating from one location. While most entrepreneurs stay at this stage, some begin to think about growth, often entailing a move to larger and/or additional sites.
- *Stage 2—Multi-site rationalization* In this stage, the successful entrepreneur starts to add to the limited number of facilities. It is during this stage that the skills required for being a

multi-site operator begin to be developed. By the end of this stage, the organization gains a certain degree of stability at a level of critical mass. Sasser *et al.* note that it is at this point that franchising starts to be considered.

- *Stage 3—Growth* Here the concept has become accepted as a profitable business idea. The company is now actively expanding through the purchase of competitors, franchising/licensing the concept, developing new company-operated facilities or a combination of the three. Growth is influenced not only by the founder's desire to succeed but also from the pressures placed upon the company by the financial community.
- *Stage 4—Maturity* The number of new outlets declines and revenues of individual facilities stabilize and, in some cases, also decline. This tends to be caused by a combination of four factors: changing demographics within the firm's market, changing needs and tastes of consumers, increased competition and 'cannibalization' of older services by service firms' newer products.
- *Stage 5—Decline/regeneration* Firms can become complacent, and unless a new concept is developed or new markets found, decline and deterioration soon follows.

Sasser *et al.* believe that by identifying a company's position in the lifecycle, the major objectives, decisions, problems and organizational transitions needed for the future can be anticipated. Thus firms can plan for necessary changes rather than react to a set of conditions that could have been predicted earlier.

6.6.3 Difficulties in applying the lifecycle concept

Although the idea of product lifecycles is appealing and seems to be validated by research, it is important to be aware of the possible failings with this conceptual approach in terms of both goods and services. It can be argued that the product/service lifecycle concept is probably more useful for strategic planning and control purposes than for developing short-term forecasts and costed marketing programmes. In reality, lifecycle patterns are far too variable in both shape and duration for any realistic predictions to be made. A second difficulty in applying the lifecycle concept lies in the inability of marketers to ascertain accurately where in the lifecycle a product actually is at any time. For example, a stabilization of sales may be a movement into maturity or simply a temporary plateau due to external causes. In fact, it is possible that the shape of the lifecycle is a result of an organization's marketing activity rather than an indication of environmental factors to which the organization should respond—in other words, it could lead to a self-fulfilling prophecy.

Another criticism of the concept is that the duration of the stages will depend upon whether it is a product class, form or brand which is being considered. For example, the lifecycle for holidays is probably quite flat, whereas those for particular formulations of holidays and for specific holiday operators' brands become progressively more cyclical.

The applicability of the lifecycle concept to services has been supported by Hise (1977), Rathmell (1974) and Sasser *et al.* (1978), although Cowell (1984) claims that a major difficulty in its application is the lack of truly valid research reinforcing the existence of such a concept for services. Furthermore, Carman and Langeard (1979) point out that most service organizations have only a very small number of core services, and consequently they suggest a degree of caution in using the lifecycle concept for services, particularly as the basis for portfolio approaches to service product planning.

Taking these points into consideration, the lifecycle concept may still be helpful in aiding a firm in its service-mix decisions. Although lifecycles may be unpredictable for services in terms of the length of time a service may remain at a particular stage, the understanding that services are likely to change in their sales and profit performance over a period of time implies a need for proactive service-mix management by the service organization.

6.7 NEW-SERVICE DEVELOPMENT

As a result of analysis and evaluation of its product mix, an organization may consider the need to extend its range of services in response to the dynamic nature of its operating environment. The following are typical circumstances when new services may become necessary:

- If a major service has reached the maturity/saturation stage of its cycle and may be moving towards decline, new services may be sought to preserve sales levels.
- New services may be developed as a means of utilizing spare capacity—for example, unoccupied rooms during off-peak periods may lead a hotel operator to develop new leisure breaks designed to fill them.
- New services can help to balance an organization's existing sales portfolio and thus reduce risks of dependency on only a few services offered within a range.
- In order to retain and develop a relationship with its customers, an organization may be forced to introduce new products to allow it to offer a comprehensive portfolio of services.
- An opportunity may arise for an organization to satisfy unmet needs with a new service as a result of a competitor leaving the market.

6.7.1 What is meant by a 'new service'?

The intangible nature of services means that it is often quite easy to produce slight variants of an existing service, with the result that the term 'new service' can mean anything from a minor style change to a major innovation. Lovelock (1984) identifies five types of 'new' services:

- *Style changes* These include changes in decor, logo or livery—the revised design of telephone kiosks introduced by BT in the mid-1980s, for example.
- *Service improvements* These involve an actual change to a feature of the service already on offer to an established market—computerization of travel-agency information and booking procedures, for example.
- *Service line extensions* These are additions to the existing service product range—new modes of study for an MBA course at a university, for example.
- *New services* These are new services that are offered by an organization to its existing customers, although they may be currently available from its competitors—building societies offering current accounts, with cheque books, standing-order facilities, etc., for example.
- *Major innovations* These are entirely new services for new markets—the provision of multi-user 'voice mail' recording services, for example.

The distinctive features of services as compared to tangible goods raise a number of special issues that need to be considered in new-service development:

- The very intangibility of services has tended to lead to a proliferation of slightly different service products. Because of this intangibility, new services can be relatively easy to develop and the variety of different services can cause confusion. As an example, banks frequently introduced 'new' mortgage offers that are only slightly differentiated from existing ones—for example, by offering a lower rate for the first two years of the mortgage.

Figure 6.6 The new-product development process

- The characteristic of inseparability between service production and consumption means that front-line operational staff have a greater opportunity to identify new service ideas that are likely to be successful.
- As services are more likely than goods to be customized to the needs of individual customers, there could be greater opportunities for marginally different new services, each having its own unique selling proposition.

6.7.2 New-service development processes

Research has indicated that a systematic process of development helps to reduce the risk of failure when new products are launched. Although a variety of different procedures have been proposed and implemented, they all tend to have the common themes of beginning with as many new ideas as possible with the end objective of producing a tested service idea ready for launch. One common sequence is shown in Figure 6.6, although in practice, many of the sequential stages shown are compressed so that their timing overlaps with other stages.

The question of whether such procedures are appropriate for services was posed by Easingwood (1986). He investigated how new-service developments in service organizations reflected the major differences between goods and services—i.e. intangibility, inseparability, variability and perishability—and found a number of differences.

Idea generation Ideas can be generated from within an organization and also from outside, either formally or informally. Easingwood found that generating new ideas is not a problem for most service firms. Inseparability means that front-line staff have a closer understanding of both service operations and customer needs, and therefore it would seem logical that a large number of new ideas would come from the operating staff.

Easingwood in fact found that the most common internal source of new service ideas was the marketing rather than the operational function. The marketing function had constant contact with both customers and competitors and thus had market information 'on-tap'. He discovered that a much smaller proportion of new ideas emanated from the operations function because 'new' services were perceived by them as a further burden which would complicate their operations. Cowell (1988) notes that although the generation of ideas is relatively easy for service organizations, the degree of novelty of idea tends to be slight. Many ideas tend to be conservative, focusing on minor modifications, geographical extensions or 'me too' ideas.

Customers can be an important source of ideas for new service, and for this purpose, a study of the interaction between service provider and customer may be worth while. MacKay and Conway (1992) consider the variety of potential influences on new services idea generation within the corporate financial services sector, and indicate that the application of a network perspective could be useful in identifying the various influences on the generation of new financial services ideas.

Idea screening   This stage involves the evaluation of the ideas generated and rejection of those that do not justify the organization's resources. Criteria are usually established so that comparisons between ideas can be made, but because each firm exists in its own particular environment, there is no standard set of evaluative criteria that fits all. Easingwood found a variety of screening practices, all with differing degrees of formality, noting that screening processes for financial services were particularly rigorous. Within this sector, each new idea would be evaluated by customer discussion groups, feedback on proposed features and advertising would be collected and financial projections calculated with some detail. It was suggested that this rigour is partly due to the difficulties in withdrawing a financial service once it is being provided.

Intangibility makes services difficult to assess, and therefore 'image' is an important means by which customers reassure themselves about the credibility of a service provider. Easingwood found that enhancement or support of an organization's image was an important criterion used by firms in the screening process.

Concept development and testing   Ideas that survive the screening stage need to be turned into service concepts. Cowell (1988) describes the translation of the service idea into a concept which the organization wishes consumers to perceive subjectively. This then is tested by obtaining reactions from groups of target customers. Cowell also notes the importance of service positioning at this stage. This involves the development of a visual presentation of the image of an organization's service in relation either to competitive services or to others in its own mix.

Business analysis   The proposed idea is now turned into a business proposal. The likelihood of success/failure is analysed, as well as resource requirements in terms of personnel, extra physical resources, etc. At this stage, many of the factors that will determine the financial success of the proposed new service remain speculative. In particular, the activities of competitors' new-product development processes could have a crucial effect on the firm's eventual market share, as well as the price that it is able to sustain for its service.

Development   This is the translation of the idea into an actual service that is capable of delivery to customers. The tangible elements as well as the service delivery systems which make up the whole service offering all have to be designed and tested. Unfortunately, testing may not always be possible, and evidence from Easingwood implies that test marketing generally among service firms is limited. One possible alternative is to introduce the new service with limited promotion just to test whether it operates effectively.

Commercialization   The organization now makes decisions on when to introduce the new service, where, to whom and how. A successful new-service development programme requires an organizational culture that is conducive to changing market conditions and which can respond quickly to such changes. Although service firms are often not as flexible as manufactured goods companies, product champions (people who have the commitment and responsibility to develop and protect new ideas to the final launch) seem to be used by both goods and services firms. In addition to product champions, Cowell (1988) suggests that there are two other important roles that need to be performed if new service development is to be successful: 'integrators' and 'referees'. Integrators are people who can step across multifunctional boundaries and encourage a coordinated effort through persuasion. Referees are the counterbalance to the entrepreneurial process. These people develop and gain acceptance for the rules by which performance will be judged.

CORDLESS PHONE SERVICE LAUNCH ENDS IN A TANGLE

The launch of a series of low-cost portable telephone services in the UK during 1989 generated much interest, but their general failure to attract the expected custom illustrates the hazards of introducing a new service.

Since the initial UK launch of cellular telephone networks in the early 1980s by Cellnet and Vodaphone, the advantages of being able to make calls from any point had proved popular with the self-employed, travelling sales personnel and business executives, among others. Beyond these segments, the service remained too expensive, and possibly overspecified for more casual users.

In January 1989 the government issued licences to four companies—Zonephone (owned by Ferranti), Callpoint (owned by a consortium of Mercury Telecommunications, Motorola and Shaye), Phonepoint (British Telecom, STC, France Telecom, Deutsche Bundespost and Nynex) and Hutchison Telecom—to operate a network of low-cost mobile phones aimed at the mass market ('Telepoint'). These would allow callers to use a compact handset to make outgoing calls only, when they were within 150 metres of a base station, these being located in public places such as railway stations, shops, petrol stations, etc.

As in the case of many new markets which suddenly emerge, operators saw advantages of having an early market share lead. Customers who perceived that one network was more readily available than any other would—all other things being equal—be more likely to subscribe to that network. Thus operators saw that a bandwagon

effect could be set up—to gain entry to the market at a later stage could become a much more expensive market-challenger exercise. With relatively low costs involved in setting up a Telepoint network, three of the four licensed operators rushed into the market, signing up outlets for terminals as well as new customers.

Such was the speed of development that the concept was not rigorously test marketed. To many, the development was too much product-led, with insufficient understanding of buyer behaviour and competitive pressures. Each of the four companies forced through their own technologies, with little inclination or time available to discuss industry-standard handsets that could eventually have caused the market to grow at a faster rate and allowed the operators to cut their costs.

Rather than thoroughly test out customer reaction to Telepoint in a small test market (as French Telecom had done with its Pointel system in Strasbourg prior to its full national launch), the operators sought to develop national coverage overnight. This was inevitably very patchy, with no outlets in some areas and heavy congestion in a few key sites. There were also the inevitable teething problems in getting the equipment to function correctly.

Worse still for the Telepoint operators, the nature of the competition had been poorly judged. Originally, a major benefit of Telepoint had been seen as removing the need to find a working telephone kiosk from which to make an outgoing call. In fact, the unreliability of public kiosks on which demand was based receded as British Telecom significantly improved them as well as increasing their availability at a number of key sites. Competition from Mercury had itself increased the number of kiosks available to users. At the top end of the Telepoint target market, the two established cellular operators had revised their pricing structure which made them more attractive for the occasion user.

The final straw for Telepoint operators came with the announcement by the government of its proposal to issue licences for a new generation of Personal Communications Networks. These would have the additional benefit of allowing both incoming and outgoing calls, and would not be tied to a limited base station range. While this in itself may not have discouraged people from buying new Telepoint equipment, it did have the effect of bringing new investment in Telepoint networks to a halt, leaving the existing networks in a state of limbo.

Faced with the apparent failure of their new-service development strategies, the Telepoint operators looked for ways of relaunching their services by refocusing their benefits on new target markets. Now that the initial target of street-based outgoing callers had all but disappeared, new ideas were developed. Hutchison Telecom, for instance, combined an outgoing handset with a paging device which would allow busi-ness executives and self-employed people to keep in touch with base—the service was in effect being positioned as a cheap alternative to the two cellular networks. Similarly, the relaunch of Phonepoint focused on meeting the needs of three key targets—small businesses, mobile professionals and commuters. Furthermore, the company aimed to achieve excellence within the London area—where a network of 2000 base stations was planned—rather than spreading its resources thinly throughout the country. Other targets had been identified for Telepoint technology. Office networks, for example, offered the chance for employees within an organization to keep in touch, without the need to be near a wired phone.

Two years after its initial launch, it had been estimated that no more than 5000 subscribers in total had been signed up for Telepoint, or roughly one per base station, instead of the hundreds per station that were needed for viability. With hindsight, it could be argued that the launch might have been more successful had the service been more rigorously tested and developed before launch and if target markets had been more carefully selected. Moreover, many of the competitors may have wished that they had carried out a more rigorous environmental analysis, in which case they may have been less enthusiastic about launching in the first place.

6.8   SERVICE DELETION

Good product management depends upon reliable marketing information to show when a product is failing to achieve its objectives. As well as maintaining successful services and investing in new ones, service organizations must also have the courage to eliminate services that are no longer likely to be of benefit to the organization as a whole. This implies a need for the following:

1. Establishment of targets for each service
2. Periodic reviews of each service's performance

3. Modification of existing services where necessary
4. Elimination of services where necessary
5. Development of new services.

New-service development has been dealt with in the previous section. This section therefore deals with service-deletion strategies.

In reality, an organization's portfolio of products/services is often the result of a number of factors:

- *Ad hoc* responses to competitive challenges
- The history and culture of the organization
- Requests from customers
- Responses to technological opportunities
- Take-overs and mergers.

In general, there is a tendency to 'add on' rather than subtract, and thus many products/services do not die but merely fade away, consuming resources of an organization which could be better used elsewhere. 'Old' products may not even cover overheads. In addition, there are a number of 'hidden' costs of supporting dying products that need to be taken into consideration:

- A disproportionate amount of management time is spent on them.
- Short and relatively uneconomic 'production' runs may be required where a service has not been deleted and there is irregular demand for it.
- They often require frequent price adjustments (and stock adjustments where tangible goods are involved).
- The search for new products and services is delayed, as so much time is spent on existing products/services that the desired allocation of time to consider new ones is inadequate.

Firms should therefore have a logical planning system that incorporates product/service deletion. It would be naive, however, to assume that deletion is a simple process. In reality, there are a number of reasons why logical deletion procedures are not readily followed:

- Often firms do not have the information for identifying whether a product/service needs to be considered for elimination. Even if an organization is aware of a potential deletion candidate, the reasons for its failure may not be known, and thus management may just leave things as they are and hope that problem will go away by itself.
- Managers often become sentimental about products/services, hoping that sales will pick up when the market improves. Sometimes, particular elements of marketing strategy will be blamed for lack of success and thus there is the belief that a change in advertising or pricing, for example, will improve the situation.
- Within organizations there may be political difficulties in seeking to delete a service. Some individuals will have vested interests in a service and may fight elimination efforts. In fact, staff may hide the true facts of a service's performance to ensure that deletion is not considered at all.
- Finally, there is sometimes the fear that the sales of other products and services are tied into the product/service being deleted. For example, a car dealer who closes down its new car-sales department may subsequently lose business in its servicing and repairs department. Furthermore, some candidates for elimination may be sold to a small number of important customers, leading to fears that deletion would cause all of their business to go elsewhere.

Factor (FWi) *weighting*	*Factor*	*Product/service* *ranking (SRi)*
	Future market potential for product/service?	
	How much could be gained from modification?	
	How much could be gained from marketing strategy modification?	
	How much useful executive time could be released by abandoning product/ service?	
	How good are the firm's alternative opportunities?	
	How much is the product/service contributing beyond its direct costs?	
	How much is the product/service contributing to the sale of other product/services?	

The product/service retention index SRI = the sum of FWi × SRi

Figure 6.7 Product-retention index

In fact, many companies tackle product/service elimination in a piecemeal fashion, only considering the matter once a service is seen to be losing money, or when there is some crisis leading to a cutback. There is clearly a need for a systematic approach. At regular intervals, every product/service should be reviewed in terms of its sales, profitability, average cost, market share, competitor share, competitor prices, etc. Hise (1977) sees this as the first vital stage for any deletion procedure. Today, information technology allows firms to calculate important percentages and ratios that can indicate how a product/service is performing in its marketplace.

Having acquired the relevant information, an organization can identify 'weak' elements of the overall product/service mix. Hise identifies a number of warning signals of which management should be aware. Some of these relate to poor sales performance, some to poor profit performance and others to more general danger such as new competitor introductions or increasing amounts of executive time being spent on one service. The presence of these warning signals merely indicates a need for further consideration and the possibilities of either service modification or total elimination. Identification of a 'weak' service does not automatically mean that deletion is required.

One possible method of deciding which products to eliminate is the development and implementation of a product/service-retention index. This can include a number of factors, each of these being individually weighted according to the importance attached to them by a particular firm. Each service is then ranked according to each factor, the product-retention index thus being equal to the sum of the products of the weighted index. An illustration of a product retention index is shown in Figure 6.7.

Two of the product-retention factors relate to potential modification approaches in terms of either the service itself or of the whole marketing strategy. Hise (1977) presents twelve non-deletion alternatives for poorly performing services:

1. Modifying the product or service. Here the emphasis is on modifying the features so that any new benefits fit with the needs and wants of the market.
2. Increasing the price. This may be a sensible strategy if there is a primary market for the product/service from which demand is fairly inelastic.
3. Decreasing the price. This is a useful approach if the existing demand curve is elastic.
4. Increasing promotional expenditure. This assumes that sales of the service are sufficiently responsive to this increased promotion.
5. Decreasing promotional expenditure. If sales are now concentrated in a small primary market, promotional savings can be made.
6. Revising the promotional mix. This may come about as a result of a re-evaluation of the original promotional programme.
7. Increasing salesforce effort so that the service can be more competitive.
8. Decreasing salesforce effort if sales are concentrated in a primary market.
9. Changing the channels of distribution.
10. Changing the physical distribution system, where there is a significant tangible element to the service offer.
11. Additional marketing research effort may indicate new markets or additional uses for the product or service. Additionally, information relating to why success has declined may also be forthcoming.
12. Licensing agreements to another firm may be a possibility.

If any of the non-deletion alternatives are chosen, the firm must decide how such options are to be implemented in terms of timing and size of any changes to the marketing mix. If, on the other hand, deletion is the chosen alternative, decisions must be made as to how this is to be implemented. This is not always a simple task and a number of options can be identified:

1. *Ruthlessly eliminate 'overnight'* The potential problem here is that there are still likely to be customers of the service. How will they respond? Will they take their business to competitors? Will they take their business for other services in the mix with them?
2. *Increase the price and let demand fade away* This could mean that the firm makes good profits on the service while demand lasts.
3. *Reduce promotion or even stop it altogether* Again this could increase profitability while demand lasts.

Whichever decision is made, an organization has to consider the timing of such a decision. These are a number of areas that a firm planning to delete a service needs to consider:

1. *Inventory level* Although services cannot themselves be inventoried, the tangible elements of the offering, of course, can be, and where these are an important element of a service offer their level should be taken into account in deciding when to delete the service.
2. *Notification of consumers* Hise believes that a firm has everything to gain and little to lose by informing consumers of the service that deletion is imminent. Such a policy at least allows people time to make alternative arrangements and this may also have the added advantage of promoting the firm's 'caring' image.
3. *Resources* Management should move freed-up resources, particularly labour, to other appropriate services as soon as is possible. This not only eliminates the possibility of idle

resources and layoffs of manpower but is also an important part of internal marketing which is so important for services firms.

4. *Legal implications* Service elimination may bring with it legal liabilities. In the case of suppliers, an organization may be committed to take supplies regardless of a deletion strategy (for example, a holiday tour operator may be contractually committed to buying aircraft seats for the remainder of a season). In the case of customers, it may not be possible to delete services provided under a long-term contract until that contract comes to an end. This can be particularly important for the financial services sector, where mortgages and pension plans usually allow no facility for a unilateral withdrawal of supply by the service producer, even though a pension policy may still have over 30 years to run.

In addition to the above considerations, firms that have decided on deletion need to be aware of possible resistance to the decision both from consumers and internally from within the organization. How such resistance is to be overcome also needs to be considered—for example, through concessions to consumers who may suffer a degree of hardship.

The above implies that firms have a choice in deciding whether a product/service needs to be deleted from the mix. In fact, a study by Hart (1988) on product deletion in British companies found that deletion decisions were generally forced on management. Hart notes that by the time managers are contemplating deletion, the circumstances may well be outside their control. She does not, however, say that circumstances are unavoidable. In fact, by reading market climate, monitoring quality of their products and assessing the fit between their current offering, the market and future possibilities, managers are afforded greater time to consider, plan and execute the deletion for minimum disruption to revenue.

The study by Hart and the work undertaken by Hise relate primarily to goods rather than services. Further research in the area of service deletion is still required, although a logical rational procedure as indicated above should provide more benefits than disadvantages to the service firm attempting to maintain a successful service product mix.

REVIEW QUESTIONS

1. Identify the key differences between the service product offering and the tangible goods offering.
2. Consider the various elements of a higher education course. Having identified the core service and the secondary service elements, could these be modified to be more customer oriented?
3. Identify services which are in the following stages of the life cycle: introduction, growth, maturity, saturation and decline. What do you think could have been done to forestall decline?
4. Of what relevance is product lifecycle theory to services marketing management?
5. By what methods could a bank obtain ideas for new-service developments?
6. Identify the factors that might influence an airline's decision whether or not to delete a loss-making route.

MANAGING THE SERVICE ENCOUNTER

OBJECTIVES

After reading this chapter, you should be able to understand:

- Reasons for and the consequences of the central role played by customer encounters in service transactions
- Factors that contribute towards critical incidents within the service encounter and strategies for recovering from service failure
- Reasons why service organizations seek to develop relationships with their customers and strategies used to achieve those relationships
- The problems of matching supply and demand caused by the perishability of service offers and strategies employed to overcome such problems

7.1 INTRODUCTION

Inseparability was introduced in Chapter 1 as one of the defining characteristics of services. The fact that the production of services cannot normally be separated from their consumption results in producer–consumer interaction assuming great importance within the service offer. The service process can itself define the benefit received by the customer—the way in which customers are handled in a restaurant forms a very large part of the benefit that they receive. In contrast, a company producing manufactured goods generally only comes into contact with its customers very briefly at the point where goods are exchanged for payment. In many cases, the manufacturer does not even make any direct contact with its customers, acting instead through intermediaries. Furthermore, the processes by which goods are manufactured are usually of little concern to the consumer.

The perishability of the service offer also distinguishes the nature of contact between service producers and consumers. While goods manufacturers can normally hold stocks in order to meet fluctuating customer demand, services cannot be stored. This requires service organizations to carefully manage the contact they have with their customers in order to avoid bottlenecks and delays in the service-production process in which the customer is actually taking part.

This chapter begins by considering the basic nature of the interaction which occurs between producer and consumer and some of the implications of this relationship that are reflected in marketing strategy. At its simplest, interaction can be seen as a series of discrete transactions between producers and consumers. However, in many situations, service producers seek to replace casual transactions with on-going relationships, and strategies for achieving such relationships are discussed. Finally, the particular problems posed by the need to manage demand spatially and temporally are examined and appropriate marketing strategies discussed.

7.2 THE SERVICE ENCOUNTER

Service encounters occur where it is necessary for consumer and producer to meet in order for the former to receive the benefits which the latter has the resources to provide. The concept has been defined broadly by Shostack (1985) as 'a period of time during which a consumer directly interacts with a service'. This definition includes all aspects of the service firm with which a consumer may interact, including its personnel, physical assets and other tangible evidence. In some cases, the entire service is produced and consumed during the course of this encounter. Such services can be described as 'high contact' and the encounter becomes the only means by which consumers assess service quality. At other times, the encounter is just one element of the total production and consumption process. For such 'low-contact' services, a part of the production process can be performed without the direct involvement of the consumer.

From the consumer's perspective, interaction can take a number of forms, dependent upon two principal factors:

- First, the importance of the encounter is influenced by whether it is the customer who is the recipient of the service, or his or her possessions.
- Second, the nature of the encounter is influenced by the extent to which tangible elements are present within the service offer.

These two dimensions of the service encounter are shown diagrammatically in Figure 7.1 and some of the implications flowing from this categorization are discussed below.

The most significant types of service encounters occur in the upper-left quadrant of Figure 7.1, where the consumer is the direct recipient of a service and the service offering provides a high level of tangibility. These can be described as high-contact encounters. Examples are provided by most types of health care where the physical presence of a customer's body is a prerequisite for a series of quite tangible operations being carried out. Public transport offers further examples within this category—the benefits of a passenger-train service are fundamentally to move customers physically. Without their presence, the benefit cannot be received. Services in this quadrant represent the most intense type of service encounter. Customer and producer must physically meet in order for the service to be performed and this has a number of implications for the service-delivery process:

- Quality control becomes a major issue, for the consumer is concerned with the processes of service production as much as with the end-result. Furthermore, because many services in this category are produced in a one-on-one situation where judgement by the service provider is called for, it can be difficult to implement quality control checks before the service is consumed.
- Because the consumer must attend during the production process, the location of the service encounter assumes importance. An inconveniently located doctor, or one who refuses to make home visits, may fail to achieve any interaction at all.
- The problem of managing demand is most critical with this group of services. Delays in service production have an adverse consequence not only for the service outcome but also for consumers' judgement of the service process.

The nature of the service encounter changes somewhat in the second category of services

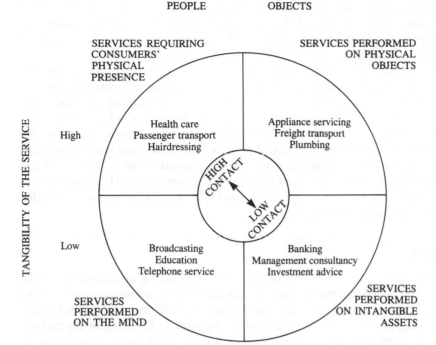

Figure 7.1   A classification of service encounter types

(lower-left-hand quadrant of Figure 7.1) which are essentially performed on customers' minds. Here, the consumer is the direct recipient of a service, but does not need to be physically present in order to receive an essentially intangible benefit. The intangibility of the benefit means that the service production process can in many cases be separated spatially from the consumption of the service. In this way, viewers of an intangible television channel do not need to interact with staff from the television company in order to receive the benefits. Similarly, recipients of educational services often do not need to be physically present during an encounter with the education provider. Open University broadcasts and other distance-learning schemes can include little direct contact.

A third pattern of service encounters can be observed in the upper-right-hand quadrant of Figure 7.1. Here, services are performed on customers' objects rather than their person—an example is the repair of appliances or the transport of goods. A large part of the production process can go unseen without any involvement of the customer, who can be reduced to initiating the service process (for example, delivering a car to a repair garage) and collecting the results (picking up the car once a repair has been completed). The process by which a car is repaired—the substantive service—may be of little concern to the customer, so long as the end-result is satisfactory. However, the manner in which they are handled during the pre- and after-service stages assumes great importance. It follows that while technical skills may be essential for staff engaged in the substantive service-production process, skills in dealing with customers assume great importance for those involved in customer encounters. Because the consumer is not physically present during the substantive service-production process, the timing and location of this part of the process allows the service organization a much greater degree of flexibility. In this way, the car repairer can collect a car at a customer's home (which is most convenient to the customer) and process it at its central workshop (which is most convenient to the service producer). As long as a service job is completed on time, delays during the substantive production process are of less importance to the customer than would be the case if the customer was personally delayed during the production of the service.

The final category of service encounters is made up of services performed on a customer's intangible assets. For these services, there is little tangible evidence in the production process. It follows that the customer does not normally need to be physically present during the production process, as is the case with most services provided by, for example, fund managers and solicitors. Here, a large part of the substantive service-production process (such as the preparation of house-transfer deeds) can be undertaken with very little direct contact between customer and organization. The service encounter becomes less critical to the customer and can take place at a distance without any need to meet physically. Customers judge transactions not just on the quality of their encounter but also to a much greater extent on outcomes (for example, the performance of a financial portfolio).

7.2.1 Critical incidents

Incidents occur each time that producers and consumers come together in an encounter. While many incidents will be quite trivial in terms of their consequences to the consumer, some will be so important that they become critical to a successful encounter. Bitner *et al.* (1990) define critical incidents as specific interactions between customers and service firm employees that are especially satisfying or dissatisfying. While their definition focuses on the role of personnel in creating critical incidents, they can arise also as a result of interaction with the service provider's equipment.

At each critical incident, customers have an opportunity to evaluate the service provider and form an opinion of service quality. The processes involved in producing services can be quite complex, resulting in a large number of critical incidents, many of which involve non-front-line staff. In the case of Scandinavian Airlines, it was estimated by Carlzon (1987, page 3) that 50 million critical incidents occurred each year between the airline and its customers. On each occasion, the airline had to prove that it could deliver to customers' expectations.

The complexity of service encounters—and the resultant quality control problems—can be judged by examining how many critical incidents are present. A simple analysis of the interaction between an airline and its customers may reveal the following pattern of critical incidents:

Pre-sales
Initial telephone enquiry
Making reservation
Issue of ticket
Post-sales, pre-consumption
Check-in of baggage
Inspection of ticket
Issue of boarding pass
Advice on departure gate
Quality of airport announcements
Quality of waiting conditions
Consumption
Welcome on boarding aircraft
Assistance in finding seat

Assistance in stowing baggage
Reliability of departure time
Attentiveness of in-flight service
Quality of food
Quality of in-flight entertainment
Quality of announcements
Safe/comfortable operation of aircraft
Fast transfer from aircraft to terminal
Post-consumption
Baggage reclaim
Information available at arrival airport
Queries regarding lost baggage, etc.

This list of critical stages of interaction is by no means exhaustive. Indeed, the extent to which any point is critical should be determined by customers' judgements, rather than relying on a technical definition by the producer. At each critical point in the service process, customers judge the quality of their service encounter.

Successful accomplishment of many of the critical incidents identified above can be dependent upon satisfactory performance by support staff who do not directly interact with customers. For example, the actions of unseen baggage handlers can be critical in ensuring that baggage is reclaimed in the right place, at the right time and intact. This emphasizes the need to treat everyone within a service organization as a 'part-time marketer' (Gummesson, 1991).

7.2.2   Blueprinting

Where service-production processes are complex, it is important for an organization to gain a holistic view of how the elements of the service relate to each other. 'Blueprinting' is a graphical approach proposed by Shostack (1984) designed to overcome problems that occur where a new service is launched without adequate identification of the necessary support functions. A customer blueprint has three main elements:

- All the principal functions required to make and distribute a service are identified, along with the responsible company unit or personnel.
- Timing and sequencing relationships among the functions are depicted graphically.
- For each function, acceptable tolerances are identified in terms of the variation from standard which can be tolerated without adversely affecting customers' perception of quality.

The principles of a service blueprint are illustrated in Figure 7.2 with a suggested application of the framework to the purchase of a cup of tea in a café.

A customer blueprint must clearly identify all steps in a service process—i.e. all contacts or interactions with customers. In Figure 7.2 these are shown in time-sequential order from left to right. The blueprint is further divided into two 'zones': a zone of visibility (processes that are visible to the customer and in which the customer is likely to participate) and one of invisibility (processes and interactions that, although necessary for the proper servicing of a customer, may be hidden from their view).

The blueprint also identifies points of potential failure in the service-production process—the critical incidents on which customers base their perception of quality. Identifying specific interaction points as potential failure points can help marketers to focus their management and quality control attention on those steps most likely to cause poor judgements of service quality.

Stage in production process	Obtain seat	Take order	Make tea	Deliver tea	Pay for tea
			Repeat if tea is unsatisfactory		
Target time (minutes)	1	1	3		1
Critical time	5	5	8		3
Is incident critical?	Y	N	N	Y	N
Participants	Customer	Customer Waiter(ress)	Cook	Customer Waiter(ress)	Customer Cashier
Visible evidence	Furnishings	Appearance of staff	Tea, crockery, manner of service delivery		Cash-collection procedures
'Line of visibility'					
Invisible processes	Cleaning of tea room		Preparation of tea Ordering of supplies		Accounting procedures

Figure 7.2 Customer service blueprint—a simplified application to the purchase of a cup of tea in a café

Finally, the blueprint indicates the level of tolerance for each event in the service process and action to be taken in the event of failure, such as repeating the event until a satisfactory outcome is obtained.

7.2.3 Role playing

The concept of role playing has been used to apply the principles of social psychology to explain the interaction between service producer and consumer (for example, Solomon et al., 1985). It sees people as actors who act out roles which can be distinguished from their own personality. Roles are assumed as a result of conditioning by the society and culture of which a person is a member. Individuals typically play multiple roles in life, as family members, workers, members of football teams, etc., each of which comes with a set of socially conditioned role expectations—a person playing the role of worker is typically conditioned to act with reliability, loyalty and trustworthiness. An analysis of the expectations associated with each role becomes a central part of role analysis. The many roles that an individual plays may result in conflicting role expectations, as where the family role of a father leads to a series of role expectations that are incompatible with his role expectations as a business manager—each role might be associated with competing expectations about the allocation of leisure time.

The service encounter can be seen as a theatrical drama. The stage is the location where the encounter takes place and can itself affect the role behaviour of both buyer and seller. A scruffy service outlet may result in lowered expectations by the customer and, in turn, a lower level of service delivery by service personnel (see Bitner, 1990). Both parties work to a script which is determined by their respective role expectations—an air stewardess is acting out a script in the manner in which she attends to passengers' needs. The script might include precise details about what actions should be performed, when and by whom, including the words to be used in verbal communication. In reality, there may be occasions when the stewardess would like to do anything but wish her awkward customers a nice day. The theatrical analogy extends to the costumes which service personnel wear. When a doctor wears a white coat or a bank manager a suit, they are emphasizing to customers the role they are playing. Like the actor who uses costumes to convince an audience that he is in fact Henry VIII, the bank manager uses the suit to convince customers that he or she is capable of taking the types of decisions made by a competent bank manager.

In a service encounter, both customers and service personnel are playing roles which can be separated from their underlying personality. Organizations normally employ personnel to act not in accordance with this personality but in a specified role. Thus employees of a bank are socialized to play the role of cautious and prudent advisers and to represent the values of the bank in their dealings with customers. Similarly, customers play roles when dealing with service providers. A customer of a bank may try to act the role of prudent borrower when approaching a bank manager for a mortgage, even though this might be in contrast to his or her fun-loving role as a family member.

Both buyers and sellers bring role expectations into their interaction. From an individual customer's point of view, there may be clear expectations of the role that a service provider should play. Most people would expect a bank manager to be dressed appropriately to play his or her role effectively, or a store assistant to be courteous and attentive. Of interest to marketers are the specific role expectations held by particular segments within society. As an example, a significant segment of young people may be happy to be given a train timetable by an enquiry office assistant and expect to read it themselves. On the other hand, the role expectations of many older people may be that the assistant should go through the timetable and read it out for them. Similarly, differences in role expectations can be identified between different countries. While customers of a supermarket in the USA would expect the checkout operator to pack their bags for them, this is not normally part of the role expectation held by UK shoppers.

It is not just customers who bring role expectations to the interaction process. Service producers also have their idea of the role that their customers should perform within the co-production process. In the case of hairdressers, there may be an expectation of customers' roles that includes giving clear instructions at the outset, arriving for the appointment on time and (in some countries) giving an adequate tip. Failure of customers to perform their role expectations can have a demotivating effect on front-line personnel. Retail sales staff who have been well trained to act in their role may be able to withstand abusive customers who are acting out of role—others may resort to shouting back.

The service encounter can be seen as a process of simultaneous role playing in which a dynamic relationship is developed. In this process, both parties can adapt to the role expectations held by the other party. The quality of the service encounter is a reflection of the extent to which each party's role expectations are met. An airline that casts its cabin crew as the most caring in the business may raise customers' expectations of their role in a manner which the crews cannot deliver. The result would be that customers perceive a poor-quality service. In contrast, the same standard of service may be perceived as high quality by a customer travelling on another airline which had made no attempt to try to project such a caring role on their crew. The quality of the service encounter can be seen as the difference between service expectations and perceived delivery. Where the service delivery surpasses these expectations, a high quality of service is perceived (although sometimes, exceeding role expectations can be perceived poorly, as where a waiter in a restaurant offers incessant gratuitous advice to clients who simply want to be left alone).

Over time, role expectations change on the part of both service staff and their customers. Customer expectations of service staff have sometimes been raised, as in the case of standards expected from many public services. In other instances, expectations have been progressively lowered, as where customers of petrol stations no longer expect staff to attend to their car, but are prepared to fill their tank and clean their windscreens themselves. Change in customers' expectations usually begins with an innovative early adopter group and subsequently trickles through to other groups. It was mainly young people who were prepared to accept the simple, inflexible and impersonal role played by staff of fast-food restaurants which many older segments have subsequently accepted as a role model for restaurant staff.

WALT DISNEY MAKES EVERYONE A STAR

The Walt Disney Company is a diversified international entertainments organization whose operations include films, consumer products and theme parks and resorts. It is in the area of theme parks and resorts that the company has acquired a reputation for providing a consistently high level of consumer satisfaction. A major reason for this success lies in the careful analysis of just what visitors to its theme parks expect and detailed specification of the service standards to be provided. In delivering high-quality services, particular attention is paid to the roles played by the employees of the organization who are responsible for front-line service encounters.

The company's business mission involves making guests happy and this mission has embedded itself in the cultural values shared by all employees. Once employed, all new employees learn about the history of the Disney Company and gain an understanding of the original philosophy of Walt Disney himself and thus the whole corporate culture. One approach used by Walt Disney to achieve its mission is to treat its theme parks as giant entertainment stages in which a series of satisfying service encounters take place. People paying to come into the park are considered not as customers but as 'guests'. Similarly, employees are considered as 'cast members' in this encounter and wear 'costumes' appropriate to their task, rather than uniforms.

After being introduced to the basic cultural values of the organization, each 'cast member' is given clear written instructions about their role expectations, where to report, what to wear and how to handle typical encounters with guests. Role playing prepares cast members for a wide range of guest requirements—for example, meeting their requests for directions or guidance on the best places to eat.

New employees are assigned a particular role whose titles indicate the strength of the 'entertainment' culture:

Custodial hosts: street cleaners
Food and beverage hosts: restaurant workers
Transportation hosts: drivers
Security hosts: police

Walt Disney's role scripting is based on careful analysis of what guests particularly value in the actions of cast members and the interactions between cast members and guests are manipulated in such a positive way that the guests' expectations are exceeded. For roles to be performed effectively, Disney provides extensive training, including several days for each employee before they come into contact with guests. Regular training sessions and newsletters are used to keep employees informed of new developments. Should training have failed to prepare an employee to cope with a guest's problem on the spot, they can contact back-up support by telephone in order to satisfy the guest's request promptly.

To ensure that management is aware of the experiences of front-line staff, each member of the management team spends a week each year as a front-line member of the workforce. In addition, each is also expected to bring his or her family for one day to experience the resort as a guest and thus perceive the experience from the guest's perspective.

Finally, employees themselves are used to monitor the quality of service encounters. Peer review by current cast members is used in the selection of new recruits, the primary criterion for selection being 'service', and all employees are expected to complete a questionnaire on their own perceptions of working for the organization. The results are then analysed and, from this, employee satisfaction is measured. The Disney philosophy is that if employees are satisfied with their encounters then so, ultimately, will be the customer.

7.2.4   The customer–producer boundary

Services are, in general, very labour-intensive and have not witnessed the major productivity increases seen in many manufacturing industries. Sometimes, mechanization can be used to improve productivity (see below), but for many personal services, this remains a difficult possibility. An alternative way to increase the service provider's productivity is to involve the customer more fully in the production process.

The inseparability of services means that customers will inevitably be an important part of the production process, especially in the case of 'high-contact' services. As real labour costs have increased and service markets become more competitive, many service organizations have sought to pass on a greater part of the production process to their customers to try to retain price competitiveness. At first, customers' expectations may hinder this process, but productivity savings often result from one segment taking on additional responsibilities in return for lower prices. This then becomes the norm for other follower segments.

Examples where the boundary has been redefined to include greater production by the customer include:

- Petrol stations which have replaced attendant service with self-service
- The Royal Mail, which gives discounts to bulk mail users who do some pre-sorting of mail themselves
- Railway operators who have replaced porters with self-service luggage trollies
- Television-repair companies who require equipment for repair to be taken to them, rather than collecting it themselves
- Restaurants which replace waiter service with a self-service buffet.

While service-production boundaries have generally been extended to involve the customer more fully in the production process, some service organizations have identified segments who are prepared to pay higher prices in order to relieve themselves of parts of their co-production responsibilities. Examples include:

- Tour operators who arrange a taxi service from customers' homes, avoiding the need for customers to get themselves to the airport
- Car repairers who collect and deliver cars to the owners' homes
- Fast-food firms who avoid the need for customers to come to their outlet by offering a delivery service

7.2.5   The role of third-party producers in the service encounter

Service personnel who are not employed by a service organization may nevertheless be responsible for many of the critical incidents that affect the quality of service encounters perceived by its customers. Three categories of such personnel can be identified:

- A service company's intermediaries can become involved in critical incidents before, during or after consumption of a service. The first contact many people have with an organization is through its sales outlets. In the case of the airline above, the manner in which a customer is handled by a travel agent is a highly critical incident, the outcome of which can affect the enjoyment of the rest of the service—for example, where the ticket agent gives incorrect information about departure times or the ticket is ordered incorrectly. The incidents in which intermediaries are involved can continue through the consumption and post-consumption phases. Where services are delivered through intermediaries, as is the case with franchisees, they can become the dominant source of critical incidents. In such cases, quality control becomes an issue of controlling intermediaries.
- Service providers themselves buy-in services from other subcontracting organizations. Service organizations buying subcontracted services must ensure that quality-control procedures apply to many of its subcontractors' processes, as well as to their outcomes. Airlines buy-in many services from subcontractors. In some cases the purchase generates very little potential for critical incidents with the airline's passengers. Where in-flight meals are bought-in from an outside caterer, the subcontractor has few (if any) encounters with the airline's customers and quality can be assessed by the tangible evidence being delivered on time. On the other hand, some services involve a wide range of critical incidents. Airlines often subcontract their passenger checking-in procedures to a specialist handling company, for whom quality cannot simply be assessed by quantifiable factors such as length of queues or amounts of lost baggage. The manner in which the subcontractor's personnel handle customers and resolve such problems as overbooked aircraft, lost tickets and general enquiries assumes critical importance.
- Sometimes staff who are not employed by the service organization or its direct subcontractors can contribute towards critical incidents in the service encounter. This occurs, for example, at airports where airport employees, air traffic controllers and staff working in shops within the airport contribute to airline passengers' perception of the total service. In many cases, the airline may have little (if any) effective control over the actions of these personnel. Sometimes it may be possible to relocate the environment of its service encounters—such as changing departure airports—but it may still be difficult to gain control over some critical publicly provided services, such as immigration and passport control. The best that a service organization can do in these circumstances is to show empathy with its customers. An airline may gain some sympathy for delays caused by air traffic controllers if it explains the reason for those delays to customers and does everything within its power to overcome resulting problems.

7.2.6   Service recovery

Almost inevitably, service companies will fail at some critical incidents. At this point, organizations need a strategy by which they can seek to recover from failure. There is a growing body of literature on the methods used by service organizations to recover from an adverse critical incident and to build up a strong relationship once again. The most important step in service recovery is to find out as soon as possible when a service has failed to meet customers' expectations. Customers who are dissatisfied and do not report their dissatisfaction to the service provider may never come back, and, worse still, may tell friends about their bad experience. Service companies are therefore going to increasing lengths to facilitate feedback of customers' comments in the hope that they are given an opportunity to make amends. Service recovery after the event may include financial compensation which is considered by the recipient to be fair, or the offer of additional services without charge, giving the company the opportunity to show itself in a better light. If service recovery is to be achieved after the event, it is important that appropriate offers of compensation are made speedily and fairly. If a long dispute ensues, aggrieved customers could increasingly rationalize their motives for never using that service organization again and tell others not only of their poor service encounter but also of the unacceptable post-service behaviour.

Rather than wait until long after a critical incident has failed, service companies should think more about service recovery during the production process. If customers' expectations of a service encounter have not been met at an early stage in the service process, there is often the possibility that it may be recovered by significantly exceeding expectations later. For example, a tour operator which has announced to its customers that they will be subject to a long delay at their departure airport may subsequently exceed their expectations by taking them for a well-planned meal or entertainment as a pleasant alternative to waiting.

It can be possible for service organizations to turn a failed critical incident into a positive advantage with its customers. In the face of adverse circumstances, a service organization's ability to empathize with its customers can create stronger bonds than if no service failure had occurred. As an example, a coach-tour operator could arrive at a hotel with a party of customers only to find that the hotel had overbooked, potentially resulting in great inconvenience to its customers. The failure to swiftly check its guests into their designated hotel could represent failure of a critical incident which results in long-term harm for the relationship between the coach-tour operator and its customers. However, the situation may be recovered by a tour leader who shows determination to sort things out to their best advantage. This could involve the tour leader demonstrating to his or her customers that they are determined to get their way with the hotel manager and to have their room allocation restored. They could also negotiate with the hotel management to secure alternative hotel accommodation of a higher standard at no additional charge, which customers would appreciate. If the process of rearranging accommodation looked like taking time, the tour leader could avoid the need for customers to be kept waiting in a coach by arranging an alternative enjoyable activity in the interim, such as a visit to a local tourist attraction.

The extent to which service recovery is possible depends upon two principal factors. First, front-line service personnel must have the ability to empathize with customers. Empathy can be demonstrated initially in the ability to spot service failure as it is perceived by customers, rather than some technical, production-oriented definition of failure. Empathy can also be shown in the manner of front-line staffs' ability to take action which best meets the needs of customers. Second, service organizations should empower front-line staff to take remedial action at the time and place which is most critical. This may entail authorizing—and expecting—staff to deviate from the scheduled service programme and, where necessary, empower staff to use resources at their discretion in order to achieve service recovery. In the case of the tour leader facing an overbooked hotel, taking customers away for a complimentary drink may make the difference between service failure and service recovery. If the tour leader is not authorized to spend money in this way, or approval is so difficult that it comes too late to be useful, the chance of service recovery may be lost for ever.

7.2.7 The role of other customers in the service encounter

Many service offers can only sensibly be produced simultaneously in large quantities, while the consumers who use the service buy only individual units of the service. It follows therefore that a significant proportion of the service is consumed in public—train journeys, meals in a restaurant and visits to the theatre are consumed in the presence of other customers. In such circumstances, there is said to be an element of joint consumption of service benefits. A play cannot be produced just for one patron and a train cannot run for just one passenger—a number of customers jointly consume one unit of service output. An environment is created in which the behaviour pattern of any one customer during the service process can directly affect other customers' enjoyment of their service. In the theatre, a member of the audience who talks during the performance spoils the enjoyment of others.

The actions of fellow consumers are often therefore an important element of the service encounter and service companies seek to manage customer–customer interaction. By various methods, organizations seek to remove adverse elements of these encounters and to strengthen those elements which add to all customers' enjoyment. Some commonly used methods of managing encounters between customers include the following:

- *Selecting customers on the basis of their ability to interact positively with other customers* Where the enjoyment of a service is significantly influenced by the nature of other customers, formal or informal selection criteria can be used to try to ensure that only those customers who are likely to contribute positively to service encounters are accepted. Examples of formal selection criteria include tour companies who set age limits for certain holidays. People booking an 18–30 holiday can be assured that they will not be holidaying with children or elderly people, whose attitudes towards loud music may have prevented enjoyment of their own lifestyle. Formal selection criteria can include inspecting the physical appearance of potential customers. Many night clubs and restaurants set dress standards in order to preserve a high-quality environment in which service encounters take place. Informal selection criteria are aimed at encouraging some groups who add to customers' satisfaction with the service environment, while discouraging those who detract from it. Colour schemes, service ranges, advertising and pricing can be used to discourage certain types of customers. Bars that charge high prices for drinks and offer a comfortable environment will be informally excluding the segment of the population whose aim is to get drunk as cheaply as possible.
- *Determining rules of behaviour expected from customers* The actions of one customer can significantly affect another customer's enjoyment of a service. Examples include smoking in a restaurant, talking during a cinema show and playing loud music on public transport. The simplest strategy for influencing behaviour is to make known the standards of expected behaviour and to rely on customers' goodwill to act in accordance with these expectations. With increasing recognition by most people in society that smoking can be unpleasant for others, social pressures alone may result in most smokers observing no-smoking signs. Where rules are not obeyed, the intervention of service personnel may be called for. Failure to intervene can result in a negative service encounter continuing for the affected party, and, moreover, the service organization may be perceived as not caring by its failure to enforce rules. Against this, intervention which is too heavy-handed may alienate the offender, especially if the rule is perceived as one that has little popular support. The most positive service encounter results from intervention which is perceived as a gentle reminder by the offender and as valuable corrective action by other customers.
- *Facilitating positive customer–customer interaction* For many services, an important part of

the overall benefit is derived from positive interaction with other customers. Holidaymakers, people attending a conference and students of a college can all derive significant benefit from the interaction with their peer group. A holiday group where no-one speaks to each other may restrict the opportunities for shared enjoyment. The service providers can seek to develop bonds between customers by, for example, introducing customers to one another or arranging venues where they can meet socially.

7.2.8   Industrializing the service encounter

Service organizations face a dilemma, for while most seek to maximize the choice and flexibility of services available to customers, they need to reduce the variability of service outcomes so that consistent brand values can be established. They must also pursue methods for increasing productivity, and, in particular, reducing the amount and cost of skilled labour involved in production processes.

Complex and diverse service offers can result in personnel being required to use their judgement and to be knowledgeable about a wide range of services. In many service sectors, giving too much judgement to staff results in a level of variability which is incompatible with consistent brand development. The existence of multiple choices in the service offer can make it very expensive for training staff to become familiar with all the options, often matched by a minimal level of income which some services generate. For these reasons, service organizations often seek to simplify their service offerings and to 'de-skill' many of the tasks performed by front-line service staff. By offering a limited range of services at a high standard of consistency, the process follows the pattern of the early development of factory production of goods. The process has sometimes been described as the industrialization of services and can take a number of forms:

- *Simplifying the range of services available* Organizations may find themselves offering services that are purchased by relatively few customers. The effort put into providing these services may not be justified by the financial return. Worse still, the lack of familiarity of many staff with little-used services could make them less than proficient at handling service requests, resulting in a poor service encounter that reflects badly on the organization as a whole. Where peripheral services do not produce significant net revenue, but offer a lot of scope for the organization to make mistakes, a case can often be made for dropping them. As an example, retailers have sometimes offered a delivery service at an additional charge, only to experience minimal demand from a small segment of customers. Moreover, the lack of training often given to sales staff (for example, on details of delivery areas, etc.) and the general complexity of delivery operations (such as ensuring that there is someone at home to receive the goods) could justify a company in dropping the service. Simplification of the service range to just offering basic retail services allows a wide range of negative service encounters to be avoided, while driving relatively few customers to competitors. It also allows service personnel to concentrate their activities on doing what they are best at—in this case, shopfloor encounters.
- *Providing 'scripts' for role performance* It was noted above that service personnel act out their role expectations in an informally scripted manner. More formal scripting allows service staff to follow the expectations of their role more precisely. Formal scripting can include a precise specification of the actions to be taken by service staff in particular situations, often with the help of machine-based systems. In this way, a telephone salesperson can be prompted what to say next by messages on a computer screen. Training in itself can help staff to understand how they should handle a service encounter—for example, the manner in which cabin crew should greet passengers boarding an aircraft.

- *Tightly specifying operating procedures* In some instances it may be difficult to set out operating procedures which specify in detail how service personnel should handle each encounter. Personal services such as hairdressing rely heavily on the creativity of individual staff and operating procedures can go no further than describing general conduct. However, many service operations can be specified with much greater detail. At a managerial level, many jobs have been de-skilled by instituting formalized procedures, which replace much of the judgement previously made by managers. In this way, bank managers use much less judgement in deciding whether to advance credit to a client—the task is decided by a computer-based credit-scoring system. Similarly, local managers in sectors such as retailing and hotels are often given little discretion over such matters as the appearance of their outlets and the type of facilities provided—these are specified in detail from head office and the branch manager is expected to follow them closely. In this way, organizations can ensure that many aspects of the service encounter will be identical, regardless of the time or place.

- *Replacing human inputs with machine-based inputs* Machines are generally more predictable in delivering services than humans. They also increasingly offer cost savings, which may give a company a competitive price advantage. Although machines may break down, when they are functioning they tend to be much less variable than humans, who may suffer from tiredness, momentary inattentiveness or periodic boredom. In addition to reducing the variability of service outcomes, machine-based encounters offer a number of other advantages over human-based ones:

  — The service provider may be able to offer a much wider range of encounter possibilities. For example, bank ATM machines allow many transactions to be undertaken at a time and place convenient to the customer.

  — It is often possible to program machinery to provide a range of services reliably in a manner which would not have been possible if the encounter was based on a human service producer. Many telephone companies now offer a wide range of automated telephone services (for example, call-interception services) which can be delivered with high levels of reliability.

  — Studies have suggested that automated encounters give many customers a feeling of greater control over these encounters. A bank customer phoning his or her local branch to ask for the balance of their account may feel that they are having to work hard to get the information from a bank employee and may feel intimidated by asking additional questions. In contrast, a caller to an automated banking information system can feel in complete control of dealings with the computer.

7.3 DEVELOPING RELATIONSHIPS WITH CUSTOMERS

Traditional marketing theory has focused attention on encounters as being a series of discrete events, too often viewed in isolation from preceding exchanges, and without analysis of both parties' expectations for future exchanges. Some services can be supplied quite adequately on the basis of a series of discrete, casual encounters. Most people ordering taxis in London or seeking a tea shop in a seaside resort would have little need for a relationship with a supplier. However, a relationship-based series of encounters can be useful for both customer and producer in a number of circumstances, some of which are identified by Berry (1983) and Lovelock (1983):

- Some services involve a multi-stage production process and it would not be sensible for a customer to switch service producers during production, thereby requiring the new supplier to have to establish what had already been carried out during previous stages. A surgeon who keeps records is able to perform an operation with the benefit of the knowledge gained during previous examinations and operations. A newly introduced surgeon may have to begin with fresh diagnostic checks.

- The service provider may be required to monitor the results of a service after it has been delivered, and therefore needs to engage in some form of relationship. An engineer who has installed a new heating unit may need to check its operation after a period of operation.
- Legislation may require that some form of relationship exists between buyer and seller before a service can be provided. Sometimes a licence allows a company to supply only *bona fide* members of a club (conditions frequently attached to licences for night clubs and casinos). In other cases, legislation may require that the supplier has taken steps to establish the true needs of the buyer before a service supply is agreed. In other words, some relationship is established (for example the Financial Services Act 1986 requires many categories of financial intermediaries to undertake an audit of customers' financial circumstances before any commitments are made).
- Where services are complex in nature, or allow significant adaptations to meet customers' differing needs, there is evidence that customers are more likely to seek a relationship with suppliers. Risk tends to increase with complexity, and a relationship is one strategy by which customers can seek to reduce the level of perceived risk.
- In some markets, customers may seek the reassurance which a relationship can bring in terms of the ability to obtain preferential treatment or semi-automatic responses to requests for service (Marshall *et al.*, 1979). For example, a customer signing up for a regular maintenance contract on domestic appliances avoids the need to formally initiate service requests each time a service is needed. By entering into such a relationship, buyers can also avoid significant transaction costs associated with multiple service ordering (Williamson, 1975).
- It has also been suggested that both suppliers and customers seek the security of relationships where the market environment is turbulent (Zeithaml, 1981).
- To the supplier of services, the development of strong relationships helps to facilitate loyalty from customers whose loyalty is challenged by competing brands. By developing a relationship with customers, suppliers add to the differentiation of their products and give their customers a reason to remain loyal (Day and Wensley, 1983). In highly competitive markets, suppliers may be able to attract new users to their services only at a high cost in terms of promotional activity and price incentives. Research has indicated that for many services, the cost of recruiting new customers exceeds the revenue earned from the first transaction. It is only by pursuing a long-term relationship that an organization is able to make profits—in other words, it has to develop an on-going relationship (Berry, 1983; Jackson, 1985).
- A more formalized relationship with customers facilitates suppliers' task of collecting feedback from their customers. Increasingly, organizations seek to move their interaction with customers along what Gronroos (1991) has described as a Marketing Strategy Continuum. The aim is to move away from delivering goods and services by a series of discrete transactions towards continuous delivery through an on-going relationship.

7.3.1   Strategies used by service organizations to develop relationships with customers

A number of attempts have been made to analyse the development of relationships, often using the principles of lifecycle theories. A theoretical model of relationship proposed by Dwyer *et al.* (1987), based on the work of Scanzoni (1979), identifies five stages of relationship development—awareness, exploration, expansion, commitment and dissolution. Their model proposes that a relationship begins to develop significance in the exploration stage, when it is characterized by attempts of the seller to attract the attention of the other party. The exploration stage includes attempts by each party to bargain and to understand the nature of the power, norms and expectations held by the other. Building on the work of Frazier (1983), Dwyer *et al.* see the expansion phase of a relationship resulting from the successful conclusion of the initial exploratory interaction between the parties. Exchange outcomes in the exploratory stage provide clues as to the suitability of long-term exchange relationships. The commitment phase of a relationship implies some degree of exclusivity between the parties and results in information search for alternatives—if it occurs at all—being much reduced. The dissolution stage marks the point where buyer and seller recognize that they would be better able to achieve their respective aims outside the relationship.

Service organizations use a number of strategies to move their customers through the stages of relationship development:

- The possibility of relationships developing can occur only where the parties are aware of each other and of their mutual desire to enter into exchange transactions. At this stage, the parties may have diverging views about the possibility of forming a long-term relationship. The supplier must be able to offer potential customers reasons why they should show disloyalty to their existing supplier. In some cases, low introductory prices are offered by service organizations which provide a sufficient incentive for disloyal customers of other companies to switch supplier. Non-price-related means of gaining attention include advertising and direct mail aimed at the market segments with whom relationships are sought. Over time, the supplier would seek to build value into the relationship so that customers would have little incentive for seeking lower-price solutions elsewhere. Inevitably, sellers face risks in adopting this strategy. It may be difficult to identify and exclude from a relationship invitation those segments of the population who are likely to show most disloyalty by withdrawing from the relationship at the point when it is just beginning to become profitable to the supplier.
- On entering into a relationship, buyers and sellers make a series of promises to each other (Gronroos, 1989). In the early stages of a relationship, suppliers' promises result in expectations being held by buyers as to the standard of service that will actually be delivered. Many studies on service quality have highlighted the way in which the gap between expected and actual service performance determine customers' perception of quality (see Chapter 8). Quality in perceived service delivery is a prerequisite for a quality relationship being developed (Crosby, 1989).
- At the first encounter, many service organizations record information about customers that will be useful in assessing their future needs. From an initial encounter, a travel agent can judge the type of service that a customer prefers and gradually refine this profile as subsequent transactions are undertaken. This can be used to build up a database from which customers are kept in touch with new-service developments of specific interest to them.
- At a relatively simple level, incentives for frequent users can help to develop short- to medium-term loyalty—many airlines, for example, reward frequent business passengers with free or reduced-price leisure tickets.
- A strategy used by some companies is to create relationships by turning discrete service delivery into continuous delivery. In this way, bus companies offer season tickets valid at all times, which avoids customers having to make a choice—where it is available—between competing bus operators.
- Financial incentives are often given to customers as a reward for maintaining their relationship. These can range from a simple money-off voucher valid for a reduction in the price of a future service to a club type scheme which allows a standard level of discount for club members. Incentives that are purely financially based have a problem in that they can defeat the service supplier's central objective of getting greater value out of a relationship. It is often expensive to

initiate a relationship, and organizations therefore seek to achieve profits at later stages by raising margins to reflect the value that customers attach to that relationship. However, in some cases, greater bonding between customer and supplier can be achieved by selling membership schemes to customers which allow subsequent discount, as is the case with a number of store discount cards. Having invested in a membership scheme, customers are likely to rationalize their motives for taking advantage of it, rather than taking their business elsewhere.

- Rather than offer price discounts, companies can add to the value of a relationship by giving other non-financial incentives. For example, many retailers offer special preview evenings for customers who have joined its membership club.
- Information about the preferences of individual customers can be retained so that future requests for service can be closely tailored to their needs. In this way a travel agent booking accommodation for a corporate client can select hotels on the basis of preferences expressed during previous transactions. By offering a more personalized service, the travel agent is adding value to the relationship, increasing the client's transaction costs of transferring to another travel agent.
- A more intensive relationship can develop where customers assign considerable responsibility to a service provider for identifying their needs. In this way, a car-service station attempts to move away from offering a series of discrete services initiated by customers to a situation where it takes total responsibility for maintaining a customer's car, including diagnosing problems and initiating routine service appointments.

In some low-contact service industries the development of relationships focuses on interaction with a very limited number of people, typically the organization's salesforce. This is characteristic of the financial services sector, where, despite a long-term relationship between a company and client, there may be very few occasions when the client has need to consult anyone other than the salesperson—the bulk of the substantive service is processed without the presence of the client. Many studies have sought to analyse the characteristics of sales personnel that are most closely associated with successful customer interaction and the ways in which these can result in the development of long-term relationships (for example, Crosby *et al.*, 1990). Two important elements used to explain relationship quality are trust in the salesperson and satisfaction with their performance so far. The role of the salesperson as a risk reducer was analysed by Zeithaml (1981), who identified quality in terms of a salesperson's ability to reduce the perceived riskiness of a highly intangible service purchase.

The emerging relationship between buyer and seller has frequently been identified with the concept of trust, defined in a marketing context by Schurr and Ozanne (1985, page 940) as 'a belief that a party is reliable and will fulfil their obligations in an exchange relationship'. While relationships may endure as a result of one or both parties having no choice but to remain with the other party (for example, in respect of a monopoly supplier), trust has been seen by Sullivan and Peterson (1982, page 30) as a crucial function in a relationship which allows tensions to be worked out. Many analyses of trust in a marketing context build upon the concept of trust used in social psychology to explain the importance of interpersonal dyads (for example, Pruitt, 1981). It has received more recent analysis in a marketing context by Dwyer *et al.* (1987) and Swan *et al.* (1985).

Although there has been much recent interest in relationship marketing—for goods as well as for services—this has tended to emphasize the producer's perspective on a relationship. It can be argued that with more knowledge and confidence, consumers are increasingly happy to venture outside a long-term relationship with a service provider. This is reflected in the observation that in 1990 43 per cent of a US sample of bank customers and 27 per cent of a UK sample had changed banks within the last five years (Lewis, 1991), running counter to earlier anecdotal observations that a relationship individuals have with their bank is more enduring than one with their spouse. With increased knowledge of financial services, consumers are more willing today to venture to another bank which offers the best personal loan for them or the most attractive credit card. Also, a long-term relationship often begins with attractive introductory discounts, and a significant segment of many service markets is prepared to move its custom regularly to the service provider offering these. The motorist who reviews his or her car insurance each year, for example, may not allow an insurance company to develop a long-term profitable relationship. In the case of many business-to-business services contracts these may be reviewed regularly as a matter of course, as in the compulsory competitive tendering which is required for many local authority services. In such circumstances, it is often not possible to add value and higher margins to a long-term relationship.

7.4 THE MANAGEMENT OF CUSTOMER DEMAND

The task of managing markets and ensuring a good fit between supply and demand is usually very much more complex for services than for goods. Because goods manufacturers are able to separate production from consumption, they have the ability to hold stocks of goods that can be moved to even out regional imbalances in supply and demand. Stocks can also be built up to cater for any peaks in demand—for example, lawnmower manufacturers can work during the winter months making lawnmowers to store to meet the sudden surge in demand each spring. Those lawnmowers not sold in that spring can be sold later in the year at a lower clearance price, or put back into stock for the following year.

Many of the strategies for managing supply and demand which are open to goods manufacturers are not available to services producers. The perishability and inseparability of the service offer means that it is not sufficient to match supply and demand over the longer term within a broadly defined geographical market. Instead, supply and demand must be matched temporally and spatially. An excess of production capacity in one time period cannot be transferred to another period when there is a shortage, nor can excess demand in one area normally be met by excess supply located in another.

The concept of demand can in itself be ambiguous, with economists and marketers adopting somewhat varying definitions of demand. It is therefore useful to begin by identifying possible demand conditions that a service organization may face. Kotler (1991) identifies eight different demand situations:

- Negative demand occurs where most or all segments in a market possess negative feelings towards a service, to the extent that they may even be prepared to pay to avoid receiving that service. Many medical services are perceived as unpleasant and are purchased only in distress, even though there may be benefit to individuals from receiving regular preventative treatments. There has been criticism of recent increases in dental charges levied on National Health Service patients on the grounds that they will reinforce the negative state of demand for regular check-ups, possibly at greater long-term cost to the individual and to the National Health Service. The task of marketing management in this situation is to identify the cause of negative feelings and to counter these with positive marketing programmes. In the case of dentists, the introduction of relaxing interior design of surgeries, background music, friendly personnel and a promotion campaign to stress both the pleasantness of modern surgeries and the valuable long-term health benefits may overcome the problems of negative demand.
- No demand occurs where a product is perceived by certain segments as being of no value. In the financial services sector, young people often see savings and pensions policies as being of no value to themselves. The task of marketing management seeking to create demand in

such segments is to reformulate the product offering and promotional methods used so that the product's benefits are more readily comprehended by the target segments.

- Latent demand occurs where an underlying need for a service exists but there is no product that can satisfy this need at an affordable price to consumers. The task of marketing management becomes one of identifying methods by which new services either could be developed, or are made available at a price that would allow latent demand to be turned into actual demand. Within the UK travel market, a latent demand for leisure travel to Australia exists, prevented from becoming actual demand by the high cost of air fares. The development of more fuel-efficient wide-bodied aircraft and the gradual liberalizing of air-licensing regulations has allowed charter operators to introduce relatively low-cost flights to Australia, thereby turning some of this latent demand into actual demand.

- Faltering demand is characterized by a steady fall in sales which is more than a temporary downturn. The task of management is to identify the causes of this downturn and to develop a strategy for reviving demand. Corner shops in the UK have often found themselves facing a faltering demand, which has sometimes been successfully transformed by the introduction of longer opening hours and by refocusing the range of goods sold.

- Irregular demand is characterized by a very uneven distribution of demand through time. The inability to store services from one period of low demand to another of high demand means that this pattern of demand poses major problems for many service industries. It can be overcome by a combination of demand management designed to reduce the irregularity of demand and supply management aimed at meeting demand as closely as practical. These issues are considered in more detail below.

- Full demand exists where demand is currently at a desirable level and one which allows the organization to meet its objectives. A hotel in a historic city with no scope for further physical expansion may have an occupancy rate that is difficult or impractical to improve. The management task moves away from increasing the volume of demand to improving its quality—by concentrating on high-value activities aimed at high-spending segments, for example.

- Overfull demand occurs where there is excess demand for a service on a permanent basis. A pop group may find that tickets for all its concerts are sold out very quickly and could be sold many times over. The marketing management task is to stifle demand in a manner which does not cause long-term harm (for example, stifling demand by high prices alone may build up an exploitative image which may be harmful in the future should demand need to be stimulated once more). It also involves increasing supply where this is possible and does not detract from the exclusive image of the product (for example, more concerts or substitutes for concerts, such as video recordings).

- Unwholesome demand occurs where an organization receives demand for a service which it would prefer not to have. It may be forced to meet the demand because of legal requirements (for example, the Post Office cannot refuse to deliver letters for customers who are very expensive to service) or because of a long-standing commitment to supply service to a customer (a medical insurance company which agreed to automatically renew premiums each year regardless of changes in the customer's state of health will consider renewal requests from sick customers to be a form of unwholesome demand). Marketing management's task here is to try to eliminate new demand through—among other things—reduced promotional activity and higher prices.

7.4.1 Managing irregular demand

The fact that services cannot be stored does not generally cause a problem where demand levels are stable and predictable. However, most services experience demand which shows significant temporal variation. Peaks in demand can take a number of forms:

- Daily variation (commuter train services in the morning and evening peaks, leisure centres during evenings)
- Weekly variation (night clubs on Saturday nights, InterCity trains on Friday evenings)
- Seasonal variation (air services to the Mediterranean in summer, department stores in the run-up to Christmas)
- Cyclical variation (the demand for mortgages and architectural services)
- Unpredictable variation (the demand for building repairs following storm damage)

In practice, many services experience demand patterns which follow a number of these peaks—a restaurant, for example, may have a daily peak (at mid-day), a weekly peak (Fridays) and a seasonal peak (December).

Financial success for organizations in competitive markets facing uneven demand comes from being able to match supply with demand at a cost that is lower than that of its competitors, or with a standard of service which is higher, or both. In free markets, service organizations must take a strategic view on the level of demand for which they seek to cater. In particular, they must decide to what extent they should even attempt to meet peak demands, rather than turn business away. The precise cut-off point is influenced by a number of factors:

- Infrequently occurring peaks in demand may be very expensive to provide for where they require the organization to supply a high level of equipment or personnel which cannot be laid off or found alternative uses during slack periods. Commuter rail operators often do not stimulate peak period demand—or even try to choke it off—because they would be required to purchase and maintain additional rolling stock whose entire overhead cost would be carried by those few journeys during the peak which they operate. Similarly, enlarged platforms at terminals may be required in order to cater for just a few additional peak trains each day.
- Peaks in demand may bring in a high level of poor-quality custom. Restaurants in tourist areas may regard the once-only demand brought by Bank Holiday day-trippers to be of less long-term value than catering for the relatively stable all-year-round trade from local residents.
- Quality of service may suffer when a service organization expands its output beyond optimal levels. For example, a bank offering a stockbroking service may suffer harm if it stimulates demand for its service at a time of peak demand, such as a flotation of a nationalized industry. Many UK building societies did this ahead of the electricity industry privatization in 1989 only to find that they had created queues and frustration, leading to negative attitudes which spilt over into the organization's core long-term business.
- On the other hand, some organizations may lose valuable core business if they do not cater for peaks. A bank which frequently suffers lunchtime queues for cash-chequing facilities may risk losing an entire relationship with customers if they transfer not only their cheque facility to a competing bank but also their mortgage and insurance business.

An indication of the financial implications for organizations of uneven patterns of demand is shown in Figure 7.3, where two levels of capacity are indicated. The optimum capacity is notionally defined as that for which a facility was designed—any additional demand is likely to result in queues or discomfort. The maximum available capacity is the upper technical limit of a service to handle customers (for example a 70-seat railway carriage can, in practice, carry up to

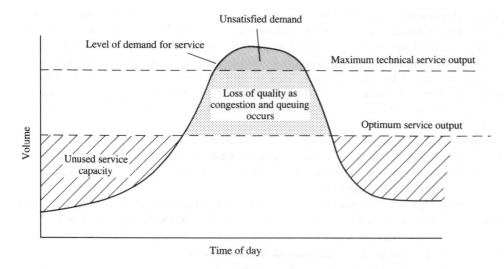

Figure 7.3   Implications of uneven service demand relative to capacity

200 people in crush conditions). At the peak, business is lost; when demand is satisfied above the optimum capacity level, customer service suffers, while in the slack period, resources are wasted.

Once a strategic decision has been made about the level of demand it is desirable to meet, tactics must be developed to bring about a match between supply and demand for each time period. The task of marketing management can be broken down conceptually into two components:

- Managing the supply of service to match the pattern of customer demand
- Managing the state of demand to even out peaks and troughs.

7.4.2   Managing service capacity

The output of service organizations is determined by the productive capacity of their equipment and its personnel. The extent to which an organization is able to adjust its output to meet changes in demand is a reflection of the elasticity of these factor inputs. Capacity is said to be inelastic over the short term where it is impossible to produce additional capacity. It is not possible, for example, to enlarge a stately home to cater for a demand peak which occurs on summer Sunday afternoons. Capacity is said to be elastic where supply can be adjusted in response to demand. Highly elastic supply allows an organization to meet very short-term variations in demand by introducing additional capacity at short notice. Sometimes, capacity can be elastic up to a certain point, but inelastic beyond that. A railway operator can provide additional trains to meet morning commuter peaks until it runs out of spare rolling stock and terminal facilities, when supply becomes very inelastic. Any discussion of the concept of elasticity of supply requires a time frame to be defined. Supply may be inelastic to very sudden changes in demand, but it may be possible to supply additional capacity with sufficient advance planning.

In the area of supply management, marketing management cannot be seen in isolation from operations management and human resource management. Typical strategies which are used within service industries for making supply more responsive to demand include the following:

- Equipment and personnel can be scheduled to switch between alternative uses to reflect differing patterns of demand for different services. A hotel complex can switch a large hall from meeting a peak demand for banquets and parties—which take place in the evenings—to meeting a peak demand for conferences that occurs during the working day. Similarly, personnel can be trained to allow different jobs to be performed at different peak periods. Tour operators often train staff to be resort representatives in the Mediterranean during the summer peak for beach holidays and skiing representatives in the Alps during the winter-skiing peak.
- Efforts are often made to switch resources between alternative uses at very short notice. For example, a store assistant engaged in restocking shelves can be summoned at short notice to perform much more perishable and inseparable service functions, such as giving advice on products or reducing check-out queues.
- Capacity can be bought-in on a part-time basis specifically at periods of peak demand. This can involve both personnel resources for example, bar staff hired in the evenings only, tour guides hired for the summer only) and equipment (aircraft chartered for the summer season only, shops rented on short leases for the run-up to Christmas).
- Operations can be organized so that as much back-up work as possible is carried out during slack periods of demand. This particularly affects the tangible component of the service offering. In this way, equipment can be serviced during the quiet periods (for example, winter overhaul programmes carried out on a holiday charter operator's fleet of aircraft) and personnel can do as much preparation as possible in the run-up to a peak (a theatre restaurant taking orders for drinks and meals before a performance and preparing them ready to serve after it).

Although it is desirable that the supply of service components should be made as elastic as possible, these components must not be considered in isolation. The benefits of elasticity in one component can be negated if they are not matched by elasticity in other complementary components of a service. For example, a strategy which allows a holiday-tour operator to increase the carrying capacity of its aircraft at short notice will be of only limited value if it cannot also increase the availability of additional hotel accommodation. Capacity management must therefore identify critical bottlenecks which prevent customers' demands being satisfied.

7.4.3 Managing the pattern of customer demand

Where demand is highly peaked, an organization could simply do nothing and allow queues to develop for its service. This is bad strategy, both in harming the long-term development of relationships and in denying short-term opportunities which peaks and troughs can present. A simple queuing strategy is most typical of services operating in non-competitive environments—for example, some aspects of the National Health Service. In competitive markets, a more proactive market-oriented strategy is needed to manage the pattern of demand, and the methods most commonly used are described below:

- Demand is frequently stimulated during the off-peak periods using all the elements of the marketing mix. Prices are often reduced during slack periods in a number of tactical forms (for example, 'off-peak' train tickets, the 'happy hour' in pubs and money-off vouchers valid only during slack periods). The product offering can itself be reformulated during the off-peak by bundling with other services or goods (activity breaks offered at weekends in business hotels to fill spare room capacity). Distribution of a service could be made more favourable to customers during slack periods. For example, during quiet times of the day or season a take-away restaurant may offer a free home-delivery service. Promotion for many service companies is concentrated on stimulating demand during slack periods. For some services where consumption takes place in public, stimulating demand in quiet periods may be important as a means of improving the quality of the service itself. In the case of theatres, more customers results not only in increased income but also a greater ambience for all customers who come for the atmosphere which the interaction of a live performer and audience creates.

- Similarly, demand is suppressed during peak periods using a reformulation of the marketing mix. Prices are often increased tactically, either directly (for example, surcharges for rail travel on Friday evenings, higher package holiday prices in August) or indirectly (removing discounting during peak periods). Promotion of services associated with peak demand is often reduced (British Rail's Network SouthEast concentrates most of its advertising on leisure travel rather than the highly peaked journey to work). Distribution and the product offering are often simplified at peak periods (for example, restaurants and cafés frequently turn away low-value business during peak periods).

7.4.4 Queueing and reservation systems

Where demand exceeds the supply capacity of a service and demand and supply management measures have failed to match the two, some form of queueing or reservation system is often desirable. A formal queueing or reservation system is preferable to a random free-for-all for a number of reasons.

First, from an operational viewpoint, advance reservation systems allow an organization to identify when peaks in demand will occur. Where there is reasonable mid- to short-term supply elasticity, supply can be adjusted to meet demand, either by bringing in additional capacity to meet an unexpected surge in demand or by laying it off where demand looks like falling below the expected level. In this way, advance reservations for a charter airline can help it to schedule its fleet to accommodate as many potential passengers as possible. A low level of advance reservations could lead to some apparently unpromising flights being cancelled, or 'consolidated'.

Second, reservation and queueing systems allow organizations to develop a relationship with their customers from an early stage. This relationship can be formed at the simplest level by using a telephone enquiry to gain some degree of commitment from a potential customer and to offer them a service at a time when both customer and supplier can be assured of achieving their objectives. Alternatively, the relationship can be developed from the time when a potential customer walks into a service outlet and joins a queue. For customers, the way they are handled in the queue forms part of their assessment of the total service quality. A number of techniques are commonly used to manage this waiting time:

- Organizations should be careful about the promises they make with regard to queueing time. Where expectations of a short wait are held out, any lengthening of the waiting time will be perceived as a service failure. This could have serious implications for customers' perceptions of subsequent stages in the service which they are about to receive. It may be better to warn customers to expect a long delay, then if the actual delay is subsequently shorter, customers will perceive this as exceeding their expectations. They will then enter the next stage of the service process with a more positive approach.
- Waiting time will appear to pass by more quickly where the customers can perceive that progress is being made—for example, by seeing that a queue is moving steadily. Uncertainty about the length of waiting time left causes anxiety and makes perceived time longer. Customers should also be able to perceive that the queue is being processed fairly.

- Attempts are made during the queueing process to take customers' minds off their wait—for example, by providing a comfortable television lounge for customers waiting for their car to be serviced.
- Where a delay is of uncertain duration, regular communication to customers makes time appear to pass by more quickly. The hardship caused by delay in waiting for a train can be lessened by appropriate communication to customers explaining the cause of the delay.
- A queue represents an opportunity for an organization to make its customers more familiar with other services which may be of interest to them at some other time. Diners waiting for a meal may have the time and interest to read about a programme of special events that associated hotels within the chain are offering.
- Sometimes the organization may be able to use a queue for one service to try to cross-sell a higher-value service. In this way, a potential customer for an economy-class air ticket may be persuaded to buy a first-class one rather than wait for the next available economy-class seat.

REVIEW QUESTIONS

1. What distinguishes 'high-contact' services from 'low-contact' ones?
2. Choose one high-contact service sector with which you are familiar and identify the critical incidents that occur during the service production–consumption process.
3. What is meant by service failure? Suggest strategies which a fast-food restaurant can employ to recover from service failure most effectively.
4. What are the potential benefits to an airline of developing relationships with its customers?
5. Identify and critically assess the effectiveness of methods used by banks to develop relationships with their customers.
6. Choose a capacity-constrained service industry and identify the options that are available to increase its elasticity of supply.

EIGHT
SERVICE QUALITY

OBJECTIVES

After reading this chapter, you should be able to understand:

- Frameworks for understanding the concept of service quality
- Methods of measuring service quality
- Approaches used to set quality standards
- Methods employed to deliver and monitor quality services

8.1 INTRODUCTION

Quality is being seen as an increasingly important element in defining a service offer. It is a significant basis which customers use for differentiating between competing services.

For tangible goods, quality can usually be assessed by examining the goods in question. However, with services, quality is less easily testable—it can normally only be assessed once a service has been consumed. For this reason, the purchase decision process for a service usually involves more risk than in the case of goods. Understanding just what dimensions of quality are of importance to customers in this evaluation process can be difficult. It is not sufficient for companies to make assumptions and deliver quality standards in accordance with their own assumptions of customers' expectations. A further problem in defining service quality lies in the importance that customers often attach to the quality of the service provider as distinct from its services—the two cannot be separated as easily as in the case of goods.

This chapter first considers the conceptual problems encountered by academics in trying to define just what is meant by service quality. Within these conceptual frameworks, methods of measuring service quality and managing its delivery are then reviewed.

8.2 DEFINING SERVICE QUALITY

Quality is an extremely difficult concept to define in a few words. At its most basic, it has been defined as 'conforming to requirements' (Crosby, 1984). This implies that organizations must establish requirements and specifications; once established, the quality goal of the various functions of an organization is to comply strictly with these specifications. However, the questions remain: whose requirements and whose specifications? Thus a second series of definitions states that quality is all about fitness for use (Juran, 1982), a definition based primarily on satisfying customers' needs. These two definitions can be united in the concept of

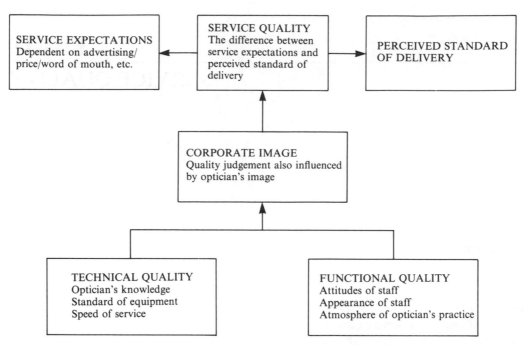

Figure 8.1 Consumer perception of technical and functional quality applied to an optician's practice (based on Gronroos, 1984 a)

customer-perceived quality. Quality can be defined only by customers and occurs where an organization supplies goods or services to a specification that satisfies their needs.

Many analyses of service quality have attempted to distinguish between objective measures of quality and those which are based on the more subjective perceptions of customers. A definition by Swan and Comb (1976) identified two important dimensions of service quality— 'instrumental' quality describes the physical aspects of the service while the 'expressive' dimension relates to the intangible or psychological aspects. More recent work by Gronroos (1984a) identified 'technical' and 'functional' quality as being the two principal components of quality. Technical quality refers to the relatively quantifiable aspects of a service. Because it can be easily measured by both customer and supplier, it forms an important basis for judging service quality. Examples of technical quality include the waiting time at a supermarket check-out and the reliability of train services. This, however, is not the only element that makes up perceived service quality. Because services involve direct consumer–producer interaction, consumers are also influenced by *how* the technical quality is delivered to them. This is what Gronroos describes as functional quality and cannot be measured as objectively as the elements of technical quality. In the case of the queue at a supermarket check-out, functional quality is influenced by such factors as the environment in which queueing takes place and consumers' perceptions of the manner in which queues are handled by the supermarket's staff. Gronroos also sees an important role for a service firm's corporate image in defining customers' perceptions of quality, with corporate image being based on both technical and functional quality. Figure 8.1 illustrates diagrammatically Gronroos's conceptualization of service quality, as applied to an optician's practice.

If quality is defined as the extent to which a service meets customers' requirements, the problem remains of identifying just what those requirements are. The general absence of easily understood criteria for assessing quality makes articulation of customers' requirements and communication of the quality level on offer much more difficult than is the case for goods. Service quality is a highly abstract construct, in contrast to goods, where technical aspects of quality predominate. Many conceptualizations of service quality therefore begin by addressing the abstract expectations that consumers hold in respect of quality. Consumers subsequently judge service quality as the extent to which perceived service delivery matches up to these initial expectations. In this way, a service which is perceived as being of a mediocre standard may be considered of high quality when compared against low expectations, but of low quality when assessed against high expectations. Much research remains to be done to understand the processes by which expectations of service quality are formed. Zeithaml *et al.* (1993) have proposed that three levels of expectations can be defined against which quality is assessed; the desired level of service, reflecting what the customer wants; the adequate service level, defined as the standard that customers are willing to accept; and the predicted service level—that which they believe is most likely to actually occur.

While the desirability of measuring service quality is now widely recognized, there is relatively little understanding of the mechanisms by which service quality leads to customer satisfaction and, in turn, to purchase intentions. An attempt to understand these linkages has been made by Cronin and Taylor (1992), who showed how service quality is an antecedent of consumer satisfaction, which, in turn, had a significant effect on purchase intentions. Their empirical investigation suggested that consumer satisfaction had a greater effect on purchase intentions than quality as more narrowly defined.

Analysis of service quality is complicated by the fact that production and consumption of a service generally occur simultaneously. Rathmell (1974) notes that there are two interfaces between the production and consumption of services. One is via the standard marketing mix and the other is through what Rathmell calls the Buyer–Seller Interaction. Along this line, Gronroos (1984a) points out that a buyer of manufactured goods only encounters the traditional marketing mix variables of a manufacturer i.e. the product, its price, its distribution and how these are communicated to the buyer. Usually, production processes are unseen by consumers and therefore cannot be used as a basis for quality assessment. In contrast, service inseparability results in the production process being an important basis for assessing quality. A further problem in understanding and managing service quality flows from the intangibility, variability and inseparability of most services which results in a series of unique buyer/seller exchanges with no two services being provided in exactly the same way.

8.3   RESEARCHING SERVICE QUALITY

The recent work of Zeithaml *et al.* (1990), which proposes an approach to delivering service quality, suggests that one of the prime causes of poor performance by service firms is not knowing what their customers expect. Many organizations are keen to provide service quality but fall short simply because they do not have an accurate understanding of what customers require from them. The absence of well-defined tangible cues makes this understanding much more difficult than it would be in the case of goods. Marketing research is a means of eliciting information about customers' expectations and perceptions of services. In this respect, service organizations should ask the following key questions;

- What do customers consider to be the important features of the service?
- What level of these features do customers expect?
- How is service delivery perceived by customers?

A number of methods for researching customers' expectations and perceptions are available, which are examined below. However, as a set of general principles for the effective measurement of service quality, Zeithaml *et al.* accentuate the need for a marketing research programme to be:

1. *Varied* Every research method has its limitations and in order to overcome this and to achieve a comprehensive insight into a problem, a combination of qualitative and quantitative research techniques should be used.
2. *On-going* The expectations and perceptions of customers are constantly changing as is the nature of the service offer provided by companies. It is therefore important that a service research process is administered on a continuous basis so that any changes can be picked up quickly and acted upon if necessary.
3. *Undertaken with employees* The closeness of staff to customers within the services sector makes it important that they are asked about problems and possible improvements as well as their personal motivations and requirements.
4. *Shared with employees* Employees' performance in delivering service quality may be improved if they are made aware of the results of studies of customer expectations, complaint analysis, etc.

8.3.1 Regular customer surveys

The incidence of surveys into the level of satisfaction that customers have experienced from service providers is increasing throughout the services sector. The increasing range of competing services available and customers' growing awareness of the fact that they are in receipt of a service for which they pay a price—whether directly or through taxation—has led them to expect to be consulted and to express an opinion about the level of satisfaction provided. Today, members of the public are in constant receipt of literature from a wide range of service providers asking for comments on the quality of service that they have received. It is probably true to say that most large service providers in both the private and public sectors have jumped on this quality bandwagon, although it is often questionable whether the most appropriate methods are employed to gather the information. Typical applications include filling in a questionnaire on the aircraft while returning from a holiday or being asked by the local council to complete a card headed Customer Service Enquiry. Such surveys usually ask recipients to relate any complaints that they may have about the services provided and any comments/ suggestions for improving them. The assumption that most people make is that data from such surveys will be used to take corrective action where expectations are not reached. It must, however, be stated that many of these surveys are of dubious quality and therefore of limited value—many are characterized by a lip-service approach to marketing, research and the issue of quality service. More rigorous and comprehensive expectation and perception studies are discussed below.

8.3.2 Customer panels

These can provide a continuous source of information on customer expectations. Groups of customers, who are generally frequent users, are brought together by a company on a regular basis to study their opinions about the quality of service provided. On other occasions they may be employed to monitor the introduction of a new or revised service. For example, a panel could be brought together by a building society following the experimental introduction of a new branch design format.

The use of continuous panels can offer organizations a means of anticipating problems and may act as an early-warning system for emerging issues of importance. Retailers have been involved in the operation of continuous panels to monitor their level of service provision as well as letting panels contribute to new-product development research. User groups also have an important part to play in many of the newly privatized industries such as gas, water, electricity and telecommunications. However, the validity of this research method is quite dependent on how well the panel represents consumers as a whole. Careful selection should therefore be undertaken to ensure that the panel possesses the same social/economic/demographic/frequency of use, etc. characteristics as the population of customers being analysed.

8.3.3 Transaction analysis

An increasingly popular method of evaluative research involves tracking the satisfaction of individuals with particular transactions in which they have recently been involved. This type of research enables management to judge current performance, particularly customers' satisfaction with the contact personnel with whom they have interacted, as well as their overall satisfaction with the service.

The research effort normally involves a mail-out questionnaire survey to individual customers immediately after a transaction has been completed. A wide range of UK service organizations are now using this approach. For example, the Automobile Association surveys customers who have recently been served by its breakdown service and the Leeds Permanent Building Society invites customers who have just used its Home Arranger Service to express via a structured questionnaire their views on the service received. An additional benefit of this research is its capability to associate service quality performance with individual contact personnel and link it to reward systems.

8.3.4 Perception surveys

These investigations use a combination of qualitative and quantitative research methods. Many professional service organizations have employed such studies in order to develop future marketing strategies. Their aim is to achieve a better understanding of how customers view an organization—to help the firm to see itself as clients see it. The initial qualitative stages of a study involve researchers in identifying the attitudes of clients (past, present and future) towards the firm as well as how the firm is perceived by the community at large (this may involve eliciting information from journalists, intermediaries and even competitors). Group discussions and/or in-depth interviews are the vehicles used for assessing the perceptions of people at this stage. In the quantitative phase of a survey, clients are asked to judge the company's performance using a battery of attitude statements. Perception studies often include an analysis of the perceptions of a firm's employees.

8.3.5 Mystery Shoppers

Mystery Shopping is a method of auditing the standard of service provision, particularly the staff involvement in such provision. A major difficulty in ensuring service quality is overcoming the non-conformance of staff with performance guidelines. This so-called service-performance gap is the result of employees being unable and/or unwilling to perform the service at the desired level. An important function of Mystery Shopper surveys is therefore to monitor the extent to which specified quality standards are actually being met by staff.

This method of researching actual service provision involves the use of trained assessors who visit service organizations and report back their observations. Audits tend to be tailored to the specific needs of a company and focus on an issue that it wishes to evaluate. The format of the enquiry is therefore something that is determined by the client and research organization in collaboration.

The constructive nature of this research technique has to be stressed, as the Mystery Shopper can quite easily be mistaken by staff as an undercover agent spying on them on behalf of the management. Gareth Jones of BEM, one of the leading research organizations providing Mystery Shopper assessments in the UK, points to a number of benefits of this type of survey (Jones, 1992). In particular, if the techniques are applied correctly, they can allow management to know what is really happening at the sharp end of their business. To be effective, Mystery Shopping surveys need to be undertaken independently, should be objective and must be consistent. The training of assessors is critical to the effective use of this research method and should include, for example, training in observation techniques which allow them to distinguish between a greeting and an acknowledgement.

8.3.6   Analysis of complaints

Dissatisfaction of customers is most clearly voiced through the complaints that they make about service provision. For many companies this may be the sole method of keeping in touch with customers. Complaints can be made directly to the provider or perhaps indirectly through an intermediary or a watchdog body. Complaints by customers, referring to instances of what they consider poor-quality service may, if treated constructively, provide a rich source of data on which to base policies for improving service quality.

However, customer complaints are, at best, an inadequate source of information. Most customers do not bother to complain, remain dissatisfied and tell others about their dissatisfaction. Others simply change to another supplier and do not offer potentially valuable information to the service provider about what factors were wrong which caused them to leave (although this could, of course, be researched by the service provider).

In truly market-oriented organizations, complaints analysis can form a useful pointer to where the process of service delivery is breaking down. As part of an overall programme for keeping in touch with customers, the analysis of complaints can have an important role to play. The continuous tracking of complaints is a relatively inexpensive source of data which enables a company to review the major concerns of customers on an on-going basis and, hopefully, rectify any evident problems. In addition, the receipt of complaints by the firm enables staff to enter into direct contact with customers and provides an opportunity to interact with them over their matters of concern. As well as eliciting customers' views on these issues in particular, complainants can also contribute views about customer service in general. In the context of complaints a notable example is provided by British Airways, who set up a facility for customers to air their grievances on videotape at Heathrow Airport, thus allowing customers to alleviate their pent-up feelings at the same time as acquiring useful information on which to act.

8.3.7   Employee research

Research undertaken among employees can enable their views about the way that services are provided and their perceptions of how they are received by customers to be taken into account. Data gathered from staff-training seminars and development exercises, feedback from quality circles, job appraisal and performance evaluation reports, etc. can all provide valuable information for planning quality service provision. One way in which formal feedback from staff can be built into a systematic research programme is the operation of a staff suggestion scheme. The proposals which staff may make about how services could be provided more efficiently and/or effectively can have an important role to play in improving service quality.

Research into employees' needs can also allow identification of policies which improve their motivation to deliver a high quality of service. Many of the techniques employed to elicit the views of employees as internal customers are, in principle, the same as those used in studies of external customers. Thus interviews and focus groups may be used in the collection of qualitative data on employee needs, wants, motivations and attitudes towards working conditions, benefits and policies. This can be followed up with appropriate quantitative analysis, such as the SERVQUAL methodology (see below), which, it is suggested, can be equally applied to internal employee studies.

The issue of obtaining involvement and participation of the workforce is considered in some detail in Chapter 9. In this respect, involving employees in the research process and its findings—for example, by using them to gather data, showing them videotapes of group discussions and interviews with customers and circulating them with the findings of research reports—can do much to improve their understanding of service quality issues throughout their organization.

8.3.8   Similar industry studies

The nature of customers' quality expectations in other similar service industries can be a useful source of information for managers. It is often apparent that customer needs may be similar between different industries, even though the service product on offer is ostensibly quite different. Many common dimensions cut across the boundaries of industries and apply to services in general—for example, courteous and competent staff, a pleasant environment and helpfulness, to name but a few. It can therefore be beneficial to investigate the nature of service provision in closely related service areas, and draw upon the findings of any research that has been made available. In particular, it is worth investigating what is known in those services sectors that have a good track record of analysing and responding to customers' needs and identifying whether it is applicable to an industry that has only recently adopted a customer-led approach. For example, it is possible to learn a lot about certain aspects of hospital service from what hotel and catering establishments have been researching and practising for some considerable time. Continuing with this theme, many service organizations that have been operating outside the private marketplace for many years can benefit from an understanding of the operations of their counterparts in other countries that have openly marketed their services in a freely competitive market. In this way, managers within the UK National Health Service may learn a lot about customer care by examining health services in the USA.

8.3.9   Intermediary research

It has already been noted that service intermediaries often have a valuable function in the process of service delivery, performing their role in quite a different manner to goods intermediaries. Research into intermediaries focuses on two principal concerns:

- First, where intermediaries form an important part of service-delivery processes, the quality perceived by customers is, to a large extent, determined by the performance of intermediaries. In this way, the perceived quality of an airline may be tarnished if its ticket agents are perceived as being slow or unhelpful to customers. Research through such techniques as

Mystery Shopper surveys can be used to monitor the standard of quality delivered by intermediaries.

- Second, intermediaries as co-producers of a service are further down the channel of distribution and hence closer to customers. They are therefore in a position to provide valuable feedback to the service principal about customers' expectations and perceptions. As well as conducting structured research investigations of intermediaries, many services principals find it possible to learn more about the needs and expectations of their final customers during the process of providing intermediary support services such as training.

8.4 COMPREHENSIVE EXPECTATION AND PERCEPTION STUDIES

Quality is clearly a complex concept which cannot satisfactorily be measured by a series of isolated *ad hoc* studies. This, and the increasing importance of quality as a means of gaining competitive advantage, has seen the emergence of comprehensive programmes to research customers' expectations and perceptions of service quality. Pre-eminent among these studies is the work of Berry, Parasuraman and Zeithaml, who have been strong advocates of the need for service organizations to learn more about their customers through a rigorous marketing research-oriented approach which focuses on the expectations and perceptions of customers.

Their research programme, which began in 1983, is still progressing, yet its findings thus far offer a number of insights into the marketing of services that should benefit practitioners throughout the services sector. They concentrate on the belief that service quality is measurable, although due to intangibility it may be more difficult to measure than goods quality. It tackles two basic dimensions of service provision—outcomes and processes—and supplements this with a number of additional dimensions of service quality which transcend these two basic dimensions. Furthermore, they make the point that the only factors that are relevant in determining service quality are those that customers perceive as being important. Only customers judge quality—all other judgements are considered to be essentially irrelevant. Thus they set out to determine what customers expect from services and what are the characteristics which define these services (effectively what is the service in the mind of the customer). Subsequently they endeavoured to develop an instrument for measuring customers' perceptions of service quality compared to their expectations. Their findings have evolved from a set of qualitative marketing research procedures culminating in the quantitative technique for measuring service quality which is known as SERVQUAL.

The SERVQUAL technique can be used by companies to better understand the expectations and perceptions of their customers. It is applicable across a broad range of services industries and can be easily modified to take account of the specific requirements of a company. In effect, it provides a skeleton for an investigatory instrument that can be adapted or added to as needed.

SERVQUAL is based upon a generic 22-item questionnaire which is designed to cover five broad dimensions of service quality that the research team consolidated from their original qualitative investigations. The five dimensions covered, with a description of each and the respective numbers of statements associated with them, is as follows:

Dimension	*Statements*
- Tangibles (appearance of physical elements)	1 to 4
- Reliability (dependability, accurate performance)	5 to 9
- Responsiveness (promptness and helpfulness)	10 to 13
- Assurance (competence, courtesy, credibility and security)	14 to 17
- Empathy (easy access, good communications and customer understanding)	18 to 22

Customers are asked to self-complete the 22 statements relating to their expectations and a perceptions section consisting of a matching set of company-specific statements about service delivery. They are asked to score in each instance, on a Likert scale from 1 (strongly agree) to 7 (strongly disagree), whether they agree with each statement. In addition, the survey asks for respondents' evaluation of the relative importance they attach to each of the dimensions of quality, any comments that they would care to make about their experiences of the service and their overall impression of it. Customers are also asked for supplementary demographic data.

To measure the level of customer satisfaction for a service provided by a particular company, the results for perceptions and expectations need to be calculated for each customer. From this, measures of service quality can be derived quite simply by subtracting expectation scores from perception scores, either unweighted or weighted to take into consideration the relative importance of each dimension of quality, or the relative importance of different customer groups. The outcome from a one-off study is a measure that tells the company whether its customers' expectations are exceeded or not.

Beyond this simple analysis, SERVQUAL results can be used to identify the components or facets of a service in which the company is particularly good or bad. It can be used to monitor service quality over time, to compare performance with that of competitors, or to measure customer satisfaction with a particular service industry generally.

An organization or industry group can use the information collected in this way to improve its position by seeking to surpasses customers' expectations on a continuous basis. Additionally, the expectations—perceptions results, along with the demographic data, may facilitate effective customer segmentation.

The SERVQUAL model highlights the difficulties in ensuring high-quality service for all customers in all situations. More specifically, it identifies five gaps where there may be a shortfall between expectation of service level and perception of actual service delivery:

Gap 1: between consumer expectations and management perception Management may think that they know what consumers want and proceed to deliver this when in fact consumers may expect something quite different.

Gap 2: between management perception and service quality specification Management may not set quality specifications or may not stipulate them clearly. Alternatively, management may set clear quality specifications but these may not be achievable.

Gap 3: between service quality specifications and service delivery Unforeseen problems or poor management can lead to a service provider failing to meet service quality specifications. This may be due to human error as well as to mechanical breakdown of facilitating or support goods.

Gap 4: between service delivery and external communications There may be dissatisfaction with a service due to the excessively heightened expectations developed through the service provider's communications efforts. Dissatisfaction occurs where actual delivery does not meet up to expectations held out in a company's communications.

Gap 5: between perceived service and expected service This gap occurs as a result of one or more of the previous gaps. The way in which customers perceive actual service delivery does not match their initial expectations.

The five gaps are illustrated in Figure 8.2, where a hypothetical application to a restaurant is shown.

While the SERVQUAL technique has attracted much attention for its conceptualization of quality measurement issues, it has also been criticized. There is little theoretical or empirical evidence to support the relevance of the expectations—performance gap as the basis for

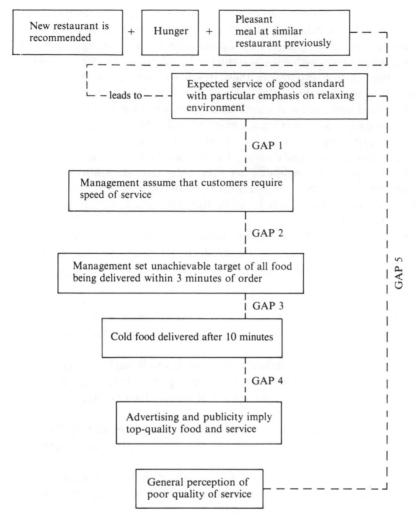

Figure 8.2 Sources of divergence between service quality expectation and delivery (modified from Parasuraman *et al.*, 1985)

measuring service quality (Carman, 1990). Instead, it has been argued that considerable research supports a more straightforward approach of measuring quality through simple performance-based approaches (Bolton and Drew, 1991; Churchill and Suprenant, 1982).

8.5   SETTING QUALITY STANDARDS

The specification of service levels serves a valuable function in communicating the standard of quality that consumers can expect to receive. It also communicates the standards that are expected of employees. While the general manner in which an organization goes about promoting itself may give a general impression as to what level of quality it seeks to deliver, more specific standards can be stated in a number of ways:

- At its most basic, an organization can rely on its terms of business as a basis for determining the level of service to be delivered to customers. These generally act to protect customers against excessively poor service rather than being used to promote high standards of excellence proactively. The booking conditions of tour operators, for example, make very few promises about service quality, other than offers of compensation if delays exceed a specified level or if accommodation arrangements are changed at short notice.

- Generally worded customer charters go beyond the minimum levels of business terms by stating the standards of performance that the organization aims to achieve in its dealings with customers. In this way, banks usually publish charters that specify in general terms the manner in which accounts will be conducted and complaints handled. The National Westminster Bank's Code of Practice for Business Banking, for example, includes general promises to inform customers in writing of any special conditions attached to loans, to discuss the price to be charged for any special services and to investigate any dissatisfaction with the service through a formalized complaints procedure.

- Specific guarantees of service performance are sometimes offered, especially in respect of service outcomes. As an example, parcel-delivery companies often guarantee to deliver a parcel within a specified time and agree to pay compensation if they fall below this standard. Many of the public utilities now offer compensation payments if certain specified services are not delivered correctly. For example, Southern Electricity aims to restore any loss of power within 24 hours of failure—if it fails in this aim, it pays compensation of £40 plus £20 for each subsequent 12-hour period of power failure. Sometimes, guarantees concentrate on the manner in which a service is produced rather than specifically on final outcomes. In this way, building societies set standards for the time they will take to give a decision on a mortgage application and to subsequently process it. While there can be great benefits from publicizing specific guaranteed performance standards to customers, failure to perform could result in heavy compensation claims, or claims for misleading advertising. Many highly specific targets are therefore restricted to internal use where their function is to motivate and control staff rather than to provide guarantees to potential customers. While the major banks give their branch managers targets for such quality standards as customer queueing time and availability of working ATM machines, it does not guarantee a specified level of service to its customers.

- Many service companies belong to a trade or professional association and incorporate the association's code of conduct into their own offering. Codes of conduct adopted by members of professional associations as diverse as undertakers, solicitors and car repairers specify minimum standards below which service provision should not fall. The code of conduct provides both a reassurance to potential customers and a statement to employees about the minimum standards that are expected of them.

- Of more general applicability is the adoption of British Standard 5750 (or its international equivalent, ISO 9002). Contrary to popular belief, a company operating to BS 5750 does not guarantee a high level of quality for its service. Instead, BS 5750 is granted to organizations who can show that they have in place management systems for ensuring a *consistent* standard of quality—whether this itself is high or low is largely a subjective judgement. Although this standard was initially adopted by manufacturing industries, it has subsequently found significant use among service companies, including education (see case study below), leisure centres and building contractors. Increasingly, industrial purchasers of services are seeking the reassurance that its suppliers are BS 5750 registered.

- In the case of some public sector services which operate in a monopolistic environment, quality standards are sometimes imposed from outside. In privately owned utilities in the UK, the relevant regulating authority has the power to set specific service targets. For example, the telephone regulatory body, Oftel, sets limits on what proportion of public telephone kiosks should be out of service at any one time. In the case of UK publicly owned services, the government has issued a series of customer charters setting out the standards of service which users of the service can expect—for example, the period of time that a hospital patient has to wait for an operation. Critics of such charters would argue that they provide little—if any—practical compensation for users of a service who suffer from poor standards of quality.

COLLEGE SETS STANDARDS FOR QUALITY

Sandwell College of Further and Higher Education was created in 1986 through the merger of Warley College of Technology and West Bromwich College of Commerce and Technology. The quality of the training provided by its 520 teaching staff to its 25 000 students was not a major item on the college agenda at the time. A major inspection in the autumn of 1988 indicated that the general standards within the college were satisfactory to good, although there were one or two small areas of concern.

The 1980s had seen significant change in Sandwell College's operating environment. The recession of the early 1980s had affected local manufacturing industry particularly badly, putting great pressure on local employers' training budgets. Those companies that did survive the depths of the recession realized that if they were to prosper, the quality of their own output would have to be raised to meet that of their overseas competitors. The attention given to the quality of these firms' output was matched only by their concern with that of their inputs.

Manufacturing firms sought to obtain British Standards Institution approval BS 5750 as a means of reassuring their customers of consistency of production processes. Firms working to this standard are expected to pass similar standards back through their supply chains. It was the college's involvement with local manufacturing industry that led it to look at the possibilities of obtaining a recognized quality standard. Obtaining BS 5750 would have the advantage of showing local industry on its own terms what the college was capable of achieving. Moreover, training managers of local employers were being increasingly selective about where they placed their training budgets and the College needed every marketing tool possible to preserve and build its business.

A Quality Assurance Unit was established within the College in November 1989 to consider the applicability of BS 5750: Part II to education and training. From the outset, the Unit recognized that the language and concepts of the standard would require radical translation and interpretation from their original manufacturing context into terms and ideas that are current within further and higher education. Among the early tasks was to define just what was the 'product' that the college was seeking to promote. Initially, there was some debate as to whether this was the course or package of training, or the value-added to the student who underwent the process of education or training. After much discussion, it was decided that the 'product' was in fact the value-added or enhancement of the student in terms of skills developed, knowledge acquired, experience gained or increased self-confidence and personal development. The 'process' was considered to be curriculum delivery.

The process of managing quality focused on course teams—these became responsible for the planning, development, review and evaluation of the educational process. Quality procedures grew out of existing good practice and allowed for the possibility of considerable diversity of procedures to meet a diverse range of courses. For example, all course teams had to obtain feedback on their course from students, but could choose how they did so, using one of four models presented by the Quality Assurance Unit or their own approved method.

In December 1990 the quality system developing within Sandwell College was audited by a team of internal auditors, in preparation for an external audit by three auditors from the British Standards Institution in April 1991. The audit involved a rigorous inspection of the quality system, looking at the procedures followed by course teams across the college's six campuses.

Sandwell College was granted BSI registration with effect from May 1991. The immediate benefit of registration has been to generate a quality assurance ethos where all the issues that affect the quality of service provided by the college are constantly on its agenda. This, in turn, has benefited the college by attracting quality-sensitive education and training work away from other private and public sector institutions in an increasingly competitive market for education and training services.

The value of the pioneering steps taken by Sandwell College were soon recognized by other colleges. Within a year of its registration, over a hundred colleges in the UK had begun working towards obtaining registration under the standard.

8.6 MANAGING THE MARKETING MIX FOR QUALITY

Service quality management is the process of attempting to ensure that the gap between consumer expectations and the perceived service delivery is as small as possible. There are a number of important dimensions to this task.

First, the marketing-mix formulation and its communication to potential customers must be as realistic as possible. Exaggerated claims merely lead to high expectations that an organization may not be able to meet and thus the service is likely to be perceived as being of a poor quality. Secondly, non-marketer-dominated factors such as word-of-mouth information, traditions, etc. also need to be considered as, once again, their presence may have the effect of increasing expectations. Finally, service companies must recognize that the relationship between customer perceptions and expectations is dynamic. Merely maintaining customers' level of perceived quality is insufficient if their expectations have been raised over time. Marketing-mix management is therefore concerned with closing the quality gap over time, either by improving the service offer or by restraining customers' expectations (see Figure 8.3).

Quality affects all aspects of the marketing mix—decisions about service specification cannot be taken in isolation from those concerning other elements of the mix. All can affect the level of customer expectations and the perceived standard of service delivery:

- *Promotion* decisions have the effect of developing consumers' expectations of service quality. Where marketer-dominated sources of promotion are the main basis for evaluating and selecting competing services, the message as well as the medium of communication can

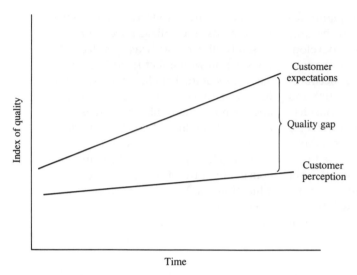

Figure 8.3   The changing quality gap

contribute in a significant way towards customers' quality expectations. Invariably, promotion sets expectations which organizations struggle to meet.

On some occasions, however, the image created by promotion may actually add to the perceived quality of the service. This is quite common for goods, where the intangible image added to products such as beer can actually lead to consumers believing that the beer is of higher quality than another of identical technical quality which has been promoted in a different way. The possibility for achieving this with services is generally less, on account of the greater involvement of customers in the production/consumption process and the many opportunities which occur for judging quality. It is, however, possible in the case of some publicly consumed services, where high-profile advertising may actually add to the perceived quality of the service. In this way, promotion of a gold credit card may add to a customer's feeling that they have bought an exclusive and prestigious facility—without the advertising, the prestigious value of the card may not be recognized by others.

- *Price* decisions affect both customers' expectations and perceptions of service quality, as well as the service organization's ability to produce quality services. In cases where all other factors are equal, price can be used by potential customers as a basis for judging quality. If two outwardly similar restaurants charge different prices for a similar meal, the presumption may be made that the higher-priced restaurant must offer a higher standard of service, which the customer will subsequently expect to be delivered. It will be against this benchmark that service delivery will be assessed.

The price charged can influence the level of quality which a service organization can build into its offering. The concept of price positioning was raised in Chapter 3, where it was noted that while any position along a line from high price/high quality to low price/low quality may be feasible, high price/low quality and low price/high quality positions are not generally sustainable over the long term. As an example, the low prices that many UK tour operators have charged relative to the levels in many overseas markets has resulted in insufficient margins to provide a high quality of service. Delays and inconvenience due to overscheduled aircraft or overbooked flights have been among the consequences.

- *Place* decisions can affect customer expectations of quality as well as actual performance. A poor-quality service sold through a high-quality agent may give heightened expectations of quality. Poor delivery may subsequently harm the image of the agent itself, which partly explains why many travel agents are reluctant to continue to act as intermediaries for tour operators with poor service quality records. The manner in which an intermediary initiates, processes and follows up the service-delivery process can often affect perceived quality received by the customer. An agent who incorrectly fills out the departure time for a coach ticket harms the quality of the service that the customer receives. For these reasons, an important element of quality management involves the recruitment and monitoring of a network of intermediaries who are able to share the service principal's commitment to quality standards.

- *Personnel* (or, more particularly, the 'contact personnel') are important elements of con-sumers' perceptions of functional quality and thus the nature of the buyer-seller inter-action becomes crucial in the management of service quality. Recruitment, training, motivation and control of personnel therefore become important elements of the marketing mix which impact on quality standards. Those employees who directly perform a service have the best possible vantage point for observing it and are the most able to identify any impediments to its quality. Whether these contact personnel have the ability to articulate these failings is another matter.

8.7   ORGANIZING AND IMPLEMENTING SERVICE QUALITY

Service quality does not come about by chance—organizations need to develop strategies for ensuring that they deliver consistent and high-quality services. A number of people have sought to identify the organizational factors that are most commonly associated with successful quality management. Kotler (1991), as a result of research involving successful service firms in the USA, proposed the following requirements:

1. A strategic concept which is customer focused.
2. A history of top-management commitment to quality, i.e seeing quality indicators as being just as important as financial ones.
3. The setting of high standards and communicating these expected standards to employees.
4. Systems for monitoring performance. Top service firms regularly evaluate their own and their competitors' performance.
5. Systems for satisfying complaining customers. It is important to respond quickly and appropriately to customer complaints.
6. Satisfying employees as well as customers. Successful organizations understand the importance of contact personnel and see an important role for 'internal marketing', i.e. 'applying the philosophies and practices of marketing to people who serve the external customers so that (1) the best possible people can be employed and retained and (2) they will do the best possible work' (Berry, 1980)

Service personnel have emerged as a key element in the process of quality management. Maintaining a consistent standard of quality in labour-based services becomes very difficult on account of the inherent variability of personnel, as compared to machines. Furthermore, it has already been noted that the inseparability of most services does not generally allow an organization to undertake quality-control checks between the points of production and consumption. In this section, strategies to reduce the variability of the human input are examined.

8.7.1   Total quality management (TQM)

TQM is an approach to improving the effectiveness and flexibility of an organization as a whole. It is a multi-disciplinary approach, in that marketing inputs to TQM processes cannot be seen in isolation from issues of Operations Management and Human Resource Management. TQM is essentially a means of organizing and involving everyone employed in an organization, in all activities, in all functions and at all levels. The approach recognizes that the activities of every staff member have an impact on the quality received by customers, including non-contact personnel, whose actions in activities such as processing invoices or orders could nevertheless have implications for customer satisfaction. Thus an important aim of TQM is the generation of a widespread awareness of customer needs among employees, and in particular the standards of quality that are expected by customers.

In addition to focusing on meeting customer requirements effectively, TQM is concerned with the efficiency with which these requirements are met. An important element of TQM therefore comprises strategies to reduce waste—defined as anything that neither adds value nor contributes towards meeting customer requirements. One target for cost reductions are 'transaction' costs. These are distinguished from production costs and represent the costs of 'governing' production systems, referring to the costs of monitoring and negotiating work contracts and their level of performance (see Williamson, 1975). In this way, many service organizations have budgeting procedures that can be slow and cumbersome in responding to changed customer expectations, resulting in greater cost or loss to the organization. For example, a local authority-owned leisure centre may consider it necessary to upgrade the standards of its squash courts in the face of competition from a newly opened privately operated facility. Permission to spend the necessary money to improve standards may require prolonged negotiations with senior managers and possibly a committee of the authority. By the time that approval is given for the quality improvement, the competition may have taken away a significant share of its market, representing a transaction cost of not having in place an effective system for Total Quality Management.

TQM may be introduced as part of a package of other quality initiatives such as just-in-time (JIT) production methods to control stock levels—now widely employed by the retail sector. Within the services sector, the concept of JIT can be extended to the deployment of staff, whereby extra personnel are brought in at short notice to meet peak demands.

TQM has many points of congruence with marketing in its internal and external manifestations. It rests upon the generation of an organizational mission or philosophy which encourages all employees and functional areas to regard themselves as providers and customers of other departments. Human Resource Management policies play a key role in facilitating TQM—for example, in the way that total quality training and quality appraisals are taken on board by line areas in their efforts to contribute to overall corporate goals. In this respect, the dissemination and fitting processes of the Harvard and Matching schools (described in Chapter 9) are important.

8.7.2   Quality circles (QCs)

Quality circles often work within a TQM framework and consist of small groups of employees who meet together with a supervisor or group leader to discuss their work in terms of production and delivery standards. If QCs are to be used in the delivery of services, the marketing aims of the service organization must be incorporated into the TQM package and the agenda of the QCs. QCs are especially suited to high-contact services where there is considerable interaction between employees and consumers. Front-line service staff who are in a position to identify quality shortcomings as they impact on customers are brought together with operational staff who may not interact directly with customers but can significantly affect service quality. By sitting down and talking together, employees have an opportunity to jointly recognize and suggest solutions to problems. In this way, a QC run by a car-repair garage would bring together reception staff who interact with the public and mechanics who produce the substantive service. By analysing a quality problem identified by the receptionists (for example, delays in collecting completed jobs), the mechanics might be able to suggest solutions (rescheduling some work procedures).

To be successful, the QC leader has to be willing to listen to and act upon issues raised by QC members. This is essential if the QC is to be sustained. Circle members must feel that their participation is real and effective, thus the communication process within the QC must be two-way. Consent can be real or perfunctory. In the latter case, if the QC appears to become only a routinized listening session, circle members may consider it to be just another form of managerial control. While circle members might consent to such control, their active participation in processes to improve service quality may be absent.

QC members need speedy and real feedback on ideas they might come up with to solve operational problems. Where a QC has successfully identified reasons why marketing objectives are not being attained, its suggestions should be commented on in a constructive manner. The effectiveness of QCs can be improved if staff-reward mechanisms are linked to performance.

8.7.3   Reducing dependency on human resources

In most service industries, opportunities exist to replace potentially variable human inputs with relatively predictable machine-based ones. While this may result in a loss of customization to meet the needs of individual customers, the quality of service outcomes and processes can generally be made more predictable. At one extreme, human contact personnel can be dispensed with completely (for example, telephone banking), while in other cases, equipment is used to moderate the behaviour of contact personnel (for example scripted computer-generated messages used by many airline reservation staff). The subject of personnel replacement policies is considered in more detail in Chapter 9.

BANK PUTS ITS MONEY WHERE ITS MOUTH IS

Until the 1970s, marketing-led approaches to quality management were not high on the agenda of most banks. They operated in an environment in which professional ethics and standards of conduct were the main constraint on their activities. Furthermore, promoting quality standards was often seen as undesirable, possibly undermining the implicit trust which, it was assumed, people had in their banks. This approach may have suited banks well until the 1970s, but since that time, the banking environment in many countries has became increasingly competi-

tive. In the context of deregulated financial markets, customers of banks were increasingly able and willing to shop around for financial services which best met their expectations. Moreover, consumers' expectations in general had been heightened in a number of consumer service markets and they saw no reason why banks should not operate to the same standards as an airline or a car-rental company.

It was against this background that from the mid-1980s many UK banks began issuing 'Customer Charters'—generally worded statements about the standards of service to be provided by the bank. To many customers, these general charters did not go far enough, and they pointed to the examples of many US banks who had begun offering quite specific customer guarantees of performance.

While many American banks had given guarantees to their customers on such matters as the accuracy of statements for some time, one bank decided to back up its quality guarantees with financial compensation schemes. The Colorado National Bank developed a quality programme which was appropriately called 'PIMWIMI' ('Put Your Money Where Your Mouth Is'). The bank made a number of specific promises to its customers:

- Customers would not wait more than 3 minutes to be served by a teller or 5 minutes for a personal banking, personal loan or customer-assistance enquiry
- Staff would offer a friendly greeting to each customer by name
- All enquiries and applications for personal loans would be turned round within no more than one working day
- Statements would be accurate.

These items were selected for inclusion in the customer guarantee as a result of previous research which had shown them to be of importance to customers. Before offering the guarantee, the bank ensured that it had the resources to deliver service to these standards.

If it failed to deliver in accordance with its guarantee, the bank promised that it would send a personal letter from the bank's President to the customer apologizing for the failure to meet the quality standard, along with a $5 note.

Within the first year of its operation the bank was not called upon to make any payment related to its guarantee of courteous service. In respect of the other elements of its guarantee, it paid out just $885 in the first three months, representing a very low rate of failure among its 256 000 transactions during the period and less than had been expected.

The principal benefit of the PIMWIMI programme was to focus the attention of the bank's employees on meeting clearly defined quality targets. The programme was linked to the bank's reward system which linked individuals' pay to the quality of service reported by customers.

REVIEW QUESTIONS

1. Discuss the reasons why quality has become an increasingly important issue in services marketing.
2. In what ways can an airline attempt to measure the quality of its services?
3. Using a public sector organization of your choice, give examples of the methods by which the organization can seek to manage service quality.
4. Giving examples, distinguish between the concepts of 'functional' and technical' quality.
5. Critically assess the usefulness of the SERVQUAL technique for measuring quality in an industry of your choice.
6. In what ways can the personnel input to services be managed in order to achieve more consistent quality standards?

MANAGING THE HUMAN ELEMENT OF THE SERVICE OFFER

OBJECTIVES

After reading this chapter, you should be able to understand:

- The role played by personnel in service production
- The relationship between personnel performance and service quality
- Human Resource Management policies and their role in improving marketing orientation among personnel
- Methods of recruiting, motivating and controlling service personnel

9.1   INTRODUCTION

The importance of people as a component of the service offering has been stressed on many occasions in previous chapters of this book. Human attributes can embed themselves in the service offer in three principal ways:

- Most service-production processes require the service organization's own personnel to provide significant inputs to the service-production process, both at the front-line point of delivery and in those parts of the production process that are relatively removed from the final consumer. In the case of many one-to-one personal services, the service provider's own personnel constitute by far the most important element of the total service offer.
- Many service processes require the active involvement of the consumer of the service and the consumer therefore becomes involved as a co-producer of the service. At its simplest, this can involve consumers in merely presenting themselves or their objects to the service provider in order for the service to be provided. For example, a customer may deliver his or her car to the garage rather than have it collected by the garage. In other cases, the customer may become involved in performing some preparatory part of the service process. For example, a road-haulage company might prepare a lorry for painting prior to sending it to a specialist paint sprayer. In the case of services performed on the body or mind, the consumer is necessarily involved in the production process. In this way a driving school can only deliver the benefits of driver training if the customer cooperates and follows the advice of the instructor.
- Other people who simultaneously consume a mass-produced service can influence the benefits that an individual receives from the service in a number of ways. First, the characteristics of other users of a service can affect the image of the service, in much the same way as owners

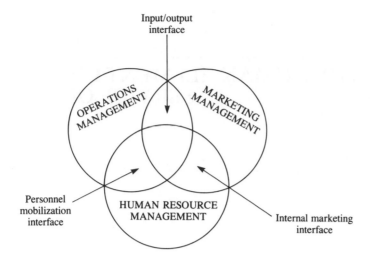

Figure 9.1 The interfaces between marketing management, operations management and Human Resource Management

of certain brands of goods can lend them some degree of 'snob' appeal. In this way, a night club can build up an exclusive image on account of the high-spending, high-profile users who patronise it. Second, the presence of other consumers in the service production–delivery process means that the final quality of the service that any customer receives is dependent on the performance of other consumers. In effect, they become co-producers of the service offering. Often fellow-consumers have an important role to play in enhancing the quality of the service offering, as where a full house in a theatre creates an ambience for all customers to enjoy, or where the presence of a large number of other exhibitors at an exhibition can make the whole event more attractive to potential exhibitors. On other occasions, other consumers can contribute negatively to the service production process, as where rowdy behaviour in a pub or people smoking in a restaurant detracts from the enjoyment of an event for other customers.

The focus of this chapter is on the first of these categories—personnel employed by the service organization. For most service providers, employees constitute a very important component of the service offering. The management of this input, in terms of recruiting the best personnel and training, motivating, rewarding and controlling them, becomes crucial in influencing the quality of service output.

Services management has often been described as the bringing together of the principles of marketing, operations management and Human Resource Management, in which it can sometimes be difficult—and undesirable—to draw distinctions between the three approaches (Figure 9.1). In this way, methods to improve the service provided by staff of a fast-food restaurant can be seen as a problem of marketing (for example, the need to analyse and respond to customer needs for such items as speed and cleanliness), or of operations management (scheduling work in a manner which reduces bottlenecks and allows a flexible response to patterns of demand), or of Human Resource Management (selecting and motivating staff in such a way that maximizes their ability to deliver a specified standard of service that meets identified customer needs).

This chapter analyses the key strategic decisions that service organizations must make in

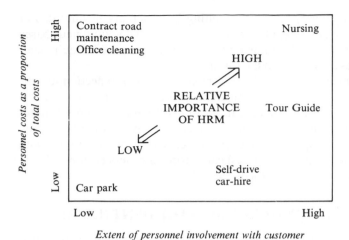

Figure 9.2   The importance of personnel within the service offer

relation to their employees. A general background to the management of the employment relationship is introduced, with an analysis of how this relationship can be managed in order to bring about a greater marketing orientation within service organizations. A more detailed analysis of the principles of Human Resource Management can be found in more specialized texts (for example, Storey, 1989, 1992). In analysing the personnel element of services processes, this chapter returns to many of the issues first discussed in Chapters 6, 7 and 8, where the service offer was defined, especially in the all-important area of quality standards.

9.2   THE IMPORTANCE OF PERSONNEL TO THE SERVICE OFFERING

It can be almost a cliché to say that, for some businesses, the employees *are* the business. If these are taken away, the organization is left with very few assets with which it can seek to gain competitive advantage in meeting customers' needs. While for some organizations the management of personnel can be seen as just one other asset to be managed, for others, Human Resource Management is so central to the activities of the organization that it cannot be seen as a separate activity. Some indication of the importance attached to Human Resource Management within any organization can be gained by examining two aspects of personnel:

1. The proportion of total costs which are represented by personnel costs.
2. The importance of personnel encounters with customers within the service offer.

In Figure 9.2 these two dimensions of personnel significance are shown in a matrix form with examples. For Human Resource Management, the most critical group of services is found where personnel accounts for a high proportion of total costs and form an important part of the service offering perceived by the consumer—many personal services such as hairdressing fall into this category. In other cases, personnel costs may be a small proportion of total costs, but can represent key individuals who can significantly affect consumers' perceptions of a service. In this way, personnel costs are typically a relatively small proportion of the costs of a telephone service, yet the performance of key front-line staff such as telephone operators or service engineers can significantly affect judgements of quality.

The human input to services can be highly variable, resulting in variability in output. For this reason, many service organizations have sought to replace personnel with equipment-based inputs, often resulting in fewer but more highly trained personnel being required. Equipment-based personnel replacement strategies are discussed later in this chapter.

The importance attached to Human Resource Management is also a reflection of the competitiveness of the environment in which an organization operates. At one extreme, the highly competitive environment which faces most West European fast-food restaurants requires organizations to ensure that their staff meet customers' needs for speed, friendliness and accuracy more effectively than their competitors. On the other hand, organizations with relatively protected markets (such as many public services) can afford to be less customer-led in the manner in which their human resources are managed.

9.3 WHAT IS MEANT BY HUMAN RESOURCE MANAGEMENT (HRM)?

The employees of a service organization are a resource that should be effectively managed if the organization's corporate goals are to be achieved. In much the same way as organizations develop strategic plans in relation to the markets they serve, they also need to do the same to develop their human resources. In labour-intensive, market-oriented service organizations, the development of Human Resource Management plans are closely linked to marketing plans. This section considers in general terms what is meant by Human Resource Management (HRM).

HRM is concerned with the deployment and provision of human resources, thus it deals with the policies, procedures and processes in the management of work organizations (Sisson, 1989, page 1). At a strategic level, Boxall (1992) identifies two approaches to Human Resource Management—the 'Matching School' and the 'Harvard School'. The former, based on the work of Frombrun et al. (1984), focuses on the importance of establishing a tight fit between HRM and business strategy, viewing HRM as something which is 'done' to employees in order to achieve predefined business goals.

In contrast, the Harvard Model (Beer et al., 1984) focuses on the crucial importance of getting general managers involved in the dissemination of an organization's central mission to all employees. The role of employees in delivering on this mission is crucial, and without this dissemination and pick-up, HRM will be merely a set of specialist independent activities without a strategic business contribution. Guest (1987, 1989, 1991, 1992) identifies strategic integration and improved quality as the human resource outcomes of strategic HRM. Thus recruitment, selection, appraisal, development and participation are not considered narrowly as components of personnel activity but are seen as parts of corporate strategy designed to improve efficiency and profitability. Hendry and Pettigrew (1986, 1990) concentrate on the analytical side of the Harvard model and assert that a more comprehensive understanding of strategy making within highly complex structures will provide a better framework for the analysis of HRM issues. Thus, they work backwards from an evaluation of HRM outcomes to focus on how HRM activities can become integrated with other functional areas such as marketing.

Human Resource Management can be contrasted with the more traditional personnel management, which is often seen as being isolated and separate from the business aims of firms. Personnel management has frequently been oriented towards control and administrative activities rather than the alignment of human resources towards achieving strategic organizational goals. In doing so, personnel management has often become too concerned at achieving its own set of subgoals that are not necessarily related to the marketing needs of an organization. In this way, the maintenance of a uniform pay structure may have been seen as a desirable objective in its own right by personnel managers, despite the fact that the marketing needs of an organization may require more flexibility in the manner in which staff are paid.

9.3.1   Soft and Hard HRM compared

Guest (1989) divided HRM into two component parts, termed 'Hard' and 'Soft' HRM. Hard HRM is primarily concerned with the economic outcomes of a business, typically measured in terms of efficiency and worker productivity. Within many service organizations, the results of restructuring their workforces can usually be assessed by these economic criteria.

Soft HRM emphasizes the importance to organizations of developing paternal approaches to their employees by stressing employees as essential assets to be developed and encouraged to participate within the organization. It is in this area that the generation of consent is vital so that employees can identify with corporate goals and see how their function contributes to these goals. Soft HRM also facilitates the process of change within an organization.

9.3.2   HRM and its relationship to marketing

The role of marketing is, above all, to achieve organizational goals by satisfying customers' needs. HRM is concerned with reaching organizational goals. It therefore follows that HRM must itself be concerned with satisfying the needs of external customers.

Within service organizations, HRM has three client groups with which it must deal efficiently if it is not to remain distinct and independent from marketing:

- *Employees* Efficiency in dealing with this group includes focusing on the methods used in such issues as recruitment and motivation which are discussed below. This group is the focus of internal marketing efforts, discussed in Section 9.9.
- *Senior management* Functional managers in all areas must be aware of the central significance of HRM activities for the success of their area and the overall achievement of the organization. This is the central message of the Harvard model of HRM.
- *External groups* This includes prospective employees and, more indirectly, potential customers, intermediaries and other interested groups such as pressure groups and government regulatory bodies. An organization may only be able to accomplish its objectives with respect to each of these groups if it has succeeded in managing its human resources effectively.

Success for the HRM function requires that it is able to demonstrate its central significance to overall corporate goals and therefore it has to integrate itself with other functions, to serve the needs of the marketplace. In services marketing, such integration has to revolve around the consumer and has three elements:

- *Identifying with client needs* The HRM department must work backwards from the position of the client or customer. An intimate knowledge of the client profile will enable the department to tailor its functional operations to facilitate such needs. HRM supports the marketing effort by such means as recruitment and the training of staff who are most able to satisfy customers' needs. The marketing function can itself feed back information to the HRM function through regular monitoring surveys of customer satisfaction. Such data can be used in staff-appraisal schemes and integrated into the organization's Total Quality Management processes.
- *Follow-up and evaluation* HRM policies and functions must be congruent with the overall corporate goal or mission. Thus they must be evaluated against performance and their contribution to goals. For example, an analysis of reasons for low levels of repeat business may show that telephone sales staff have a poor level of sales skills. This may, in turn, result in revised training being introduced for such staff.

- *HRM and organizational gain* It must be recognized that the activities of all functional areas should contribute to overall organizational gain. If this is not the case, offending activities should be terminated or amended. This may cause some ill feeling between functions if functional areas do not take a global view of their contribution to the success of an organization.

In this light the HRM department must be able to evaluate its own contribution and the contribution of other functions, recommending and facilitating improvements and/or termination if necessary. Organizational change and development has to be seen as a continual process, not something which happens as a one-off event. The marketing and HRM functions must facilitate an air of continual improvement, something that is at the heart of Total Quality Management (see Section 8.7.1).

9.4 MOTIVATION, CONSENT AND PARTICIPATION

Motivation, consent and participation form essential focal points for an organization's HRM strategy. HRM stresses the individual employee and their importance to the organization, and this importance cannot be made real if employees do not feel motivated to share organizational goals.

Motivation concerns the choices that employees make between alternative forms of behaviour so that they, as employees, attain their own personal goals. The task of management is to equate the individual's personal goals with those of the employing organization—that is, getting employees morally involved with the service which they help to produce. This, in turn, requires employees to consent to the management of their work activity. Where this consent is obtained, employees can be motivated by some form of participation in the organization. Such participation gives the employee a small stake in the organization, be it financial or in the form of discretionary control over the performance of their work function.

Management seeks to obtain controlled performances from its employees in an effort to meet corporate and HRM goals. In the Harvard model this is facilitated by the dissemination and pick-up process, where the organization's central philosophy becomes integral to the activity of all managers. In the Matching model, the attainment of corporate goals is achieved by integrating HRM into strategic management and business policy. The challenge for HRM managers in both cases is to make HRM market oriented and integral by demonstrating its relevance to all members of management.

9.4.1 Consent

The term 'consent' covers a variety of management-led initiatives and strategies that seek to give it authority without actively emphasizing its coercive power. For many services provided on a one-to-one basis, direct monitoring and supervision of employees by management may be impossible to achieve in any case. Active consent is therefore of great use to the management of service organizations.

In the UK during the twentieth century there have been various forms of employee participation and involvement designed to aid management in the generation of consent. Such initiatives include scientific management, industrial management, the Human Relations approach, welfare, paternalism, professionalized and proceduralized personnel management as prescribed by the Donovan Commission (1968) and, more recently, HRM. Each initiative has its own prescription for the generation of consent.

Scientific management approaches seek cooperation between employer and employee in terms of the division of labour, whereby individual employees work in predefined workstations as directed by management. Advocates of scientific management saw mutual benefits for the employee and employer. For the former, specializing in one work activity would give the opportunity to earn more, especially through piece-rate pay systems, while management would benefit through greater work control and higher productivity. What Taylor (1964), the leading advocate of scientific management did not expect, was the hostility of employees to what is often described as the process of de-skilling. Within the services sector, many attempts have been made to de-skill jobs in accordance with the scientific management prescription. However, it is necessary to balance the benefits of specialization and improved efficiency against employees' sense of alienation from their job, which occurs where they are involved in only a very small part of a service-delivery process. In this way, scientific management might suggest that coach tours could be operated more efficiently by allocating different sections of a tour to different drivers who are specialists in their own area. However, a much greater sense of involvement from employees may occur if drivers are trained to be able to deliver the whole service themselves from beginning to end.

Paternalism is often associated with Quaker employers such as Cadbury or Rowntree, who attempted to show that they were interested in their workforce at home as well as at work. Within the services sector, many retail employers such as Marks & Spencer take a paternalistic attitude towards their employees by providing such benefits as on-site hairdressing services or temporary accommodation for their employees. These and other benefits, such as subsidized social clubs, are designed to encourage employee identification with the company, and therefore loyalty, which legitimizes managerial authority and hence consent to it.

In contrast to the economically based consent strategies of scientific management, the Human Relations approach looks at people as a social animals. Mayo, in his study of General Electric in the USA argued that productivity was unrelated to work organization and economic rewards as suggested by scientific management (Mayo, 1949). He emphasized the importance of atmosphere and social attitudes, group feelings and the sense of identification which employees had. Mayo suggested that the separation of employees which scientific management had created prevented them from experiencing a sense of identification and involvement that is essential for all humans. Hence one solution was to design group structures into production processes. Such processes were thought to assist in the generation of employees' loyalty to their organization via the work group.

Mayo's work is similar in focus to that of Herzberg (1966) and Maslow (1943, 1954). Maslow suggested that humans have psychological as well as economic needs. To Herzberg, humans have lower- and higher-order needs. The former are the basic economic needs of food and shelter whereas the latter are more psychologically based in terms of recognition and contribution to the group and organization.

All the management initiatives and strategies described in this section are, in part, efforts to generate employee consent to management authority without management exercising its authority via coercion. For a more detailed discussion of consent, see Fox (1988).

9.4.2   Moral involvement

Moral involvement refers to some mechanism whereby employees can identify with the corporate goals of their employer and relay their feelings about these goals back to management. Essentially, employees need some institutional process through which, directly or indirectly, they can voice their concerns over decisions that affect them.

Mechanisms to develop moral involvement are closely related to policies that generate consent, and can operate collectively, as with collective bargaining or professional recognition via professional associations. Management can generate moral involvement via joint consultation with employees on decisions made by management. Alternatively, they can be individual through quality circles, team briefings, appraisals or the 'open-door' policies encouraged by the Human Relations approach. HRM highlights the importance of the individual worker to the success of the organization and therefore stresses individual training and development.

9.4.3 Motivation

Motivation concerns goals and rewards. Maslow (1943) argues that motivation is based on individuals' desire to satisfy various levels of need. These levels range from the requirement to realize potential and self-development to the satisfaction of basic needs such as hunger, thirst and sex. Rewards for reaching goals can be tangible (for example, money) or intangible (for example, commendations or awards which add to status or self-esteem). An organization has to bring about a congruence between its own goals and those of its employees. This is the basis for designing an appropriate motivation package.

9.4.4 Participation

An employee's participation in an organization may be limited to purely economic matters—payment is received in return for work performed. Alternatively, participation may manifest itself through more qualitative measures such as employee involvement in decision making through quality circles or team briefings. Participation can take the form of a devolution of some areas of traditional personnel activity to line management so that the employees actually doing the work and those responsible for managing particular sections feel that they are somehow involved in—among other things—selecting, recruiting and appraising employees under their operational control.

9.5 THE FLEXIBLE FIRM

It was noted in Chapter 7 that demand for many services can be highly variable, with peaks and troughs which can be daily, weekly, annual, seasonal, cyclical or unpredictable in pattern. A number of methods of managing demand have been suggested in previous chapters, including differential pricing to encourage off-peak consumption and reformulating the service offer to provide added benefits during off-peak periods. On the supply side, great importance is attached to the flexible management of service personnel in such a way that they can respond rapidly to meet changes in the volume of service demand.

As well as being able to achieve short-term flexibility, service organizations must also have the flexibility over the longer term to shift their human resources from areas in decline to those where there is a prospect of future growth. For example, in order to retain its profitability a bank must have the ability to move personnel away from relatively static activities such as cash handling and current-account chequing towards the more profitable growth area of financial services.

Flexibility within a service organization can be achieved by segmenting the workforce into core and peripheral components. Core workers have greater job security and have defined career opportunities within an internal labour market. In return for this job security core workers may have to accept what Atkinson (1984) terms 'functional flexibility', whereby they become responsible for a variety of job tasks. As part of a Hard HRM approach, the work output of this group is intensified. For this to be successful, employees require effective training and motivation which, in turn, has to be sustained by effective participation methods.

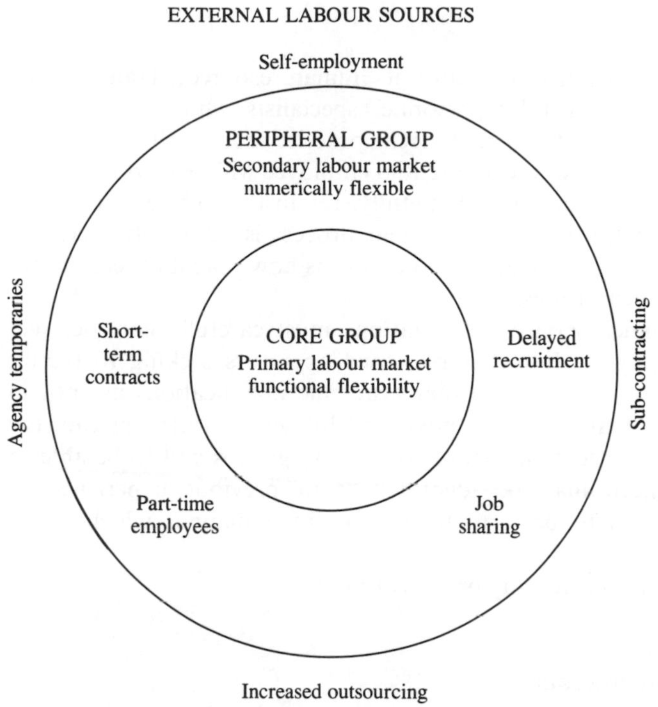

EXTERNAL LABOUR SOURCES

Self-employment

PERIPHERAL GROUP
Secondary labour market
numerically flexible

CORE GROUP
Primary labour market
functional flexibility

Short-term contracts

Delayed recruitment

Agency temporaries

Sub-contracting

Part-time employees

Job sharing

Increased outsourcing

Figure 9.3 Components of a flexible firm

Peripheral employees, on the other hand, have lesser job security and limited career opportunity. In terms of Atkinson's prescription they are 'numerically flexible', while financial flexibility is brought about through the process of 'distancing'. In this situation a firm may utilize the services and skills of specialist labour but acquire it through a commercial contract as distinct from an employment contract. This process is referred to as subcontracting. The principal characteristics of the flexible firm are illustrated in Figure 9.3.

As a strategic tool, the model of the flexible firm has important implications for service organizations which experience fluctuating demand. However, critics of the concept—Pollert (1988) and Marginson (1989)—suggest their the strategic role attributed to the flexibility model is often illusory, with many organizations introducing 'flexibility' in a very opportunistic manner.

9.6 MANAGING THE EMPLOYMENT RELATIONSHIP

Attention is now given to the application of a number of the important principles of Human Resource Management referred to above. Emphasis is placed on the impact of such personnel practices on the marketing activities of service organizations through the methods of recruiting, selecting, training and rewarding staff.

9.6.1 Recruitment

Recruitment is the process by which an organization secures its human resources. Traditionally, the recruitment function has been performed by personnel specialists who, as functional specialists, are removed from line management. Current HRM practice favours the integration of the recruitment function into the line areas where a potential employee will be working.

The focus of recruitment activity is to attract and, hopefully, retain the right employee for the right job within the organization. Clearly, the recruitment process is intimately linked to that of selection. The process of selection (described below) concerns how potential recruits are tested in terms of the job and person specifications.

In order to recruit the right personnel, service organizations must carefully consider just what they want from particular employees. For example, tour operators seeking to recruit representatives to work in overseas resorts recognize that academic qualifications are not in themselves an important characteristic that should be possessed by new recruits. Instead, the ability to work under pressure, to empathize with clients, to work in groups and to be able to survive for long periods without sleep may be identified from previous experience as characteristics that allow representatives to perform their tasks in a manner which meets customers' expectations.

Cole (1988) identifies five recruitment tasks for any organization:

- Development of recruitment policies
- Establishment of routine recruitment procedures
- Establishment of job descriptions
- Development of a person specification
- Advertising of job vacancies.

Traditionally, all five areas have been considered to be the preserve of the personnel department. Within an HRM approach, recruitment policies, job descriptions and person specifications can all become the responsibility at least in part of line managers, largely on the grounds that these are better able to understand the needs of the organization.

9.6.2 Selection

The recruitment process is concerned with attracting a sufficient number of appropriate candidates for potential selection. The process of selection is concerned with identifying and, hopefully, employing the most suitable candidate. Again by referring to Cole (1988), six elements within the selection process can be identified:

- Examining candidates' CVs or application forms
- Shortlisting candidates
- Inviting candidates for interview
- Interviewing and testing candidates
- Choosing a candidate for employment
- Offering and confirming the employment.

As with the process of recruitment, the pre-interview selection, shortlisting, interviewing and choosing of a candidate can all be wholly or in part devolved to the line areas. Again it is argued that line managers are closer to understanding the requirements of a job and can use previous experience in selecting new recruits.

9.6.3 Training and development

Hard HRM emphasizes labour as a factor of production to be used as effectively as any other input. This effective use of labour can be attained in a variety of ways—for example, by forcing labour to become more flexible or to work more intensively. However, there is a danger that this process might cause labour to become alienated and poorly motivated. Soft HRM, on the other hand, stresses the need to train and develop labour as the organization's most valuable assets. Both Soft and Hard HRM are concerned with the corporate aims of efficiency and profitability. The most effective organizations are those that can use elements of Soft HRM to ensure that they do in fact get the economic benefits of Hard HRM. Thus, the two dimensions of HRM as identified by Guest are not mutually exclusive but highly integrated with Soft HRM operating as the front end of Hard HRM. Training and development are essential elements within the process of ensuring effective economic performance by employees.

Training refers to the acquisition of specific knowledge and skills that enable employees to perform their job effectively. Thus the focus of staff training is the job. In contrast, staff development concerns activities that are directed to the future needs of the employee, which may themselves be derived from the future needs of the organization. For example, workers may need to become familiar with personal computers, fax machines and other aspects of information technology which, as yet, are not elements within their own specific job requirements.

If a service organization wishes to turn all its employees who interface with the public into part-time marketers it must include such an objective within its overall corporate plan and identify the required training and development needs. This is essential if any process of change is to be actively consented to by the workforce. Initially this may be merely an awareness-training programme whereby the process of change is communicated to the workforce as a precursor to the actual changes. It may involve making employees aware of the competitive market pressures that the organization faces and how the organization proposes to address them. This initial process may mean giving employees the opportunity to make their views known and to air any concerns they may have. This can help to generate some moral involvement in the process of change and could itself be the precursor to an effective participation forum.

If marketing is to become a function which is integrated into the jobs of all employees, marketing managers cannot merely state this need at strategic HRM meetings. It is also essential that programmes are developed by which such strategies can be operationalized. In many cases, it may be possible to specify these needs in terms of the levels of competence required in performing particular tasks. For example, in the case of bank counter staff, personnel may be required to be aware of a number of specific financial services offered by the bank and be able to evaluate customers and make appropriate suggestions for service offers. Failure to develop general sales skills and to disseminate knowledge of specific services available could result in lost opportunities for the organization.

A practical problem facing many service organizations who allocate large budgets to staff training is that many other organizations in their sector may spend very little, relying on staff being poached from the company doing the training. This occurs, for example, within the banking sector, where many building societies set up cheque-account operations using the skills of staff attracted from the 'big four' UK banks. The problem also occurs in many construction-related industries and in the car-repair business.

While the ease with which an organization can lose trained staff may be one reason to explain UK companies' generally low level of spending on training and development, a number of policies can be adopted to maximize the benefits of such expenditure to the organization.

Above all else, training and development should be linked to broader Soft HRM policies which have the effect of generating longer-term loyalty by employees. Judged by Hard HRM policies alone, training can be seen as a short-term risky activity which adds relatively little to the long-term profitability of an organization.

Where Soft HRM policies alone are insufficient to retain trained staff, an organization may seek to tie an individual to it by seeking reimbursement of any expenditure if the employee leaves the organization within a specified time period. Reimbursement is most likely to be sought in the case of expenditure aimed at developing the general abilities of an individual as opposed to their ability to perform a functional and organizational specific task. Thus an organization might seek to recover the cost of supporting an individual to undertake an Open University degree but not a product-specific sales training course. In some instances, an employer may be able to recoup some or all of the initial cost of training from a government-funded scheme. While industry-specific training boards have now been largely abolished in the UK, assistance is available through—among other bodies—local Training and Enterprise Councils.

Where an organization is an industry leader it may have no alternative but to accept a certain level of wastage in return for maintaining a constant competitive advantage over other organizations, and hence achieving higher levels of profitability. In this way, the travel-agency chain Thomas Cook provides a level of training which is considered to be one of the best in the sector. A travel clerk who is trained by Thomas Cook can readily find employment with one of its competitors. Against such potential loss—which itself is offset by the Soft HRM policies adopted by the company—Thomas Cook enjoys a very high reputation with the travel-buying public. This, in turn, has allowed it to position itself as a high-quality service provider, removing much of the need to take part in price discounting which has harmed many of its rivals.

9.6.4 Career development

Another mechanism that can assist an organization in its goals of recruiting and retaining staff is a clearly defined career-progression pathway. In Atkinson's (1984) model this mechanism is of greater relevance to core employees, as opposed to the large number of 'peripheral' workers (for example, catering assistants, part-time shop assistants and hotel housekeeping staff) for whom short-term reward systems are likely to assume greater importance than the possibility of career progression.

Career progression refers to a mechanism that enables employees to visualize how their working life might develop within a particular organization. Clearly defined expectations of what an individual employee should be able to achieve within an organization and clear statements of promotion criteria can assist the employee in this regard. Additionally, the creation and use of an internal labour market—for instance, through counselling and the dissemination of job-vacancy details—are vital. An organization can introduce vertical job ladders or age- or tenure-based remuneration and promotion programmes to assist in the retention of core employees.

During periods of scarcity among the skilled labour force, offers of defined career paths may become essential if the right calibre of staff are to be recruited and retained. As an example, many retailers who had previously operated relatively casual employment policies introduced career structures for the first time during the tight labour market of the late 1980s. Conversely, during the following period of recession it became very difficult for employers to maintain their promises with a consequent demotivational effect on staff. In a similar way, the falling profitability of UK branch banking in the early 1990s has brought about considerable disillusionment among core bank employees who see their career progression prospects made considerably more difficult than they had expected, despite good work performance on their part.

9.6.5   Rewarding staff

The process of staff recruitment and, more crucially, the retention of staff is directly influenced by the quality of reward on offer. The central purpose of a reward system is to improve the standard of staff performance by giving employees something they consider to be of value in return for good performance. What employees consider to be good rewards is influenced by the nature of the motivators which drive each individual. Thus one standardized reward system is unlikely to achieve maximum motivation among a large and diverse workforce.

Rewards to employees can be divided into two categories—non-monetary and monetary. Non-monetary rewards cover a wide range of benefits, some of which will be a formal part of the reward system—for example, subsidized housing or sports facilities and public recognition for work achievement (as where staff are given diplomas signifying their level of achievement). At other times, non-monetary rewards could be informal and represent something of a hidden agenda for management. In this way, loyal, long-standing restaurant waiters may be rewarded by being given relatively easy schedules of work, allowing unpopular Saturday nights to be removed from their duty rotas.

The Soft HRM approach does not recognize these non-monetary benefits as being part of a narrowly defined reward system. Instead, they are seen as going to the root of the relationship between staff and employer. Thus subsidized sports facilities are not merely a reward but part of the total work environment that encourages consent, moral involvement and participation by the workforce. In the case of the hidden agenda of informal non-monetary rewards, the Soft HRM approach would see these as being potentially harmful to the employment relationship by reducing the level of consent from the workforce at large.

Monetary rewards are a more direct method of improving the performance of employees and form an important element of Hard HRM policy. In the absence of well-developed Soft HRM policies, monetary rewards can form the principal motivator for employees. A number of methods are commonly used in the services sector to reward employees financially:

- Basic hourly wages are used to reward large numbers of 'peripheral' workers. These are generally rewarded according to their inputs rather than outputs. Compared to the manufactured goods sector, it is generally more difficult to measure service outcomes and to use these as a basis for payment, but, nevertheless, it sometimes occurs. Delivery drivers employed by a courier firm may, for instance, be paid a fixed amount for each parcel delivered. In many cases, strict payment by output could have potentially harmful effects on customers. The delivery driver may concentrate on delivering as many parcels as quickly as possible, but with little regard for courtesies when dealing with people.
- A fixed salary is more commonly paid to the core workers of an organization. Sometimes this is related to length of service. For example, many public sector service workers in the UK receive automatic annual increments not related to performance. As well as being administratively simple, a fixed salary avoids the problems of trying to assess individuals' eligibility for bonuses, which can be especially difficult where employees work in teams.
- A fixed annual salary plus a variable commission is commonly paid to service personnel who are actively involved in selling, as a direct reward for their efforts. A problem for organizations who use this approach is that a salesperson who aims to maximize his or her commission earnings is often not involved in the service-production/delivery process and therefore not in a position to maximize customer satisfaction and thereby secure repeat

business. Where service-production employees are in fact involved in selling (for example, many restaurant waiting staff), this form of payment can be a motivator to good service delivery as well as increasing sales.

- Performance Related Pay (PRP) is assuming increasing importance within the service sector. PRP systems seek to link some percentage of an employee's pay directly to their work performance. In some ways PRP represents a movement towards the individualization of pay.

  A key element in any PRP system is the appraisal of individual employees' performance. For some workers, outputs can be quantified relatively easily—for example, the level of new accounts opened forms part of most bank managers' performance-related pay. More qualitative aspects of job performance are much more difficult to appraise—for example, the quality of advice given by doctors or dentists. Qualitative assessment raises problems about which dimensions of job performance are to be considered important in the exercise and who is to undertake the appraisal. If appraisal is not handled sensitively, it could be viewed by employees with suspicion as a means of rewarding some individuals according to a hidden agenda. There is also the problem in many service industries that service outcomes are the result of joint activity by a number of employees and therefore the team may be a more appropriate unit for appraisal than the individual employee.

  Nevertheless, some form of performance-related pay is generally of great use to service organizations. It can allow greater management control and can enable management to identify quickly good or bad performers. If handled appropriately, it can also assist in the generation of consent and moral involvement, because employees will have a direct interest in their own performance.

- Profit-sharing schemes can operate as a supplement to the basic wage or salary and can assist in the generation of employee loyalty through greater commitment. Employees can be made members of a trust fund set up by their employer, where a percentage of profits are held in trust on behalf of employees, subject to agreed eligibility criteria. Profit-sharing schemes have the advantage of encouraging staff involvement in their organization. Such schemes do, however, have a major disadvantage where, despite employees' most committed efforts, profits fall due to some external factor such as an economic recession. There is also debate about whether profit sharing really does act as a motivator to better performance in large companies, or merely becomes part of basic pay expectations. In the UK, examples of profit-sharing schemes have been set up by Tesco, British Gas and Sainsbury.

- In many service organizations an important element of the financial reward is derived from outside the formal contract of employment. This in particular refers to the practice of tipping by customers in return for good service. The acknowledgement of tipping by employers puts greater pressure on front-line service staff to perform well and, in principle, directly places the burden of appraisal on the consumer of a service. It also reduces the level of basic wages expected by employees. Against this, reliance on tipping poses a number of problems. Support personnel may be important contributors to the quality of service received by customers but may receive none of the benefits of tipping received by front-line staff. A chef may be an important element of the benefit received by a restaurant customer, but tipping systems tend to emphasize the quality of the final delivery system. On the other hand, attempts to institutionalize tipping by levying service charges and sharing proceeds among all service staff may reduce individual motivation. A fixed service charge also reduces the ability of consumers to make payments based on perceived quality. A further problem of relying on tipping is that customers may be displeased by the prospect of feeling obliged to pay a tip, and for this reason many service providers prohibit their employees from receiving tips. While customers from some countries—such as the USA—readily accept the principle of tipping, others—including the British—are more ambivalent. In the public sector, attempts at tipping are often viewed as a form of bribery.

MORE MANAGED HEALTH-CARE SYSTEMS USE INCENTIVE PAY TO REWARD 'BEST DOCTORS'

Doctor Finlay, of the popular television series, would have shuddered at the thought of being paid according to how well he was liked by his patients. Doctors in Britain have largely followed a few basic principles when getting paid. They negotiate a level of fees for services to be provided, in return for which they expect to perform their duties to the best of their abilities and in accordance with their code of ethics. Doctors employed by the National Health Service (NHS), as well as self-employed general practitioners have negotiated with the NHS by focusing on the costs of providing their services and the idea of a fair rate of pay for highly qualified staff. Performance-related pay has not yet appeared to any significant extent on doctors' pay agendas in Britain. However, it is becoming increasingly common in the USA, demonstrating some of the benefits—as well as problems—of evaluating performance within the personal services sector.

In the USA a large share of doctors' services are bought by Health Maintenance Organizations (HMOs) which, in turn, obtain their funding from employers' health insurance payments. HMOs vary in the way they pay contracting doctors, but they have traditionally been either on the basis of a fixed fee per patient per year or a fee per visit. Doctors would typically expect to have 5000 patients on their lists—a single HMO may account for half of these. US Healthcare Inc. is one of a growing number of HMOs that has introduced an incentive scheme to the way it pays its doctors. Each year, it carries out a questionnaire survey of its subscribing members to see how they like their doctors and links doctors' payments to these results. In 1992, its doctors re-

ceived a bonus in respect of their performance which averaged 15 per cent.

Among the questions that the company uses in its questionnaire for assessing doctors' performance are:

- How easy is it to make appointments for check-ups?
- How long is the waiting time in a doctor's surgery?
- How much personal concern does the doctor show?
- How readily can patients follow up test results?
- Would doctors recommend their doctor to others?

In addition, the company monitors the percentage of each doctor's patients who transfer to another doctor during the course of the year.

Incentive pay schemes for doctors are gaining popularity, spurred by a belief that they may help to upgrade the quality of medical care provided by HMOs and other managed care programmes. However, a number of questions have been raised about the legitimacy of this approach. Sceptics do not like the idea of basing incentives on patients' sense of 'quality', arguing that patients rely too much on fringe issues such as a receptionist's attitude or a doctor's punctuality. The sceptics would prefer to see assessment based on more sophisticated studies of illnesses, treatments and patient outcomes, something which is much more difficult to evaluate. Another problem often raised is that individual doctors' incentive payments can disrupt doctors' ability to work together in a collegial way. The Harvard Community Health Plan is typical of a number which introduced and then withdrew incentive schemes following arguments between doctors about the size of their respective bonuses. Another group of sceptics argue that where incentive payment schemes have been introduced for doctors, they have had only a short-term effect in changing doctors' behaviour.

Paying doctors partly on the basis of the quality of their service is in its early stages in the USA and many advocates of incentive payment schemes hope that current shortcomings can be remedied by more sophisticated measuring systems in the future. What happens in the USA today will doubtless be observed by the UK's National Health Service, keen to introduce a competitive market-like environment within the service.

9.6.6   Monitoring and controlling staff

Where production methods are based largely upon human inputs, the control of the workforce assumes great importance as a means of controlling service quality. The problem of control is particularly great with service industries, as it is usually not possible to remove the results of poor personnel performance before their effects are felt by customers. While the effects of a poorly performing car worker can be concealed from customers by checking his or her tangible output, the inseparability of the service production/consumption process makes quality control difficult to achieve.

Control systems are closely related to reward systems in that pay can be used to control performance—for example, bonuses forfeited in the event of performance falling below a specified standard. In addition, warnings or, ultimately, dismissal form part of a control system. In an ideal service organization which has a well-developed Soft HRM policy, employees' involvement in their work should lead to considerable self-control or informal control from their peer group. Where such policies are less well developed, three principal types of control are used—simple, technical and bureaucratic:

- Simple controls are typified by direct personal supervision of personnel—for example, a head waiter can maintain a constant watch over junior waiters and directly influence performance when this deviates from standard.
- Technical controls can be built into the service-production process in order to monitor individuals' performance. For example, a supermarket check-out can measure the speed of individual operators and control action (for example, training or redeployment) taken in respect of those shown to be falling below standard.
- Bureaucratic controls require employees to document their performance—for example, the completion of work sheets by a service engineer of visits made and jobs completed. Control action can be initiated in respect of employees who, on paper, appear to be underperforming.

In addition to these internal controls, the relationship which many front-line service personnel develop with their customers allows customers to exercise a degree of informal control. College lecturers teaching a class would, in most cases, wish to avoid the hostility from their students that might result from consistently delivering a poor standard of performance. In other words, the class can exercise a type of informal control.

9.7   INDUSTRIAL RELATIONS

The service sector spans from small family businesses to large multinational organizations, covering external environments that range from protected and regulated to highly competitive. As a reflection of this diversity, there is great variety in the manner in which managements negotiate employment conditions with their workforces. For service organizations employing large numbers of staff, much of the employment relationship has traditionally been conducted collectively between the employer and groups of employees.

9.7.1   Collective bargaining

The essential features of collective bargaining are threefold.

- First, a collective bargaining system recognizes trade unions with whom management negotiates on substantive issues such as pay and procedural issues (for example, discipline and redundancy). Thus, collective bargaining formally recognizes the presence within the organization of an outside body—the trade union.
- Second, the pluralist approach to the employment relationship emphasizes a divergence of interests between the employer and employees. This divergence is considered best settled via a process of compromise and negotiation.
- Third, a recognition that industrial action of some type—for example, overtime bans, 'go-slows' and strike—may be used in order to pursue employee interests. This third feature of collective bargaining is overexaggerated by the media, some academics and politicians. As an element in collective bargaining, it becomes a consideration only if the first two elements have failed.

There is a presumption by many that collective bargaining is not suited to many areas of employment in the service sector. It is more accurate to argue that the mechanisms used to administer and manage the employment relationship within the services sector do not encourage the use of collective bargaining as a method of participation. A number of reasons can be identified for this:

- Many service providers operate on a small scale, making collective agreements unnecessary.
- The concept of collective action has often appeared alien to the cultural values of many service workers. Bank workers, travel agents and accountants typify service industries where collective attitudes are relatively weak on the part of both the employer and employee.
- Flexibility in production requires many service industries to employ large numbers of part-time staff who are less likely to be organized collectively.
- Similarly, many service sectors have in their workforce a high proportion of female workers who are less likely to behave collectively.
- The very personal relationship which can develop between service personnel and their clients can result in them identifying more with their client than with their peer group of workers.

Efforts to stress a closer identification with business objectives via HRM do not sit easily with the presence of an outside body which stresses the significance of collective action. Service organizations that do not feel secure with trades unions are likely to attempt to marginalize their impact through their de-recognition and the creation of organization-specific employee relations policies described below. Within the service sector, many organizations have moved on from the traditional view of industrial relations to the situation where they speak of 'Employee Relations'.

9.7.2 Employee relations

Marchington and Parker (1990) identified three reasons for the use of the term 'Employee Relations':

- The term has become fashionable and appears to be less adversarial than 'industrial relations'. Thus, there has been growth in its use, although slippage in the use of the word occurs in some cases without any change in behaviour.
- It is increasingly employed by personnel practitioners to describe the part of their work which is concerned with the regulation of relations between employer and employee. The internal regulation of this relationship is seen in many organizations to supersede any external regulation, through collective bargaining and/or trade union membership. This can be the case even though trade union membership still exists in a particular organization.
- Employee relations focus on that aspect of managerial activity which is concerned with fostering an identification with the employing organization and its business aims. It therefore concerns itself with direct relations between employees and management—that is, independently of any collective representation by trades unions.

Employee relations may in fact become one element within a wider corporate and HRM strategy, which has already been identified as being likely to include the marketing of the services or goods that the organization produces.

The movement towards employee relations and the changed emphasis of managerial strategy and employee participation are the core of what HRM is all about. Hard HRM is primarily concerned with the economic reality of competition in the 1990s. Therefore, in terms of Hard HRM, employee relations and alternative forms of employee participation are designed to extract and facilitate increased worker efficiency and productivity. In terms of Soft HRM, employee relations and alternative forms of participation are designed to motivate, reward and stimulate employees to deliver on the Hard HRM goals of the organization. Thus, in terms of internal marketing and business aims the two types of HRM as defined by Guest (1989) are not mutually exclusive but operate along a spectrum.

9.8 STRATEGIES TO INCREASE EMPLOYEE PARTICIPATION

The methods which an organization uses to encourage participation among its employees are likely to be influenced by the type of person it employs and the extent to which their jobs present opportunities to exercise autonomy (that is, the extent to which employees are able to control their own work processes) and discretion (the degree of independent thinking they can exercise in performing their work). Participation entails giving employees some direct personal stake in the overall business objectives of their organization and forms the focus for the regulation of the employment relationship as referred to by Marchington and Parker (1990). In some ways it is the focus of strategic HRM. If management strategy is effective there should be little difference between the aims of an organization's business plan and those of employees. Management strategy should seek to make the two congruent by facilitating increased participation.

In general, participation by employees refers to the inclusion of non-managerial employees in an organization's decision-making processes. This section considers various forms of participation and comments on their suitability for service organizations.

In practice, organizations are more likely to be concerned with securing greater employee involvement by making individual employee objectives more congruent with those of the whole organization rather than through what could be described as collective participation. This type of involvement may be available to all employees, but the extent to which their participation is real and effective may depend on where they are positioned in the employment hierarchy, that is, whether they are within the core or the peripheral groups of workers. Increased participation is brought about by a combination of consultation and communication methods, and team briefings:

- 'Open-door' policies encourage employees to air their grievances and make suggestions directly to their superiors. The aim of this approach is to make management accessible and 'employee friendly'. To be effective, the Human Relations approach would require employees to feel that they do in fact have a real say in managerial matters. As a consequence, management must appear to be open and interested in employee relations. It is likely that this approach to managerial style and strategy will emphasize open management through some of the methods described below.
- Team briefings are a system of communication within the organization where a leader of a group provides members (up to about 20) with management-derived information. The rationale behind briefing is to encourage commitment to and identification with the organization. Team briefings are particularly useful in times of organizational change, although they can be held regularly to cover such items as competitive progress, changes in policy and points of future action. Ideally, they should result in information 'cascading' down through an organization. The difference between briefing and quality circles (see below) centres on their respective contents. Briefing sessions are likely to be more general and relate to the whole organization, whereas QCs are concerned with the specific work activity of a particular group of employees. Any general points of satisfaction or dissatisfaction can be aired in briefings and then taken up in specific quality circles.
- Quality circles (QCs) are small groups of employees who meet together with a supervisor or group leader in an attempt to discuss their work in terms of production quality and service delivery. QCs often work within a Total Quality Management approach (see Chapter 8). To be successful, the QC leader has to be willing to listen to and act upon issues raised by QC members. This is essential if the QC is to be sustained. Circle members must feel that their participation is real and effective, thus the communication process within the QC must be two-way. If quality circles appear to become only a routinized listening session, members may consider them to be just another form of managerial control.
- Total Quality Management (TQM) policies (discussed in more detail in Chapter 8) rest upon the generation of an organizational mission or philosophy that encourages all employees and functional areas to regard themselves as providers and customers of other departments. The central idea behind TQM is the generation among all staff of a greater awareness of customer needs, the aim of which is to improve quality and/or reduce production or internal transaction costs. Employees are encouraged to act outside of what they may see as a narrowly defined role, to appreciate the impact that their actions will have on the total service perceptions of the organization's customers.
- The pattern of ownership of an organization can influence the level of consent and participation. Where the workforce owns a significant share of a business, there should, in principle, be less cause for 'us and them' attitudes to develop between management and the workforce. For this reason, many labour-intensive service organizations have significant worker-shareholders and there is evidence that such companies can outperform more conventionally owned organizations (see case study below).

OWNER-DRIVERS STEER BUS COMPANIES TO BIGGER PROFITS

Bus companies went through a bad period during the 1980s. Increasing levels of car ownership, legislation deregulating the bus industry and finally the recession at the end of the decade resulted in many business failures. Against this bleak background, research undertaken by Dolan and Brierley (1992) showed how two companies—People's Provincial of Fareham and Derbyshire-based Chesterfield Transport—had capitalized on their worker-ownership to perform better than their more conventionally owned rivals.

Employee-ownership of bus companies assumed great importance following the government's decision to sell off the state-owned National Bus Company and legislation that encouraged local authorities to do the same with their bus fleets. By 1990, nearly a third of bus-operating turnover was accounted for by companies where employees owned 30 per cent or more of the shares. People's Provincial and Chesterfield Transport were among the relatively small number where employees—rather than management—were the principal shareholders.

To the employees, a financial investment in the two companies studied proved attractive. Over a period of five years, the value of employees' investments in People's Provincial doubled, while with Chesterfield Transport, it increased by over fourfold within two years.

To the companies as a whole, the research highlighted four important benefits that had resulted from worker-ownership:

- All workers had access to financial information, resulting, for example, in a more constructive approach to negotiations on work schedules and pay. Workers felt that information was not being withheld from them in order to give management an advantageous negotiating position.
- Traditional hierarchies were broken down, which gave much greater operational flexibility to the companies. As an example, inspectors and management would accept it as normal to change their duties and drive buses when the need arose. This was particularly important, as the uneven pattern of demand required great flexibility.
- Costs were held down because staff recognized that they would benefit directly from the resulting increase in profits. Similarly, they became more willing to pass on ideas about ways in which services could be improved or costs saved.
- An indication of the greater commitment to the company was provided by lower levels of absenteeism and a reduced need for formal disciplinary measures to be taken. Employees could see the reasons for a high level of service performance and were able to share in the resulting benefits.

The authors concluded that employee ownership—by increasing the level of participation—can give companies a competitive advantage in service industries where flexibility in production and commitment to standards of service quality are important.

9.9   INTERNAL MARKETING

The aims of all employees within an organization must be made congruent with those of the organization, in other words, some form of consent must exist between employer and employees. This can only be effectively achieved via communication and participation mechanisms. Internal marketing has increasingly been seen as a method of developing this consent.

Internal marketing describes the application of marketing techniques to audiences within the organization. It has been defined by Berry (1980) as 'the means of applying the philosophy and practices of marketing to people who serve the external customers so that (i) the best possible people can be employed and retained and (ii) they will do the best possible work'. In terms of the marketing of services, internal marketing has two aspects:

- First, all employees operating in their functional areas interact with other functional specialists in a quasi-trading manner. In this way, the personnel department can be seen as providing recruitment expertise for an organization's accounting department, while the latter can be regarded as providing payment systems on behalf of the personnel department. Therefore, each functional group within an organization engages in trade with other functional groups as though those functions were external customers.
- Second, all functional staff must work together in support of an organization's mission and business strategy. All staff must be able to share a common purpose and be able to work alongside rather than against other functional specialists in achieving the organization's aims. The mission of an organization must therefore be communicated to employees in much the same way as brand values are communicated to external customers.

Internal marketing has come to be associated with efforts to sell the message of an organization to its internal audience, using much the same techniques as in the organization's relationships with external audiences. In reality, of course, true internal marketing would encompass all the HRM policies described above which are designed to attract, select, train, motivate, direct, evaluate and reward personnel. In this way, internal marketing becomes a core business philosophy in the same way as the traditional marketing philosophy involves more than merely using the tools of promotion.

The focal point of the narrower understanding of internal marketing lies in communicating values of an organization to its employees in order to increase their level of consent and moral involvement. The following are commonly observed internal marketing techniques used by service organizations:

- The organization's mission statement should be clearly formulated and communicated to employees. Mission statements were considered in detail in Chapter 3, where it was noted that they should provide a general statement about the organization's essential purpose.
- Internal newsletters help to develop a sense of involvement of individuals within a business and can be used to inspire confidence by reporting significant new developments. Newsletters are commonly used to inform the workforce about achievements of individual employees.
- External advertising should regard the internal labour force as a secondary target market. The appearance of advertisements on television can have the effect of inspiring confidence of employees in their management.
- Staff uniforms and the physical environment in which they work can be used to inspire staffs' confidence in the organization and to convey the personality of the organization which it is desired to achieve.

MARKS & SPENCER—ACHIEVING RESULTS THROUGH CLARITY OF PURPOSE

Satisfying customer needs is of paramount importance to Marks & Spencer. This need is integral to all activities performed by the firm's employees, irrespective of the specialist function in which they work. As employers, Marks & Spencer sees itself as a facilitator, defining the mission of its business and providing services for its employees in order to facilitate them in performing their work effectively.

Among the reasons for Marks & Spencer's emergence as one of the most profitable UK retailers is the consent and participation which it has achieved from its employees for the central organizational mission of achieving excellence. Soft HRM policies are used to develop a sense of loyalty from employees and, in this respect, Marks & Spencer is regarded as a leader in the provision of important fringe benefits to its employees. Part of the distinctive Marks & Spencer culture that pervades all its workers is based on its efforts at disseminating its mission statement. This is conveyed to all employees through various means—notices displayed at critical points around its stores, items in staff newsletters and training programmes, among others.

Soft HRM policies have worked to make employees highly receptive to its mission statement—frequent repetition in key places serves to reinforce employees' commitment. As a result, most of the organization's employees are knowledgeable about—and work towards achieving—the following mission:

- To offer customers a selective range of high-quality well-designed and attractive merchandise at reasonable prices.
- To encourage suppliers to use the most modern and efficient techniques of production and quality control dictated by the latest discoveries in science and technology.
- With the cooperation of suppliers, to ensure the highest standards of quality control.
- To plan the expansion of stores for the better display of a widening range of goods for the convenience of customers.
- To simplify operating procedures so that business is carried on in the most efficient manner.
- To foster good human relations with customers, suppliers and staff.

9.10 REDUCING DEPENDENCY ON HUMAN RESOURCES

Employees represent an expensive and difficult asset to manage and, furthermore, the quality of output received by final consumers can be perceived as being highly variable. Service organizations therefore frequently pursue strategies to reduce the human element of their production process. The aim of employee-replacement schemes can be to increase consistency or to reduce costs—the latter could be important where an organization is pursuing a cost-leadership strategy, allowing it to gain a competitive advantage. Often, humans are replaced for a combination of these reasons.

A number of strategies to reduce dependency on the organization's employees can be identified:

- At one extreme, the human element in a service production and delivery process can be completely replaced by automatic machinery. Examples include bank ATM machines, vending machines and automatic car washes. Constraints on employee replacement come from the limitations of technology (for example, completely automatic car washes can seldom achieve such high standards of cleanliness as those where an operator is present to perform some operations inaccessible to machinery); the cost of replacement machinery (it is only within the past few years that the cost of telecommunications equipment has fallen to the point where mass-market automatic telephone banking has become a possibility); and the attitudes of consumers towards automated service delivery (many segments of the population are still reluctant to use ATM machines, preferring the reassurance provided by human contact).

- Equipment can be used alongside employees to assist them in their task. This often has the effect of de-skilling their task by reducing the scope they have for exercising discretion, thereby reducing the variability in quality perceived by customers. In this way, computerized accounting systems in hotels reduce the risk of front-of-house staff incorrectly adding up a client's bill. Similarly, the computer systems used by many airline-reservation staff include promptings which guide their interaction with clients.

- The inseparability of the service offer means that consumers of a service are often also involved as co-producers of that service. The involvement of the service provider's personnel can be reduced by shifting a greater part of the production process to the consumer. In this way, most petrol service stations expect customers to fill their own car with fuel, rather than have this task undertaken by its own staff. Similarly, a television-repair company may require customers to bring goods to its premises for repair. In both cases, the customer has greater control over the quality of service by undertaking part of it themselves.

REVIEW QUESTIONS

1. What are the principal ways in which the management of personnel is likely to be different in a service organization, as compared with a manufacturer?
2. Discuss the ways in which a fast-food restaurant can increase the level of participation among its staff.
3. Using an industry with which you are familiar, identify methods by which the effects of variability of the personnel inputs can be minimized in order to produce a consistent standard of output.
4. What is the link between personnel and service quality?
5. What are the shortcomings of traditional personnel management for the effective marketing of services?
6. Using examples, show how Human Resource Management policies can help to overcome the problems associated with peaked patterns of demand.

MAKING SERVICES ACCESSIBLE

OBJECTIVES

After reading this chapter, you should be able to understand:

- Factors affecting the choice of service outlet sites, and the extent to which service production and consumption are spatially flexible
- Methods used to reduce the effects of inseparability on service production and delivery
- The role of intermediaries in making services accessible to consumers
- The diversity of service intermediaries and the factors that influence their selection
- The principles of physical distribution management as they affect the tangible elements of service offers

10.1 INTRODUCTION

The methods by which a service is made available to customers is an important defining characteristic of the service offer. The method by which banks, restaurants and shops make their service offers accessible to customers often *is* the service. Without a strategy to make a service accessible to customers, a service is of no value. The inseparability of services makes the task of passing on service benefits much more complex than is the case with manufactured goods. Inseparability implies that services are consumed at the point of production, in other words, a service cannot be produced by one person in one place and handled by other people to make it available to customers in others. A service cannot therefore be produced where costs are lowest and sold where demand is greatest—customer accessibility must be designed into the service-production system.

In this chapter, strategies to make services accessible to customers will be analysed by focusing on four important but related issues:

- Where and when is the service to be made available to the consumer?
- What is the role of intermediaries in the process of service delivery?
- How are intermediaries selected, motivated and monitored?
- How are tangible goods which form a part of many service offers to be made available to final consumers?

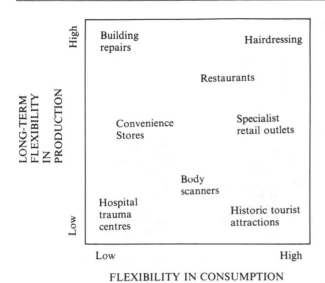

Figure 10.1   Locational flexibility in production and consumption of inseparable services

10.2   SERVICE-LOCATION DECISIONS

In this section, choices facing service providers about the place and time at which a service is to be provided are considered. First, it should be repeated that because consumers of services are usually involved as co-producers of the service, the time and place at which they are expected to take part in this process become important criteria for evaluation. Production-location decisions therefore cannot be taken in isolation from an analysis of customers' needs. While service organizations often have a desire to centralize production in order to achieve economies of scale, consumers usually seek local access to services, often at a time which may not be economic for the producer to cater for. Service-location decisions therefore involve a trade-off between the needs of the producer and those of the consumer. This is in contrast to goods manufacturers, who can manufacture goods in one location where production is most economic, then ship them to where they are most needed.

For some services, production is very inflexible with respect to location, resulting in relatively production-led locational decisions. In other cases, production techniques may, by their nature, allow much greater flexibility, but location decisions are constrained by the inflexibility of consumers to travel to a service outlet, either because of their physical inability or merely their unwillingness. In the case of some intangible, low-contact services, it is possible to separate production from consumption, using some of the methods described later in this chapter. In such cases, services can be produced in the most economic location and made available wherever customers are located.

An attempt to develop a typology of service-location decisions is shown in Figure 10.1, where inseparable services are classified in a matrix according to their degree of flexibility in production and consumption.

10.2.1   Flexibility in production

The extreme case of inflexibility in production is provided by services where the whole purpose of the service is to be at one unique location—for example, tourism-related services based on a

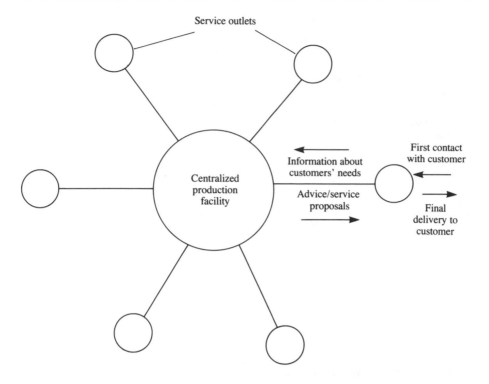

Figure 10.2 A hub-and-spoke system of service production and delivery

unique historic site by their very nature cannot be moved. A further group of services are locationally inflexible because they can only sensibly be produced in large-scale centralized production facilities. This can be the case where the necessary supporting equipment is expensive and offers opportunities for significant economies of scale. Where this equipment is also highly immobile, customers must come to a limited number of central service points to receive service. This is true with much of the specialized and expensive equipment needed for complex medical care, such as body scanners which tend to be provided at a small number of central locations. In cases where the equipment offers less scope for economies of scale and is more easily transported, service production can be distributed more widely. This explains why breast-screening services are frequently taken to users, while users must travel to body scanners.

Some service organizations operate a 'hub-and-spoke' system where the benefits of large-scale, centralized production of specialized services is combined with locally accessible outlets (Figure 10.2). In the case of banking, specialized business and investment services can often only be competitive if they are produced in units which have a sufficiently high critical mass to support the payment of an expert in that field of activity and to cover associated overheads. The major British banks have accordingly developed specialized Business Advisory Centres in a few key locations. Their services are made available through local branches by a combination of telephone, mail, computer link or a personal visit from the centrally based expert. Similarly, much of the processing work involved in producing a service can be transferred to an efficient regional centre, leaving local outlets to make the service available to the public. In this way, many building societies have transferred mortgage processing from High Street branches, leaving the latter to act as little more than sales outlets.

As well as internal economies of scale, external economies are sometimes an important influence in a firm's location decisions. One kind of external economy occurs where a location close to other service producers reduces a firm's input costs. For this reason, many diverse financial services companies have congregated in the City of London. A ship-broking agency may find significant benefits from being located within walking distance of the Baltic Exchange, Lloyd's insurance market and banks for sources of finance. Similarly, clusters of advertising agencies, graphic designers, typographers and typesetters can be found to maximize benefits from internal trading, to the benefit of suppliers and customers alike. However, the importance of such external economies of scale to locational decisions is declining due to technological developments which allow production to be separated from consumption. In both of the above examples, service benefits can now be delivered electronically without any need for direct interaction. A further source of external economies of scale can result from locating in a recognized local marketplace, as occurs where jewellers or estate agents are in one neighborhood of a town. Because the existence of the marketplace is widely recognized, any firm locating within it will need to spend less on promotion to attract potential customers.

Production considerations are likely to be a less important influence on location decisions where economies of scale are insignificant. In a market environment, competitive advantage will be gained by maximizing availability through more widespread distribution outlets rather than cost saving through centralization. To illustrate this, hairdressing offers little scope for economies of scale and competitive advantage is gained by providing small outlets that are easily accessible to customers.

Finally, the competitiveness of the market environment can affect the locational flexibility of service producers. A service producer which is able to be flexible in its location decisions may nevertheless be unwilling to be flexible if its customers have little choice of supplier. For this reason, many government-provided services (for example, housing administration) are provided through centralized administrative offices which may be inconveniently located for most users.

10.2.2 Flexibility in consumption

Decisions on service location are also influenced by the extent to which consumers are willing or able to be flexible in where they consume a service. Inflexibility on the part of consumers can arise for a number of reasons:

- Where a service is to be performed on a customer's possessions, those possessions may themselves be immovable, requiring the supplier to come to the customer (for example, building repairs).
- Sometimes the customer may also be physically immobile (for example, physically disabled users of health-care services).
- For impulse purchases, or services where there are substantial competitive alternatives, customers are unlikely to be willing to travel far to seek out a service.
- For specialist services, customers may show more willingness to be flexible in where they are prepared to receive the service, compared to routine purchases for which they would be unwilling to travel.

In reality, most service consumers' decisions involve a trade-off between the price of a service, the quality of delivery at a particular location, the amount of choice available and the cost to the consumer in terms of time and money involved in gaining access to a service. For a consumer of a few odd items of groceries, price and choice are likely to be relatively unimportant compared to ease of access—hence the continued existence of many small corner shops. For the consumer seeking to purchase the week's groceries, price and selection may become much more important relative to ease of access. For more specialized services, such as the purchase of expensive hi-fi equipment, consumers may be willing to travel longer distances to a retailer which offers competitive prices and/or a wide selection of equipment.

It follows therefore that access strategies should be based on the identification of market segments made up of users with similar accessibility needs. Access strategies can then be developed which meet the needs of each segment:

- Age frequently defines segments in terms of the level of access sought. For many elderly users of personal care services there is sometimes an unwillingness or an inability to leave home, making home availability of a service a sought attribute. For other groups, such as older teenagers, the very act of getting away from home to receive a service may be attractive. This could explain the current revived interest in going out to see a film at a cinema in the face of the competing alternatives provided by local video-rental shops or satellite television services.

- Segmentation on the basis of an individual's economic status can be seen in the willingness of more affluent segments to pay premium prices in order to consume a service at a point and a time convenient to themselves rather than the service provider. Evidence of this is provided by home-delivery food services which target groups with high discretionary incomes.

- Psychographic segmentation can be seen in the way groups of people seek out services that satisfy their lifestyle needs. As an example, some segments of the population are prepared to travel large distances to a restaurant whose design and ambience appeals to them.

- The cultural background of some individuals can predispose them to seek a particular kind of accessibility. This can be seen in the reluctance of some groups to become involved in service-delivery methods which remove regular personal contact with the service provider. Insurance companies that collect premiums from the homes of customers may give reassurance to some segments who have been brought up to distrust impersonal organizations, whereas a periodic visit to a bank or an annual payment by post may satisfy the needs of other segments.

- Access strategies can be based on the type of benefit which users seek from a service. As an example, customers are often prepared to travel a considerable distance to a restaurant for a celebration meal, but would expect it to be easily accessible for a business lunch.

- High-frequency users of a service may place a greater premium on easy accessibility than casual ones.

- In the case of business-to-business services, the level of access to a service can directly affect the customer's operating costs. A computer-repair company which makes its services available at buyers' offices avoids the costs which the latter would incur if it had to perform part of the service—delivery and collection—itself.

For some services, the location of the service-delivery point is the most important means of attracting new business. This can be true for low-value services for which consumers show little willingness to pre-plan their purchase or to go out of their way to find. Location is also very important in the case of impulse purchases. Petrol-filling stations, tea shops in tourist areas and guest houses are typically chosen as a result of a customer encountering the service outlet with no prior planning. It is unlikely, for instance, that many motorists would follow media advertisements and seek out a petrol station which is located in a back street—a visible location is a vital factor influencing consumers' choice.

The perishability of service offers results in their time accessibility being important as well as their spatial location. Again, customers can be segmented according to their flexibility with respect to the time at which they are prepared to consume a service. At one extreme, some segments for some services may be prepared to wait until a specified time to receive the service. As an example, ardent fans of a pop group would probably buy a ticket for a concert regardless of the time and date that it takes place. In other cases, no purchase would be made if a service is not instantly available. For example, a taxi operator that makes its service available only at specified times will probably lose all custom outside these times to other operators.

Service accessibility by time can be used to give an organization competitive advantage in much the same way as spatial accessibility. When building societies started offering banking services from the mid-1980s, their longer opening hours gave them a competitive advantage over banks and attracted many disloyal bank customers who found banking hours of 9.30 a.m. to 3.30 p.m. too restrictive. Having lost significant elements of their core business to building societies, banks were forced to respond by opening certain branches on Saturdays and extending their opening hours in the afternoon.

10.2.3   Service-location models

Before a network of service outlets can be designed, an organization must clearly define its accessibility objectives. In particular, it must have a clear idea of the volume of business, market share and customer segments that it seeks to attract. Accessibility objectives derive from the positioning strategy for a service. A high level of accessibility may for example, only be compatible with business objectives if it is also associated with a premium-price position. A high level of accessibility may also reduce and change the role played by promotion within the marketing mix. In contrast, a strategy that involves a low level of accessibility may need to rely heavily on promotion to make potential customers aware of the location of service outlets. Examples of accessibility objectives include:

- To provide a hotel location in all towns with a population of 100 000 or more people
- To develop supermarket sites that are within 10 minutes' driving time of at least 50 000 people
- To locate retail sites where pedestrian or vehicular traffic exceeds a specified threshold.

Service-location decisions are used at both a macro and a micro level. At the macro level, organizations seek the most profitable areas or regions in which to make their service available, given the strength of demand, the level of competition and the costs of setting up in an area. Micro-level decisions refer to the choice of specific sites.

Macro analysis begins with a clear statement of the profile of customers that an organization is targeting. Areas are then sought that have a geodemographic profile closely matching that of the target market. At its simplest, indicators can be used to identify potentially attractive locations. As a simple example, a financial services company seeking to set up a national chain of outlets offering home-equity loans to elderly people may select the most promising areas on the basis of three pieces of information—the average value of houses in an area (available from the Chartered Institute of Surveyors' regular monitoring report), the percentage of the population who are elderly (available from the Census of Population) and the percentage of the population who are owner–occupiers (available from *Regional Trends*). The attractiveness of a market could be indicated by a weighted index of these factors and subjected to a more detailed analysis of competitor activity in each area. A number of more specialized segmentation methods have been developed which allow organizations to evaluate the profile of an area. An example is the ACORN method of geodemographic profiling developed by CACI Systems, which is based on an analysis of post codes.

Methods used by an organization to select service-outlet locations tend to become more complex as the organization grows. In the early stages of growth, simple rule-of-thumb methods may be acceptable. With further growth, simple indexes and ratios are commonly used. With more service outlets established, an organization can begin to gather sufficient data to analyse the performance of its existing outlets, and from this to develop models that can be used to predict the likely performance of proposed new locations. Regression techniques are employed to identify relationships between variables and the level of significance of each variable in explaining the performance of a location. The development of regression models requires considerable initial investment in creating an information base and calibrating the model, but once calibrated, they can help to reduce the risk inherent in new service-location decisions. It should be noted, however, that models cannot be extrapolated to cover types of decisions that were not envisaged in the model as originally calibrated. For example, a model calibrated for UK site-location decisions may be inappropriate for making similar decisions for sites in France.

REGRESSION MODEL HELPS SUPERMARKET PLAN FUTURE STORE SITES

The level of risk associated with opening a new supermarket in a fiercely competitive environment can be considerable. While a small general retailer may be able to rent shop space on low-risk, short-term leases, modern supermarkets often require considerable investment in purpose-built facilities that meet customers' ever-increasing needs and expectations. A study by Jones and Mock (1984) of a small American supermarket chain illustrates the value of regression-modelling techniques. The supermarket chain being studied had previously relied on rule-of-thumb methods for store allocation, but as the size of its new stores increased, so too had the level of risk. As its business grew, it was also able to gather more data to understand the factors that are associated with the success of a particular store.

The regression modelling started by grouping sites according to similarities in their environments. On the basis of socio-economic data, five distinctive environments were identified—city centre, suburbs, old-established shopping streets, the urban fringe and non-metropolitan locations. To find which of the many variables available were the most relevant for each retailing environment, a series of cross-tabulations between individual key variables was carried out. The relevant variables were then put into a series of stepwise regression models, one for each environment, allowing the identification of the variables that were most significant in explaining sales performance. In the case of suburban stores, variation in store sales was best explained by three measures—the percentage of the neighbourhood that had recently been developed, accessibility of the site by car and the number of competitors located within three blocks. Each increase of 1 per cent in the share of new houses resulted in an additional weekly sales turnover of $120, whereas each nearby competitor reduced sales by $656.

A number of additional problems in the application of regression-modelling techniques can be noted. Because such techniques require large amounts of data for calibration, they are only really suited to high-volume services. It can also be difficult to identify the key variables that cause variation in sales turnover, or to exclude interaction among the variables. Finally, regression is essentially an incremental planning technique which is less appropriate for designing networks of service outlets, such as may occur following the merger of two service organizations resulting in a need to rationalize outlets. For the latter, an alternative approach is to use a spatial-location model.

Spatial-location models measure the geographical dispersion of demand and seek to allocate this demand to service outlets on the basis that the probability of a consumer using a particular outlet will be:

- Positively related to the attractiveness of that outlet, and
- Negatively related to its distance from the points where demand is located.

These principles are developed in the following model (Huff, 1966) which has frequently been used as a basis for retail location models, but also has applications in locating leisure facilities and health services, etc.:

$$P_{ij} = \frac{\dfrac{A_j^a}{d_{ij}^b}}{\sum_{n=1}^{i} \dfrac{A_j^a}{d_{ij}^b}}$$

where P_{ij} = the probability of a trip from origin i to destination j, A_j = the attractiveness of destination j, d_{ij} = the distance between origin i and destination j, and a and b = parameters to be empirically determined.

The intuitive appeal and simplicity of such a model can hide a number of conceptual and practical problems in their application which has triggered considerable research in an attempt to operationalize the basic model. The concept of attractiveness can be difficult to measure. Fishbein (1967) has pointed out that although an individual may have a belief that a location is attractive, this attractiveness may not be of importance to that particular individual. Distance itself can be difficult to determine and can be measured either objectively (for example, mileage or average travelling times) or subjectively according to users' perceptions of distance. As an example of research into the distance components of such models, Mayo and Jarvis (1981) argue that subjectively perceived distances increase proportionately less than the objective measured distance.

Spatial location-allocation models are powerful tools which emphasize long-term marketing strategies rather than short-term decisions about opening or closing a specific location. They can be used to evaluate all possible combinations of location possibilities in relation to the geographical pattern of demand. The criteria for selecting the most efficient network of outlets usually involve balancing the need to maximize its attractiveness to customers against the service provider's requirement to minimize the cost of operating the network. Sophisticated computer models allow assumptions about consumer behaviour to be varied—for example, the maximum distance that people are prepared to walk to an outlet. Such models are expensive to develop in view of the data requirements and the need to use specialized staff to develop them. Where the risks associated with a poor location decision are low, it may be more cost effective to use rule-of-thumb methods than to commission such a model. In the UK, the high cost of acquiring and refurbishing property in the mid-1980s led to spatial-location models becoming very popular as risk reducers. However, the fall in property-related costs—and associated risk levels—in the early 1990s saw many companies (such as Sketchley's Dry Cleaners) dropping their use and reverting to more cost-effective rule-of-thumb methods or regression models.

Spatial-allocation models do, however, continue to be used in both the private and public sectors (for example, in planning a network of clinics that minimizes patients' travel distances).

RATIONALIZING PETROL-STATION OUTLETS

Goodchild and Noronha (1987) report on a study to evaluate the most efficient network of service-station outlets in a small north American town. The merger of two chains had left the new one with a total of 31 outlets in the town, but it was considered that the new chain would be most profitable if it operated only 20 outlets. The company decided that four of the newest and highest-volume locations would be retained, leaving it the task of deciding which 16 of the remaining 27 locations should be retained. Rather than evaluating on a site-by-site basis using multiple-regression techniques, the company used a spatial location-allocation model on account of its interactive ability to adjust sales volumes of all outlets in the network simultaneously.

The potential demand for petrol was measured by reference to:

- The residential population in each of 600 census enumeration areas in the city.
- The traffic flow (number of cars × length of link) in each of 560 road links.
- Against these positive determinants of demand, a distance decay effect was introduced to the model, indicating that demand would decrease as customers' distance from a service outlet increased.

A model was developed of the form:
Demand, $j =$

$$A\Sigma_i \frac{\text{Population } i}{(1 - ad_{ij})} + B\Sigma_k \frac{\text{Traffic } k}{(1 - ad_{kj})}$$

where demand at service station j was calculated as the sum total of population at all i enumeration districts divided by a factor reflecting the distance of the outlet from each enumeration district $(1 - ad_{ij})$, plus the sum total of traffic on all links, divided by a factor reflecting the distance of the outlet from each link $(1 - a\,d_{kj})$. A and B are weights that could be modified to favour either local catchment area demand or traffic flow demand. The location-allocation procedure was able to indicate the sales and market share at each site—including competitors—and how a site may be even more effective if it is slightly relocated. The analysis can be repeated using different distance-decay parameters and different weights for A and B in the equation to reflect different marketing strategies. An emphasis on local catchment area demand (high value for A) favoured central locations, while an emphasis on traffic flow generates more dispersed site locations.

10.2.4 Reducing locational dependency

The traditional idea that service production and consumption are inseparable would appear at first to pose problems in achieving both maximum productive efficiency and maximum accessibility to a service. One method of resolving this apparent problem is to try to make production and consumption separable—that is, to design a service which can be produced where it is most efficient and consumed where it is most needed. It can sometimes be conceptually quite difficult to identify just where a service is produced, but a number of methods can be identified by which production can be removed from the point of consumption:

- Telecommunications can be used to allow the substantive element of a service to be produced at a central processing unit and made available at any point of consumers' choice. Information databases used by businesses and pre-recorded telephone information used by personal consumers fit into this category. Banks have recognized the distribution implications of telephone banking services and most of the large banks in the UK have created systems that allow private and business customers to receive spoken telephone statements and to transfer funds from one account to another, or to pay bills to outside organizations from any telephone. Some banks have offered more sophisticated services by allowing customers to receive information and give instructions via a telephone line and the customer's own personal computer terminal. The locational implications of such delivery systems are quite significant. It will doubtless prove possible to reduce the size of banks' costly branch networks as some segments of the population and some categories of the banks' services are distributed to any point which the consumer chooses. As well as offering distribution at any place, telephone delivery systems can operate from an efficient central base capable of offering 24-hour service delivery on every day of the year. Some systems (for example, Midland Bank's First Direct) use human operators, requiring a shift system to be operated, while others (National Westminster Bank's ActionLine) employ computer-based interaction and require minimal human input. The latter demonstrated the attractiveness of all-hours banking with the disclosure that over 400 customers used its telephone banking service on Christmas Day 1991.
- Postal services can be used to make intangible services available at almost any location, in much the same way as telecommunications-based accessibility strategies. The development of database marketing has allowed direct mail to be used as a means not only of promotion but also of increasing accessibility. Insurance companies now make many services such as personal loan cheques and insurance cover available at the homes of consumers while the service itself is processed at a remote office.
- A more novel means of separating production and consumption is to provide a surrogate for a service that allows the service itself to be provided at a time and place of the consumer's choice. The best example of a surrogate is provided by a credit card. Providing short-term credit is a service offered by credit-card companies, yet the companies are not required to take part in every act of service delivery—that is, every time customers use their card to pay a bill in a shop or a restaurant. The credit card acts as a mediating device between a shopkeeper and his or her customer by stating that the credit-card company agrees at some future point to transfer funds into the shopkeeper's bank account and the shopper agrees to send to the credit-card company payment for the goods purchased plus the cost as agreed of any ancillary services such as extended credit. The service of providing credit is thus made available at a potentially enormous range of outlets and not simply those operated by the credit-card company.

10.3   THE ROLE OF INTERMEDIARIES IN DISTRIBUTING SERVICES

In the context of manufactured goods marketing, the concept of an intermediary can be understood as being a person who handles goods as they pass from the organization that manufactured them to the individual or business that finally consumes them. The intermediary may physically handle the goods, dividing them into progressively smaller volumes as they pass through channels of distribution, or it may simply buy and sell the rights to goods in the role of a commodity dealer.

Any discussion of service intermediaries immediately raises a number of conceptual issues;

- Services cannot be owned, therefore it is difficult to speak of rights to service ownership being transferred through channels of distribution.
- Pure services are intangible and perishable, therefore stocks cannot exist.
- The inseparability of most services should logically require an intermediary to become a co-producer of a service.

A distinction should be made between intermediaries as co-producers and their role as mere sales agents. While the former are an active part of the production process, the latter do not actually deliver a service itself, only the right to a service. As an example, a shop selling postage stamps is not significantly involved as a co-producer of postal services. It can be difficult to distinguish between these two situations—a theatre ticket agency in addition to merely selling the right to a service may provide a valuable service for consumers in procuring specific seats.

Service intermediaries perform a number of important functions on behalf of service producers (the latter are often referred to as 'service principals'). The role expectations of intermediaries vary according to the nature of the service in question and some of the most important are as follows:

- As a co-producer of a service, an intermediary assists in making a service available to consumers at a place and time that is convenient to them. An estate agent providing a cheque-cashing facility for a building society is assisting in the process of producing and making financial services available to consumers. In other cases, an intermediary may become the dominant partner involved in co-production. A national key-cutting or shoe-heeling service may place almost the entire service production process in the hands of intermediaries, leaving the principal to provide administrative and advertising support and to monitor standards.
- Intermediaries help to make a service locally available. A mortgage can be said to be created at the head office of a bank or building society where bulk funds are acquired and documentation produced, but for many customer segments, the mortgage must be made available through an intermediary with a local outlet where potential customers could discuss their requirements. This could be the bank's own branch staff or an appointed intermediary.
- Intermediaries usually provide sales support at the point of sale. For some customers of personal services, a two-way personal dialogue with a local intermediary may be more effective in securing a sale than advertising messages derived centrally from a service principal.
- Consumers may prefer to buy services from an intermediary who offers a wide choice, including those provided by competing service principals. A holiday-tour company seeking to sell its holidays direct to the public may encounter resistance from segments of the population who prefer to have choices presented to them at one location.
- Consumers may enjoy trusting relationships with intermediaries and prefer to choose between competing alternatives on the basis of the intermediaries' advice. In the financial services sector, intermediaries develop trust with their clients in guiding them through often

1. 'PUSH' STRATEGY

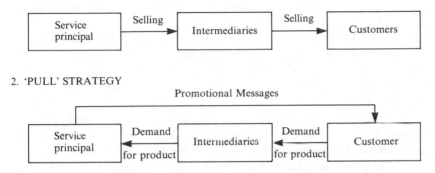

2. 'PULL' STRATEGY

Figure 10.3   Push and Pull strategies for making services available to consumers

complex choices. To be successful with such segments of buyers, a financial services company must establish its credentials with the intermediary if its products are to enter the final consumer's choice set.

- An intermediary as co-producer of a service often shares some of the risk of providing a service. This can come about where a service principal requires intermediaries to contribute some of their own capital to the cost of acquiring equipment and both share any subsequent operating profit or loss.
- The use of independent intermediaries can free up capital which a service principal can re-invest in its core service-production facilities. An airline which closes its own ticket shops and directs potential customers to travel agents is able to reinvest the proceeds in updating its aircraft or reservation systems, which may give it greater competitive advantage than having its own ticket outlets.
- Once the initial service act is completed, there may be a requirement for after-sales service to be provided. Intermediaries can make this support more accessible to the consumer and assist the service principal as co-producer of the after-sales support. Insurance is a good example, where many segments of the insurance-buying public feel happier with easy local access to a local agent who can give advice about making a claim. The agent, in turn, simplifies the task of the insurance company by handling much of the paperwork involved in making a claim.

10.4   PUSH AND PULL RELATIONSHIPS WITH INTERMEDIARIES

'Push' and 'Pull' channels of distribution are familiar concepts in the marketing of manufactured goods, but they also have application within the service sector. A traditional 'Push' channel of distribution involves a service principal aggressively promoting its service to intermediaries by means of personal selling, trade advertising and the use of trade incentives. The intermediary, in turn, aggressively sells the service to final consumers, often having to strike a balance between maximizing the customer's benefit and maximizing the incentives offered to the intermediary by the service principal. This approach sees the service as essentially a commodity—the consumer starts with no preference of service principal and seeks the best value available from an intermediary. A push channel is typical of the way in which basic third-party, fire and theft motor insurance is made available to customers. For most customers, insurance is a 'distress' purchase where the only perceived difference between policies is the price. Many people rely on their intermediary to suggest the lowest-cost insurance available to them. Intermediaries, in turn, will be tempted to sell most aggressively those policies on which they receive the most attractive commission payments.

For service principals, push strategies can be quite risky, as any product-differentiation policy can only be effective if the intermediary clearly communicates the unique benefits to potential customers, rather than relying on price alone as the point of differentiation. To try to reduce this risk, service principals can aim messages directly at consumers, seeking to establish at an early stage in the buying process the values for which their brand stands. Having developed an attitude towards a brand, consumers are more likely to ask specifically for that brand from an intermediary or to express a preference for it when offered a choice by the intermediary. For a pull strategy, the intermediary's role is reduced to one of dispensing pre-sold branded services. The UK pensions industry has seen considerable activity by companies such as Prudential, Legal & General and Standard Life seeking to build up favourable images of their services so that potential customers enter discussions with intermediaries with a favourable predisposition towards the insurance company. Push and Pull strategies are compared in Figure 10.3.

It can sometimes be difficult to distinguish between pure push and pull strategies. A company may act as an intermediary for some services but as a service principal for other, similar, services. As well as selling a service for a principal as an intermediary, the latter could buy-in rights to services as though the principal was in fact a subcontractor. In this way, small local travel agents sometimes put together package holidays aimed at segments of their own market. An agent which acts as intermediary for the sale of other tour operators' coach holidays might buy-in hotel, coach and sightseeing services direct from other companies and sell the entire tour under its own brand name. The travel agent effectively becomes a principal. While there is potential benefit from being able to earn both the retail agent's and the tour operator's profit margin, this strategy poses potential risk for the intermediary, who must cover all the fixed costs of the principal, rather than earning a commission on every service sold.

10.5 SERVICE CHARACTERISTICS AS AN INFLUENCE ON CHANNEL DESIGN

Services are not homogeneous, and this is reflected in the choice of intermediaries. While some services can be handled by a large number of intermediaries, others cannot easily be dealt with by intermediaries at all. The characteristics of services and of customers' expectations need to be considered before an accessibility strategy is developed:

- Some services experience highly variable outcomes, making efforts to control quality through intermediaries very difficult to achieve. This is particularly true of personal services such as hairdressing, which are most commonly provided by small businesses direct to final consumers without the use of intermediaries.
- Some services may be highly specialized and likely to be neglected by intermediaries with inadequate training or knowledge. A principal may gain no competitive advantage if intermediaries are incapable of giving appropriate sales and co-production support. Where a service is complex, the service principal must pay careful attention to the selection of intermediaries or, alternatively, deal directly with consumers. Within the package-holiday industry, skiing and activity holidays are quite specialized services for which most travel agents have inadequate knowledge to handle effectively. Some operators of these holidays have chosen to work through specialized intermediaries such as outdoor pursuit agencies, while many more prefer to deal directly with their target markets.

- Margins available on a service may be insufficient to support many intermediaries, if any at all. Domestic and industrial cleaning services often operate on very low margins, resulting in most services being provided direct to consumers.
- Legislation or voluntary codes of conduct may limit the choice of intermediary available to a service principal or make it impossible to act through them at all. The Financial Services Act 1986 is a good example of legislation which directly constrains the distribution opportunities available for certain services. The Act requires that specified financial services may only be handled by authorized intermediaries. Voluntary codes also provide an additional constraint for some services. An example is that operated by the Association of British Travel Agents (ABTA) governing the manner in which package holidays can be sold. ABTA does not generally allow its retail agent members to sell any overseas holidays of tour operators who are not themselves members of ABTA. As most travel agents in the UK are members, the distribution options of a non-ABTA tour operator are quite constrained.

TAKING A BET IN THE HIGH STREET

Gambling on horses has long been seen as a vice against which the public needs to be protected by making access to betting services difficult. Against this, private sector profit-motivated organizations have been keen to make the benefits of horse racing more widely available to markets where a need has been identified and this need can be satisfied profitably.

In the UK, government passed legislation during the nineteenth century which outlawed corrupting 'betting offices' and restricted the placing of bets to racecourses. However, despite measures to eradicate off-course betting, an underlying demand for gambling services was reflected in the ingenuity of punters and entrepreneurs alike to distribute the benefits of horse-race betting more widely. These included the use of 'runners', who would collect the working man's bet and place it at the racecourse, and the use of credit betting, which was not covered by the restrictive legislation.

The Betting, Gaming and Lotteries Act 1963 had the effect of legalizing off-course betting shops for the first time. However, the manner in which betting services could be distributed off-course remained highly constrained. Local auth-

ority planning permission was required before a betting shop could be established, but frequently proved difficult to obtain in the face of neighbourhood opposition. The facilities that betting-shop operators could provide within any location were strictly regulated, and thus it was made illegal to offer refreshments or any comfortable furnishings that may have made the outlet seem an attractive place to spend more time. Opening hours were restricted—they were not allowed to be open after 6.30 p.m. or on Sundays. Finally, it was very difficult for a betting shop to promote its location—rules made it difficult to use external signage to draw attention.

Nevertheless, cash-betting offices increased in number, opening up a new market to the small-scale punter who wished to bet near his or her home in the same way as purchasing fast-moving consumer goods. Cash-betting offices therefore offered the opportunities for large operators to develop chains of betting shops.

By 1986, it has been estimated that over 90 per cent of all horse-race betting activity was conducted off-course (Munting, 1989). With the passing of the Betting, Gaming and Lotteries Act 1985, greater freedom was given for the big three betting chains (Ladbrokes, William Hill and Coral) to position their chains as entertainment outlets offering a much broader leisure experience. Betting shops were now allowed to provide live television broadcasts of races as well as offering refreshments and a higher standard of comfort which were designed to encourage customers to stay longer and to bet more. In a bid to diversify, many shops offered related gambling services, such as football pools and bets on events as diverse as election results and the weather. Ironically, however, betting shops remained barred from providing gaming machines, commonly found in many pubs.

With liberalization of the design of betting shops, the big three chains employed design consultants to develop a distinctive image and positioning for their chains. Particular effort was placed on refurbishing the outlets located in areas of highest competition. Locational decisions have reflected trends in betting shops' marketing environment. Town-centre sites have tended to become larger, reflecting the desire to create leisure centres of broad appeal. For example, in 1991, William Hill opened an outlet in the centre of Birmingham, which with a floor space of 550 m² was claimed to be the largest betting centre in Europe. However, the decline of city-centre employment has resulted in new-shop development being concentrated in suburban residential areas. More recently, the development of communications technology has made the direct distribution of horse-race betting facilities to punters' homes a more attractive option, with bets being taken over the telephone using prearranged credit facilities.

Further liberalization of regulations governing the distribution of betting services provides both opportunities and threats for existing operators. While many recent developments have presented opportunities, an example of a potential problem is the suggestion that betting shops should be able to sell alcohol to their customers. This has raised the prospect of betting services being provided as an ancillary service within pubs. Doubtless, if this suggested reform did come about, the large betting organizations would adapt to the changed circumstances, possibly by rationalizing their branch network and coming to arrangements with pub operators to distribute betting services through their outlets.

10.6 DEVELOPING A STRATEGY FOR INTERMEDIARIES

The development of a strategy to make services accessible to users begins with a clear analysis of an organization's accessibility objectives for a particular service. Accessibility strategies could be designed around meeting the following typical objectives:

- To gain market share for an existing service in an established market
- To gain entry to a new market
- To prevent penetration of an established market by a market challenger

The following sections discuss the merits of a number of types of intermediaries, and their ability to contribute towards the service principal's accessibility objectives. One option is for the service principal to make a service available directly to consumers without the involvement of intermediaries. In some of the circumstances described in the previous sections, this could be the most appropriate strategy—for example, where the service is complex and the service principal wishes to ensure that greater accessibility through intermediaries is not achieved at the expense of quality standards. In other cases, service principals can better achieve accessibility objectives by working with intermediaries. Here, decisions must be made about what is the most appropriate type of intermediary for the service in question.

10.7 DIRECT SALE

Direct sale is a particularly attractive option for service providers where the service offering is complex and variable and where legal constraints make the involvement of intermediaries difficult. The attractions of direct sale are numerous:

- The service provider is in regular direct contact with consumers of its service, making faster feedback of customer comments a possibility. This can facilitate the process of improving existing services or developing new ones.
- It can be easier for service principals to develop relationships with customers if they are in regular contact. Databases can be built up to provide a profile of individual customers, allowing for more effective targeting of new service offers. Banks—which have traditionally dealt directly with their personal customers—in theory have the information on which to target their customers with offers that reflect their age, income and stage in the family lifecycle. Over the longer term, a bank could present a series of offers which may not yield short-term profits but could be used to build a long-term profitable relationship.
- Intermediaries may jealously guard their customers from the service principal, in the fear that any initial contact between the service principal and consumer could result in the role of the intermediary being diminished. Having spent time and effort attracting their customer, they do not wish to see the service principal picking up the long-term benefits of repeat business without the revenue-earning involvement of the intermediary. The service principal therefore loses a lot of valuable feedback. In the travel industry, agents deliberately do not pass on the addresses of customers' names to the tour-operating company with whom they are booked, disclosing only a telephone number for emergency use.
- In the public sector, political considerations or fears over confidentiality may prevent services being provided by private sector intermediaries. Definitions of what is politically acceptable change over time. In the UK many have considered that school catering, refuse collection and leisure-centre services are vital public services which could only be supplied directly by public sector bodies. It is now routinely accepted that all these can be provided through service intermediaries of one form or another, although debate continues about whether more contentious services such as prisons and security services should be provided through private sector intermediaries. From the opposite approach, the use of public sector organizations as intermediaries has been increasingly accepted as normal. As an example, doctors' surgeries and hospitals are being used to make a widening range of private health-related services available, including a chain of Travel Clinics operated in conjunction with British Airways.
- The service principal can retain for itself the profit margin than would have been paid to an intermediary. This could be beneficial where its own distribution costs are lower than the commission that it would have paid to an intermediary.

Quite often, service principals choose to make their services available both directly and through intermediaries. This can be an attractive option as it allows the principal to target segments which may have very different buying behaviour. For example, one segment of the holiday-buying public may seek the reassurance provided by being able to walk into and talk to a travel agent, while another segment may be more confident, price-sensitive and short of time, for whom direct booking with a tour operator by telephone is attractive. Against the advantages of segmenting the market in this way can come significant problems. Intermediaries can become demotivated if they see a principal for whom they are working as agent selling the same services direct to the public. To make matters worse, direct-sale promotional material often emphasizes the benefits of not using an intermediary, typically lower prices and faster service. Occasionally, agents' trade associations have threatened to boycott the products of principals who act in this way. Eagle Star Insurance, for example, encountered initial hostility when it launched Eagle Star Direct in apparent competition with its agents. One solution is to split an organization into two distinct operating units with their own brand identity, one to operate through intermediaries and the other to sell direct to the final consumer. This was the solution adopted by the Thomson holiday group, who, in addition to selling holidays through travel agents under the Thomson and Horizon brand names (among others), also sell basically similar holidays direct to the public under the Portland brand name.

AGENTS TARGETED FOR INSURANCE COMPANY'S EXPANSION

During the 1980s, epitaphs were being written for the traditional insurance broker. A significant segment of the population increasingly saw brokers as inefficient barriers to communication between the insurance company and its customers—it was one more stage at which delay could occur in handling a claim, or at which vital documents could go missing. Furthermore, insurance brokers were often perceived as inefficient and a visit to a broker often entailed lengthy periods of waiting to be attended by staff of mediocre ability.

From the viewpoint of the insurance companies themselves, there was an increasing desire to enter into a dialogue with customers directly, cutting out the inefficiencies which could occur by acting through intermediaries. Modern computerized databases were increasingly making it possible for companies to target customers directly and to sustain a relationship with them. Added to this, a direct relationship potentially reduced the variability inherent in insurance brokers' efforts at selling policies and in acting as co-producers of companies' policies. Direct sales also offered companies the chance to save the com-

mission paid to brokers on each policy sold.

The 1980s therefore saw the emergence of many direct-sell insurance companies who had begun offering attractive insurance deals, particularly in the home, motor and health sectors. Some, such as the Royal Bank of Scotland subsidiary, Direct Line Insurance, had already made significant inroads into the home and motor sectors. Many of the major insurance companies, such as Eagle Star, had created separate subsidiaries specifically to promote direct sales to the public.

There remained, however, a large segment of insurance buyers who remained unmoved by the efforts of the direct-sell companies. For this segment, the reassurance of face-to-face contact and the ability of a broker to shop around on behalf of the customer were undoubtedly attractions. Therefore while many insurance companies sought to reduce the role of intermediaries in distributing their policies, others attempted to develop sales through them. One example of a company which has sought to work with brokers rather than against them is Independent Insurance Ltd, a general insurance company who in 1987 expanded significantly with the acquisition of Allstate Insurance Ltd.

A key part of Independent's strategy to gain competitive advantage rested on the quality of service which customers received at its network of agencies. The company found itself with an extensive and lumbering network of over 10 000 agents, varying in degrees of commitment to Independent. The majority of these had very little detailed knowledge of the services offered by Independent. Most merely kept information in files in case customers asked for it, rather than proactively promoting its policies. The result was that Independent spent a lot of money supporting a network of agents, many of whom produced quite insignificant levels of business.

In 1987, Independent decided to cut the size of its agency network from 10 000 to 4 000, having identified which category of broker had been most effective at generating business. It had also found from its research that agents were increasingly looking for a high level of support from insurance companies. The result was the development of a smaller network of focused agents, supported in a way that was not possible with the previous size of network.

A focal point for bringing quality to its smaller network of agencies was the development of a partnership between them and the company. Agents had traditionally worked quite independently, but the company sought to add to this the possibility of collaboration in joint ventures. One collaborative approach was an invitation to agents to join the newly created 'Independent Club', which offered members free staff training, regular newsletters, the services of Independent's marketing department (for example, to develop local advertising campaigns), a profit-sharing scheme and priority attention from the company for Club members. To demonstrate the importance that the company attached to the development of relationships with its agents, it chose a high-profile launch for the Club. Instead of relying on the traditional visit by sales personnel to agents' premises, the company arranged to bring 150 of its key agents to a central point for a lavish launch event. A video aimed at instilling confidence in agents was given to all Club members.

In addition to motivating its agents, the Club was also used as a means of gathering marketing research. At the qualitative level, Club members were invited by the company to brainstorming sessions at which proposals for new or modified services were discussed. During 1989 alone, the company launched 30 new products, or product modifications, with inputs from agents playing a significant role. Meetings of Club members possessed many of the characteristics of quality circles—traditionally confined within an organization, but extended here to include intermediaries who are vital co-producers of the company's service.

The development of a quality agency network was undoubtedly a reason for the growth in turnover of Independent, from £27 million in 1986 to £62 million in 1989. The growth achieved through its agents has led it to develop a newly segmented club—The Merit Club. This is aimed at a select group of agents who will be targeted as outlets for more specialized policies which members of the original Club may not be fully prepared to deliver to the standards of quality expected by the company.

10.8 SELECTION OF INTERMEDIARIES

Service intermediaries take many forms in terms of their size, structure, legal status and relationship to the service principal. Because of this diversity, attempts at classification can become confused by the level of overlap present. In this section, attention is focused on the characteristics of four important types of intermediary—agents, retailers, wholesalers and franchisees.

10.8.1 Service agents

An agent is someone who acts on behalf of a principal and has the authority to create a legal relationship between the customer and service principal as if it was made directly between the two. Principals are vicariously liable for the actions of their agents. Agents are usually rewarded for their actions by being able to deduct a commission before payment is passed on to their principal, although in many cases, agents may be paid a fixed fee for the work actually done—for example, in preparing a new market prior to the launch of a new service.

For service principals, the use of agents offers many advantages:

- capital requirements for creating a chain of distribution outlets are minimized, allowing reinvestment in core service production.
- Consumers may expect choice at the point of service purchase and it is usually easier for an independent agent to do this rather than the service principal to set up distribution outlets which sell competing products. (In the case of many financial services, the Financial Services Act 1986 makes it difficult for banks and building societies to both sell their own products and those of competitors—they must choose between being 'tied' to one principal (or their own products) or offering a genuine choice to customers.)
- Where a service principal is entering a new market it may lack the knowledge which allows it to understand buyer behaviour and the nature of competition in that market. Many overseas financial institutions with a poor understanding of the UK mortgage market chose to make mortgage services available by means of independent mortgage brokers and, in some cases, established UK building societies.
- In overseas markets it may be illegal for a service principal to deal directly with the public, a problem that can be remedied by acting through a local licensed agent.
- In some cases, special skills are required by a service principal that would be very costly to develop in-house. A shipping company may not have the need for a full-time employee to be based at the Baltic Exchange charter market and it would therefore be more sensible to employ an agent who is a member of the Exchange to sell shipping capacity as and when required, on either a commission or a fixed-charge basis. Similarly, merchant banks sell shares on the Stock Exchange through specialist stockbrokers.

10.8.2 Retail outlets

The notion of a retailer in the service sector poses conceptual problems, for it has already been established that a retailer cannot carry a stock of services—one of the important functions of a retailer of goods. The distinction between a retailer and an agent or franchisee (see below) can be a fine one. In general, a retailer operates in a manner which does not create legal relations between the service principal and the final customer—the customer's relationship is only with the retailer.

Many services which pass through retailers have a significant goods element. As an example, many film-processing companies sell their services through retail chemists under the brand name of the chemist. The latter takes a profit margin while allowing the film-processing company to make its service available locally. Many services, such as key cutting and fast-food catering, are often retailed in the form of a franchise agreement which is discussed more fully below.

Sometimes service retailers undertake another of the traditional goods retailer's function in taking a risk. A retailer can buy the right to a block of service transactions and if these rights are not sold by the time the service is performed, the value of these rights disappears. This can happen where a ticket agent buys a block of tickets on a no-return basis from an event organizer.

10.8.3 Service wholesalers

Similar conceptual problems apply to the role of the wholesaler. For services, the term is most sensibly understood where an intermediary buys the right to a large volume of service transactions and then proceeds to break these down into smaller units of rights to a service for handling by retailers or other intermediaries. Hotel-booking agencies who buy large blocks of hotel accommodation earn their margin by buying in volume at low prices and adding a mark-up as a block booking is broken down into smaller units for sale to retailers or agents. As with retailers, it can be difficult to distinguish a wholesaler from an agent. A hotel wholesaler may in fact have some rights to return unsold accommodation to the hotels concerned and may include in their dealings with customers a statement that the transaction is to be governed by conditions specified by the service principal.

10.9 FRANCHISED SERVICE DISTRIBUTION

The term 'franchising' refers to a relationship where one party—the franchisor—provides the development work on a service format and monitors standards of delivery, while coming to an arrangement with a second party—the franchisee—who is licensed to deliver the service, taking some share of the financial risk and reward in return. Vertical franchising occurs where a manufacturer allows a franchisee an exclusive right to make the goods it has produced available to the public. The more recent business-format franchising occurs where an organization allows others to copy the format of its own operations.

The International Franchise Association defines a franchise operation as:

a contractual relationship between the franchisor and franchisee in which the franchisor offers or is obliged to maintain a continuing interest in the business of the franchisee in such areas as know-how and training; wherein the franchisee operates under a common trade name, format or procedure owned by or controlled by the franchisor, and in which the franchisee has made or will make a substantial capital investment in his business from his own resources.

(Adams and Prichard, 1987)

The private services sector has recognized the value of franchising and witnessed significant growth. A *Key Note* report in 1987 stated that the total turnover of UK business format franchises in 1985 was £1.7 billion, and the British Franchise Association (1989) has estimated that this figure is growing at a rate of about 30 per cent per annum. The rapid growth of franchise operations is indicated by the fact that of the top 40 business format franchise operations in the UK, just over one half have been in operation for less than 10 years (Charter and Fernique, 1990). Franchising offers particular opportunities for service industries which are people-intensive—it combines the motivation of self-employed franchisees with the quality control and brand values of the franchisor.

Franchise agreements cover a diverse range of services, from car hire to fast food, kitchen-design services, veterinary services and hotels. Of the top 10 business franchise operations (in terms of turnover), all are involved in essentially service-based activities, ranging from fast food to car hire and car servicing (Golzen and Barrow, 1986). Although most franchisees are self-employed individuals or small companies, they can also be very large organizations. As an example, it is quite common to find corporate franchisees who operate a large number of hotels for a franchisor, making the franchisee a very large organization. Franchising also has applications within the public sector (see below).

10.9.1 The nature of a franchise agreement

The franchise agreement sets out the rights and obligations of the franchisor and franchisee. It typically includes the following main clauses:

- The nature of the service that is to be supplied by the franchisee is specified. This can refer to particular categories of service which are to be offered. For example, a car-repair franchise would probably indicate which specific service operations (such as brake replacement, engine tuning, etc.) are covered by the franchise agreement.
- The territory in which the franchisee is given the right to offer a service is usually specified. The premium that a franchisee is prepared to pay for a franchisee usually reflects the exclusivity of its territory.
- The length of a franchise agreement is specified—most franchises run for a period of 5 to 10 years with options to renew at the end of the period.
- The franchisee usually agrees to buy the franchise for an initial fee and agrees the basis on which future payments are to be made to the franchisor. The level of the initial fee reflects the strength of an established brand. A high initial fee for a strong established brand can be much less risky for a franchisee than a low price for a relatively new franchise. Payment of on-going fees to the franchisee is usually calculated as a percentage of turnover. The agreement also often requires the franchisee to buy certain supplies from the franchisor. Agreements vary widely: for example, the British School of Motoring makes no initial charge to franchisees but subsequently charges a fixed fee of from £120 per week, which includes much of the equipment that the franchisee uses.
- The franchisee agrees to follow instructions from the franchisor concerning the manner of service delivery. Franchisees are typically required to charge according to an agreed scale of prices, maintain standards of reliability, availability and performance in the delivery of the service and ensure that any franchisee-produced advertising follows the franchisor's guidelines.
- The franchisee usually agrees not to act as an intermediary for any other service principal, insisting that their franchised outlets show the same loyalty to the organization as if they were actually owned by it. Thus the operator of a Pizzaland franchise cannot use a franchised outlet to sell the services or goods of a competing organization such as Burger King. Franchising implies a degree of control that the franchisor has over the franchisee, unlike a retail agent, who usually has considerable discretion over the manner in which they conduct their business. For the franchisor, considerable harm could result from its promotion being used to draw potential customers into the franchisee's outlets, only for them to be cross-sold a service over which the franchisor has no control nor is likely to receive any financial benefit. However, in many cases, service franchises are sold on the understanding that they will form just one small part of the franchisee's operations. For example, a franchise to operate a courier service's collection point may be compatible with the business of a service station or newsagent.

- The franchisor agrees to provide promotional support for the franchisee. The aim of such support is to establish the values of the franchisor's brand in the minds of potential customers, thereby reducing the promotion which the franchisee is required to undertake. The franchise agreement usually requires certain promotional activity of the franchisee to be approved by the franchisor.
- The franchisor usually agrees to provide some level of administrative and technical support for the franchisee. This can include the provision of equipment (for example, printing machines for a fast-print franchise) and administrative support such as accounting.
- Franchise agreements usually give either party the right to terminate the franchise and for the franchisee to sell their franchise. The right to terminate can act as a control mechanism should either party fail to perform in accordance with the conditions of the franchise. A successful franchisee would want a clause in an agreement allowing him or her to sell the goodwill of a franchise that they have developed over time.

10.9.2 Franchise development

Once franchising has taken hold within an organization, it tends to expand rather than contract. If a franchisor has built up a successful brand format, coupled with successful management, it can usually achieve greater returns on its capital by selling the right to use its name rather than operating its own outlets. The British School of Motoring, for example, steadily increased the proportion of its outlets that are franchised from 24 per cent in 1980 to 85 per cent in 1990. Other strongly managed brands that have followed this route include Sketchley Dry Cleaning, Holland & Barrett Health Food shops and Swinton Insurance.

There is a limit to which operations can be franchised and most franchisors choose not to franchise their operations entirely. There are two important reasons for this. First, new-product development is usually easier to carry out in-house rather than at a distance through a franchise. In this way it avoids alienating franchisees should experimental new services fail. Second, some operations may be too specialized to expect a franchisee to have the standard of training to ensure a consistent standard of delivery and the franchisor may choose to retain responsibility for providing these.

Maintaining and motivating franchisees is a constant challenge for franchisors. Franchisees can become only too aware of the payments that the franchisor takes from them on an on-going basis and may be tempted not to renew their franchise at the end of their agreement and either to go it alone or to sign up with another franchise operation. Where brands are strong, the former route can be very risky. For example, Benetton retail franchisees who have used their premises to provide their own competing service format have lost customers when the franchisor creates a new outlet in the locality. Payment of franchise fees represents good value to a franchisee for as long as it receives good back-up from the franchisor and a steady supply of customers who are attracted by the reputation of the franchise brand.

SHELL CHOOSES FRANCHISEES TO PUT THE SERVICE BACK INTO SERVICE STATIONS

Petrol is a commodity that cannot easily be differentiated. During the 1970s and 1980s, oil companies had sought to increase their share of retail petrol sales by attempting to differentiate their corporate image, and occasion-ally the product itself. The Shell Oil Company had tried both corporate and product differentiation strategies to boost its market share but remained subject to severe price competition in an overpopulated petrol-station market.

During the late 1980s, the strategy of Shell focused increasingly on the manner in which petrol was retailed. Instead of simply being a point at which a commodity was dispensed, Shell sought to position its outlets as places where customers could enjoy a wide range of services in a pleasant environment. The blueprint for the proposed service mix of its service stations included the provision of mini-markets and facilities for obtaining hot snacks as well as the more traditional petrol-station services such as car washes. Research had shown that a significant segment of the petrol-buying population was not very price-sensitive. This included individuals buying petrol which is later reimbursed by their employers and those who only infrequently need to purchase it. For these segments, the quality of service received at an outlet was more important than price alone. Shell needed a strategy for managing its sites that would put the service back into its service stations and to ensure that customers could be sure of the same high standards of service whichever Shell station they visit. Shell aimed to be the Marks & Spencer of the forecourt world with not only good products on sale but also high-quality customer service.

Like most other oil companies, Shell had traditionally granted licences to operators to run its company-owned sites. The licence focused on the agreement to supply petrol with little stipulation about the manner in which it was to be sold, other than basic operational and safety rules. However, in May 1990, Shell launched a franchise scheme called SHARE (Standards, High Quality and Retailer Excellence) which allowed individuals to buy a 10-year franchise to operate a site. The franchisee pays a sum of money for a franchise which he or she is free to develop within limits specified by Shell, and subject to meeting minimum standards of service. In return, Shell provides business and marketing support to the franchisee.

Forecourt shops are seen by Shell as a growth area and the company has given valuable support to franchisees in their operation. This support has included the development of store designs which are based on customer research, negotiation with supliers to get advantageous deals for franchisees, promotional and merchandising support and assistance with bookkeeping and administrative duties.

One person who saw the advantages of the SHARE scheme was Andrew Brown, who had run a Shell company-owned site on the outskirts of Alcester, Warwickshire, for a number of years. A proposed bypass would have had the effect of drastically reducing traffic flows past the site. Out of this apparent problem, Brown saw a possible opportunity, for land was available for development at an important new junction of the bypass where traffic flows were expected to reach 40 000 vehicles per day by 1995. He therefore set about buying the site and obtaining planning permission for a new service station ahead of the opening of the new bypass.

Unlike the existing station, the new site is operated on a franchise basis with a 10-year fuel-supply agreement running in tandem with the franchise. It opened in May 1991 after Andrew Brown had undergone a mandatory franchisee training programme at the Shell Management Training Centre in Coventry, which gave him the foundations for running a successful SHARE service station and the ability and motivation to maintain the constant high standards required. The programme covered new ideas in multi-tasking, the setting up of rotas and keeping to them and methods of ensuring standards of cleanliness and staff selection that were very different from those that most company-owned site managers had previously been practising.

Andrew Brown has successfully developed a wide range of services on the new site, including a shop and car wash. The franchise arrangement had worked to the mutual benefit of both partners, prompting them to begin negotiations to convert a second company-owned site at nearby Stratford-on-Avon into a similar franchise operation.

10.9.3   Public Sector Franchising

Public services are increasingly being delivered by franchise agreements in order to capitalize on the motivation of smaller-scale franchisees described above. Franchising can take a number of forms:

- The right to operate a vital public service can be sold to a franchisee who, in turn, can charge users of the facility. The franchisee will normally be required to maintain the facility to a specified standard and to obtain government approval of prices to be charged. In the UK, the government has begun offering private organizations franchises to operate vital road links, including the Dartford river crossing and Severn Bridge. In the case of the latter, an Anglo-French consortium has acquired the right to collect tolls from users of the bridge and in return must carry out routine maintenance work on it and develop a second river crossing.
- Government can sell the exclusive right for private organizations to operate a private service which is of public importance. Private sector radio and television broadcasting is operated on a franchise basis where the government invites bids from private companies for exclusive rights to broadcast in specified areas and at certain times.
- Where a socially necessary but economically unviable service is provided in a market—mediated environment, government can subsidize provision of the service by means of a franchise. An example of this can be seen in the way subsidies are paid by local authorities for uneconomic but socially necessary bus services. Following the Transport 1985, local authorities wishing to support such services can invite tenders from interested bus operators to provide thcm. Successful bidders are awarded a franchise type of contract that allows the bus operator to keep the revenue which it generates from passengers, subject to meeting the minimum requirements of the local authority in terms of timetables, reliability, etc.
- Even though a public service is not market mediated at the point of delivery, production methods may nevertheless be market mediated, and part of the production function may be provided through a franchise agreement. Such an arrangement can have benefits for customers where the franchisee is rewarded partly on the basis of feedback from users. A recent application of this type of franchise can be found in the field of higher education (see Palmer, 1992).
- In the UK, possibly the longest-established public sector franchise is seen in the Post Office. In addition to government-owned 'Crown' post officcs, 'sub'-post offices have traditionally been operated on a franchise basis in smaller towns. Franchises have been taken up by a variety of small shops and newsagents and generally offer a more limited range of postal services compared to Crown offices.

HIGHER EDUCATION EXPANDED AND MARKETED THROUGH FRANCHISED CHANNELS

Universities and the former polytechnics in England and Wales faced a challenge in 1989 when the Secretary State for Education set a target for the proportion of students studying at higher education level to double by the year 2014. One solution to the inevitable pressure that this would place on universities has been the development of a franchised system of delivering degree and HND programmes through local colleges of further education.

While there had been many long-standing examples of collaboration between the further and higher education sectors in providing specialized courses (for example, agricultural engineering), the new interest in franchising borrowed many of the practices from private sector service franchising. The new wave of franchising involved a local college of further education delivering all or part of a higher education programme in a manner prescribed by the university. For the latter, franchising offered a number of attractive benefits:

- Franchising allowed the institution to overcome short-term capacity constraints imposed by buildings and staff availability, particularly where spare resources existed within the FE sector.
- Parts of some degree programmes—such as first-year foundation courses—may be relatively easy to provide as they require less specialized staff and equipment to deliver them. It becomes possible to provide these elements of a course more cheaply at colleges of further education which are not burdened with the overhead costs associated with research and specialized library resources. A university may be finan-

cially better off by taking a 10 per cent franchise fee and letting somebody else deliver a course, rather than taking the whole of a student's fee income and having to pay the costs of delivery itself.
- On the marketing side, franchising allows higher education to be made locally available, for all or part of a course. This may offer important new opportunities for some segments of the population—for example, mature students, who may be put off by the prospect of moving away from home into the uncertain world of higher education.

For local colleges of further education there were also numerous attractions to taking on a higher education franchise:

- Faced with the prospect of a decline in the number of 16–18-year-olds on which colleges had traditionally relied, participation in the expanding higher education sector allowed full use of facilities to be maintained.
- The addition of higher education courses added to the status of the college and could become a valuable stimulus to staff.

Many franchised operations grew rapidly during the late 1980s—for example, the Lancashire Polytechnic scheme started with 11 students in 1984, but by 1991 accounted for 531 students in nine franchised colleges.

Both the university and the local college become involved in the marketing of franchised courses. The franchised college can appeal to its local population on the basis of being a caring local community facility, while the university can add to this at both a local and a national level. If the reputation of the university is itself weak, the task of recruiting students for franchised colleges will be more difficult.

At the heart of an educational franchise is the requirement to maintain consistent standards so that a student studying at a franchised college receives substantially the same education as one at the franchising university. Vetting of colleges at the outset is crucial to ensure that they have the staff, accommodation and technical resources capable of delivering the specified course. Once a scheme is running, close monitoring is required from the university on such matters as assessment standards and the quality of teaching materials delivered.

Quality control of franchise colleges was an issue highlighted in an HMI report into higher education provision within the further education sector (HMI, 1991). The report indicated that quality control had failed from the beginning of many franchise operations—for example, through poor

specification of requirements at the outset and some of the essential quality requirements not having been met. The importance of clear and unambiguous guidelines for course operation and regular monitoring systems was emphasized. A number of universities that had tried to introduce totally new courses to franchised colleges without having had any experience of delivering the course themselves encountered much the same difficulties as would any private sector franchisor.

A franchise relationship between university and college will last for as long as it is in both organizations' interests for it to do so. A college could, in many cases, run a course on its own without reference to a university, but against the saving in franchise fees must be set the greater cost and difficulty of recruiting students who may be unaware of the qualities of the college. Students may perceive a franchised course that is validated by a university as being much more valuable than one offered by a local college in its own name.

10.10   ACCESSIBILITY THROUGH CO-PRODUCTION

Some service organizations choose to make their services available to consumers in combination with other goods and services with the collaboration of another producer. The outputs of the two organizations can be quite diverse. For example, a finance company could offer loan facilities in conjunction with customers buying hi-fi equipment. Other examples include a combined train fare and museum admission ticket and a combined hotel and travel offer.

On other occasions, a service can be made available in combination with similar services provided by potential competitors. The basis for doing this is that the combined value of the enlarged service offer will generate more business and ultimately be of benefit to all service providers involved. In this way, many regional travel tickets allow passengers to travel on the trains and buses of potentially competing operators, thereby making public transport as a whole a relatively attractive option. Similarly, banks benefit by sharing cash-dispenser networks. Those sharing gain a competitive advantage over a bank that chooses to go it alone with its own dedicated but smaller network. In Britain, as in most Western countries, restrictive practices legislation restricts such co-production where it is deemed to restrict competition in a manner that is against the public interest.

10.11   DEVELOPMENTS TO INCREASE ACCESSIBILITY

The means by which an organization makes its services available to consumers need to be periodically reviewed to reflect the changing marketing environment, especially the nature of competition, technological developments and new legislative constraints and opportunities. The needs of the service as it passes through its lifecycle and the changing strengths and weaknesses of the organization may also call for a reassessment of strategy. Here, a number of important factors affecting future service accessibility decisions are considered:

- New technology can allow a much greater integration of intermediaries to cut down on slow bureaucratic procedures. As an example, new data-processing techniques allow airlines and tour operators to provide much quicker and more comprehensive facilities through travel agents, overcoming many of the previous communications constraints imposed by mail and telephone methods of making services available.
- Having established itself in a market through an independent intermediary, a service principal may seek to gain more influence over its outlets by acquiring its own. An example of this is found in the UK mortgage market, where greater competition during the mid-1980s led many financial service providers to acquire their own chains of estate agents, for whom an important objective was to sell the principal's own financial services.
- In many service industries the effects of new technology and the desire of organizations to develop closer relationships with their customers can result in a reduction in the number of intermediaries used and the greater use of direct marketing techniques.

AIRLINES FIND SALVATION IN TICKET DISTRIBUTION

A major development in services distribution systems in recent years has been the creation of multi-user computer-based systems.

Their growth has had a particularly significant effect on the way travel services are distributed through agents. Until quite recently, the installation of computer terminals in agents' premises was costly, but recent falls in the price of hardware and software have allowed even small agencies to obtain the necessary equipment.

Computerized Reservation Systems (CRS) give airlines and tour operators the opportunity to gain competitive advantage over their competitors in a number of ways. Many of them realized that an agent would recommend a service principal who could rapidly respond to their request. Here, a reliable, easy-access, user-friendly CRS offered advantages over much slower telephone conversations. There were also cost considerations, both for the agent who was able to improve its productivity and to the service principal who could cut the cost of operating its reservations system. Computerized reservations systems also allowed the latter to match supply with demand more effectively and to collect payment from agents more quickly.

The early days of computerized reservations systems saw tour operators and airlines developing systems in apparent isolation from each other, resulting in a nightmare scenario for travel agents of the need to invest time and space in several different VDU terminals. In Britain, this threat was initially reduced by the development of multi-access systems, which allow a number of service principals to share a central computer system. Agents would dial a central computer which then switched their message to the appropriate service principal. Travicom was such a system, backed by British Airways, which was linked to over 30 airlines worldwide.

More recently, the development of single-access computerized reservations systems has created a new generation of information intermediaries. A handful of worldwide systems allow travel agents to access comprehensive information on flight availability, departure times, car hire and hotel accommodation. The largest system—Sabre—is owned by American Airlines and in 1991 it took bookings for 1.6 million flights daily and dealt with twenty times that many enquiries for over 740 airlines who use its service. The development of worldwide computerized reservation systems is reflected in the merger between them that has created a number of highly efficient, comprehensive world-class systems. In Europe, the market for computerized reservation systems is dominated by Amadeus (owned by Lufthansa, Air France and Iberia) and Galileo (based in the UK but owned by 11 European and US airlines). The latter announced in March 1992 that it was to merge with the US-based Apollo system, to create a new system with 40 per cent of the US and 30 per cent of the European markets. Further mergers (for example, between Sabre and Amadeus) have only failed because of the technical incompatibility of the different systems.

Although most CRS systems were initially developed by airlines to make access to their services easier, once they had grown significantly, they tended to become autonomous services in their own right, and not merely an outlet for the airline's core service. Not only did agents demand a comprehensive and unbiased information service, anti-trust legislation in the USA and other countries insisted that such systems should show no bias towards the airline's own services.

Airlines' computerized reservation systems have come of age, and apart from allowing airlines to manage their businesses more efficiently, they enable them to earn additional valuable income by selling their services to third parties. In 1991, the income that American Airlines earned from its Sabre system was more than it received from its entire cargo operation and its profitability was greater than the entire flying operations. In the early 1990s, the unprofitability of many airline operations resulted in a common joke among many of them that they would rather sell their fleet of aircraft and concentrate solely on providing information services.

10.12 MAKING THE TANGIBLE COMPONENTS OF THE SERVICE OFFER AVAILABLE TO CONSUMERS

For some services, tangible goods are a vital element of the overall offering and a strategy is needed for making them available to consumers. Managing the availability of tangibles assumes importance for a number of reasons:

- Tangibles may be vital in giving pre-sales evidence of a service offering in the form of printed brochures, order forms, etc. An indication of the logistical problems in making brochures available to potential customers is provided by the task facing Thomson Holidays. If the company was to distribute 50 copies of its main summer holiday brochure to each of over 7000 ABTA travel agents in Britain, it would need to move over 350 000 brochures. The fact that Thomson produces multiple brochures aimed at different segments of the holiday market makes the logistical task even greater.

- Tangibles often form an important component of a service offer, and failure to deliver them reduces the quality of a service or makes it impossible to perform at all. This is true of fast-food restaurant chains for whom perishable raw materials have to be moved regularly and rapidly.
- Sometimes the fundamental purpose of a service process is to make goods available. Retailers and equipment—rental companies provide a service, but without a strategy to move the associated goods effectively, this service becomes of little value.
- The freight transport service sector exists solely to move goods.

Where tangibles form an important part of a service offer their efficient and effective distribution can give an organization a competitive advantage. An inefficient and unreliable distribution system can negate a restaurant chain's efforts at improving service quality if it is unable to deliver advertised meal offers. There are many texts covering the subject of physical distribution management in detail (e.g. Martin (1986), Rushton and Oxley (1989)). Here, a brief overview of the key elements of a physical distribution system is offered.

10.12.1 Physical distribution management

The design of a physical distribution system begins by setting objectives. Ideally, a system should make the right goods available in the right places at the right time. Against this must be balanced the need to minimize the cost of distribution, therefore objectives are stated in a form which involves a trade-off. For example, a holiday-tour operator may realistically aim to deliver 80 per cent of brochure requests to travel agents within 3 working days at the minimum possible cost. Distribution objectives, in turn, are based on an assessment of distribution needs. While a fast-food restaurant chain may be happy to live with a 3-day delivery objective for orders for packaging materials, 24-hour delivery may be required for perishable foods. The importance of rapid and reliable delivery of fresh food would be reflected in a greater willingness to pay premium prices for a service that is capable of meeting objectives. Failure to deliver could have a harmful effect on sales and reputation.

Physical distribution system can be seen as comprising six basic elements that can be manipulated to design an optimum system. These are shown in Figure 10.4 and the management decisions which need to made in respect of each of these are considered below.

Suppliers A marketing-oriented service organization must balance the need to have supply sources close to customers against economics of scale which may be obtained from having one central point of supply. Where markets are turbulent, the distribution system may favour suppliers who are closest to the customer rather than necessarily the cheapest sources of production. During a period of market turbulence, a domestic tour operator may source brochures at home rather than wait for them to be delivered from a possibly cheaper source overseas.

Outlets These can range from the individual household through to the largest hypermarket. If the unique offer of a service is home delivery, strategy must identify the most efficient and effective means of moving associated tangibles to customers' homes.

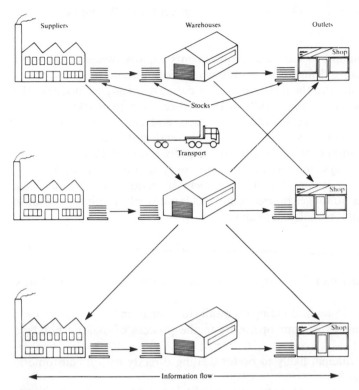

Figure 10.4 Elements of a physical distribution system

Stocks These need to be held in order to provide rapid availability of goods and contingencies against disruptions in production. Stocks also occur because of the need to achieve economies of scale in production, resulting in initially large stockholdings that are gradually reduced until the next production run. Seasonal patterns of production and consumption may also contribute towards fluctuating stock levels. The need to make stock readily available has to be offset against minimizing the cost of stockholding which can result from capital charges, storage charges and the risk of obsolescence.

Warehouses These are incorporated into a system to provide a break-of-bulk point and to hold stocks. A company must decide on the number and nature of the warehouses that are incorporated into its system, particularly the balance between the need for local and accessible warehouses against efficiency savings that favour large warehouses. Automation of warehouses with the development of computerized picking systems is increasingly favouring larger ones. A typical national supermarket in the UK would now include just half a dozen strategically located warehouses in its distribution system to serve a national chain of outlets.

Transport This moves stocks from manufacturers to retail outlets and sometimes—as in the case of mail order or home delivery of milk—to final consumers. Transport is becoming an increasingly important element of distribution systems, with goods tending to travel for longer average distances within the system. Road haulage has become the dominant form of goods transport within Britain, accounting in 1990 for over 60 per cent of all tonnage carried (Department of Transport, 1991).

Information flow   The need to respond to customer requirements rapidly, while at the same time keeping down stockholding levels, demands a rapid flow of information. The development of JIT systems has only been possible with the improvement of data-processing techniques. The introduction of bar codes has achieved notable results in this respect. A supermarket can now know minute by minute the state of stocks for all its products and can order replacement stocks—by an electronic data link—for delivery from a regional distribution centre the following day. The regional distribution centres can similarly rapidly re-order stocks from their suppliers. The development of JIT systems has allowed not only a more reliable level of availability of goods to the final consumer but also retailers to reduce warehouse space provided within shops. Because it is no longer necessary to hold large stocks locally, warehouse space can be turned over to more valuable sales-floor space.

REVIEW QUESTIONS

1. What are the most important factors influencing the location decision for a proposed new gymnasium?
2. Of what value are modelling techniques in deciding on retail store location?
3. In what ways does a travel agent assist tour operators in the process of making holidays available to its customers?
4. In what situations is a service principal likely to prefer dealing directly with its customers, rather than through intermediaries?
5. Using examples, contrast the role of 'push' and 'pull' methods of making services available within the services sector.
6. Analyse the potential problems and opportunities for a dry-cleaning company seeking to expand through franchising.

PRICING OF SERVICES

OBJECTIVES

After reading this chapter, you should be able to understand:

- The role of price in developing the marketing mix for services
- Factors influencing an organization's price decisions, including organizational objectives, cost levels, strength of demand, level of competition and external price regulations
- The development of price strategies for services
- Methods of implementing a programme of tactical pricing
- Specific issues raised in the pricing of public and internally traded services

11.1 INTRODUCTION

For services distributed through market mechanisms, price is the financial mediating device by which exchange takes place between service providers and their customers. Within the services sector, the term 'price' often passes under a number of names, sometimes reflecting the nature of the relationship between customer and provider. Professional service companies therefore speak of fees, while other organizations use terms such as fares, tolls, rates, charges and subscriptions. The art of successful pricing is to establish a price level which is sufficiently low that an exchange represents good value to consumers yet high enough to allow a service provider to achieve its financial objectives.

The importance of pricing to the development of marketing strategy is reflected in the diverse range of strategic uses to which it is put:

- At the beginning of the life of a new service, pricing is often used to gain entry to a new market. As an example, a firm of estate agents seeking to extend its operations to a new region may offer initially very low commission rates in order to gain awareness and entry to the local market.
- Price is used as a means of maintaining the market share of a service during its life and is used tactically to defend its position against competitors.
- Ultimately, for organizations working to financial objectives, prices must be set at a level that allows them to meet their financial objectives.

While most services are market mediated through the price mechanism, services are more likely than goods to be made available to consumers by methods where price is not the focal point of the exchange. Many public sector services are provided to the end-user at either no charge or at one that bears little relation to the value of a service to the consumer or producer. Public services such as museums and schools that have sought to adopt marketing principles often do not have any control over the price element of the marketing mix. The reward for attracting more visitors to a museum or pupils to a school may be additional centrally derived grants, rather than income received directly from the users of the service.

11.2 ORGANIZATIONAL INFLUENCES ON PRICING DECISIONS

It was noted in Chapter 3 that organizations show a wide variation in the objectives they seek to achieve. An analysis of corporate objectives is a useful starting point for understanding the factors which underlie price decisions. Some commonly found organizational objectives and their implications for price decisions are analysed below.

11.2.1 Profit maximization

It is often assumed that all private sector organizations exist primarily to maximize their profits and that this will therefore influence their pricing policies. In fact, the concept of profit maximization needs to be qualified with a time dimension, for marketing strategies which maximize profits over the short run may be detrimental to achieving long-term profits. An organization charging high prices in a new market may make that market seem very attractive to new entrants, thus having the effect of increasing the level of competition in subsequent years and thereby reducing long-term profitability. Also, the time frame over which profitability is sought can affect pricing decisions. If a new service is given an objective to break even after just one year, prices may be set at a low level in order to capture as large a share of the market as quickly as possible, whereas a longer-term profit objective may have allowed the organization to tap relatively small but high-value segments of its markets in the first year and save the exploitation of lower-value segments until subsequent years. The concept of profit maximization has a further weakness in the service sector, where it can be difficult to establish clear relationships between costs, revenue and profits (see below).

11.2.2 Market-share maximization

It is frequently argued (for example, Cyert and March, 1963) that it is unrealistic to expect the managers of a business to put all their efforts into maximizing profits. To begin with, there can be practical difficulties in establishing relationships between marketing strategy decisions and the resulting change in profitability. Second, management often does not directly receive any reward for increasing its organization's profits. Its main concern is to achieve a satisfactory level of profits rather than the maximum possible. It can be argued that managers are more likely to benefit from decisions that increase the market share of their organization, (for example, through increased promotion prospects and job security), even though greater overall profits could probably have been achieved by more ruthlessly pruning those activities that made no contribution towards overheads.

An objective to maximize market share may be very important to service industries where it is necessary to achieve a critical mass in order to achieve economies of scale, and therefore a competitive advantage. The price competition which accompanied the evolving structure of DIY retailing in the UK in the 1980s was based on the desire of the main competitors to achieve economies of scale in buying, distribution and promotion, and thereby achieve long-term profitability.

11.2.3   Survival

Sometimes the idea of maximizing profits or market share is a luxury to a service provider—the main objective is simply to survive and to avoid the possibility of going into receivership. Most businesses fail when they run out of cash flow at a critical moment when debts become due for payment. In these circumstances, prices may be set at a very low level simply to get sufficient cash into the organization to tide it over its short-term problems. During the Gulf War in 1991, demand for air travel fell significantly, putting severe pressure on the resources of many airlines who suffered doubly from the increase in aviation fuel prices. In a bid to stay afloat, many were forced to lower fares considerably simply in order to keep cash flowing into the business over what they thought would be the last hurdle before regaining a long-term growth path.

11.2.4   Social considerations

Profit-related objectives still have little meaning for many public sector services. At one extreme, the price of many public services represents a tax levied by government based on wider considerations of the ability of users to pay for the service and the public benefits of providing that service. Thus, in the UK, most basic health services are provided without charge to the end-user, but various additional services, such as private rooms in National Health Service hospitals, are charged on the basis that those who can afford such facilities should provide more resources to be used for the central health-care functions of the service. Where public services are provided in a more market-mediated environment, pricing decisions may nevertheless be influenced by wider social considerations. An example is provided by non-vocational educational classes run by local authorities, where adult literacy may be seen as something to be encouraged and therefore offered at no charge, or only a very nominal one. On the other hand, authorities may consider it unjustified to subsidize golf-tuition classes which would probably be attended by people who could afford to pay a relatively high price, thereby providing more resources for the education authority's wider social objectives.

It can sometimes be difficult to establish the extent to which public sector service organizations are operating to social as opposed to financial objectives, for even with clearly specified financial objectives, politicians are prone to interfere in pricing decisions. British Rail's InterCity operation has clear financial objectives, but this did not prevent the government intervening at the end of 1991 to hold down proposed fare increases on certain commuter routes into London. At the time it was argued by the government that the proposed increases were unreasonable as the quality of service had not increased correspondingly, but cynics noted that in the run-up to a general election, this interference in pricing had the greatest beneficial effects in a number of marginal parliamentary constituencies.

Although social objectives are normally associated with public sector services, they can sometimes be found within the private sector. Services provided by employers for their staff are often priced at a level that does not reflect their true value, but instead contributes towards staffs' total benefit package. Examples include staff restaurants and sports clubs that are often priced at much lower levels than their normal market value.

In practice, organizations work to a number of objectives simultaneously. For example, a market-share objective over the short term may be seen as a means towards achieving a long-term profit-maximizing objective.

11.3   FACTORS INFLUENCING PRICING DECISIONS

An organization's objectives determine the desired results of pricing policies. Strategies are the means by which price is used to achieve these objectives. Before discussing pricing strategy, it is

Figure 11.1   The key influences on price decisions

useful to lay the groundwork by analysing the underlying factors that influence price decisions. Four important bases for price determination can be identified:

- What it costs to produce a service
- The amount that consumers are prepared to pay for it
- The price that competitors are charging
- The constraints on pricing that are imposed by outside agencies

The cost of producing a service represents the minimum price that a commercial organization would be prepared to accept over the long term for providing it. The maximum price achievable is that which customers are prepared to pay for the service—this will itself be influenced by the level of competition that is available to customers to satisfy their needs elsewhere. Government regulation may intervene to prevent organizations charging the maximum price that consumers would theoretically be prepared to pay. These principles are illustrated in Figure 11.1.

11.3.1   Costs as a basis for pricing

Many empirical studies have shown the importance of costs as a basis for determining prices within the service sector. For example, Zeithaml *et al.* (1985) in their study of service firms in the USA found that it was the dominant basis for price determination.

At its most simple, a 'cost-plus' pricing system works by using historical cost information to calculate a unit cost for each type of input used in a service-production process. Subsequent

Total drivers' wage costs	£125000	
Total drivers' hours worked	45000	
Cost per driver's hour		£2.77
Total vehicle running costs	£100000	
Total mileage operated	250 000	
Vehicle operating costs per mile		£0.40
Total other overhead costs	£30000	
Overhead per mile operated		£0.12
Required return on sales turnover	15%	

For a price quotation based on a 200-mile journey requiring 12 hours of driver's time:

Total price =

200 miles × £0.40	=	£80.00
12 hours × £2.77	=	£33.24
Overheads (based on mileage):		
200 hours × £0.12	=	£24.00
Total	=	£137.24
Add 15% margin	=	£20.59
TOTAL PRICE	=	£157.83

Figure 11.2 'Cost-plus' method of price setting for a coach operator

price decisions for specific service outcomes are based on the number of units of inputs used, multiplied by the cost per unit, plus a profit margin. This method of setting prices is widely used in service industries as diverse as catering, building, accountancy and vehicle servicing. An example of how of a coach-hire operator might calculate its prices on this basis is shown in Figure 11.2.

There are many reasons why 'cost-plus' type pricing methods assume great importance in the services sector:

- Prices are easy to calculate and allow the delegation of price decisions for services that have to be tailored to the individual needs of customers. For example, every building, vehicle-repair or landscape gardening job is likely to be unique and a price for each job can be calculated by junior staff using standard unit costs for the inputs required to complete the job at a predetermined profit margin.
- Where an agreement is made to provide a service, but the precise nature of the service that will actually be provided is unknown at the outset, a contract may stipulate that the final price will be based in some way on costs. Thus a garage agreeing to repair a car brought in by a customer with an unidentified engine noise could not realistically give a price quotation before undertaking the job and examining the nature of the problem. In these circumstances, the customer may agree to pay an agreed amount per hour for labour, plus the cost of any parts which the garage buys in.
- Trade and professional associations often include codes of conduct that allow the service provider to increase prices only beyond those originally agreed in an estimate on the basis of the actual costs incurred. Solicitors and accountants, for example, who need to commit more resources to complete a job than was originally allowed for in their quotation are bound by their professional bodies to pass on only their reasonable additional costs.

Against these attractions, pricing services on this basis presents a number of problems:

- In itself, cost-based pricing does not take account of the competition that a particular service faces at any particular time, nor of the fact that some customers may value the same service more highly than others.
- Calculating the costs of a particular service can in fact be very difficult, and often more so than in the case of goods. One reason for this is the structure of costs facing many services businesses. The costs of producing a service can be divided into those that are variable and those that are fixed. Variable costs increase as service production increases, whereas fixed costs remain unchanged if an additional unit of service is produced. Fixed costs therefore cannot be attributed to any particular unit of output. Between these two extremes are semi-fixed costs which remain constant until a certain level of output is reached, when expenditure on additional units of productive capacity is needed. The particular problem of many service industries is that fixed costs represent a very high proportion of total costs, resulting in great difficulty in calculating the cost of any particular unit of service.

The importance of fixed costs for a number of service industries is illustrated in Table 11.1, where variable costs are defined as any cost that varies directly as a result of one extra customer consuming a service for which there is currently spare capacity. Thus one more passenger on a domestic flight from London to Aberdeen will only result in nominal additional variable costs of an additional in-flight meal and the airport departure tax that has to be paid for each passenger. The cost of cabin crews and aircraft depreciation would not change, nor would those more remote fixed costs such as head-office administration and promotion.

It can be argued that over the long term, all costs borne by a business are variable. In the case of the airline, if the unit of analysis is a particular flight rather one individual passenger, so the proportion of costs that are variable increases. Thus if the airline withdrew just one return journey between the two points, it would save fuel costs, making fuel a variable cost. It would probably also save some staff costs, but may still have to incur aircraft-depreciation costs and those of the more remote head-office administration. If the whole route was closed, even more costs would become variable—staff employed at the terminal could be cut, as could the flight crews. It may be possible for the airline to avoid some of its aircraft-depreciation costs by reducing the size of its fleet. Even promotional costs would become variable as part of the airline's advertising would no longer need to be incurred if the service was closed completely.

High levels of fixed costs are associated with a large amount of interdependency between the services that make use of the fixed-cost elements. Thus the cost of maintaining a retail bank branch network is fixed over the short to medium term, yet the network provides facilities for a wide range of different service activities—current accounts, mortgages, business loans and foreign currency business, to name but a few. Staff may be involved in handling each of these activities in the course of a working day and it is likely that no special space is reserved exclusively for each activity. For many of these activities, the short-term direct costs are quite negligible—for example, the direct cost of one order to change pounds into dollars is little more than the cost of a receipt slip. But users of this service would be expected to contribute towards the overhead costs of staff and space. There is frequently no obvious method by which these fixed costs can be attributed to specific units of output, nor even to particular types of service. The fixed costs for money exchange could, for instance, be allocated on the basis of the proportion of floor space occupied, proportion of staff time used, proportion of total turnover, or some combination of these bases. Allocation bases are often the result of judgement and political infighting. They can change as a result of argument between cost-centre managers, who invariably feel that their product is contributing excessively to fixed costs and may put forward an argument why their pricing base is putting them at a disadvantage in the marketplace against competitors who have a simpler cost structure. In the end, cost allocation is a combination of scientific analysis and bargaining.

Table 11.1 Fixed and variable costs in selected service industries

Service	Fixed costs	Variable
Restaurant	Building maintenance Rent and rates Waiters and cooks	Food Washing-up costs
Bank mortgage	Staff time Building maintenance Corporate advertising	Sales commission Paper and postage
Domestic air journey	Aircraft maintenance and depreciation Head-office administrative costs	Airport departure tax In-flight meal
Hairdresser	Building maintenance Rent and rates	Shampoos used

While it may be possible to determine costs for previous accounting periods, it can be difficult to predict what future costs will be. This is a particular problem for services contracted to be provided at some time in the future. Unlike goods, it is not possible to produce the service at known cost levels in the current period and to store it for consumption at some future time. Historical cost information is often adjusted by an inflation factor where service delivery is to be made in the future, but it can be difficult to decide what is the most appropriate inflation factor to use for a specific input. Where input costs are highly volatile (for example, aviation fuel), one solution is for a service producer to pass on part of the risk of unpredictable inflation to customers. Charter airlines frequently do this by requiring customers to pay for any increase in fuel costs beyond a specified amount.

Marginal cost pricing A special kind of cost-based pricing occurs where firms choose to ignore their fixed costs. The price that any individual customer is charged is based not on the total unit cost of producing it but only on the additional costs that will result directly from servicing that additional customer. For services with a high elasticity of demand, it is used where the bulk of a company's output has been sold at a full price which recovers its fixed costs, but in order to fill remaining capacity, the company brings its prices down to a level which at least covers its variable, or avoidable, costs. Marginal cost pricing is widely used in service industries with low short-term supply elasticity and high fixed costs. It is common in the airline industry, where the perishability of a seat renders it unsaleable after departure. Rather than receive no revenue for an empty seat, an airline may prefer to get some income from a passenger, so long as the transaction provides a contribution by more than covering the cost of additional food and departure taxes.

Against the attraction of filling spare capacity and getting a contribution towards fixed costs where otherwise there would have been none, marginal cost pricing does have its problems. The greatest danger is that it can be taken too far, allowing too high a proportion of customers to be carried at marginal cost, with insufficient customers charged at full price to cover the fixed costs. Many airlines and holiday-tour operators have fallen into the trap of selling holidays on this basis, only to find that their fixed costs have not been fully covered. Another problem is that it may devalue customers' perception of a service. If a service promoted for its prestige value can be sold for a fraction of its original price, it may leave potential customers wondering just what is the true value of the service. It may also cause resentment from customers who had committed themselves to a service well in advance, only to find that their fellow-consumers obtained a lower price by booking later (and thereby also making marketing planning much more difficult for many service operators). Companies can try to overcome problems of marginal cost pricing by differentiating the marginally costed product from that purchased at full price. Holiday-tour operators, for instance, reduce the price of last-minute standby holidays but offer no guarantee of the precise accommodation to be used—or even the resort—unlike the full-price holiday, where these are clearly specified.

11.3.2 Demand-based pricing

The upper limit to the price of a service is determined by what customers are prepared to pay for it. In fact, different customers often put differing ceilings on the price for a service. Successful demand-oriented pricing is therefore based on effective segmentation of markets to achieve the maximum price from each segment. Price discrimination can be carried out on the basis of:

- Segmentation between different groups of users
- Segmentation between different points of use
- Segmentation between different types of use

Price discrimination between different groups of users Effective price discrimination requires groups of consumers to be segmented in such a way that maximum value is obtained from each segment. Sometimes this can be achieved by simply offering the same service to each segment but charging a different price. Thus a hairdresser can offer senior citizens a haircut that is identical to the service provided to all other customer groups in all respects except price. The rationale could be that this segment is more price-sensitive than others and therefore additional profitable business can only be gained by sacrificing some element of margin. By performing more haircuts, even at a lower price, a hairdresser may end up having increased total revenue from this segment, while still preserving the higher prices charged to others.

On other occasions, the service offering is slightly differentiated and targeted to segments who are prepared to pay a price that reflects its differential advantages. This is particularly important where it is impossible or undesirable to restrict availability of a lower price to certain predefined groups. Thus airlines operating between London and New York offer a variety of fare and service combinations to suit the needs of different segments. One segment requires to leave at short notice and is typically travelling on business. For the employer, the cost of not being able to travel at short notice may be high, so this group is prepared to pay a relatively high price in return for ready availability. A subsegment of this market may wish to arrive refreshed ready for a day's work and be prepared to pay more for the differentiated first-class accommodation. For non-business travellers, another segment may be happy to accept a lower price in return for committing themselves to a particular flight three weeks before departure. Another segment with less income to spend on travel may be prepared to take the risk of obtaining a last-minute standby flight in return for a still lower-priced ticket.

The intangible and inseparable nature of services make the possibilities for price discrimination between different groups of users much greater than is usually the case with manufactured goods. Goods can easily be purchased by one person, stored and sold to another. Thus if price segmentation allowed one group to buy bread at a discounted price it would be possible for this group to buy bread and sell it on to people in higher-priced segments, thus reducing the effectiveness of the segmentation exercise. Because services are produced at the point of consumption, it is possible to control the availability of services to different segments. Therefore a hairdresser who offers a discounted price for the elderly segment is able to ensure that only such people are charged the lower price. The elderly person cannot go into the hairdressers to buy a haircut and sell it on to a higher-price segment.

BRITISH RAIL ARRIVES AT MARKET-BASED PRICES

British Rail has often been accused of confusing its customers by offering so many different fares. For a return journey from Leicester to London, no fewer than 23 different fares are charged. A number of market segments have been identified and a distinctive marketing mix has been developed for each. The business traveller typically has a need for the flexibility of travelling at any time of the day and because an employer is often picking up the bill, this segment tends to be relatively insensitive to the price charged. Some segments of the business market demand higher standards of quality and are prepared to pay a higher price for 'First-Class' travel or for an executive package that includes additional services such as meals and car parking. Leisure segments are, on the whole, more price-sensitive and are prepared to accept a lower standard of service offered. For example, the student segment is charged a lower fare in return for accepting restrictions on the number of trains on which tickets can be used.

A keen eye is kept on the competition in determining prices. The student is more likely than the business person to accept the coach as an alternative and therefore the Leicester-to-London student rail fare of £14 is pitched against the equivalent student coach fare of £10.75, the higher train fare being justified on the basis of a superior service offering. For the business traveller, the comparison is with the cost of running a car, parking in London and, more importantly, the cost of an employed person's time. Against these costs, the full fare of £41 appears to be relatively good value. For the family market, the most serious competition is presented by the family car, so a family discount railcard allows the family as a unit to travel for the price of little more than two adults.

The underlying cost of a train journey is difficult to determine as a basis for pricing. The provision of the track and terminals represents high fixed costs that can be allocated to individual trains by a number of methods. British Rail recognizes that trains operating in the morning and afternoon peak periods cost more to operate as the fixed costs of track, terminal and vehicles used solely for the peak period cannot be spread over other off-peak periods. The underlying costs of running commuter trains has been publicly cited by British Rail as the reason for increasing season ticket charges by greater than the rate of inflation during recent years, although the fact that commuters often have no realistic alternative means of transport may have also been an important consideration in raising prices.

The political environment has had an important effect on British Rail's pricing policies. Before the 1960s, railways were seen as a public service and fares were charged on a seemingly equitable basis which was related to production costs. Fares were charged strictly on a cost per mile basis, with a distinction between first and second class, and a system of cheap day returns which existed largely through tradition. From the 1960s, British Rail has moved away from social objectives with the introduction of business objectives. With this has come a recognition that pricing must be used to maximize revenue rather than to provide social equality. However, government intervention occasionally comes into conflict with British Rail's business objectives. For example, the latter was instructed to curtail fare increases during the 1980s as part of the government's anti-inflation policy, and again in the autumn of 1991 to reduce some proposed Inter-City fare increases on account of the poor quality of service on some routes.

The strict relationship between distance and price no longer exists following the advent of market-led fares. In its applications of pricing policy, British Rail has been held out as an example of good railway business practice. Many overseas governments still hold that railways are a vital part of their public infrastructure and that rail fares should reflect wider public needs and not be determined solely by market forces.

Price discrimination between different points of consumption   Service organizations frequently charge different prices at different service locations. The inseparability of service production and consumption results in service organizations defining their price segments on the basis of both the point of consumption and the point of production. Service producers often take the production outlet as a basis for price discrimination in its own right. An example of this is found in chains of retail stores, who, in addition to using price to target particular groups of customers, also often charge different prices at different stores. For example, Marks & Spencer charges higher prices for some of its products in its central London stores than in its provincial ones. For its overseas branches, it is faced with very different markets again, requiring separate price lists. Some retailers with a combination of large superstores and small convenience stores can justify charging higher prices in its convenience stores. A town-centre branch of a Gateway supermarket is likely to attract people calling in for a few items for which they would be less prepared to shop around than if they were doing a week's shopping.

Some production locations may offer unique advantages to consumers. Unlike goods, the service offering cannot be transferred from where it is cheapest to produce to where it is most valued, hence service providers can charge higher prices at premium sites. Hotels fall into this category, with high premiums charged by chains for those hotels located in 'honeypot' areas. A hotel room in the centre of Stratford-upon-Avon offers much greater benefit to consumers who wish to visit the theatre without a long drive back to their accommodation. Hotel prices for comparable standards of hotel therefore fall as distance from the town centre increases.

Travel services present an interesting example of price discrimination by location, as operators frequently charge different prices at each end of a route. Thus the New York-to-London air-travel market is quite different from the London-to-New York one. The state of the respective local economies, levels of competition and customers' buying behaviour may differ between the two markets, resulting in different pricing policies in each. Because of the personal nature of an airline ticket and the fact that discounted return tickets specify the outward and return dates of travel, airlines are able to avoid tickets being purchased in the low-priced area and used by passengers originating from the higher-priced one.

Within Britain, price discrimination by area is frequently used by British Rail for journeys to and from London. Fares from provincial towns to London are frequently priced at a lower rate than equivalent fares from London, reflecting—among other things—the greater competitive advantage that British Rail has in the London-based market.

Price discrimination by time of production   Goods produced in one period can usually be stored and consumed in subsequent ones. Charging different prices in each period could result in customers buying goods for storage when prices are low and running down their stockpiles when prices are high. Because services are instantly perishable, much greater price discrimination by time is possible.

Services often face uneven demand which follows a daily, weekly, annual, seasonal, cyclical or random pattern. At the height of each peak, pricing is usually a reflection of:

- The greater willingness of customers to pay higher prices when demand is strong, and
- The higher cost that often results from service operators trying to cater for short peaks in demand.

The greater strength of demand which occurs at some points in a daily cycle can occur for a number of reasons. In the case of rail services into the major conurbations, workers must generally arrive at work at a specified time and may have few realistic alternative means of getting there. A railway operator can therefore sustain a higher level of fares during the daily commuter peak period. Similarly, the higher rate charged for telephone calls during the day is a reflection of the greater strength of demand from the business sector in that period. As well as price discrimination between different periods of the day, it can also occur between different periods of the week (for example, higher fares for using many British Rail services on a Friday evening) or between different seasons of the year (holiday charter flights over Bank Holiday periods).

Price discrimination by time can be effective in inducing new business at what would otherwise be a quiet period. Hotels in holiday resorts frequently lower their prices in the off-peak season to tempt additional price-sensitive customers. Similarly, many public utilities lower their charges during off-peak periods (for example, lower electricity tariffs are available during the night).

In most cases of price discrimination by time there is also some relationship to production costs. An argument of telephone operators and electricity generators is that the marginal cost of producing additional output during off-peak periods is relatively low. As long as peak demand has covered the fixed costs of providing equipment, off-peak output can be supplied on a marginal cost basis (see above).

11.3.3 Competitor-based pricing

There are very few situations in which an organization can set its prices without taking account of the activities of its competitors. Just who the competition is against which prices are to be compared needs to be carefully considered, for competition can be defined in terms of the similarity of the service offered, or merely similar in terms of the needs that a product satisfies. For example, a chain of video-rental shops can see its competition purely in terms of other rental chains, or it could widen it to include the cinema and satellite television services, or wider still to include any form of entertainment.

Having established what market it is in and who the competition is, an organization must establish what price position it seeks to adopt relative to its competitors (see Chapter 3). This position will reflect the service's much wider marketing-mix strategy, so if the company has invested in providing a relatively high-quality service whose benefits have been effectively promoted to target users, it can justifiably pitch its price level at a higher level than its competitors.

For services targeting similar subsegments of a market, the pricing decisions of competitors will have a direct bearing on an organization's own pricing decisions. Price in these circumstances is often used as a tactical weapon to gain short-term competitive advantage over rivals. In a market where the competitors have broadly similar cost structures, price cutting can be destabilizing and result in costly price wars with no sustainable increase in sales or profitability. An example of price being used to gain short-term competitive advantage is provided by the Midland Bank's decision to offer free banking for customers who kept their accounts in credit. While the Midland's market share increased in the short term, it was neutralized during the following year when competing banks offered free banking to match that originally offered by Midland. The market eventually stabilized with all the main competitors offering free banking and all had lost revenue as a result.

Going-rate pricing   In some services markets that are characterized by a fairly homogeneous service offering, demand is so sensitive to price that a firm would risk losing most of its business if it charged just a small amount more than its competitors. On the other hand, charging any lower would result in immediate retaliation from competitors, resulting in no-one being any better off. An example of this situation is found in areas where a number of restaurants cluster closely together, all offering a basically similar service at a similar price. For the price-sensitive diner, the 'Dish of the Day' may be set at the going rate, while more specialized dishes for which there is less direct competition are priced at a premium.

Where cost levels are difficult to establish, charging a going rate can avoid the problems of trying to calculate costs. As an example, it may be very difficult to calculate the cost of renting out a video film, as the figure will be very dependent upon assumptions made about the number of uses over which the initial purchase cost can be spread. It is much easier to take price decisions on the basis of the going rate among nearby competitors.

Sealed-bid pricing   Many industrial services are provided by means of a sealed-bid tendering process where interested parties are invited to submit a bid for supplying services on the basis of a predetermined specification. In the case of many government contracts, the organization inviting tenders is often legally obliged to accept the lowest-priced tender, unless exceptional circumstances can be shown. Price thus becomes a crucial concern for bidders, regardless of their efforts to build up long-term brand values which in other markets might have allowed them to charge a premium price. The first task of a bidding company is to establish a minimum bid price based on its costs and required rate of return, below which it would not be prepared to bid. The more difficult task is to put a maximum figure on what it can bid. This will be based on expectations of what its competitors will bid, based on an analysis of their strengths and weaknesses.

In Britain, the Local Government Acts of 1980 and 1988 and the Housing and Local Government Act 1989 have required an increasingly comprehensive list of local authority services to be opened up to compulsory competitive tendering. The list began with refuse collection, but has subsequently been extended to include housing maintenance, grounds maintenance, the operation of sports and leisure centres and most recently, the provision of accounting and architectural services. The desire of many organizations to gain business by underbidding has resulted in many financial failures part-way through the operation of a contract.

11.4   DISTORTIONS TO MARKET-LED PRICING DECISIONS

It is often too simplistic to say that organizations set prices on the basis of market forces and naive to presume that markets themselves are perfectly competitive. In practice, services are more likely than goods to be supplied in non-competitive environments and this results in government intervention in pricing decisions. The nature and consequences of such market distortions are discussed below.

11.4.1   Pricing in non-competitive markets

In most Western countries there is a presumption that competition is necessary as a means of minimizing prices charged to consumers. While price competition may appear to act in the short-term interests of consumers, this normally restrains the combined profits of competitors. It is common therefore for competing organizations to seek to come to some sort of agreement among themselves about prices to be charged in order to avoid costly price competition.

To counter this, most Western governments have actively sought to eliminate practices that reduce the level of competition in a market. In the UK, the Resale Price Maintenance Act 1964 and the Restrictive Trade Practices Act 1976 (and, at a European level, Articles 85 and 86 of the Treaty of Rome) between them limit the ability of services producers to collude with their fellow-producers in fixing prices. Agreements which have the effect of regulating prices are only allowed by the Restrictive Trade Practices Court if it can be shown that they are—on balance—in the public interest. Thus a Monopolies and Mergers Commission investigation of 1992 into car retailing acknowledged that restrictive franchises had the effect of keeping prices higher than in many other countries, but essentially recommended retaining the present system on account of compensating benefits to the public. On the other hand, an investigation into the package-holiday industry in 1985 concluded that the way in which tour operators dictated minimum selling prices of holidays to their travel agents did not allow for price competition among agents, and considered such agreements to be, on balance, against the public interest.

The Office of Fair Trading has power to order an investigation by the Monopolies and Mergers Commission of any anti-competitive practices that may have the effect of restricting choice or causing prices to be higher than they need be. A recent referral in respect of the credit-card industry, for example, criticized the existing pricing structure, stating that it involved cross-subsidization between different groups of consumers and imposed unnecessary restrictions on retailers handling credit-card sales. In response to this, most credit-card companies revised their pricing structure by lowering interest charges levied on those who use their cards as a means of credit and balancing this by a fixed annual charge on all cards, including those held by customers who use their card solely as a means of payment.

Many covert price-fixing agreements have been alleged by the Monopolies and Mergers Commission and referred to the Restrictive Practices Court where such activities have been declared illegal. As an example, during 1984, the court sought injunctions to stop the ferry operators Sealink and Townsend Thoresen fixing fares on routes between Northern Ireland and Scotland, while two years later an agreement between the four largest betting-shop operators not to compete on price was declared illegal. At a local level, many services providers have understandings—if not outright agreements—which have the effect of limiting price competition. In this way, local estate agents and building contractors have frequently been accused of covert collusion not to engage in price competition, although obtaining evidence of such collusion can be very difficult.

11.4.2   Regulation as a factor influencing pricing decisions

In addition to some publicly provided services where prices are set as a matter of social policy, many private sector services companies must take account of various regulations in setting their prices. These can be classified as:

- Direct government controls to regulate monopoly power
- Government controls on price representations

Direct government controls to regulate monopoly power   During the 1980s, the privatization of many UK public sector utilities resulted in the creation of new private sector monopolies. To protect the users of these services from exploitation the government response has been twofold. First, it has sought to increase competition, in the hope that this in itself will be instrumental in moderating price increases. In this way, the electricity-generating industry was divided into a number of competing private suppliers (National Power, Powergen, Nuclear Electric, Scottish Power and Scottish Hydro), while conditions were made easier for new generators to enter the market. In some cases, measures to increase competition have had only limited effect, as in the very limited competition faced by the newly privatized British Telecom from Mercury Communications—the latter has only had a significant effect on moderating British Telecom prices for large business users.

For many of the newly privatized monopolies, effective competition proved to be an unrealistic possibility. The result has been the creation of a series of regulatory bodies that can determine the level and structure of charges made by these utilities. Thus British Telecom, British Gas and the regional water companies are controlled by Oftel, Ofgas and Ofwat, respectively. In the case of British Gas, Ofgas regulations allow the company to increase gas-supply charges in line with changes in energy prices, but the price for ancillary services such as standing charges and repairs can rise only by the rate of inflation, less 2 per cent. The regulatory bodies have power to prohibit any practices which allow the companies to exploit their monopoly position. In 1989, Ofgas investigated complaints from industrial users of gas that price discrimination was being practised against those users who had no alternative source of energy supply, favouring those for whom a choice was available. Ofgas held that this was an anti-competitive practice and ordered British Gas to publish a tariff of gas prices that would be applied to all industrial users.

LOWER CHARGES AT BT

British Telecom (BT) has often been accused of having a licence to print money through its domination of the UK telecommunications market. In arriving at pricing decisions, BT has to balance a number of factors. In the short term, it has a relatively protected market with very little price pressure from competitors. However, this protected market will not last for ever, especially as increasing competition from newly licensed cable and portable telephone networks is likely to put greater pressure on its prices during the next decade. BT has therefore sought to set its prices to make the most of its monopoly while it enjoys it. Against this, most of its prices are regulated by the government watchdog Oftel, whose Director-General must respond to public and political pressure. A widespread feeling that BT prices are higher than in most Western countries, plus reports of very large salaries earned by the senior executives of BT, has caused BT to act cautiously for fear of provoking the regulator to impose unduly harsh price controls on the company. Some price incentives—such as its provision of the free 'Child-line' telephone service—are designed to present a better image of a caring BT in an attempt to fend off more extreme demands for price controls. Other initiatives such as lower charges on trunk routes or off-peak reductions offered on Sunday afternoons during November and December 1992 are designed to boost revenue against competitive pressure or where demand is price-sensitive.

Nevertheless, BT recognizes the power that its regulating body has over its prices, but has generally sought to agree these with Oftel rather than have them imposed. In June 1992, Oftel accepted a proposal from BT which affected its prices in a number of ways:

- Increases in a basket of all BT services were to be limited to the increase in the Retail Price Index (RPI), less 7.5 per cent.
- Rental charges for ordinary exchange lines were to be limited to the RPI, less 2 per cent.
- For all other individual services within the basket of services, no single item was to be raised by greater than the level of the RPI. This agreement was included in response to previous complaints that average price increases had hidden the fact that this still allowed some individual prices to increase quite significantly, often at the expense of captive groups of customers.
- To protect infrequent users of telephone services, a low-user scheme was revised to benefit those private customers who use less than 240 units per quarter.

Government controls on price representations In addition to controlling or influencing the actual level of prices, government regulation can have the effect of specifying the manner in which price information is communicated to potential customers. At a general level, the Consumer Protection Act 1987 requires that all prices shown should conform to the Code of Practice on pricing. Misleading price representations that relegate details of supplementary charges to the small print or give an attractively low lead in prices for services that are not in fact available are made illegal by this Code. There are other regulations which affect specific industries. The Consumer Credit Act 1974 requires that the charge made for credit must include a statement of the Annual Percentage Rate (APR) of interest. Also within the financial services sector, the Financial Services Act 1986 has resulted in quite specific requirements in the manner in which charges for certain insurance-related services are presented to potential customers.

11.5 PRICING STRATEGY

The factors that underlie pricing decisions have now been described. This section now analyses how these factors can be manipulated to give strategic direction to pricing policy so that organizational objectives can be met. The challenge here is to make pricing work as an effective element of the marketing mix, combining with the other mix elements to give a service provider a profitable market position. An effective strategy must identify how the role of price is to function as a service goes through different stages in its life, from the launch stage through growth to maturity.

This analysis of pricing strategy will consider first, the development of a strategy for a new service launch, and second, price adjustments to established services. In practice, of course, it is often not easy to distinguish the two situations, as where an existing service is modified or relaunched.

11.6 NEW-SERVICE PRICING STRATEGY

In developing a price strategy for a new service, two key issues need to be addressed:

- What price position is sought for the service?
- How novel is the service offering?

The choice of price position cannot be separated from other elements of the marketing mix—Chapter 3 analysed some of the issues involved in selecting a position for a new service. For many consumer services, the price element can itself interact with the product-quality element of a positioning strategy. This can happen where consumers have difficulty in distinguishing between competing services before consumption, and the price charged is seen as an important indication of the quality of the service. Private consumers choosing a painter or decorator with no knowledge of their previous work record may be cautious about accepting the cheapest quotation, on the basis that it may reflect an inexperienced decorator with a poor record.

The novelty of a new service offering can be analysed in terms of whether it is completely new to the market or merely new to the company providing it but already available from other sources. In the case of completely new services the company will have some degree of monopoly power in its early years, as where one bank introduces a new ATM facility to a town which is the only such facility for many miles. On the other hand, the launch of a 'me too' service to compete with established services is likely to face heavy price competition from its launch stage. The distinction between innovative and copycat services is the basis of two distinct pricing strategies—'price skimming' and 'saturation pricing', which are now examined.

11.6.1 Price skimming

Most completely new product launches are aimed initially at the segment of users who can be labelled 'innovators' consumers who have the resources and inclination to be trendsetters. This group includes the first people to buy innovative services such as telephone banking and portable telecommunications. Following these will be a group of early adopters, followed by a larger group often described as the 'early majority'. The subsequent 'late majority' group may take up the new service only when the product market itself has reached maturity. 'Laggards' are the last group to adopt a new service and only do so when the product has become a social norm and/or its price has fallen sufficiently. A diffusion model is illustrated in Figure 12.2.

Price-skimming strategies seek to gain the highest possible price from the early adopters. When sales to this segment appear to be approaching saturation level, the price level is lowered to appeal to the early adopter segment that has a lower price threshold at which it is prepared to purchase the service. This process is repeated for the following adoption categories.

The art of effective pricing of innovative services is to identify who the early adopters are, how much they are prepared to pay and how long this price can be sustained before competitors come on the scene with imitation services at a lower price. A price-skimming strategy works by gradually lowering prices to gain access to new segments and to protect market share against new market entrants. This pricing strategy is closely related to the concept of the product lifecycle. A typical price-skimming strategy showing price levels through time is shown in Figure 11.3(a).

It can be argued that diffusion patterns for new industrial services are generally different from those for consumer services. There is less of a desire to be a trendsetter for its own sake and a greater rationality in purchase decisions, limiting the opportunities for price skimming to

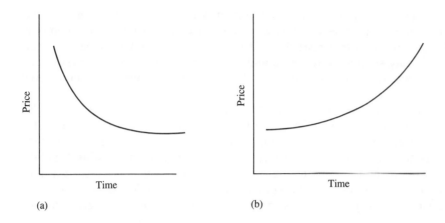

Figure 11.3   Pricing strategies compared: (a) price skimming; (b) saturation pricing

situations where commercial buyers can use innovative service inputs to gain an early competitive advantage.

For many innovative services, the trend of falling prices may be further enhanced by falling costs. Lower costs can occur due to economies of scale (for example, the cost per customer of providing the technical support for a home-shopping service declines as fixed costs are spread over more volume of throughput) and also to the experience effect. The latter refers to the process by which costs fall as experience in production is gained (see Abell and Hammond, 1979, page 107). It is of particular strategic significance to service industries, since by pursuing a strategy to gain experience faster than its competitors, an organization lowers its cost base and has a greater scope for adopting an aggressive pricing strategy. The combined effects of these two factors can be seen in the UK portable telephone market, where high initial prices have been brought down by the ability of network operators to spread their capital costs over increasing numbers of users. Also, operators have learnt from experience how a given level of service can be provided more efficiently—for example, through adjusting transmitter locations.

11.6.2   Saturation pricing

Many 'new' services are launched as copies of existing competitors' services. In the absence of unique product features, a low initial price can be used to encourage people who show little brand loyalty to switch service suppliers. Once an initial trial has been made, a service provider would seek to develop increased loyalty from its customers, as a result of which they will be prepared to pay progressively higher prices. A saturation pricing strategy is shown diagrammatically in Figure 11.3(b).

The success of a saturation pricing strategy is dependent upon a sound understanding of the buying behaviour of the target market, in particular:

- *The level of knowledge that consumers have about prices* for some services, such as the rate of interest charged on credit cards, consumers typically have little idea of the charge they are currently paying, or indeed of the 'going rate' for such charges. Therefore any attempt to attract new customers on the basis of a differential price advantage may prove unsuccessful. Other incentives (for example, free gifts or money-off vouchers for reduced-price holidays) may be more effective in inducing new business. Sometimes companies providing a diverse range of services may offer low prices on services where price comparisons are commonly made but charge higher ones on other related services where consumer knowledge is lower. Customers of solicitors may shop around for a standard service such as house conveyancing but may be more reluctant to do so when faced with a non-routine purchase such as civil litigation.

- *The extent to which the service supplier can increase prices on the basis of perceived added value of the service offering;* the purpose of a low initial price is to encourage new users of a service to try a service and return later, paying progressively higher prices. If the new competitor's service is perceived to offer no better value than that of the existing supplier, the disloyalty which caused the initial switching could result in a switching back at a later date in response to tactical pricing. Worse still, a new service could be launched and experience teething troubles in its early days, doing nothing to generate a perception of added value.
- *The extent to which the service supplier can turn a casually gained relationship into a long-term committed one;* incentives are frequently offered to lessen the attractiveness of switching away from a brand. This can take the form of a subscription rate for regular purchase of a service, or offering an ever-increasing range of services which together raise the cost to consumers of transferring their business elsewhere. Banks may offer easy transfers between various savings and investment accounts and, in doing so, aim to reduce the attractiveness of moving one element of the customer's business elsewhere.

In some cases where co-production of benefits among consumers is important, a high initial uptake may itself add value to the service offering. A telecommunications operator offering data-exchange facilities will be able to provide a more valuable service if large numbers of users are contracted to its system, offering more communications possibilities for potential new users. In the same way, airport landing slots become increasingly valuable to an airline operator as an airport becomes progressively busier, as each airline is able to offer a more comprehensive and valuable set of potential connections to customers. In both cases, a low initial price may be critical to gain entry to a market, while rising prices is consistent with increasing value to the users of the service.

11.6.3 Evaluating strategic pricing options

In practice, pricing strategies often contain elements of skimming and saturation strategies. The fact that most new services are in fact adaptations and are easy to copy often prevents a straightforward choice of strategy. Even when a price strategy has been adopted and implemented, it may run off-target for a number of reasons:

- Poor market research may have misjudged potential customers' willingness to pay for a new service. As an example, National Westminster Bank sought to charge personal customers £3.50 per quarter for using its innovative telephone banking service 'Actionline'. Take-up was less than expected, with the result that the charge was abolished after less than one year. The service provider may have misjudged the effect of price competition from other services, which, although different in form, satisfied the same basic needs.
- Competitors may emerge sooner or later than expected. The fact that new services can often be easily and quickly copied can result in a curtailment of the period during which an organization can expect to achieve relatively high prices. As an example, an optician opening the first eye-care centre in an expanding market town may expect to enjoy a few years of

higher price levels before competitors drive them down, only to find that another optician had a similar idea and opened a second eye-care centre shortly afterwards.

- The effects of government regulation may be to extend or shorten the period during which a company has a protected market for its new market. The announcement by the British government in 1991 that it was to license a number of new cellular telephone networks had the effect of bringing forward the time when the existing operators have to face direct competition on price.

11.6.4   Price leader or follower?

Many services markets are characterized by a small number of dominant suppliers and a large number of smaller ones. Perfect competition and pure monopoly are two extremes that rarely occur in practice. In markets which show some signs of interdependency among suppliers, firms can often be described as price makers or price followers. Price makers tend to be those who, as a result of their size and power within a market, are able to determine the levels and patterns of prices which other suppliers then follow. Within the UK insurance industry, the largest firms in the market often lead changes in rate structures. Price takers, on the other hand, tend to have a relatively low size and market share and may lack product differentiation, resources or management drive to adopt a proactive pricing strategy. Smaller estate agents in a local area may find it convenient to simply respond to pricing policies adopted by the dominant firms. To take a proactive role themselves may bring about a reaction from the dominant firms which they would be unable to defend on account of their size and standing in the market.

11.7   SERVICE-MIX PRICING

Multi-output service providers usually seek to set the price of a new service in relation to the prices charged for other services within their mix. A number of product relationships can be identified as being important for pricing purposes:

- Optional additional services
- Captive services
- Competing services

Optional additional services are those which a consumer chooses whether or not to add to the core service purchase, often at the time that the core service is purchased. As a matter of strategy, an organization could seek to charge a low lead-in price for its core service but to recoup a higher margin from the additional optional services. Simply breaking a service into core and optional components may allow for the presentation of lower price indicators, which through a process of rationalization may be more acceptable to some customers. Research may show that the price of the core service is the only factor which potential customers take into account when choosing between alternative services. In this way, many travel agents and tour operators cut their margins on the core holiday that they sell but make up some of their margin by charging high prices for optional extras such as travel insurance policies and car hire.

Captive services occur where the core service has been purchased and the additional services can be supplied only by the original provider of the core service. Where these are not specified at the outset of purchasing the core service, or are left to the discretion of the service provider, the latter is in a strong position to charge a high price. Against this, the company must consider the effect the perception of high exploitative prices charged for these captive services will have on customer loyalty when a service contract comes due for renewal. An example of captive service pricing is provided by many car-insurance companies who, after selling the core insurance policy, can treat the sale of a 'green card' (which extends cover beyond the geographical limits defined in the policy) as a captive sale.

Competing services within the mix occur where a new service targets a segment of the population which overlaps the segments served by other products within the organization's mix. By a process of 'cannibalization', a service provider could find that it is competing with itself. In this way, an airline offering a low-priced direct service from Glasgow to Frankfurt may find that the low price—in addition to generating completely new business—has a side-effect in abstracting traffic from its connecting services from Glasgow to London and from London to Frankfurt.

11.7.1 Price bundling

Price bundling is the practice of marketing two or more services in a single package for a single price. Bundling is particularly important for services on account of two of their principal characteristics. First, the high ratio of fixed to variable costs that characterize many service organizations makes the allocation of costs between different services difficult and sometimes arbitrary. Second, there is often a high level of interdependency between different types of service output from an organization. In this way, the provision of a cashpoint card and cheque guarantee card becomes an interdependent part of the current bank-account offering for which most UK banks do not charge separately.

Price bundling of diverse services from an organization's service mix is frequently used as a means of building relationships with customers. In this way, a mortgage could be bundled with a household contents insurance or legal protection policy. Where the bundle of service represents ease of administration to the consumer, the service organization may be able to achieve a price for the bundle that is greater than the combined price of the bundle's components.

'Pure' bundling occurs where services are available only in a bundled form (for example, where a tour operator includes insurance in all its package holidays) whereas 'mixed' bundling allows customers to choose which specific elements of the service offering they wish to purchase.

In his study of price bundling, Guiltinan (1987) showed that as service firms expand their range of service outputs, simple cost-based or price-follower strategies become too simplistic for two reasons. First, as the number of services offered increases, the opportunities for differentiation and bundling are enhanced. Second, the high ratio of fixed to variable costs typical of many service industries make average costing increasingly arbitrary as fixed-cost allocations change with the expansion of the service range. Bundling reduces the need to allocate fixed costs to individual services.

11.8 TACTICAL PRICING

Pricing strategy determines the role of price within the marketing mix over the strategic planning period. In practice, manoeuverability around the central strategy will be needed to allow detailed, local application of the overall strategy. This is the role of tactical pricing. The distinction between strategic and tactical pricing can sometimes be difficult to draw. In highly competitive, undifferentiated services markets, the development of tactical plans can be all-important and assume much greater importance than for a service where an organization has more opportunity for developing a distinctive strategic price position. Some of the tactical uses of pricing are analysed below:

- Tactical pricing can provide short-term competitive advantage. Periodic price reductions can be a means of inducing potential customers to try a service, whether it is new or established. The price cut can be a general across-the-board reduction or it could be targeted (for example, by the use of vouchers). The extent of the uptake will be dependent on the importance of price comparisons, how often consumers of that type of service typically make casual purchases and are not tied to a relationship with another supplier (for example, lower single bus fares may result in little additional demand if a large proportion of travellers are tied to a season ticket with another operator) and consumers' perceptions of the price offer. Economic rationality may expect that sales of a service will increase as its price is reduced. However, the price reduction may reduce the perceived value of a service, leading to a feeling that its quality has been eroded. Subsequent price increases may give the impression that the service is overpriced if it could be offered previously at a lower price. There may also be significant price points at which a service is perceived as being of good value. A transatlantic air ticket priced at £199 may be perceived as offering much better value than one at £200.

  Even if economic rationality is assumed on the part of consumers, it can be difficult to predict the effects of a price change. Comparison with previous occasions when price was adjusted assumes that all other factors are the same, whereas in reality, many factors, such as the availability of competitors' services and general macro-environmental considerations require some judgement to be made about how a similar price cut may perform this time around.

- Tactical pricing can be used to remove unplanned excess supply. The strategic price position sought by an organization may be incapable of achievement on account of excess supply, within both the organization and the market generally. A temporary price cut can be used to bring demand and supply back into balance. The excess supply of air seats that occurred following the outbreak of the Gulf War in 1991 resulted in airlines responding tactically with very low prices in order to attract segments who may not otherwise have had the resources to travel. Pricing can also be used to capitalize on excess demand relative to supply. In addition to removing discounts and increasing prices, firms can remove low-margin elements from their service mix in order to maximize their returns from high-margin lines.

- Short-term tactical pricing can be used to protect markets against new entrants. Where a new entrant threatens the existing market of an established supplier, the latter may react with short-term price reductions where price comparisons are commonly made. If the new entrant is a small, opportunist company seeking to make inroads into the larger dominant firm's market, a low price may force the new company to respond with low prices, putting strain on its initial cash flow and possibly resulting in its withdrawal from the market, if not ceasing to trade completely. Following deregulation of bus services in the UK in 1986, many established bus companies found themselves challenged by relatively small companies. A common response was to run 'free buses' ahead of the new entrant's service. The new entrant often did not have the resources to match this pricing tactic for any length of time and often quickly withdrew from the market.

- Differential pricing with respect to time which may have been part of the strategic pricing plan can be implemented by a number of tactical programmes. Off-peak discounts are frequently used in such industries as rail travel, telecommunications and hotels. The converse of peak surcharges can also be employed—for example, the supplementary charge levied by British Rail for travel on certain West Country holiday trains on the busiest weekends of the year. Other options include offering added-value price bundles at certain periods (for example, shopping vouchers for off-peak ferry passengers) and subtly altering a service offering and making it available only at certain times (a restaurant may slightly differentiate lunch from dinner and charge more for the latter on account of the willingness of customers to pay more for a social evening meal).

- Similarly, differential pricing with respect to place must be translated from a strategic plan to a tactical programme. Implementing differential pricing by area is relatively easy for services on account of the difficulty in transferring service consumption. Hotels and shops—among others—often use different price lists for different locations, depending upon the local competitive position, and such lists are often adjusted at short notice to respond to local competitive pressure. Sometimes a common base price is offered at all of an organization's service outlets, and tactical objectives are achieved by means of discounts that are available only at certain locations. Reduced-price vouchers offered by a national hotel chain may have their validity restricted to those locations where demand is relatively weak. Local tactical pricing can cause problems where national promotion is price-led. In this case, a number of services can be advertised at a nationally uniform rate, while related services are priced according to local market conditions.

- For differential pricing between different consumer segments, the problem of turning a strategy into a tactical programme hinges on the ease with which segments can be isolated and charged at different prices. Because services are consumed at the point of production, it is often easy to confine price differences within small segments of a market. In this way, British Rail is able to ensure that only students are able to use reduced-price student tickets by asking for identification as the service process is being undertaken. Sometimes the implementation of a highly segmented pricing programme can cause problems for services providers where compromise needs to be made between the desire for small, homogeneous segments and for segments which are of a worthwhile size to service. As an example, British Rail places all elderly people in one segment which is offered a low-price Senior Citizen Railcard. However, the simplicity of this large homogeneous segment is offset by the fact that many people in it are well off and less price-sensitive, and may even be travelling on business. There is also the problem with this form of price segmentation that goodwill can be harmed where arguments develop over a customer's eligibility to a particular price offer.

- Tactical pricing programmes are used to motivate distributors. Where a service is provided through an intermediary, the difference between the price that a customer pays and the amount that the service principal receives represents the intermediary's margin. In some cases, price sensitivity of the final consumer is low but awareness of margins by the intermediary high, requiring tactical pricing to be directed at maintaining intermediaries' margins relative to those offered by competitors. An example is provided by holiday insurance offered by travel agents. Customers do not typically shop around for this ancillary item of a package holiday, but travel agents themselves decide which policy to recommend to their clients largely on the basis of the commission level they can earn. Price charged to the final consumer can also affect an intermediary's motivation to sell a principal's service. If the agent perceives the selling price to be too high, they may give up trying to promote it in favour of a more realistic and attractive competitor. On the other hand, if the price is too low, intermediaries working on a percentage commission basis may consider that the reward for them is not worth their effort. The glut of cheap air fares to Spain offered by tour operators during 1987 with prices from just £29 resulted in many travel agents being unable to cover their agency costs on a transaction and therefore they did not actively push these low-priced offers to their customers.

11.9 PRICING STRATEGIES FOR PUBLIC SECTOR SERVICES

It was noted at the beginning of this chapter that price is often a very constrained element of the marketing mix for public services where there is much less freedom to implement the strategies and tactics of pricing described above. The concept of public services can be ambiguous in the context of marketing, and this is especially so with pricing. Some publicly provided services can operate in a market-mediated environment where pricing policies do not differ significantly from those of the private sector. Indeed, legislation frequently requires such services to act as though they were a private sector operator. Local authority-operated bus services are such an example. Other public services can only be sensibly distributed by centrally planned methods where price loses its role as a means of exchange of value.

The pricing of services which by their very nature, require a high degree of central planning but which are expected to exhibit some degree of marketing orientation present particular challenges for marketers. It may be difficult or undesirable to implement a straightforward price–value relationship with individual service users for a number of reasons:

- External benefits may be generated by a service that are difficult or impossible for the service provider to appropriate from individual users. For example, road users within the UK are not generally charged directly for the benefits they receive from the road system. At present, the only significant case where direct charges are levied occurs at toll bridges. Charges for using the remainder of the network are based on a fixed annual road-fund licence charge, variable contributions to general taxation through taxation on fuel and semi-variable contributions through taxation on the purchase and maintenance of motor vehicles. Pedestrians and cyclists are not charged for using the road system. The present methods of charging for roads reflects the technical difficulties in appropriating charges from users and the political problem that access to road space is deemed to be a 'birthright' which should not be restricted by direct charging. Nevertheless, in some countries, the technical and political environment has allowed governments to charge more directly for road space used. In France, for example, many motorways are operated by private sector organizations who charge tolls regulated by the government. In order to attract more usage of their motorways, effort is put into making them more pleasant than the parallel non-toll roads, by such means as the provision of rest areas. In other cases, attempts have been made to charge for the use of urban roads according to the level of congestion present. Such a scheme is in operation in Singapore and has been proposed for the central area of Cambridge. It is interesting to note that inter-urban rail travel in Britain is distributed by market-mediated mechanisms in which price plays a key role, whereas road facilities are distributed by centrally planned mechanisms where price is relatively unimportant. It is possible that, with improved technology, many external benefits could be internalized by charging users directly for the services they consume.
- The benefits to society at large may be as significant as those received by the individual who consumes a service. An early argument for the free provision of doctors' services was that society as a whole benefited from an individual being cured of a disease and therefore not spreading it to other members of the community. Similarly, education and training courses may be provided at an uneconomic charge in order to add to the level of skills available within an economy generally.
- Pricing can be actively used as a means of social policy. Subsidized prices are often used to favour particular groups. For example, prescription charges are related to consumers' ability to pay, with exemptions for the very ill and unemployed, among others. Communication programmes are often used by public services to make the public aware of the preferential prices to which they may be eligible. Sometimes the interests of marketing orientation and social policy can overlap. Reduced admission prices to museums for the unemployed may, at

the same time, help a disadvantaged group within society while generating additional overall revenue through segmenting the market in terms of ability to pay.

Problems can occur in public services which have been given a largely financial, market-oriented brief but in which social policy objectives are superimposed, possibly in conflict. It was mentioned earlier that political considerations have affected the business-led pricing strategy of British Rail. Museums, leisure centres and car-park charges have frequently been at the centre of debate about the relative importance to be attached to economic and social objectives. One solution that has sometimes been adopted is to divide a service into two distinct components, one part being an essentially public service which is provided for the benefit of society at large and the other comprising those elements that are indistinguishable from commercially provided services. In this way, museums have often retained free admission or nominally priced charges for the serious, scholarly elements of their exhibits, while offering special exhibitions which match the private sector in the standard of production and the prices charged. Similarly, public libraries have distinguished between basic book lending, which is provided at no charge as public policy, and video and music rental, where price is used as one element of this marketing to gain competitive advantage over private sector competitors. In some cases, organizations have been completely restructured to reflect the different role which price plays in mediating relationships between the organization and its users. In this way, the Royal Mail was divided into four operating units during 1990, of which one—Royal Mail Letters—retained the social objective to deliver letters within the UK for a fixed price, regardless of distance or location, while the parcels division—ParcelForce—priced its services according to the needs of a very competitive market.

11.10 INTERNAL MARKET PRICING

The development of matrix-type organizations (see Chapter 4) can result in significant internal trading occurring within an organization. Services that are commonly traded internally include photocopying, cleaning, transport and catering. Very often, the price at which services are traded between a department that uses a resource and one that produces that resource does not reflect a competitive market price—indeed, a market as such may not exist. Setting transfer prices can raise a number of issues for an organization, even where external market prices can be readily ascertained. Allowing users of resources to purchase their services from the cheapest source— internal or external—could result in the in-house supplier losing volume to a point where it ceases to be viable, yet its retention may still be required in order to perform specialized jobs that cannot be easily handled by outside contractors. By allowing part of its requirements to be bought-in from outside, an organization may increase the loss incurred by its internal supplier while adding to the profits of outside companies. The internal pricing of services therefore needs to reconcile the possibly conflicting requirements of the in-house production unit to make profits and maintain some capacity against the resource users' requirements to minimize their total expenditure.

A number of possible solutions to the problem of internal pricing can be identified (see Eccles, 1983):

- If an external market exists, a 'shadow' price can be imputed to the transfer, reflecting what the transaction would have cost if it had been bought-in from outside.
- Where no external market exists, bargaining between divisional managers can take place, although the final outcome may be a reflection of the relative bargaining strength of each manager.
- Corporate management could instruct all divisions to trade on an agreed full-cost-pricing basis.
- A system of dual pricing can be adopted where selling divisions receive a market price

(where this can be identified) while the buying division pays the full cost of production. Any difference is transferred to corporate accounts.

- A proportion of the internal service producer's fixed costs can be spread over all resource users as a standing charge, regardless of whether they actually use the services of the unit. This would enable the internal supplier to compete on price relatively easily, while still allowing resource users for whom a higher standard of service is worth paying a premium to buy-in their requirements from outside.

Public services that are provided free of charge to users are often traded within the public sector using price as a means of reconciling the accounts of those groups responsible for service delivery with those responsible for service production. In this respect, an area that has received considerable attention recently is the National Health Service, which is responsible for providing a wide range of services to the public at either no charge or only a nominal one. Instead of being centrally planned, the provision of hospital facilities is now subject to negotiated contracts between hospitals who provide care services and the health authorities and fund-holding general practitioners, who are responsible for buying-in services on behalf of patients. The fund-holding health authorities and GPs clearly want their funds to buy the best available care for their patients at the lowest possible price. The early days of internal trade within the National Health Service saw many of the pricing problems commonly associated with internal trading. The wide discrepancies in prices quoted by different hospitals for the same operation reflected a lack of costing information on which prices were based and the high level of overhead costs associated with many medical facilities. The prospect emerged of whole hospitals being suddenly closed because of their lack of price competitiveness, undoing the benefits of centralized planning which had sought to balance supply and demand for specialized facilities at a regional level. This led the government initially to limit the freedom of fund-holders to move their patients from the hospitals with which they had traditionally dealt to those charging lower prices.

CALLS GROW FOR REFORM OF ELECTRICITY PRICING

Less than a year after privatization of the electricity industry in England and Wales, customers—particularly large industrial users—found themselves complaining bitterly about rising prices and the manipulation of prices by the two dominant electricity generators—National Power and PowerGen. At the heart of the grievance was the electricity industry's internal trading system into which generators sell electricity and from which customers—large and small—buy. This system, known as the Pool, had resulted in volatile upwards movements in prices, yet to a level which, the generators claimed, was still not adequate to cover their costs. Some very large customers had negotiated higher prices direct with the generators, in return for which they were protected from the volatility of Pool prices.

The Pool is a committee made up mainly of the supplying generating companies and the electricity distribution companies. Prices are set on a half-hourly basis by a computer system run by the National Grid Company (itself jointly owned by the distribution companies). Computers also decide, based on information provided by the generators, which plants will run in any given half-hour period. The complex process begins at 10 a.m., when the generators say which power plants they can make available for the next day and for how long. They also say how much they will charge for power from each plant. Computers draw up a schedule of which plants should run, starting with the cheapest and gradually moving up the price curve as demand dictates. The price for electricity from the last plant is the basic price paid for all power generated in the half-hour. But the system also depends on how many plants the generators say they can make available overall. This is because the grid company wants to be sure that enough plant can be brought into use should there be a surge in demand. When supply and demand seem tight because not enough plant is available, the generators get an extra-capacity payment, reflecting the scarcity value of their capacity. It has been suspected that one generator has been declaring relatively few plants available, thus boosting the Pool price of electricity. But by later 'redeclaring' that more plant is available, the company can sell more power, while still getting the higher price. The rules which allow this redeclaration also allow the generator to keep the capacity charge, even though it is based on an earlier declaration.

Another problem in setting prices is the computer software, which has proved to be faulty on occasions. In one period, the effect of mistakenly calling on the expensive plants for supply caused the Pool price to rise to 16p per unit compared with the average of between 2p and 3p.

Other complexities in electricity Pool pricing arise from the role of the state-owned Nuclear Electric, which supplies a significant share of electricity to the Pool and which enjoys a subsidy in the form of an 11 per cent levy on power derived from fossil fuels generated by its competitors.

This case highlights the problems that can occur in setting prices where complex trading arrangements exist. Large industrial users felt aggrieved by the prices that they were charged as a result of this process and prompted the Office of Electricity Regulation (Offer), which is the government's watchdog on the electricity industry, to order an inquiry into Pool pricing at the end of 1991.

REVIEW QUESTIONS

1. What is the relationship between product lifecycle theory and pricing strategy?
2. Give examples to illustrate situations where price competitiveness may be largely absent in services markets.
3. Analyse the product mix of a diverse service organization and identify the pricing strategies used to increase total revenue.
4. Using examples, compare the advantages and disadvantages of cost-plus and marginal-cost pricing.
5. Using a service company of your choice, analyse how price discrimination is practised between different groups of customers.
6. Examine the role that is likely to be played by pricing for a local authority-owned leisure centre.

TWELVE

PROMOTING SERVICES

OBJECTIVES

After reading this chapter, you should be able to understand:

- The role played by promotion in the marketing mix for services
- The impact of core-service attributes on promotional decisions
- The principal elements of the promotion mix and their relationship within promotional campaigns
- Methods used to set promotional objectives, develop promotional strategies, implement programmes and monitor results

12.1 INTRODUCTION

Well-developed marketing strategies and tactics should have the effect of reducing reliance on promotion as a means of achieving customer take-up of a service. A well-formulated service offer, distributed through appropriate channels at a price that represents good value to potential customers, places less emphasis on the promotion element of the marketing mix. Nevertheless, few services—especially those provided in competitive markets—can dispense with promotion completely. The purpose of this chapter is to examine the nature of the strategic and tactical decisions that service organizations must take in formulating this element of the marketing mix.

This chapter considers some of the basic principles of promotion decisions, but places particular emphasis on the distinctive needs of services. These can be related back to some of the distinguishing characteristics of services, in particular:

- The intangible nature of the service offer results in consumers perceiving a high level of risk in the buying process.
- Promotion of the service offer cannot generally be isolated from promotion of the service provider.
- Visible production processes—especially service personnel—become an important element of the promotion mix.
- The intangible nature of services and the heightened possibilities for fraud results in their promotion being generally more constrained by legal and voluntary controls than is the case with goods.

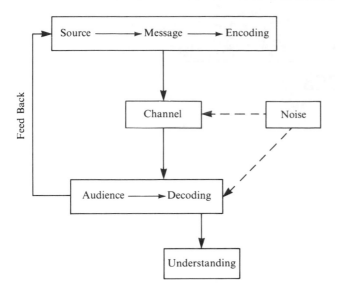

Figure 12.1   The communication process

The promotional function of any service organization involves the transmission of messages to present, past and potential customers. At the very least, these customers need to be made aware of the existence of a service. Eventually, in some way, they should be influenced towards purchase.

12.2   THE COMMUNICATION PROCESS

Promotion involves an on-going process of communication between an organization and its target markets. The process is defined by the answers to the following questions:

- *Who* is saying the message?
- *To whom* is the message addressed?
- *How* is the message communicated?
- To what *effect* was the communication made?

The elements of this process are illustrated in Figure 12.1 and are described in more detail below.

12.2.1   To whom is the message addressed?

The most important element of the communication process is the audience at which communication is aimed. This audience determines what is to be said, when it is to be said, where it is to be said and who is to say it. The target audience of a communication must be clearly defined and this can be done in a number of ways:

- The most traditional method of defining audiences is in terms of social, economic, demographic and geographical characteristics. In this way, audiences are characterized using parameters such as age, sex, social class, area of residence, etc.

- Audiences can be defined in terms of the level of involvement of potential recipients of the communication. For example, a distinction can be made between those people who are merely **aware** of the existence of a service, those who are **interested** in possibly purchasing it and those who **wish to purchase** the service.
- An audience can be identified on the basis of target customers' usage frequency (for example, regular users of an airline are likely to respond to communications in a way different from occasional users).
- Similarly, audiences can differ in the benefits that they seek from a category of service. British Rail aims different messages at leisure users who may seek benefits such as meeting distant friends, compared to business users for whom speed and reliability may be of greatest importance.
- In the case of services supplied to corporate buyers, audiences can be defined in terms of the type and size of business and its geographical location. More importantly, the key decision makers and influencers must be identified and used in identifying the audience. For example, for many corporate travel services, secretaries can be important in choosing between competing services rather than the actual service user, and should therefore be included in a definition of the target audience.

Having defined its target audience, the communicator must then research a number of its important characteristics. For services, one vital aspect to explore is the audience's image of the organization and its services and the degree of image consistency among that audience. An image tends to persist over time, with people continuing to see what they expect to see rather than what actually exists. The image of a service firm and its offers can be significantly influenced by how it is presented and therefore contact personnel play a vital role in the development of this image.

Of course, some elements of an organization's image can be derived through channels other than the formal communication process. Davis *et al.* (1979), for example, found that when differentiating between retail services, customers preferred to be guided by information from friends and other personal contacts rather than the usual promotion mix. This seems to be reinforced by more recent studies on other services, particularly professional ones.

A second important characteristic of the audience justifying research is its degree of perceived risk when considering the purchase of a new service. For highly risky services, customers are likely to use more credible sources of information (for example, word-of-mouth recommendation) and engage in a prolonged search through information sources. People differ markedly in their readiness to try new products and a number of attempts have been made to classify the population in terms of their level of risk taking. Rogers (1962) defines a person's 'innovativeness' as the 'degree to which an individual is relatively earlier in adopting new ideas than the other members of his social system'. In each product area, there are likely to be 'consumption pioneers' and early adopters, while other individuals only adopt new products much later. This has led to a classification of markets into the following adopter categories:

- Innovators
- Early adopters
- Early majority
- Late majority
- Laggards

The adoption process is represented as a normal distribution when plotted over time. After a slow start, an increasing number of people adopt the innovation. The number then reaches a

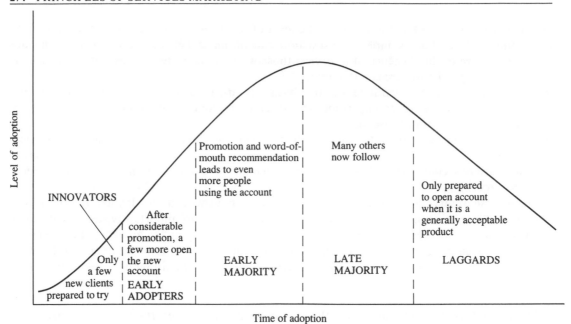

Figure 12.2 Buyer-adoption pattern for a new type of bank account (based on Rogers, 1962)

peak before diminishing as fewer non-adopters remain. A typical adoption distribution pattern is illustrated in Figure 12.2. Innovators are venturesome in that they try new ideas at some risk. Early adopters are opinion leaders in their community (see below) and adopt new products early but carefully. The early majority adopt new ideas before the average person, taking their lead from opinion leaders. The late majority are sceptical, tending to adopt an innovation only after the majority of people have tried it. Finally, laggards are tradition bound, being suspicious of changes. They adopt a new service only when it has become sufficiently widespread that it has now taken on a measure of tradition in itself.

Although adoption processes for goods and services are, in principle, similar, differences can result from services being perceived as riskier than goods. Cowell (1984) notes that services tend to be perceived as more personal than goods and their higher perceived risk occurs because evaluation of quality and value before purchase is difficult. Effective promotion of services must therefore start by understanding the state of mind of potential customers and the information they seek in order to reduce their exposure to risk.

12.2.2 Audience response

Having identified the target audience and its characteristics, the communicator must consider the type of response required from it. This response will have an influence on the source, message and channel of communication.

In most cases, customers are seen as going through a series of stages before finally deciding to purchase a service. It is therefore critical to know these buyer-readiness stages and to assess where the target is at any given time. The communicator will be seeking any one or more of three audience responses to the communication:

- *Cognitive responses* The message should be considered and understood

Table 12.1 Models of buyer states

Domain	AIDA model	Hierarchy of effects (*Lavidge and Steiner, 1961*)	Innovation-adoption model (*Rogers, 1962*)
Cognitive	Awareness	Awareness Knowledge	Awareness
Affective	Interest Desire	Liking Preference	Interest Evaluation
Behavioural	Action	Conviction Purchase	Trial Adoption

- *Affective responses* The message should lead to some change in attitude
- *Behavioural responses* Finally, the message should achieve some change in behaviour (a purchase decision)

Many models have been developed to show how marketing communication has the effect of 'pushing' recipients of messages through a number of sequential stages, finally resulting in a purchase decision. The stages defined in three widely used models of communication—'AIDA', the Hierarchy of Effects and Innovation Adoption models—are shown in Table 12.1.

Communication models portray a simple and steady movement through the various stages, although it should not be seen as ending when a sale is completed. It was noted in Chapter 7 that service organizations increasingly seek to build relationships with their customers, so the behavioural change (the sale) should be seen as the starting point for making customers aware of further offers available from the organization.

Smooth progress through these stages is impeded by the presence of a number of 'noise' factors which are discussed below. The probabilities of success in each stage cumulatively decline due to noise and therefore the probability of the final stage achieving purchase behaviour is very low.

12.2.3 Communication source

The source of a message—as distinct from the message itself—can influence the effectiveness of any communication. Aaker and Myers (1982) identified three major features of sources that influence communication effectiveness:

- If a source is perceived as having power, then the audience response is likely to be compliance.
- If a source is liked, then identification by the audience is a probable response. Important factors here include past experience and reputation of the service organization, in addition to the personality of the actual source of the communication. A salesperson, any contact personnel, a TV/radio personality, etc. are all very important in creating liking.
- If a source is perceived as credible then the message is more likely to be internalized by the audience. Credibility can be developed by establishing a source as important, high in status, power and prestige or by emphasizing reliability and openness.

12.2.4   The message

A message must be able to move an individual along a path from awareness through to eventual purchase. For a message to be received and understood, it must gain attention, use a common language, arouse needs and suggest how these needs may be met. All this should take place within the acceptable standards of the target audience. However, the service itself, the channel and the source of the communication also convey a message and therefore it is important that these do not conflict.

Three aspects of a communication message can be identified—content, structure and format. It is the content that is likely to arouse and change attention, attitude and intention, and therefore the appeal/theme of the message is important. The formulation of the message must therefore include some kind of benefit, motivator, identification or reason why the audience should think or do something. Appeals can be rational, emotional or moral.

Messages can be classified into a number of types, according to their dominant themes. The following are common focal points for them:

- *The nature and characteristics of the organization and the service on offer* For example, the television advertisements for Cathay Pacific Airlines emphasize the high quality of their in-flight service.
- *Advantages over the competition* A British Rail television campaign during the early 1990s emphasized the relative spaciousness and high standards of its seating compared to its airline competitors.
- *Adaptability to buyers' needs* Many insurance companies stress the extent to which their policies have been designed with the requirements of particular age segments of the population in mind.
- *Experience of others* In this way, testimonials of previous satisfied customers are used to demonstrate the benefits resulting from use and the dependability of the service provider. For example, the Midland Bank has used the opinions of ordinary people in its television advertising to extol the virtues of its Meridian bank account.

Recipients of a message must see it as applying specifically to themselves and they must have some reason for being interested in it. The message must be structured according to the job it has to do—the points to be included in the message must be ordered (strongest arguments first or last) and consideration given to whether one- or two-sided messages should be used. The actual format of the message will be very much determined by the medium employed—for example, the type of print if published material, type of voice if broadcast media is used, etc.

12.2.5   Noise

The creator of a message needs to encode it into some acceptable form for an audience to decode and comprehend. Unfortunately, there is likely to be interference between the stages of encoding and decoding, and although it is difficult to eliminate totally such interference in the communication process, an understanding of the various elements of this 'noise' should help to minimize its effects. The potential for 'noise' to hinder the effective communication is usually greater for services than for manufactured goods. Because of the intangible nature of services, expectations of service delivery must be created in peoples' minds without the help of tangible evidence which can be used to describe manufactured goods.

The nature of 'noise' factors can be examined in terms of a simple 'black box' model of buyer behaviour (Figure 12.3). A communication of some sort (either marketer or non-

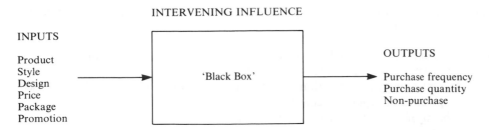

Figure 12.3   'Black box' model of buyer behaviour

marketer dominated) is seen as a stimulus to some form of customer response. Response can be expressed in terms of quantity purchased, frequency of purchase or even non-purchase. The final response, however, is not a straightforward one to the initial stimulus. This stimulus is distorted within the 'black box' process, resulting in different individuals responding in different ways to a similar stimulus. The variables at work within the black box are the noise factors and can be divided into two major types:

- Those that relate to the individual, i.e. psychological factors
- Those that relate to other groups of people, i.e. sociological factors.

Psychological factors   No two individuals are the same in terms of their psychological make-up. Each person undergoes different experiences influencing their personalities, their perceptions of the world, their motives for action and their attitudes towards people, situations and objects. Therefore it is not surprising to find that different people will interpret communications differently.

An individual's experience of a service or service organization is an important influence on how messages about that service are interpreted. Both positive and negative experiences predispose an individual to decode messages in a particular way. Also, the personality of specific members of an audience can significantly influence interpretation of a message. For example, an extrovert may interpret a message differently from an introvert. Similarly, an individual's motives can influence how a message is decoded.

A number of authors (for example, Maslow, 1954; Bayton, 1958) classify motives into those that are biological (such as the need to satisfy hunger, thirst, etc.) and those that are psychological and learned. Maslow speaks of safety, social, esteem and self-actualization requirements while Bayton distinguishes between ego-bolstering, ego-defensive and affective needs. Both agree that in different situations, one of these needs becomes dominant over the others and influences perceptions of the outside world. As an example, an individual who has just come home from work hungry and is about to eat dinner is unlikely to be amenable to information communicated by a life-assurance salesperson that may satisfy some higher-order need for family security.

Sociological Factors   In addition to possessing inherent personal characteristics which influence behaviour, individuals are affected by the presence of other people around them. The conditioning process brought about by the existence of these groups of people can be analysed in terms of the attitudes that individuals develop. Attitudes are learnt and are usually formed as a result of past experience—they are extremely enduring and very influential in determining how a message is perceived. For example, an individual may have a negative attitude towards a particular bank as a result of having previously been refused overdraft facilities by that bank. This negative attitude is likely to distort the individual's interpretation of any marketing communication from the bank. In this context, therefore, the communication should involve an attempt to shift attitude as well as merely to inform.

Attitudes are predispositions to act in a particular situation and involve three elements: cognitive, affective and conative:

- The cognitive element of an attitude involves the knowledge and understanding of the object, person or situation to which there is an attitude.
- The affective element refers to the emotional content of an attitude and is usually expressed in terms of either positive or negative feelings.
- The conative element of an attitude relates to the preparedness on the part of the individual holding the attitude to act positively or negatively if a particular situation involving the object or person arose.

Services marketers have great difficulty in overcoming negative attitudes towards themselves or their services because of the very subjective way in which services are evaluated before, during and after consumption. The possibilities for attitude change are therefore likely to be greater if the service involves tangible aspects that can be produced/offered/displayed. Such tangible elements need to show clearly that quality has improved.

People develop attitudes from a number of sources. In addition to the family, there are many other social groupings that influence how consumers see the world and thus the purchase decisions they make. Great importance is attached to the concept of reference groups. Chisnall (1985) defines reference groups as 'groups with which an individual closely identifies so that they become for him/her, standards of evaluation and the sources of personal behavioural norms'. Reference groups can be divided into those of which an individual is a member ('membership groups') and those to which membership is aspired ('aspirational groups'). Both types of reference group influence how an individual perceives his or her environment and their decisions on goods and services purchases. The existence of reference groups also influences the way in which individuals interpret communications. Hyman (1960) also speaks of a 'reference individual' or 'opinion leader' (Lazarsfeld *et al.*, 1948) who assimilates the communication message and then 'trickles' it down to other members of an audience. This type of process is most important where the cost of a service is high, the amount of service information is low, the service involves significant social and symbolic value and the purchase involves a high level of perceived risk.

Other important sociological influences on behaviour include culture and social class. Individual members of different cultures and classes are likely to interpret messages in different ways. Thus communications offering credit facilities may be interpreted with suspicion within certain social groups who have been conditioned to live within their means, whereas members of other social groups may welcome the opportunities represented by the message.

Past experience, personality, motivation, attitudes and the influence of reference groups can all produce a 'noise' effect and thus distort audience interpretation of a message. Individuals are constantly being bombarded with numerous stimuli (visual, auditory, tactile, etc.), but are likely to select only the stimuli perceived as being important to them:

- Selective perception occurs where communication is perceived in such a way that it merely reinforces existing attitudes and beliefs.
- Selective exposure occurs where individuals make active decisions as to which stimuli they wish to expose themselves. For example, a staunch Conservative Party supporter may consciously avoid a Labour Party political television broadcast.
- Selective reception occurs when an individual remembers only those aspects of the message perceived as being important.

Even if an individual decides to give attention to a message, understands it and remembers it, comprehension may still be different from that which the communicator expected. This perceptual distortion could be caused by those noise factors previously noted, poor encoding on the part of the communicator or poor understanding by the audience itself. It is therefore important to pre-test any marketing communication.

Noise is an extremely difficult variable to eliminate totally from any communication process. However, an understanding of its existence and its potential in hindering effective communication is vital in developing a communication strategy. The best way of minimizing these noise effects is to develop a detailed understanding of the target audience.

12.3 DEVELOPING THE PROMOTIONAL MIX

Having considered 'who says what to whom and with what effect', the next area of concern is 'how?' Developing the promotional mix entails selecting and blending different channels of communication in order to achieve the promotional objectives of the marketing mix. Specifying the objectives of a communication is important if appropriate messages are to be targeted accurately through the most appropriate channels in the most cost-effective manner possible. Typical promotional objectives might be:

- To develop an awareness of and an interest in the service organization and its service products
- To communicate the benefits of buying a service
- To influence eventual purchase of the service
- To build a positive image of the service firm
- To differentiate the service from its competitors
- To remind people of the existence of a service and/or the service firm.

Ideally, these objectives should be quantified as far as possible. Thus promotional objectives for a new type of motor insurance policy may begin with an objective to achieve awareness of the brand name by 30 per cent of the 25–55-year-old insurance-buying public within one year of launch.

The promotion mix refers to the combination of channels that an organization uses to communicate with its target markets. Communication is received by audiences from two principal sources—those within an organization and external sources. The latter includes word-of-mouth recommendation from friends, editorials in the press, etc. which, it has already been noted, may have high credibility in the service-evaluation process. Sources originating within an organization can be divided into those from the traditional marketing function (which can be divided into personal two-way channels such as personal selling and impersonal one-way channels such as advertising), and those from front-line production resources. Because services normally involve consumers in the production process, the promotion mix has to be considered more broadly than is the case with manufactured goods. Front-line operations staff and service outlets become a valuable channel of communication. The elements of the services promotion mix are illustrated in Figure 12.4.

The choice of a particular combination of communication channels will depend primarily on the characteristics of the target audience, especially its habits in terms of exposure to messages. Other important considerations include the present and potential market size for the service (advertising on television may not be appropriate for a service that has a local niche market, for example), the nature of the service itself (the more personal the service, the more effective the two-way communication channel) and, of course, the costs of the various channels.

A very important consideration is the stage that a service has reached in its lifecycle (see

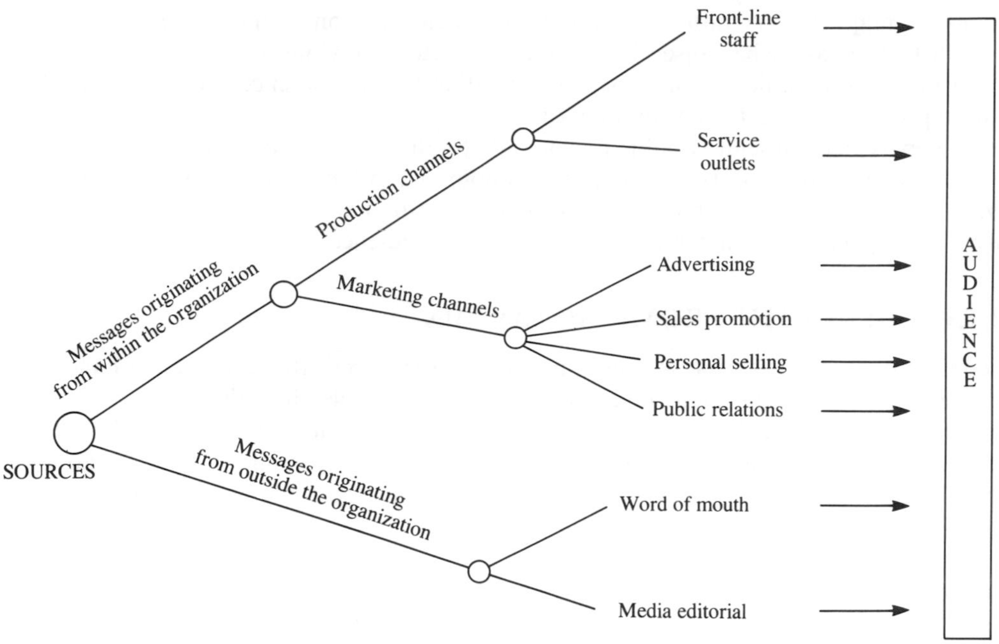

Figure 12.4 Communication channels

Chapter 6). Advertising and public relations are more likely to form important channels of communication during the introductory stage of the lifecycle where the major objective is often to increase overall audience awareness. Sales promotion can be used to stimulate trial and, in some instances, personal selling can be employed to acquire distribution coverage. During a service's growth stage, the use of all producer-derived communication channels can often be reduced, as demand during this phase tends to produce its own momentum through word-of-mouth communications. However, competition can grow during this stage and on into the maturity stage, calling for an increase in advertising and sales promotion activity. Finally, when the service is seen as going into decline, advertising and public relations are often reduced, although sales promotion can still be quite usefully applied. Sometimes services in decline are allowed to die quietly with very little promotion. In the case of many long-life financial services which a company would like to delete but cannot for contractual reasons, the service may be kept going with no promotional support at all.

In the following sections each of the elements of the promotion mix through which communications can be directed is discussed. Before the traditional elements of advertising, sales promotion, personal selling and public relations are considered, attention is given to the role of operational inputs to the promotion mix of service firms.

12.4 THE PRODUCER–CUSTOMER INTERFACE OF THE SERVICES PROMOTION MIX

Inseparability results in consumers being involved in a series of encounters with service producers. During each of these encounters a service organization has an opportunity to communicate with its customers. Without any effort on the part of an organization, customers will pick up messages, whether they are good or bad. With more planning, an organization can ensure that every encounter is turned into an opportunity to convey positive messages that encourage repeat business from customers and encourage them to pass on the message to others. Two important sources of non-marketer-derived messages can be identified within the extended promotion mix of services—front-line employees and the physical environment of the service encounter.

12.4.1   The promotional role of employees

The important role played by front-line operational personnel as 'part-time marketers' has been stressed in this book on many previous occasions. It has also been noted that the activities of such staff can be important in creating an image of an organization which can live on to influence target customers' perceptions.

Staff who have front-line encounters with customers should be trained to treat these encounters as promotional opportunities. Without appropriate training and explanation of expectations, a call for such employees to promote their service can be little more than rhetoric. Training might seek to develop a number of skills in front-line staff:

- An ability to spot cross-selling possibilities can call for empathy on the part of front-line staff. A bank clerk who sees a customer repeatedly using a service that is not adequately fulfilling his or her needs could be trained to cross-sell another service which better meets the customer's requirements. Training should make such employees aware of the services available and give them skills in effectively approaching customers and referring them to appropriate personnel.
- Many operational staff have quite clearly defined sales roles. For example, waiters may be expected to encourage customers to spend more on their visit to a restaurant.
- The general manner of staffs' interaction with customers is important in encouraging customers to return and to tell their friends about their good experience. Again, training should emphasize those behaviours that have a positive effect on customers' evaluation of their encounter.
- Staff can directly facilitate future business by encouraging customers to book a repeat service or by giving them literature to pass on to friends.

Of course, it is difficult to draw a distinction between operational and marketing staff in terms of their contribution towards the promotion of an organization. Organizational boundaries should not prevent operational staff being considered an important element of promotion mix planning.

12.4.2   The promotional role of service outlets

From the outside, service outlets can be seen as billboards capable of conveying messages about the services that take place within them. They are therefore powerful tools in appealing to both customers and non-customers. The general appearance of an outlet can promote the image of a service organization—a brightly coloured and clean exterior can transmit a message that the organization is fast, efficient and well run. Outlets can be used to display advertising posters which, in heavily trafficked locations, can result in valuable exposure. Many retailers with town-centre locations consider that these opportunities are so great that they do not need to undertake more conventional promotion. Among the large UK retailers, until the 1980s

Marks & Spencer paid for very little promotional activity, arguing that over half the population passed one of its stores during any week, thereby exposing them to powerful 'free' messages. Although the company's promotional mix now includes more paid-for advertising, store locations are still considered to be valuable promotional media.

Service outlets can also provide valuable opportunities to show service-production processes to potential customers, something which is much more difficult to achieve through conventional media. A fast-printing shop displaying sophisticated printing equipment and a tyre retailer's large stocks and tidy appearance all help to promote an organization's processes as much as their outcomes.

12.5   ADVERTISING AND THE MEDIA

Advertising is mass, paid communication which is used to transmit information, develop attitudes and induce some form of response on the part of the audience. It seeks to bring about a response by providing information to potential customers, by trying to modify their desires and by supplying reasons why they should prefer that particular company's services.

The planning process for advertising comprises a number of stages. King (1975) proposed five:

1. *'Where are we now?'* In the first stage, an organization seeks to establish how its brand or service offering is perceived in peoples' minds. This can be ascertained through marketing research.
2. *'Why are we there?'* An organization should seek to establish how a particular position was reached by examining and identifying causal relationships.
3. *'Where could we be?'* This reflects an organization's objectives in terms of such factors as market share, awareness levels, etc.
4. *'How can we get there?'* This refers to the planning of advertising strategy and its tactical implementation.
5. *'Are we getting there?'* Having implemented an advertising programme, results must be evaluated and control action taken to address any discrepancy.

An essential element of this process is the setting of objectives for an advertising campaign. These should reflect the areas of accountability for those who implement the programme and a number of key elements in defining advertising objectives have been noted by Govoni *et al.* (1986). These should include:

- A concise definition of the target audience
- A clear statement of the desired response or responses to be generated among the target audience
- An expression of goals in quantitative terms
- A projection of achievements attributable to advertising
- An expressed understanding of advertising's role with respect to the rest of the promotion programme
- An acknowledgement that the goals are demanding yet achievable
- A statement of time constraints

Although it is common to think that advertising can increase sales, it is extremely difficult to prove that this alone can do so. Sales, after all, can be the result of many intervening variables, some of which are internal to the organization (public relations activity, pricing policy), while others are external (the state of the national economy). It is therefore too simplistic to set advertising objectives simply in terms of increasing sales by a specified amount. Given the existence of diverse adopter categories and the many stages in the communication process described earlier, more appropriate objectives can often be specified in terms of levels of awareness or comprehension.

12.5.1   Media characteristics

The choice of media is influenced by the characteristics of each medium and their ability to achieve the specified promotional objectives. The following are some of the most common types of media and their characteristics.

Newspapers   Daily newspapers tend to have a high degree of reader loyalty, reflecting the fact that each national title is targeted to specific segments of the population. This loyalty can lead to the printed message being perceived as having a high level of credibility on the part of the reader. Therefore, daily papers may be useful for prestige and reminder advertising. They can be used for creating general awareness of a product or a brand as well as providing detailed product information. In this way, building societies use newspapers for adverts both designed to create brand awareness and liking for the organization as well as giving specific details of savings accounts. The latter may include an invitation to action in the form of a freepost account opening coupon. Daily newspapers, however, are normally read hurriedly and therefore lengthy copy is likely to be wasted. Sunday newspapers also appeal to highly segmented audiences and are generally read at a more leisurely pace than daily ones. They are also more likely to be read at home and shared by households, which may be important for appealing to family-based service purchase decisions.

Local newspapers offer a much greater degree of geographical segmentation than is possible with national titles. Within their circulation areas, they also achieve much higher levels of readership penetration. In the case of 'freesheets', total penetration is achieved, although actual readership levels are more open to question. While national advertising through local newspapers is expensive and inefficient, it is useful for purely local service providers, as well as national organizations who wish to target local areas with local messages or to pre-test national advertising copy.

Magazines/journals   Within Britain, there is a wide range of magazine and journal titles available to advertisers. While some high-circulation magazines appeal to broad groups of people (for example, *Radio Times*), most titles are specialized in terms of their content and targeting. In this way, *Which Mortgage* can prove to be a highly specific medium for building societies to promote mortgages. Specialist trade titles allow messages to be aimed at service intermediaries. For example, a tour operator seeking to promote a holiday offer may first gain the confidence and support of travel agents through such magazines as *Travel Trade Gazette*.

Although advertising in magazines may at first seem relatively expensive compared to newspapers, they represent good value to advertisers in terms of the large number of readers per copy and the highly segmented nature of their audiences.

Outdoor advertising   This is useful for reminder copy and can support other media activities— the effect of an advertisement on television can be prolonged if recipients are exposed to a reminder poster on their way to work the following day. If strategically placed, the posters can appeal to segmented audiences—for example, London Underground sites in the City of London are seen by large numbers of affluent business people. The sides of buses are often used to support new service facilities (for example, new store openings) and have the ability to spread their message as the bus travels along local routes. Posters can generally be used to convey only a simple communication rather than complex details.

Television   This is an expensive but very powerful medium. Although it tends to be used mainly for the long-term task of creating brand awareness, it can also create a rapid sales response. The very fact that a message has been seen on television can give credibility to the message source, and many smaller service companies add the phrase 'as seen on TV' to give additional credibility to their other media communications. The power of the television medium is enhanced by its ability to appeal to both the senses of sight and sound, and to use movement and colour to develop a sales message.

The major limitation of television advertising is its cost. For most local service providers, television advertising rates start at too high a level to be considered. The high starting price reflects not only high production costs but also the difficulty in segmenting television audiences, either socio-economically or in terms of narrowly defined geographical areas. Also, the question must be asked as to how many people within the target audience are actually receptive to television advertising. Is the target viewer actually in the room when an advertisement is being broadcast? If the viewer is present, is he or she receptive to the message? The increasing use of video recorders and remote controls could have important implications for the effectiveness of television advertising in the future (see Yorke and Kitchen, 1985).

Cinema   Because of the captive nature of cinema audiences, this medium could potentially have a major impact. It is frequently used to promote local services such as taxi services and food outlets whose target market broadly corresponds to the audience of most cinemas. However, without repetition, cinema advertisements have little lasting effect, but do tend to be useful for supporting press and television advertising.

Commercial radio   Radio advertising has often been seen as the poor relation of television advertising, appealing only to the sense of sound. The threshold cost of radio advertising is much lower than for television, reflecting much more local segmentation of radio audiences and the lower production costs of radio adverts. A major advantage over other media is that the audience can be involved in other activities—particularly driving—while being exposed to an advertisement. Although there are often doubts about the extent to which an audience actually receives and understands a message, it forms a useful reminder medium when used in conjunction with other media.

12.5.2   Media-selection criteria

In addition to the characteristics of the media themselves, a number of other important factors are taken into account in selecting the media mix for a particular advertising campaign. These factors are:

- The characteristics of the target audience
- The level of exposure of the target audience to the medium
- The impact that advertising will have on the target audience
- The extent to which the effects of a particular advertising message 'wear out' over time
- The cost of advertising through a particular medium

Target audience   The media habits of the target audience must be fully understood. If a firm's target market is not in the habit of being exposed to a particular medium, much of the value of advertising through that medium will be wasted. As an example, attempts to promote premium credit cards to high-income segments by means of television commercials may lose much of their value because research suggests that the higher socio-economic groups tend to spend a greater proportion of their viewing time watching BBC rather than commercial channels. On the other hand, they are heavy readers of Sunday newspaper magazine supplements.

Information about target audiences' media habits is obtained from a number of sources. Newspaper readership information is collated by the National Readership Survey. For each newspaper, this shows reading frequency and average issue readership (as distinct from circulation) broken down into age, class, sex, ownership of consumer durables, etc. Television viewing information is collected by the Broadcasters' Audience Research Board (BARB). This indicates the number of people watching particular channels at particular times by reference to two types of television ratings (TVRs)—one for the number of households watching a programme/advertising slot and one for the people watching.

Using such sources of information, the media characteristics of a particular target audience can be ascertained and a media plan can be produced that achieves maximum penetration of the target audience.

Advertising exposure The number of advertising exposures of a particular communication is determined by two factors: cover/reach and frequency. 'Cover' or 'Reach' is the percentage of a particular target audience reached by a medium or a whole campaign, while 'frequency' is the number of times a particular target audience has an 'opportunity to see/hear' (OTS/OTH) an advertising message. The combination of these two factors results in an index of advertising exposure which is usually stated in terms of 'Gross Rating Points' (GRPs). For example, if an objective is to reach 50 per cent of the target audience three times a year, this would be stated as a GRP of 150 (i.e. 50 × 3).

Within a given budget, there has to be a trade-off between coverage/reach and frequency. A greater stress on reach means less emphasis on frequency and vice versa. The actual balance at any given time will depend on advertising objectives. Frequency *may* be a more important objective in situations where a new brand requires increased awareness, to increase loyalty to a non-dominant brand, to match the frequency of competitors' advertising or to increase the level of understanding of a complex message.

Advertising impact Although impact is usually more closely related to the message than the medium, different media vehicles can produce different levels of impact of an identical message. Where a service organization links a powerful tangible image to its service offering (e.g. McDonald's use of the Ronald McDonald character) the impact will be greatest with a visual medium that has movement and colour.

Wearout The concept of advertising exposure assumes that all advertising insertions have equal value. However, the effect of additional insertions may in fact decline, resulting in diminishing returns for each unit of expenditure. There is usually a 'threshold' level of advertising beneath which little audience response occurs. Once over this threshold, audience response tends to increase quite rapidly through a 'generation' phase until eventually a saturation point is reached. Any further advertising leads to a negative or declining response, i.e. 'wearout'. Generally, wearout is more a function of the message, but if wearout for the same message does vary between media, this should be taken into account when choosing between media. Wearout may be alleviated by broadening the variety of media being used (although this is likely to increase marginal costs) or, alternatively, by incorporating a more 'creative' approach in the message. A typical relationship between advertising repetitions and audience response is illustrated in Figure 12.5.

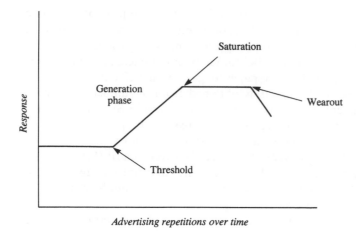

Figure 12.5 Advertising wearout

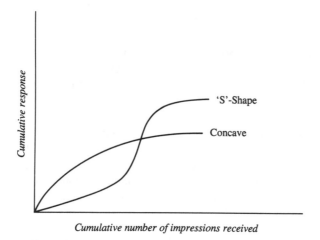

Figure 12.6 Advertising response functions

The possibilities for overcoming the effects of wearout are dependent upon the pattern of audience responses. Two response functions over time are shown in Figure 12.6. The 'S'-shape response pattern implies that there is a need for a large amount of advertising initially to ensure that a threshold is reached. This could be achieved by an initial 'burst' campaign, slowly reducing over time. On the other hand, the concave response pattern implies that a more regular 'drip' campaign would be the most appropriate. Symon and Arndt (1980) undertook extensive research to ascertain which function is more likely to occur in practice. Their findings indicated greater evidence in favour of the concave rather than the 'S'-shaped response pattern.

Cost The cost of using different media varies markedly, and while a medium which at first appears to be expensive may in fact be good value in terms of achieving promotional objectives, a sound basis for measuring cost is needed. There are generally two related cost criteria:

- Cost per Gross Rating Point—this is usually used for broadcast media and is the cost of a set of commercials divided by the Gross Rating Points.
- Cost per Thousand—this is used for print media to calculate the cost of getting the message seen by one thousand members of the target market

These measures can be used to make cost comparisons between different media vehicles. However, a true comparison needs to take into consideration the different degrees of effectiveness each medium has. In other words, the strength of the media vehicle needs to be considered, as does the location, duration, timing and—where relevant—size of the advertisement plus a variety of more complex factors. These are all combined to form 'media weights' which are used in comparing the effectiveness of different media. Cost effectiveness therefore, is calculated using the following formula:

$$\text{Cost effectiveness} = \frac{\text{Readers/viewers in target} \times \text{Media weight}}{\text{Cost}}$$

12.5.3 Determining the advertising budget

Advertising expenditure could become a drain on an organization's resources if no conscious attempt is made to determine an appropriate budget and to ensure that expenditure is kept within it. A number of methods are commonly used to determine an advertising budget:

- *What can be afforded* This is largely a subjective assessment and pays little attention to the long-term promotional needs of a service. It regards advertising as a luxury which can be afforded in good times, to be cut back during lean ones. In reality, this approach is used by many smaller service companies to whom advertising spending is seen as the first and easy short-term target for reducing expenditure in bad times.
- *Percentage of Sales* By this method, advertising expenditure rises or falls to reflect changes in sales. In fact, sales are likely to be influenced by advertising rather than vice versa, and this method is likely to accentuate any given situation. If sales are declining during a recession, more advertising may be required to induce sales, but this method of determining the budget implies a cut in advertising expenditure.
- *Comparative Parity* Advertising expenditure is determined by the amount spent by competitors. Many market sectors see periodic outbursts of promotional expenditure, often accompanying a change in some other element of firms' marketing mix. During the late 1980s price competition triggered an increase in advertising by airlines operating between the UK mainland and Ireland, with each airline responding to their competitors' increase in advertising expenditure. However, merely increasing advertising expenditure may hide the fact that it is the other elements of the marketing mix that need adjusting in order to gain a competitive market position in relation to competitors.
- *Residual* This is the least satisfactory approach and merely assigns to the advertising budget what is left after all other costs have been covered. It may bear no relationship whatever to promotional objectives.
- *Objective and Task* This approach starts by clearly defining promotional objectives. Tasks are then set which relate to specific targets. In this way, advertising is seen as a necessary— even though possibly risky—investment in a brand, ranking in importance with other more obvious costs such as production and salaries. This is the most rational approach to setting a promotional budget.

12.5.4 Developing the advertising campaign

An advertising campaign brings together a wide range of media-related activities so that instead of being a discrete series, they can act in a planned and coordinated way to achieve promotional objectives. The first stage of campaign planning is to have a clear understanding of promotional objectives (see above). Once these have been clarified, a message can be developed that is most likely to achieve these objectives. The next step is the production of the media plan which specifies:

- The allocation of expenditure between the different media.
- The selection of specific media components—for example, in the case of print media, decisions need to be made regarding the type (tabloid versus broadsheet), size of advertisement, whether use of a Sunday supplement is to be made and whether there is to be national or local coverage.
- The frequency of insertions.
- The cost of reaching a particular target group for each of the media vehicles specified in the plan.

Finally, the advertising campaign must be coordinated with the overall promotional plan—for example, by ensuring that sales-promotion activities reinforce advertising messages.

While the principles of planning a campaign for a service organization are, in principle, the same as would be followed by a manufacturing company, the intangible, inseparable and variable natures of services do need to be borne in mind when planning a campaign. Advertising alone is unlikely to be successful in helping customers to make services purchase decisions, but their effectiveness can be increased by following a few guidelines. The following have been proposed by George and Berry (1981):

- *Use clear and unambiguous messages* The very intangibility of services can make it very difficult to communicate information defining the service offer. This is particularly true of highly complex services. Here, advertising copy should emphasize the benefits of a service and how these match the benefits sought, i.e. a customer orientation rather than a product/service one.
- *Build on word-of-mouth communication* An important influence on service customer decision making is recommendation from others, therefore advertising should be used to enhance this. For example, advertising can be used to persuade satisfied customers to let others know of their satisfaction. Organizations can develop material that customers can pass on to non-customers or persuade non-customers to talk to present customers. Finally, advertising campaigns can be aimed at opinion leaders who will then 'trickle down' information about the service to the rest of the reference group.
- *Provide tangible cues* Organizations selling manufactured goods tend to differentiate their products from those of their competitors by emphasizing intangible features such as after-sales service, guarantees, etc. Service marketers, however, tend to differentiate their services by emphasizing tangible cues or 'physical evidence'. Cowell (1984) notes that the use of well-known personalities and objects can act as surrogates for the intangible features of the service. He also points out the importance of a service organization developing a continuous theme in its advertising. The use of consistent logos, catchphrases, symbols and themes can help to overcome the transitory nature of intangibility and ensure a durable company identity in the customer's mind. Firestone (1983) believes that there is a need for customers to identify strongly with a company and therefore a company's image should be relevant to customer needs, values and attitudes.
- *Promise what can be delivered* The intangible nature of services results in customers holding abstract expectations about the standard of service delivery. Customers judge a service to be

of poor quality where perceived delivery does not meet these expectations. Advertising should therefore not overpromise.

- *Aim advertising also at employees* Most services are labour-intensive and advertisers need to be concerned with the encouragement of employees to perform and of customers to buy. Advertisements that emphasize personal service can motivate contact personnel to perform their duties more effectively as well as influencing consumer choice.
- *Remove post-purchase anxiety* Consumption of a service usually involves a high degree of customer involvement and therefore there is a greater likelihood of post-purchase dissonance occurring than is the case with most goods purchases. There is little tangible evidence to use in the post-purchase evaluation process and therefore advertising should be used to reinforce positive post-purchase feelings.

12.6 SALES PROMOTION

Sales promotion involves those activities, other than advertising, personal selling and public relations, that stimulate customer purchase and the effectiveness of intermediaries. Although it can be used to create awareness, sales promotion is usually used for the later stages of the buying process, that is, to create interest, desire and—in particular—to bring about action. Sales promotion can complement other tools quite successfully within the promotion mix—for example, by reinforcing a particular image or identity developed through advertising. It is normally most effective when it is used in conjunction with advertising—for example, by capitalizing on the amiable disposition of potential customers produced by positive publicity.

Over the last few years there has been a rapid increase in the use of sales promotion, due to a number of reasons:

- Internally, there has been a greater acceptance of the use of sales promotion by top management and more people are now qualified to use it. In addition, there is greater pressure today to obtain a quick sales response, something that sales promotion is good at achieving.
- There has been a general proliferation of brands with increased competitive pressure. As a result of this and the changing economic environment, consumers are more 'deal oriented' and this has led to intermediary pressure for better incentives from service principals.
- It has been argued by many that advertising efficiency is declining due to increasing costs and media clutter.
- New technology in targeting has resulted in an increase in the efficiency and effectiveness of sales promotion.

The public and professional services sectors have also accepted the role of sales promotion in many areas—for example, leisure centres and opticians, respectively. As a promotional tool, sales promotion is likely to continue to grow in the future.

12.6.1 The role of sales promotion

Sales promotion contributes in a number of ways to achieving overall promotional objectives. While it can be used merely to gain attention for a service, it is more likely to be employed as an incentive incorporating an offer which represents value to the target audience. It can also act as an invitation to engage in a transaction now rather than later. Sales promotion usually attracts brand switchers but is unlikely to turn them into loyal brand users without the use of other elements of the promotion mix. In fact, it is usually considered that sales promotion is used to break down brand loyalty, whereas advertising is used to build it up. Sales promotion can gain new users or encourage more frequent purchase but it cannot compensate for inadequate advertising, poor delivery or poor quality.

12.6.2 Sales-promotion planning

As in the case of advertising, effective sales promotion involves an on-going process with a number of stages:

- *Establishment of objectives* Sales-promotion objectives vary according to the target market. If the target is the customer, objectives could include the encouragement of increased usage or the building of trial among non-users or other brand users. For intermediaries, objectives could be to encourage off-season sales or offsetting competitive promotions. Sales-promotion activity could also be aimed at internal personnel, making up part of the reward system described in more detail in Chapter 9.
- *Selection of promotional tools* Promotional objectives form the basis for selecting the most appropriate sales-promotion tools. The cost and effectiveness of each tool must be assessed with regard to achieving these objectives in respect of each target market. The tools available to the service marketer are described in more detail below.
- *Planning the sales-promotion programme* The major decisions that need to be made when designing the sales-promotion programme relate to the timing of the promotion and how long this tool is to be used. Also important are the size of incentive, rules for eligibility and, of course, the overall budget for the promotion.
- *Pre-testing* This needs to be undertaken to ensure that potentially expensive problems are discovered before the full launch of a promotion. Testing in selected market segments can highlight problems of ambiguity, response rates and give an indication of cost effectiveness.
- *Implementation* The programme for implementation must include two important time factors. First, it must indicate the 'lead time'—the time necessary to bring the programme up to the point where the incentive is made available to the public. Second, the 'sell in time', which is the period of time from the date of release to when approximately 90–95 per cent of incentive material has been received by potential customers.
- *Evaluation* The performance of the promotion needs to be assessed against the objectives set. If objectives are specific and quantifiable, measurement would seem to be easy. However, extraneous factors could account for the apparent success of many sales-promotion activities. For example, competitive actions or seasonal variations may have influenced customers' decision making. It can also be extremely difficult to separate out the effects of sales-promotion activity from other promotional activity—or indeed from other marketing-mix changes.

12.6.3 Sales-promotion tools

A wide and ever-increasing range of sales-promotion tools is employed by service organizations. Some of the more commonly used tools aimed at the final consumer include the following:

- *Free samples/visits/consultations* These encourage trial of a service and can be valuable where consumers are loyal to an existing service supplier. It could, for example, be used by a video film-rental chain to entice potential customers into their branch so that they can learn something about the nature of the service on offer. In the case of new services that are perceived as being expensive and of poor value to a consumer, they can encourage trial—this has been used by satellite television companies, for example. Taken to extremes, the excessive offering of free samples can demean the value of the service on offer and of the service provider. Customers may become reluctant to pay for a service which they have seen being given away freely.

- *Money-off price incentives* These are used to stimulate demand during slack periods where price is considered to be a key element in customers' purchase decision. Price incentives can be used tactically to counteract temporary increases in competitor activity. They can also be employed to stimulate sales of a new service shortly after launch. Price incentives tend to be expensive to the service provider, as the incentive is given to customers regardless of its motivational effect on individual customers. A leisure park reducing its prices for all is unable to extract the full price from those customers who may have otherwise been willing to pay that price. There is also a danger that price incentives can become built into consumers' expectations and their removal may result in a fall in business.
- *Coupons/vouchers* These allow holders to obtain a discount off a future purchase and can be targeted at quite specific groups of users or potential users. To encourage trial by potential new users, vouchers can be distributed to non-users who fit a specified profile. In this way, the operator of a solarium might arrange for vouchers to be given to customers of a cooperating hairdressing salon. To encourage repeat usage, vouchers can be given as a loyalty bonus. Voucher offers tend to be much more cost effective than straight price incentives because of their ability to segment markets. In this way, a leisure park operator is able to recognize that a visitor from overseas may see the full price as being only a small part of their total holiday cost and representing good value, while a local family might need an incentive to make more frequent visits to the park.
- *Gift offers* These allow an organization to augment its service offer with an additional gift which can satisfy a number of objectives. In order to promote initial enquiry and to give tangible cues of the service company's offering and image, many firms—especially in the financial services sector—offer a gift for merely enquiring about their service. Items offered by insurance companies for merely requesting a quotation often include pocket calculators and pens. A gift can also be used to bring about immediate action—for example, a free clock radio if a policy is taken out within a specified period. For existing customers, gifts can be used to develop and reward loyalty—vouchers collected at shops can often be used to obtain services provided by another company, thus satisfying both organizations' sales promotion objectives. Sometimes, a company may charge for a gift, making the sales-promotion self-financing. The gift could also carry a message that makes the service tangible to the user and others. In this way, some petrol retailers and football clubs—among others—sell ranges of promotional clothing, paid for by a combination of vouchers and cash.
- *Competitions* The inclusion of a competition in a service offer adds to the value of the total offer. Instead of simply buying an insurance policy, customers buy the policy plus a dream of winning a prize to which they attach significance. Competitions can be used both to create trial among non-users and to retain loyalty among existing users (for example, a competition for which a number of proofs of purchase are necessary to enter).

Sales-promotion activity aimed at intermediaries includes the following:

- *Short-term increases in sales commission* These, together with sales bonuses, can be used to stimulate sales during slack periods or to develop loyalty from intermediaries in the face of competitor activity.
- *Competitions and gifts* These can be powerful motivators where the individual sales personnel benefit directly from the incentive and use their sales skills to promote the brand with the greatest value of incentive.
- *Point-of-sale material* To stimulate additional sales, a service principal can provide a range of incentives to help intermediaries. Examples include tour operators who agree to send a

representative to a travel agency to provide additional information and reassurance for customers, or to host a film evening for the agency's clients.

- *Cooperative advertising* a service principal often agrees to subscribe to local advertising by an intermediary, often in conjunction with a significant event—for example, the opening of a new outlet by the intermediary or the launch of a new service.

BOOTS USED TO GIVE A KICK-START TO RAILWAYS

The recession in the UK during the early 1990s saw many service companies facing hard times. Both consumer and business spending had fallen in a wide range of sectors and those companies that had not gone out of business were left fighting more aggressively than ever before for the diminishing markets available to them. Retailing and travel were two sectors that had been affected particularly badly by a downturn in expenditure. It was against this background that two organizations—Boots and InterCity—got together to stimulate their respective markets by the use of collaborative sales-promotion activity.

Boots owns Britain's largest chain of retail chemists which over the years had diversified into a number of related product areas—for example, audio and hi-fi sales, optician services and kitchenware. Research undertaken during the late 1980s had shown that over two-thirds of all households visited a Boots branch regularly. However, a long-standing problem which Boots faced was that when customers came into their shops, they tended to spend very little, typically £2–3 on small items such as shampoo or toothpaste. Boots saw its major marketing task as being to increase the level of expenditure per visit, as well as developing customer loyalty in the face of threats from growing competitors such as Superdrug.

InterCity had become a profitable business during the late 1980s. However, the onset of the recession had first taken away much of its high-value first-class business traffic and, later, much of the lower-priced leisure traffic that had helped to fill its trains during off-peak periods. Faced with tightening budgets, people were making fewer discretionary leisure journeys. Furthermore, recent fare rises had increased the public's perception of InterCity as an expensive service, making it even more difficult to maintain market share in a falling market.

At the beginning of 1992, Boots and InterCity got together to offer a joint sales-promotion incentive. Every time a customer spent over £5 at a Boots store they were given a voucher which allowed one person to make a free return journey on InterCity, provided a travelling companion paid for an identical ticket. The sales promotion appeared to meet both organizations' promotional needs. For Boots, it encouraged customers to spend just a little more in order to qualify for a free train ticket. It also helped to generate additional traffic within its stores in the first place by offering added-value benefits compared to what was on offer from its competitors. For InterCity, the terms of the incentive allowed it to achieve a number of objectives. It saw the promotion as essentially a tool to fill spare capacity during quiet periods. For this reason, the eligibility excluded the busy Easter holiday period and those trains that were likely to be heavily used by commuters. Many of its leisure customers perceived InterCity prices as being too high and a coupon offer allowed the chance of segmenting its markets without risking the loss of revenue from passengers who would have been willing to pay the full price. In this way, the voucher could only be used in conjunction with 'Saver' and 'Supersaver' fares. This had the effect of reducing the chance of commuters and business travellers using vouchers for their regular journeys, as these tickets cannot, in general, be used on peak-hour trains used by commuters. The fact that tickets had to be reserved at least 24 hours in advance reduced their attractiveness to business or affluent leisure travellers who would prefer the freedom to travel on any train at short notice. For InterCity, the conditions of the incentive were also used to promote a more positive image of its service. For a number of years InterCity had built up a reputation for being overcrowded, with frequent reports about passengers being forced to travel in the guard's van or sitting on the floor in gangways. The requirement that passengers must reserve seats (free of charge) in advance not only had the effect of allowing British Rail to manage its demand more effectively it also allowed previous non-users or irregular users to receive positive images of service quality.

The sales promotion finished as planned at the end of spring 1992 and was judged to have been a success by both sides. Indeed, a similar incentive was introduced in September 1992 which ran for a longer period and additionally included free travel on many more local services operated by Regional Railways.

12.7 PERSONAL SELLING

Personal selling is a powerful two-way form of communication. It allows an interactive relationship to be developed between buyer and seller in which the latter can modify the information presented in response to the needs of the audience. Personal selling allows for the cultivation of a friendship between buyer and seller, which can be an important element of a relationship marketing strategy. It can also be powerful in creating a feeling of obligation by the customer to the salesperson, thereby helping to bring about a desired response.

Although the principles of personnel selling are basically the same for goods and services industries, services sales personnel are more likely to combine their sales duties with other functional duties, for example in the way that a travel agent—as well as being an expert on travel-reservation systems—is expected to perform a selling role.

12.7.1 The salesperson's activities

The actual selling act is only a small part of a salesperson's role. Salespeople invariably produce reports, service customers, handle complaints, send in leads, etc. In addition to their specific selling role, two further principal roles can be identified—servicing and intelligence.

The servicing element can be an important contributor to the development of long-term customer relationships where the service in question is perceived as being highly risky. Such relationships need to be regularly attended to, even if there is no short-term prospect of a sale. In a study of the life-assurance sector, George and Myers (1981) found that customers viewed their purchases as being highly risky and therefore unpleasant. As a consequence, they attached particular importance to the level of support they received from a salesperson in particular and their organization in general. There have now been many studies to identify the factors that contribute towards relationship satisfaction between buyer and seller (for example, Crosby et al., 1990).

As well as being the mouthpiece of an organization, sales personnel can also be its ears. They can be extremely useful in marketing research, for example by reporting on customers' comments, or providing information about competitors' activity. Organizations should develop systems for capturing information collected by sales personnel.

In respect of their selling role, a number of types of selling situations can be identified:

- Trade selling, where their role is to facilitate sales through intermediaries.
- Technical selling, which involves giving advice and technical assistance to customers. This type of salesperson becomes a consultant and assumes importance in many types of business-to-business service sales—for example, business travel services.
- Missionary selling, where the salesperson is not expected to take orders but to 'prepare the ground' by building goodwill.
- New business selling—this involves the acquisition of new accounts and may sometimes involve 'cold calling'.

The task of selling can be broken down into a number of sequential stages:

- *Prospecting, i.e. finding new customers* Sales leads can be developed in a number of ways—for example, records of past customers, past enquiries and referrals from existing customers and suppliers. Cold-call leads from local newspapers, trade directories, etc. are also a possibility.
- *Preparation and planning* A salesperson should attempt to gain as much information as possible about a prospect before actual contact takes place—for example, in regard to their previous buying behaviour or aspirations. In the case of business-to-business sales the most appropriate members of the decision-making unit should be identified for contact.
- *The sales presentation* This is the focal point for the interaction and is considered in more detail below.
- *Handling objections* Objections to the sales presentation can be rational (for example, objections to the price or the service itself) or irrational (objections based on resistance to change, apathy, prejudice, etc.) and need to be acknowledged, isolated and discussed.
- *Closing the sale* This is a difficult stage in that knowing how and when to close is a skill in itself.
- *Follow-up* This stage is often neglected but is essential to ensure customer satisfaction and repeat business. A letter of thanks or a phone call can help to reduce post-purchase dissonance, which is especially valuable for services where benefits are to be delivered in the distant future.

12.7.2   The sales presentation

A sales presentation has to achieve a number of objectives, from initially gaining attention, through to developing interest, bringing about a desire for the service and finally action to purchase. By following a few guidelines, the effectiveness of a sales presentation as a two-way interactive promotional tool can be increased (see Kotler and Andreasen, 1991; George *et al.*, 1983).

- The sales person should be recognized as a surrogate for the service. For low-contact services such as life insurance, the salesperson may be perceived as being *the* service. Appearance and demeanour are therefore very important in creating the right impression of the service offer.

- As well as giving information, the salesperson should also ask questions and listen to customers' answers. One-way communication removes the interactive advantage of personal selling and may fail to identify a customer's true needs.
- Service features should be linked to benefits as they will be valued by customers. This is particularly important for highly complex and abstract services.
- Complex information should be used selectively. Overcomplication may overwhelm customers and leave them feeling belittled by the salesperson. Such detailed information is more effectively used in response to specific questions.
- The presentation should not be price oriented but should allow a potential customer to balance the overall costs with the overall benefits possible. There is a suggestion that price sensitivity is generally less important for services than for goods (George and Myers, 1981).
- The sales presentation should help to make tangible an intangible service. Samples of supporting goods, brochures or audiovisual aids can often give a better and more credible description of a service process than a salesperson alone. They will also help to keep the client's attention.
- The salesperson should show a deep knowledge of their particular area, therefore the training of sales personnel in technical as well as sales skills is important. Without a respect for their knowledge, customers are less likely to have confidence in the salesperson or the services they are selling.
- The sales presentation should not offer what cannot be delivered. This applies to both goods and services but is particularly important where abstract expectations of service quality are not matched by actual performance. Overpromising may increase short-term sales, but the resulting poor-quality assessment would harm longer-term relationship possibilities. It may sometimes therefore, be better to underpromise and overdeliver.
- Customers should be given early opportunities to assess service quality, either by producing evidence of previous outcomes (for example, previous performance of an investment fund) or by sampling the service process.
- An organization's image and reputation should be used to support sales arguments for high-credence services.
- External reference sources should be used to support a sales argument.

12.8 DIRECT MARKETING

Direct marketing has been defined by the UK Direct Marketing Association as 'an interactive system of marketing which uses one or more media in acquiring a measurable response at a given location'. Its aim is to create and exploit a direct relationship between service producers and their customers. In recent years there has been a considerable increase in the use of direct marketing for promoting services, largely due to the development of new technology that enables organizations to target their messages accurately. In the UK, direct marketing has been taken up in a big way by the financial services sector, particularly pensions and insurance companies. Travel companies, retailers and hotels have been more recent adopters of direct marketing methods on a large scale. While direct marketing may include personal selling, it is the other elements of direct marketing that are of interest here, including telemarketing, direct mail, directories and videotech.

The key elements of a direct marketing system are the following:

- An accurate record of the names of existing customers, former customers and prospective customers classified into different groups.
- A system for recording the results of communications with targets. From this, the effectiveness of particular messages and the responsiveness of different target groups can be assessed.

- A means of measuring and recording actual purchase behaviour.
- A system to follow up with continuing communication where appropriate.

The two most common forms of direct marketing used by service organizations are telemarketing and direct mail.

12.8.1 Telemarketing

Telemarketing involves two-way communication by telephone—'outbound' telemarketing occurs where suppliers take the initiative and 'inbound' where customers act in response to another stimulus, such as a newspaper advertisement. In both the USA and the UK there has been a rapid increase in the use of inbound telemarketing using free 0800 numbers, particularly by the financial services sector. Inbound telemarketing is very powerful when combined with other media action and an incentive for customers to act promptly. Outbound telemarketing has sometimes been used as an alternative to personal selling, especially where some customers are seen as potentially less profitable than others and telemarketing is used for these instead of more expensive personal selling.

The effectiveness of telemarketing can be assessed by measuring the cost per telephone call, the cost per telephone hour and the number and quality of enquiries received. Furthermore, by asking questions of enquirers, the source of particularly effective supporting advertisements can be identified. It can often be possible to measure the cost effectiveness of telemarketing in terms of the value of sales generated, especially where there is little extraneous media advertising which could itself have explained sales success.

12.8.2 Direct mail

Direct mail describes the way in which an organization distributes printed material aimed at specifically targeted potential customers with a view to carrying on direct interchange between the two parties. Its use is becoming increasingly popular among service industries and a number of important advantages which it has over the other promotional tools can be identified:

- It can be used very selectively to target quite specific groups of potential private or business customers.
- The sales message can be personalized to the needs of individual recipients.
- Direct mail offers a very versatile and creative medium and is flexible in the range of materials that can be used.
- It can be timed effectively to fit in with the overall marketing strategy and is quick to produce.
- It is also quick in terms of producing results.

Direct mail can be employed to achieve a number of promotional objectives, including the generation of enquiries, keeping prospects interested, informing customers of new developments and improving the effectiveness of the salesperson (i.e. it can be used as a 'door opener').

Compared to advertising, the direct mail message can be more detailed. Much more space is available on a direct mailshot and this allows long and complex messages to be presented—a point which partly explains its popularity with financial services companies whose sales messages are typically very complex. The response medium serves a variety of purposes. It can be used to obtain expressions of interest, to obtain sales orders and to measure the effect of the promotion. It is therefore extremely important to know who has responded and what the response actually is. It is also important to consider non-respondents and why they did not respond. Leaflets, inserts, pop-ups, etc. can also be included in the mailshot.

With the use of reply-paid envelopes and freephone numbers, response from recipients of direct mail is facilitated. The results of individual targeted mailshots can be assessed quite easily and through further refinement of customer profiling and targeting, the cost of contact per person can be reduced to a low level.

12.9   PUBLIC RELATIONS

Public relations is an indirect promotional tool whose role is to establish and enhance a positive image of an organization and its services among its various publics. It is defined by the Institute of Public Relations as 'the deliberate, planned and sustained effort to establish and maintain mutual understanding between an organization and its publics'. It seeks to persuade people that a company is an attractive organization with which to relate or do business, which is important for services as it has already been noted that services are evaluated very subjectively and often rely on word-of-mouth recommendation. Public relations facilitates this process of subjective evaluation and recommendation.

Because public relations is involved with more than just customer relationships, it is often handled at a corporate rather than the functional level of marketing management and it can be difficult to integrate public relations fully into the overall promotional plan. As an element within the promotion mix, public relations presents a number of valuable opportunities as well as problems. Some of its more important characteristics are as follows:

- *Low cost* The major advantage of public relations is that it tends to be much cheaper in terms of cost per person reached than any other type of promotion. Apart from nominal production costs, much public relations activity can be carried out at almost no cost, in marked contrast to the high cost of buying space or time in the main media. In this way, many small service organizations use public relations as a cheap way of gaining exposure and building awareness of themselves and their service offer.
- *Audience specificity* Public relations can be targeted to a small, specialized audience if the right media vehicle is used.
- *Believability* Much public relations communication is seen as credible because it comes from an apparently impartial and non-commercial source. Where information is presented as news, readers or viewers may be less critical of a message than if it were presented as a biased advertisement.
- *Difficult to control* A company can exercise little direct control over how its public relations activity is subsequently handled and interpreted. If successful, a press release may be printed in full, although there can be no control over where or when it is printed. At worst, a press release can be misinterpreted and the result could be very unfavourable news coverage.
- *Competition for attention* The fact that organizations compete for a finite amount of attention puts pressure on the public relations effort to be better than competitors.

12.9.1   The publics of public relations

Public relations can be distinguished from customer relations because its concerns go beyond the creation of mutually beneficial relationships with actual or potential customers. The following additional audiences for public relations can be identified:

- *Intermediaries* These may share many of the same concerns as customers and need reassurance about the company's capabilities as a service principal. Service organizations can develop this reassurance through the use of company newsletters, trade journal articles, etc.

- *Suppliers* These may need assurances that the company is a credible one to deal with and that contractual obligations will be met. Highlighting favourable annual reports and drawing attention to major new developments can help to raise the profile and credibility of a company in the eyes of its suppliers.
- *Employees* Here, public relations overlaps with the efforts of internal marketing (see Chapter 9) and assumes great importance within the services sector where personnel become part of the service offer and it is important to develop participation and motivation among employees. In addressing its internal audiences, public relations uses such tools as in-house publications, newsletters and employee-recognition activities.
- *Financial community* This includes financial institutions that have supported, are currently supporting or who may support the organization in the future. Shareholders—both private and institutional—form an important element of this community and must be reassured that the organization is going to achieve its stated objectives.
- *Government* In many cases, actions of government can significantly affect the fortunes of an organization and therefore relationships with government departments—at local, national and supra-national level—need to be carefully developed. This can include lobbying of Members of Parliament, communicating the organization's views to government enquiries and civil servants and creating a favourable image for itself by sponsoring public events.
- *Local communities* It is sometimes important for an organization to be seen as a 'good neighbour' in the local community. Therefore, the organization can enhance its image through the use of charitable contributions, sponsorship of local events, being seen to support the local environment, etc.

12.9.2 The tools of public relations

As far as planning a promotional campaign is concerned, a wide range of public relations tools are available. The suitability of each tool is dependent upon the promotional objectives at which they are directed. In general, the tools of public relations are best suited to creating awareness of an organization or liking for its services and tend to be less effective in directly bringing about action in the form of purchase decisions. While there can be argument as to just what constitutes public relations activity, some of the important elements used within the promotion mix are as follows:

- *Press releases* The creation and dissemination of press releases is often referred to as 'publicity'. Kotler (1991) defines publicity as the 'activity of securing editorial space, as divorced from paid space, in all media read, viewed or heard by a company's customers or prospects, for the specific purpose of assisting in the meeting of sales goals'. Because of its important contribution towards the promotion mix, this tool is considered in more detail below.
- *Lobbying* Professional lobbyists are often employed in an effort to inform and hence influence key decision makers who may be critical in allowing elements of a marketing plan to be implemented. Lobbying can take place at a local level (for example, a bus company seeking to convince a local authority of the harm that would result to the public in general if streets in a town centre were closed to buses); at a national level (the campaign mounted by London Underground during 1992 to create awareness among ministers of the benefits to London commuters of a government decision to fund the extension of the Jubilee underground railway line); and at a supra-national level (the representations made by many holiday companies and their trade associations against a proposed EC Directive on package holidays which would have had the effect of increasing their price).

- *Education and training* In an effort to develop a better understanding—and hence liking—of an organization and its services, many service organizations aim education and training programmes at important target groups. In this way, banks frequently supply schools and colleges with educational material that will predispose its recipients to their brand when they come to open a bank account. Open days are another common method of educating the public by showing them the complex 'behind the scenes' production processes involved.
- *Exhibitions* most companies attend exhibitions not with the intention of making an immediate sale but to create an awareness of their organization that will result in a sale over the longer term. Exhibitions offer the chance for potential customers to talk face to face with representatives of the organization and the physical layout of the exhibition stand can give valuable tangible evidence about the nature of the service on offer. Exhibitions are used for both consumer and business-to-business services. As an example of the latter, the annual World Travel Market in London offers the chance for a wide range of tourism-related service industries to meet quite narrowly targeted customers and to display tangible cues of their service offering (for example, brochures and staff).
- *In-house journals* Many service organizations have developed their own magazines which are given to customers or potential customers. By adopting a news-based magazine format, the message becomes more credible than if it were presented as a pure advertisement. Often, outside advertisers contribute revenue which can make such journals self-financing—this commonly happens with in-house magazines published by banks. Travel operators often publish magazines that are read by a captive travelling public.
- *Special events* In order to attract media attention, organizations sometimes arrange an event which is in itself newsworthy and will create awareness of the organization. An example is the non-stop flight made by a Quantas aircraft between Britain and Australia during 1991. Although the company had adapted the aircraft and the journey could not be made under normal operating conditions, the fact that it was a first made it newsworthy and created significant awareness of Quantas. Of course, if badly managed, a special event can turn into a public relations disaster.
- *Sponsorship* There is argument about whether this strictly forms part of the public relations portfolio of tools. It is, however, being increasingly used by services companies and is described in more detail below.

12.9.3 Press relations (publicity)

The aim of publicity is to create over the longer term a feeling of mutual understanding between an organization and the media. This understanding with the media is developed by means of:

- *Press releases* This is the most frequent form of press relations activity and is commonly used to announce new service launches, new appointments or significant achievements.
- *Press conferences* These are used where a major event is to be announced and an opportunity for a two-way dialogue between the organization and the media is considered desirable.
- *Availability of specialist commentators* Faced with a news story on which the media wishes to report, a newspaper or radio station may seek specialists within an industrial sector who are knowledgeable on the issues involved. For example, a tour operator may be asked by a local newspaper to comment upon the consequences of a hurricane in an overseas resort. This helps both the reporter and the service organization in question, whose representative is fielded as an expert.

Publicity has the advantage of being a relatively inexpensive promotional tool which can reach large audiences with a high degree of credibility. Against this, a major disadvantage is the lack of control that the generator of publicity has over how the publicity is subsequently handled, in terms of appearance, timing and content (it is likely to be edited). Because of the competition from other organizations for press coverage, there can be no guarantee that any particular item will actually be used.

An important element of press relations is avoiding negative publicity. Because services can be highly variable, there is always the possibility that the media will report one unfavourable incident and leave its audience thinking that this is the norm for a particular organization. This is particularly a problem for highly visible public or quasi-public services for which readers enjoy reading bad news stories to confirm their own prejudices.

External events may also lead to poor publicity, or the negative actions of similar service organizations may result in a generally poor reputation of the sector as a whole. In all situations, an organization needs to establish contingency plans to minimize any surprise and confusion resulting from the publicity. Bad publicity is more likely to be effectively managed if an organization has invested time and effort in developing mutually supportive good relations with the media.

12.9.4   Preparing the publicity strategy

As with all aspects of the communication mix, publicity will achieve maximum effectiveness if a clear plan is formulated which identifies objectives, has a clear strategy and implementation programme and effective monitoring:

- Publicity objectives typically include the desire to raise awareness of a new service launch or to identify the organization with a desired image.
- Planning involves identifying items that should be brought to the attention of a wider audience by means of publicity.
- Implementing the plan requires a great deal of care and may involve carefully building up mutual trust with important media editors.
- Evaluation is difficult as publicity is usually used in conjunction with other promotional tools. It is easier to evaluate if publicity is used before other tools. There are, however, a number of publicity response measures that can be employed. For example, 'exposures' relate to the number of times news about the the company has been carried by the media. However, this does not give any indication of how many people actually saw or heard the information. Alternatively, surveys of awareness, comprehension and attitudes before and after publicity could be undertaken and these may give some indication of the response to publicity.

PROMOTING NORTHERN IRELAND

Northern Ireland has a desperate need to attract inward investment to overcome the social problems associated with the UK's highest level of unemployment. However, the image perceived by influential developers is inevitably dominated by over 20 of 'troubles'. This has ensured that while the province has regularly remained in the news and has a high recognition factor among the public, it is recognized for the wrong reasons. A major task, therefore, is to alter attitudes and remove preconceived prejudices. Unfortunately, bombs and bullets make far more attractive news stories than the beautiful countryside, fishing and low start-up costs for investors.

The Industrial Development Board of Northern Ireland is a government service organization which has been charged with stimulating economic development in the province. A vital part of this unenviable task entails promoting a favourable image of the province to overseas investors and to try to counterbalance the negative images which seem to be so deeply ingrained. As well as the pleasant countryside and low start-up costs, the Board seeks to make the most of the province's cheap, good labour, high educational standards and lack of industrial disputes.

To present a more positive image of the province, public relations is used extensively to communicate with potential investors. Out of an international marketing budget of £5.5 million, advertising in itself accounts for only single-figure percentages. The main reason for this is that people see advertising as paid-for propaganda and therefore the messages lack credibility. Public relations accounts for the bulk of its expenditure, and even where advertising is used, it is generally linked to public relations activity—for example, in the form of 'advertorial' features. The IDB uses a public relations consultancy which aims to counteract the negative media coverage and to demonstrate to businesses that investing in Northern Ireland can lead to financial success. Success stories are highlighted, such as Ford, DuPont and British Telecom, who are all prepared to endorse the message. The promotional approach is to cultivate good contacts with influential journalists and decision makers. In an attempt to cultivate favourable coverage in business journals, site visits are frequently arranged on the grounds that actually experiencing the region at

first hand is the only true way of overcoming the fears and prejudices produced by the media. The greater part of the IDB public relations budget is spent on hospitality and contact events. Presentations and dinners are regularly organized for professional bodies.

Direct mail is also used, particularly in the European and American markets. Fact sheets describing the positive features of Northern Ireland are sent to the target audiences and the message is targeted according to the audience. For example, a mailshot to the USA emphasized the fact that the high security levels result in a relatively low crime rate.

Personal selling is used to supplement the public relations effort. One of the greatest assets of Northern Ireland is claimed to be its people, so the opportunity to meet a representative not just of the IDB but of Northern Ireland as a whole gives an opportunity to evaluate one of the claims made about the province. Indeed, it is often said that Northern Irish professionals tend to have the 'gift of the gab', and this is put to good effect.

Finally, word-of-mouth recommendation is facilitated through the Northern Ireland Partnership. This is an international group of senior business people who have links with the region and have agreed to help attract investment into the province. Personal endorsement can help to overcome some of the negative images produced by the many years of conflict.

12.10 SPONSORSHIP

One way that service organizations can try to 'make' their service tangible is to attempt to get customers to link the image of its organization or of specific services with a more tangible event or activity. While publicity can successfully perform this function, sponsorship can also have long-term value.

Sponsorship involves investment in events or causes so that an organization can achieve objectives such as increased awareness levels, enhanced reputation, etc. Sponsorship activities include such examples as a bank sponsoring cricket matches (the NatWest Trophy) and the sponsorship of specific television programmes (such as Legal & General Insurance sponsoring the north-west weather forecast on Granada Television).

Sponsorship is attractive to service companies as it allows the relatively known characteristics of an event or activity being sponsored to help enhance the image of an organization's own inherently intangible services. As an example, an insurance company wishing to associate itself with high quality may seek to sponsor the activities of a leading arts organization noted for the quality of its productions. In this way, the Royal Insurance Company's sponsorship of the Royal Shakespeare Company gives potential customers an indication of the standards of quality with which it is associated. A further advantage of sponsorship is that it allows a company to avoid the general media clutter usually associated with advertising. Furthermore, audiences can be segmented and a sponsorship vehicle chosen whose audience matches that of the sponsoring company, in terms of socio-economic, demographic and geographic characteristics. In this way, a regional insurance broker may sponsor a local theatrical group operating solely in its own business area.

It is difficult to evaluate sponsorship activities because of the problem of isolating the effects of sponsorship from other elements of the promotion mix. Direct measurement is only likely to be possible if sponsorship is the predominant tool. Sponsorship should therefore be seen as a tool that complements other elements of the promotion mix.

REVIEW QUESTIONS

1. To what extent does the intangibility of a service influence the promotional methods used by a service organization?
2. Why do you think that certain professional services still consider sales promotion to be unethical?
3. What is the link between 'internal marketing' and the promotion of services?
4. To what extent can the application of direct marketing be effective in the promotion of a university?
5. Public relations may be a more effective promotional tool for services than other communication methods. If this is true, why do you think this may be the case?
6. Identify the problems likely to be faced by an airline in evaluating the effectiveness of its promotion for a newly introduced service.

INTERNATIONAL MARKETING OF SERVICES

OBJECTIVES

After reading this chapter, you should be able to understand:

- The nature of international trade in services and reasons for its development
- Methods used by service organizations to assess the attractiveness of overseas opportunities
- The development of marketing-mix strategies that are sympathetic to overseas market needs
- Strategies for entering and developing overseas service markets

13.1 INTRODUCTION

At some point, many service organizations recognize that their growth can continue only if they exploit overseas markets. A company that has successfully developed its marketing strategy should be well placed to extend this development into overseas markets. Many of the fundamental principles of marketing management that have been applied to the domestic market will be of relevance in an international setting. The processes of identifying market opportunities, selecting strategies, implementing those strategies and monitoring performance involve principles fundamentally similar to those that apply within the domestic market. The major challenge to service companies seeking to expand overseas lies in sensitively adapting marketing strategies that have worked at home to the needs of overseas markets whose environments may be totally different to anything previously experienced.

The purpose of this chapter is to identify the main differences facing the task of marketing management when services are provided in an international rather than a purely domestic environment. Some of the key differences between trade in goods and trade in services are emphasized, particularly the diverse nature of buyer–seller interaction which causes international trade in services to take a number of forms.

13.2 THE IMPORTANCE OF INTERNATIONAL TRADE IN SERVICES

International trade in services is becoming increasingly important, representing not only opportunities for domestic service producers to earn revenue from overseas but also threats to domestic producers from overseas competition. Some indication of the importance of international trade in services for Britain can be seen in the trade statistics. In 1990, the UK earned £117 billion from selling services overseas, compared to £102 billion from selling goods. More importantly, the UK had a small surplus (£4.2 billion) in services, compared with a growing deficit in goods (£18.6 billion). A closer examination of trade statistics indicates the relative importance of the main service sectors. The most important in terms of overseas sales continues to be financial services, with credits ('exports') of £15.6 billion in 1990, set against debits ('imports') of £5.9 billion, although the export/import ratio has deteriorated in favour of imports during recent years. Travel-related sectors were the next most significant group recorded by national statistics, although here, the UK is now a net importer of services (with debits of £9.9 billion, against credits of £7.7 billion) and the trade balance has been steadily deteriorating. Sea transport and civil aviation each account for about £4 billion of debits and credits each year.

13.3   DEFINING INTERNATIONAL TRADE IN SERVICES

Conceptual difficulties can occur in attempting to analyse international trade in services. While trade in manufactured goods can be represented by stocks of goods moving in one direction and payment (in cash or in goods) in the other, the intangible nature of most services makes it difficult to measure a physical flow—trade statistics cannot rely on records of goods passing through Customs. Any analysis of international trade in services is complicated by the diverse nature of producer/supplier interaction, stemming from the inseparability of service production/consumption processes.

International trade statistics for services hide the fact that trade can take a number of forms. Sometimes credits are earned by customers from overseas travelling to an organization's domestic market in order to consume a service (for example, an overseas tourist visiting the UK). On other occasions, they are earned by domestic producers taking their production processes to customers in overseas markets. A further category of services can be identified which allow production and consumption to be separated—for these services, producers and consumers do not need to meet in order for international trade to occur. The form that international trade takes can be seen as dependent on the mobility of both producer and consumer and the separability of the production/consumption process (see Figure 13.1).

Immobility in service production processes occurs where it is either not possible or sensible to produce a service in an overseas market—customers in these markets must travel if they are to receive the service. This is typical of many tourism-related services that are based on a unique historic site. In other cases, it is customers who are inflexible, requiring the production process to be taken overseas to wherever customers are located (for example, building contractors must travel to a building requiring renovation).

Because of the diverse ways in which international trade takes place, estimates of the total value of international trade in services are much more unreliable than for manufactured goods, and frequently subject to subsequent revision. From the diversity of producer/consumer interaction, three important patterns of trade can be identified:

1. *Production of a service in one country for consumption in another* While manufactured goods are commonly traded on this basis, this can only occur for services where production and consumption can be separated. This has often been achieved using postal and telephone communications. In this way, an insurance policy for a ship can be produced at Lloyd's in London but the benefits of the policy relayed to the policyholder anywhere in the world. Similarly, many information services can be traded between countries by modern telecommunications. It can be difficult for official statistics to record accurately both the outward flow of services and the inward flow of money for this type of trade.
2. *Production of a service by a domestic company in an overseas market for overseas consumption* Where the problem of inseparability cannot be overcome, a domestic service

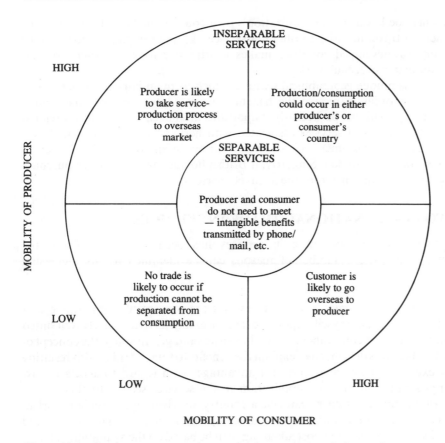

Figure 13.1   Producer–consumer interaction in overseas trade for services

producer may only be able to access an overseas market by setting up production facilities in that market. Examples of services in this category include catering and cleaning services which must deliver a tangible outcome at a point of the customer's choice. The various methods by which a company can set up overseas service outlets are discussed in more detail later in this chapter. While this type of international trade can be of great importance to service organizations, it only appears in a country's balance of payments in the form of capital movements, remitted profits and trade in the tangible components of a service offer.

3. *Production of a service at home for sale to overseas customers for consumption in the domestic market* It is often expensive or impossible to take a service-production process to overseas customers, therefore customers travel overseas to consume a service. This can occur for a number of reasons:

- Demand for a highly specialized service may be very thinly dispersed, making it uneconomic to take staff and equipment to the market. As an example, it is common for patients to travel long distances to visit specialist doctors in London's Harley Street.
- The laws of an overseas country may make the provision of a service in that market illegal, forcing those seeking the service to travel overseas. Countries which forbid abortion operations often do so to the benefit of abortion clinics in countries such as Britain, where a more liberal regime applies.

- Production costs may be lower in an organization's own country, making it attractive for overseas customers to travel in order to obtain a service. As an example, the lower price of labour in many less-developed countries makes it attractive for shipowners to send their ships away for major overhaul work.
- A country may possess unique geographical features which form an important element of a service offer, and in order to receive the benefits of related services customers must travel to that country. This is particularly important in the case of tourism-related industries, where the benefits of services associated with heritage sites or climatic differences cannot be taken to consumers. If American citizens wish to visit the Tower of London, they must travel to London. Similarly, if British holidaymakers want to purchase a holiday with guaranteed sunshine, they must travel overseas.

13.4 REASONS FOR INTERNATIONAL TRADE IN SERVICES

However it is measured, international trade in services has been increasing. From the perspective of national economies, a number of reasons can be identified for its increasing importance:

- Services are traded between economies in order to exploit the concept of comparative cost advantage. This holds that an economy will export those services that it is particularly well suited to producing and import those where another country has an advantage. Although the concept of comparative cost advantage was developed to explain the benefits to total world wealth resulting from each country exploiting its comparative cost advantages with regard to access to raw materials and energy supplies, it also has application to the services sector. In this way, a favourable climate or outstanding scenery can give a country an advantage in selling tourism services to overseas customers, a point not lost to tourism operators in the Canary Islands and Switzerland, respectively. A comparative cost advantage can be based on the availability of low-cost or highly trained personnel (cheap labour for the shipping industry and trained computer software experts for computer consultancies, respectively). Sometimes the government of a country can itself directly create comparative cost advantages for a service sector, as where it reduces regulations and controls in an industry, allowing that industry to produce services for export at a lower cost than its more regulated competitors (for example, many 'offshore' financial services centres impose lower standards of regulation than their mainstream competitors).
- The removal of many restrictions on international trade in services (such as the creation of the Single European Market) has allowed countries to exploit their comparative cost advantages. Nevertheless, restrictions on trade in services generally remain more significant than those on manufactured goods.
- Increasing disposable household incomes result in greater consumption of those categories of services that can only be provided by overseas suppliers, especially overseas travel and tourism. Against this, economic development within an economy can result in many specialized services that were previously bought-in from overseas being provided by local suppliers. Many developing countries, for example, seek to reduce their dependence on overseas banking and insurance organizations.
- Cultural convergence which has resulted from improved communications and increasing levels of overseas travel has led to a homogenization of international market segments. Combined with the decline in trade barriers, this has allowed many service providers to regard segments of their overseas markets as though they are part of their domestic market.

For an individual company, development of overseas markets can be attractive for a number of reasons. These can be analysed in terms of 'pull' factors which derive from the attractiveness of a potential overseas market and 'push' ones that make an organization's domestic market appear less attractive:

- For firms seeking growth, overseas markets represent new market segments which they may be able to serve with their existing range of products. In this way, a company can continue to produce services at which it is good. Finding new overseas markets for existing or slightly modified services does not expose a company to the risks of expanding simultaneously both its product range and its market coverage.
- Saturation of its domestic market can force a service organization to seek overseas markets. This can come about where a service reaches the maturity stage of its lifecycle in the domestic market while being at a much earlier stage of the cycle in less-developed overseas markets. While the market for fast-food restaurants may be approaching saturation in a number of Western countries—especially the USA—they represent a new service opportunity in the early stages of development in many Eastern European markets.
- Environmental factors may make it difficult for a company to fully exploit its service concept in its domestic market, forcing it to look overseas for opportunities. As an example, the initial planning restrictions imposed on French hypermarket operators forced them to exploit their concept overseas.
- As part of its portfolio management, an organization may wish to reduce its dependence upon one geographical market. The attractiveness of individual national markets can change in a manner unrelated to other national markets. For example, costly competition can develop in one national market but not in others, world economic cycles show lagged effects between different economies and government policies—through specific regulation or general economic management—can have counterbalancing effects on market prospects.
- The nature of a service may require an organization to become active in an overseas market. This particularly affects transport-related services such as scheduled airlines and couriers. A UK scheduled airline flying between London and Paris would most likely try to exploit the non-domestic market at the Paris end of its route.
- Industrial companies operating in a number of overseas countries may require their services suppliers to be able to cater for their needs across national boundaries. A business customer may wish to engage accountants who are able to provide auditing and management accounting services in its overseas subsidiaries. For this, the firm of accountants would probably need to have created an operational base overseas. Similarly, firms selling in a number of overseas markets may wish to engage an advertising agency who can organize a global campaign in a number of overseas markets.
- Similarly, there are many cases where private consumers demand a service that is internationally available. An example is the car-hire business, where customers frequently need to be able to book a hire car in one country for collection and use in another. To succeed in attracting these customers, car-hire companies need to operate internationally.
- Some services are highly specialized and the domestic market is too small to allow economies of scale to be exploited. Overseas markets must be exploited in order to achieve a critical mass that allows a competitive price to be reached. Specialized aircraft-engineering and oil-exploration services fall into this category.
- Economies of scale also result from extending the use of service brands in overseas markets. Expenditure by a fast-food company on promoting its brand image to UK residents is wasted when those citizens travel abroad and cannot find the brand that they have come to

value. Newly created overseas outlets will enjoy the benefit of promotion to overseas visitors at little additional cost.

PHILIPPINES GETS A SHARE OF EMERGING WORLD TRADE IN DATA

Improved communications show how easily a country can gain or lose its competitive advantage within the services sector, generating new flows of international trade. During the 1980s, a variety of factors led to data processing emerging as a major industry, new to the international market.

In the 1980s, organizations of all kinds found an increasing need to enter data into computerized databases—records of customer sales, services performed, details of rolling stock movements, to name but a few. In the early days, most firms regarded this as a backroom function which they could perform most cost effectively by using their own staff on their own premises. With time, an increasing volume of data to be processed and the growing sophistication of data-analysis systems, many service companies emerged to take the burden of data processing from client companies.

At first, most data-processing companies operated close to their clients. However, by the late 1980s, large volumes of data began entering international trade to be processed by companies in overseas countries where costs were lower, working regulations more relaxed and trades unions virtually non-existent. An important factor accounting for this development in international trade was the rapid pace of technological developments. Processed data could now be transmitted back to a client company very quickly using satellites or fibre-optic links.

Data processing has established a firm foothold as an exportable service in areas such as the Caribbean, the Philippines and, to some extent, the Irish Republic. Each of these countries is characterized by relatively low wage rates with skills that are at least as good as those of workers in more developed countries.

The development of the Kansas, US-based Saztec Company illustrates the way in which international trade can be developed. Saztec has won data-processing contracts from major organizations throughout the world, including a number of UK government departments, such as the Home Office and the Treasury. Yet these services are generally produced far away from either the company's or the client's base. The company employs over 800 people in the Philippines, who earn an average of £75 per month—one-fifth of the salary paid to its staff in Kansas. Staff turnover at less than 1 per cent is much lower than the 35 per cent annual rate in Kansas. Furthermore, the company is able to obtain a higher quality of output by the military-style organization and control of its staff—something that would not be accepted in the USA.

The Philippines has become an important exporter of data-processing services by exploiting its comparative cost advantage in labour inputs—something that is useful in capturing high-volume, basic data input where accuracy and cost are paramount. Another country that has considerably developed this service sector is Jamaica, which, in addition to exploiting its low labour costs, offers the advantages of a sophisticated infrastructure—such as satellite links—and generous tax incentives. Ireland, in contrast, has exploited the fact that it has a relatively highly educated and English-speaking work-force who earn about half that of their counterparts in the UK or the USA. A number of firms—such as Wright Investor Services—have been set up in Ire-land to do more sophisticated financial analysis on behalf of the large London-based banks and insurance companies.

13.5 ANALYSING OPPORTUNITIES FOR OVERSEAS DEVELOPMENT OF SERVICES

Overseas markets can represent very different opportunities and threats compared to those to which an organization has been accustomed in its domestic market. Before a detailed market analysis is undertaken, an organization should consider whether the environment of a market is likely to be attractive. By analysing in general terms such matters as political stability or cultural attitudes, an organization may screen out potential markets for which it considers further analysis cannot be justified by the likelihood of success. Where an exploratory analysis of an overseas marketing environment appears to indicate some opportunities, a more thorough analysis might suggest important modifications to a service format which would need to be made before the service could be successfully offered to the market.

This chapter first identifies some general questions that need to be asked in assessing the marketing environment of overseas countries and then considers specific aspects of researching such markets.

13.6 THE OVERSEAS MARKETING ENVIRONMENT

The combination of environmental factors that have contributed to success within an organization's domestic market may be absent in an overseas market, resulting in the failure of attempts to export a service format. In this section, questions to be asked in analysing an overseas marketing environment are examined under the overlapping headings of the political, economic, social, demographic and technological environments.

13.6.1 The political environment

Government and quasi-government organizations influence the legislative and economic frameworks within which companies operate. Although the most important political influences originate from national governments, inter-government agreements can also be important in shaping a national market.

National government framework At a national level, individual governments can influence trade in services in a number of ways:

- At the most general level, the stability of the political system affects the attractiveness of a particular national market. While radical change rarely results from political upheaval in most Western countries, the instability of many Eastern European governments leads to uncertainty about the economic and legislative framework in which services will be provided.
- Licensing systems may be applied by governments in an attempt to protect domestic producers. Licences can be used to restrict individuals practising a particular profession (for example, licensing requirements for accountants or solicitors may not recognize

experience and licences obtained overseas) or they can be used to restrict foreign owners setting up a service operation (for example, the UK government does not allow overseas investors to own more than 25 per cent of shares in UK scheduled airlines).

• Regulations governing service standards may require expensive reconfiguration of the service offer to meet local regulations or may prohibit its provision completely. Gambling-related and medical services often fall into this category.

Import controls can be used to restrict the supply of goods that form an integral part of a service. A restaurant seeking overseas outlets may be forced to source its materials locally, leading to possible problems in maintaining consistent quality standards and also perhaps losing economies of scale.

• Service-production possibilities can be influenced by government policies. Minimum wage levels and conditions of service can be important in determining the viability of a service. For example, many countries restrict the manner in which temporary seasonal staff can be employed, making the operation of a seasonal holiday hotel inflexible and uneconomic.

• Restrictions on currency movements may make it difficult to repatriate profits earned from an overseas service operation.

• Governments are major procurers of services and may formally or informally give preference in awarding contracts to locally owned service organizations.

• Legislation protecting trade marks varies between companies. In some countries, such as Greece, the owner may find it relatively difficult to protect itself legally from imitators.

Beyond the nation state, international institutions can have important consequences for the international marketing of services. Some of the more important are described below.

The European Community (EC)   Although the EC was conceived as a vehicle for reducing trade barriers, this has so far benefited mainly trade in raw materials and manufactured goods. Many non-tariff barriers have existed to restrict the amount of services trade that takes place between EC member states. However, the Single European Act 1987 sought to remove many of these barriers. Most importantly, licensing arrangements are being harmonized so that a company seeking to set up in another member state will no longer need to go through a lengthy approval process in that country. Licences of one state are increasingly being accepted as valid for companies seeking to operate in other member states. This can potentially benefit a wide range of service organizations such as insurance companies and banks which are heavily regulated and can increasingly regard Europe as one large domestic market. Service organizations are also increasingly affected by the requirement that large public service contracts should be put out to EC-wide tendering. This has already resulted in cross-border competition for highway building and maintenance contracts.

According to *Lloyds Bank Economic Bulletin in* January 1989, the probable 'gainers' in the UK are likely to include the insurance and airline industries. These are industries in which UK companies appear to have a comparative cost advantage and/or where trade barriers are high. The disappearance of such barriers is thus likely to benefit these sectors and will provide an incentive for firms to take advantage of their relative strength by expanding into Europe, in some cases through acquisition or merger.

Nevertheless, uncertainties still remain for UK firms seeking expansion within the EC. The lack of a common currency means that companies earning money overseas can never be sure how much this will translate to in sterling, a particular problem where income is in one currency and expenditure in another. The cost alone of exchanging money can put non-domestic companies at a competitive disadvantage—the development of a single European currency will therefore be watched with interest. The EC has also developed social goals with the Social Chapter of the Treaty of Maastricht. This is a declaration of basic rights for workers, such as rights to trade union representation and minimum wages, planned for implementation in 1993. If implemented (the UK has in fact been alone among EC states in refusing to implement it), it would have a significant effect on some service organizations by imposing higher production costs.

The General Agreement on Tariffs and Trade (GATT) The origins of GATT lie in the early post-war period when the signatories to the agreement sought to achieve greater international economic prosperity by exploiting fully the comparative cost advantages of nations by reducing the barriers which inhibited international trade. All the signatories agreed not to increase tariffs on imported goods beyond their existing levels and to work towards the abolition of quotas which restricted the volume of imports.

GATT has proceeded to reduce tariffs and quotas through several rounds, the most recent of which—the Uruguay Round—has sought to reduce barriers to international trade in services. Because of the multi-lateral nature of the GATT negotiations, attempts to liberalize trade in services can be impeded by arguments in completely unrelated areas of trade. For example, attempts to liberalize trade in financial services have been linked to demands for action to reduce agricultural subsidies given by some countries.

Other international agreements and institutions A wide range of other agreements and institutions affect service organizations. At their simplest, they include bilateral agreements between two countries—for example, the Bermuda Agreement which governs the allocation of transatlantic air rights between Britain and the USA. However, even here, change can be slow when there are many items on a hidden agenda. More complex multi-lateral agreements between governments can create policies and institutions that directly affect the marketing environment of firms. Examples include the International Civil Aviation Organization and the Universal Postal Union.

13.6.2 The economic environment

A generally accepted measure of the economic attractiveness of an overseas market is the level of GNP per capita. The demand for most services increases as this figure rises. However, organizations seeking to sell services overseas should also consider the distribution of income within a country which may identify valuable niche markets. For example, the relatively low GNP per head of South Korea still allows a small and relatively affluent group to create a market for high-value overseas holidays.

An organization assessing an overseas market should place great emphasis on future economic performance and the stage which a country has reached in its economic development. While many Western developed economies face saturated markets for a number of services, less-developed economies may be just moving on to that part of their growth curve where services begin to appeal to large groups of people.

A crucial part of the analysis of an overseas market focuses on the level of competition within that market. This can be related to the level of economic development achieved within a country—in general, as an economy develops, its markets become more saturated. This is true of the market for household insurance, which is mature and highly competitive in North America and most Western European countries, but relatively new and less competitive in many developing economies of the Pacific Rim, allowing better margins to be achieved.

The level of competitive pressure within a market is also a reflection of government policy towards the regulation of monopolies and the ease with which it allows new entrants to enter a market. The government of a country can significantly affect the competitive pressure within a market by legislation aimed at reducing anti-competitive practices.

13.6.3 The social and cultural environment

Together, the social and cultural environments represent the values of a society. An understanding of culture and, in particular, an appreciation of cultural differences is clearly important for marketers. Individuals from different cultures not only buy different services but may also respond in different ways to the same service. Examples of differing cultural attitudes and their effects on international trade in services include the following:

- Buying processes vary between different cultures. For example, the role of women in selecting a service may differ in an overseas market compared to the domestic one, thereby possibly requiring a different approach to service design and promotion.
- Some categories of services may be rendered obsolete by certain types of social structure. For example, extended family structures common in some countries have the ability to produce a wide range of services within the family unit, including caring for children and elderly members. Extended families also often reduce the need for bought-in financial services by circulating funds within a very closed system.
- A service that is taken for granted in the domestic market may be seen as socially unacceptable in an overseas one. Interest charged on bank loans may be regarded as a form of usury in some Muslim cultures.
- Attitudes towards promotional programmes differ between cultures. The choice of colours in advertising or sales outlets needs to be made with care because of symbolic associations (for example, the colour associated with mourning/bereavement varies across cultures).
- What is deemed to be acceptable activity in procuring sales varies between cultures. In Middle Eastern markets, for example, a bribe to a public official may be considered essential, whereas it is unacceptable in most Western countries.

In short, culture not only conditions an individual's response to products and influences the nature of the purchase process, it also exercises considerable influence on the structure of consumption within a given society. It should also be remembered that no society is totally homogeneous. Every culture contains smaller subcultures, or groups of people with shared value systems that are based on common experiences and situations. These identifiable subgroups may be distinguished by race, nationality, religion, age, geographical location or some other factor, and share attitudes and behaviour that reflect subcultural influences.

13.6.4 The demographic environment

An analysis of the population of an overseas market will reveal first whether it is increasing in terms of the total number of people available to purchase services. On average, the population of Western Europe grew by 1.6 per cent during the period 1985–90, but this hides a number of differences. Western Germany, although it has a high level of GNP per capita, grew in numerical terms by only 1.04 per cent, while Belgium actually contracted during the same period (by 1 per cent). The strongest growth was shown by Italy and Ireland (3.5 per cent and 5.7 per cent respectively). Much greater growth still was experienced in other parts of the world, especially Latin America (11.8 per cent) and Oceania (7.9 per cent). Of most importance is the projected population growth rate during the planning period.

Within these population totals, structures can differ significantly. For example, there are considerable differences within the EC in the proportion of the population which is either young or elderly, with consequent implications for demand for age-related services. As an example, the proportion of the population aged 60 and above ranges from 15 per cent in the Irish Republic to 21 per cent in the UK. In contrast, the Irish Republic has the greatest proportion of under-15s (30 per cent), compared to West Germany, which has the lowest (15 per cent).

In addition, the geographical distribution of the population and structure of household units may be significantly different from that which had contributed to success in the domestic market. For example, EC statistics show a number of interesting contrasts in geodemographic characteristics between member states.

- Very significant differences occur in home-ownership patterns, with implications for demand for a wide range of home-related services. The proportion of households living in rented accommodation ranges from 21 per cent in Spain to 53 per cent in West Germany, while the proportion with a mortgage ranges from 8 per cent in Spain to 44 per cent in the UK.
- The proportion of the population living within metropolitan areas varies from 13 per cent in Italy to 44 per cent in France. The resulting differences in lifestyles can have implications for services as diverse as car repairs, entertainment and retailing.
- The distribution of self-employed people ranges from 45 per cent in The Netherlands to 17 per cent in Italy, with implications for the sale of personal pension schemes, etc.

13.6.5 The technological environment

An analysis of the technological environment is important for service organizations who require the use of a well-developed technical infrastructure and a workforce which is able to use technology. Communications are an important element of the technological infrastructure. Poorly developed telephone and postal communications may inhibit attempts to make credit cards more widely available, for instance.

13.7 SOURCES OF INFORMATION ON OVERSEAS MARKETS

The methods used to research a potential overseas market are, in principle, similar to those for a domestic market. Companies would normally begin by using secondary data about a potential overseas market which is available to them at home. Sources readily available through specialized libraries, government organizations and specialist research organizations include Department of Trade and Industry information for exporters, reports of international agencies such as the Organization for Economic Cooperation and Development (OECD), chambers of commerce and private sources of information such as that provided by banks. Details of some specific sources are shown in Table 13.1.

Initial desk research at home will identify those markets that show greatest potential for development. A company will then often follow this up with further desk research of materials available locally within the short-listed markets, often carried out by appointing a local research agency. This may include a review of reports published by the target market's own government and specialist locally based market research agencies.

As in home markets, secondary data have limitations in assessing market attractiveness. Problems in overseas markets are compounded by the greater difficulty in gaining access to data, possible language differences and problems of definitions that may differ from those with which an organization is familiar. In the case of services which are a new concept in an overseas market, information on current usage and attitudes to the service may be completely

Table 13.1 Some examples of sources of secondary information on overseas markets

Government agencies
    Department of Trade and Industry market reports
    Overseas governments – for example, US Department of Commerce
    Overseas national and local development agencies
International agencies
    European Community (Eurostat, etc.)
    Organization for Economic Cooperation and Development (OECD)
    GATT
    United Nations
    International Monetary Fund
    Universal Postal Union
    World Health Organization
Research organizations
    Economist Intelligence Unit
    Dun and Bradstreet International
    Market research firms
Publications
    Financial Times country surveys
    Business International
    International Trade Reporter
    Banks' export reviews
Trade associations
    Chambers of commerce
    Industry-specific associations – for example, IATA

lacking. For this reason, it would be difficult to use secondary data to try to assess the likely response from consumers in many Eastern European countries to a proposed chain of out-of-town superstores.

Primary research is used to overcome shortcomings in secondary data. Its most important use is to identify cultural factors that may require a service format to be modified or perhaps abandoned altogether. A company seeking to undertake primary research in a new proposed overseas market would almost certainly use a local specialist research agency. Apart from overcoming possible language barriers, a local agency would better understand attitudes towards privacy and the level of literacy that might affect response rates for different forms of research. However, the problem of comparability between markets remains. For example, when a Japanese respondent claims to 'like' a product, the result may be comparable to a German consumer who claims to 'quite like' it. It would be wrong to assume on the basis of this research that the product is better liked by Japanese consumers than German ones.

Primary research is generally undertaken overseas when a company has become happy about the general potential of a market but is unsure of a number of factors that would be critical for success. An example would be whether intermediaries are willing and able to handle their new service, or whether traditional cultural attitudes will present an insurmountable obstacle for a service not previously available in that market. Instead of commissioning its own specific research, a company may go for the lower-cost route of undertaking research through an omnibus survey. These are regularly undertaken among panels of consumers in overseas markets (for example, the Gallup European Omnibus) which carry questions on behalf of a number of organizations.

13.8 INTERNATIONAL SERVICES MARKETING MANAGEMENT

Many of the issues raised in Chapters 3 and 4 in respect of domestic operations apply equally to the management of overseas services. The process of defining the organization's mission, analysing opportunities, setting quantifiable goals, implementing and monitoring results is just as important in overseas operations, if not more so.

The mission statement has a valuable function in communicating the central purpose of the organization. A simple, straightforward mission statement is vital in creating a common sense of purpose among diverse international groups of workers who may be expected to produce a globally uniform service output.

Objectives must be clearly stated for each overseas market, preferably in a quantified form. These must be set with due regard for local conditions by being achievable. A globally uniform return on investment objective may be inappropriate in locally competitive markets where a service firm nevertheless wants a presence in order to secure international coverage. For this reason, a hotel chain may develop in a popular area to satisfy the needs of its regular users and retain their international loyalty, even though it will not be able to achieve its normal profit objective.

Like any new venture, objectives are essential if performance is to be monitored and any corrective action taken. Because overseas markets are generally much less certain than domestic ones it is important that any variance from target is rapidly analysed and corrective action taken. There must be a clearly defined process by which failing services can be assessed for their prospects of long-term viability or withdrawn from an overseas market. For instance, assumptions on which a market entry decision were based may have proved to be false and no amount of local reformulation of a service will allow it to break even.

A major issue in the international management of services marketing concerns the extent to which an organization's headquarters should intervene in the management of overseas subsidiaries. A commonly heard complaint from marketing managers of the latter is that they are given insufficient freedom to respond to local market conditions. Against this is the argument that intervention from headquarters is vital in order to secure the development of a consistent standard of service output in a planned way. Where a service is quite specialized to a national market and international brand building is relatively unimportant (for example, municipal contract cleaning services) there is strong argument for delegation of management responsibilities on a geographical basis. On the other hand, where the service appeals to an international audience, there is a stronger case for introducing international product- or market-management structures to which overseas managers are answerable.

13.9 REFINING THE MARKETING MIX FOR OVERSEAS MARKETS

Having analysed an overseas market and decided to enter it, an organization must make marketing-mix decisions that will allow it to penetrate that market successfully. These focus on the extent to which the organization will adapt its service offering to the needs of the local market, as opposed to the development of a uniform marketing mix that is globally applicable in all its markets.

The process of globalizing a service offer can be somewhat different from the case with tangible goods on account of the greater variability of services. In addition to being highly variable, services can be extremely flexible—they are more likely than goods to be designed around the specific requirements of small groups of consumers using a basically common formula. Whether services firms choose to standardize their products globally or to adapt them to the needs of local markets is dependent on the nature of the services they offer. Some fast-food restaurants, for example, have adapted their menus, architectural designs and staff-training methods to suit local needs, while retaining a common process formula worldwide. Compared to manufactured goods, it has been argued that services can enjoy the best of both worlds, retaining their competitive advantage by remaining true to their basic managerial approach, while changing their product to meet local needs (see Palmer 1985).

One approach to globalizing services is the process of 'industrializing' the service through the replacement of people with machines and a systems approach to management. Levitt (1976) finds an explanation of the worldwide success of McDonald's restaurants in the 'same systematic modes of analysis, design, organization and control that are commonplace in manufacturing'. This process has occurred not just within the restaurant sector but also in the construction, hotel, professional and technical service sectors. Standardization is often accompanied by a high degree of centralization, sometimes creating further management problems when local managers are instructed to sacrifice their local autonomy in order to benefit the organization globally.

13.9.1 Product and promotion decisions

At the heart of international marketing-mix strategy are product and promotion decisions. Keegan (1989) identifies five possible strategies for adapting the product offering and promotional effort in overseas markets based on the extent to which each of these vary from the global norm:

1. *Maintain a uniform product and promotion worldwide* This approach develops a global marketing strategy as though the world was a single entity. Its benefits are numerous. Customers travelling from one market to another can immediately recognize a service provider and the values for which its global brand stands. If, on the other hand, the service formulation is different in an overseas market, a traveller visiting an overseas outlet may be confused about the qualities of the brand. As an example, a car-rental company with an established position in its home market as the operator of a very modern fleet of cars could harm its domestic image if it pursued a strategy of operating older ones in an overseas market. Standardization of the service offer can also yield benefits of economies of scale which include market research and the design of buildings and uniforms, etc. The use of a common brand name in overseas markets for either the service provider or for specific services also benefits from economies of scale. Travellers to overseas markets will already be familiar with the brand's values as a result of promotion in the domestic market. However, care must be taken in selecting a brand name which will have no unfortunate connotations in overseas markets—the 'Big Mac' for example, translates in French as 'the big pimp'. There can also be problems where legislation prevents an international slogan being used. In France, for example, law No. 75–1349 of 1975 makes use of the French language compulsory in all advertising for services—this also applies to associated packaging and instructions, etc.
   In the case of transport services which operate between different markets it may be not be feasible to adapt the service offering to each of the local markets served, and either a compromise must be reached or the needs of the most important market given precedence. Airlines flying between two countries may find the pricing of in-flight services, the decor of the aircraft and catering having to satisfy very different markets needs at either end of the route.

2. *Retain a uniform service formulation, but adapt promotion* This strategy produces an essentially uniform global service but adapts promotional effort to meet the sensitivities of local markets. The manner in which brand values are communicated in advertisements is a reflection of the cultural values of a society. For this reason, an airline may use a straightforward, brash hard-sell approach in its American market, a humorous one in its British market and a seductive approach in its French market, even though the service offer is identical in each. Similarly, certain objects and symbols used to promote a service may have the opposite effect to that which may be expected at home. Animals, which are often used in Britain to promote a range of home-based goods and services, present a caring and comfortable image, but in some markets such as Japan, they are seen as unclean, disgusting objects.

3. *Adapt the service offering only* This may be done to meet specific local needs or legislation while retaining the benefits of a global image. For this reason, a car-rental company may offer a range of predominantly compact cars in areas where average journeys are short (for example, the Channel Islands) while supplying jeeps and vans in countries such as the USA where motoring costs are lower and distances generally much greater.

4. *Adapt both product and promotion* In practice, a combination of a slight modification to service and promotion is needed in order to meet both differing local needs and differences in local sensitivity to advertising.

5. *Develop new services* Markets may emerge overseas for which a domestic company has no product offering that can easily be adapted. In the field of financial services, the absence in some overseas countries of state provision for certain key welfare services may create a market for insurance-related products (for example dental health insurance cover) which is largely absent in the domestic UK market where the welfare state is relatively comprehensive. Similarly, the social and economic structure of a country can result in quite different products being required. For example, the pattern of property ownership in Malaysia has given rise to a novel two-generation property mortgage not generally found in West European markets.

13.9.2   Pricing decisions

The issue of whether to globalize or localize the service offer arises again in respect of pricing decisions. On the one hand, it may be attractive for an organization to be able to offer a standard charge for a service regardless of where in the world the service is consumed. Consumers will immediately have an idea of how much a service will cost and this helps to develop a long-term relationship between client and company. A common pricing policy will help to project that company as a global brand. However, the reality is that many factors cause global service operators to charge different prices in the different markets in which they operate. There is usually no reason to assume that the pricing policies adopted in the domestic market will prove to be equally effective in an overseas one. Furthermore, for those services produced overseas that are consumed mainly by the local population it may be of no great importance that comparability between different markets is maintained.

There are a number of factors which affect price decisions overseas:

- Competitive pressure varies between markets, reflecting the stage of market development that a service has reached and the impact of regulations against anti-competitive practices.
- The cost of producing a service may be significantly different in overseas markets. For services which employ people-intensive production methods variations in wage levels between countries will have a significant effect on total costs. Personnel costs may also be affected by

differences in welfare provisions for which employers are required to pay. Other significant cost elements that often vary between markets include the level of property prices or rental costs. The cost of acquiring space for a service outlet in Britain, for example, is usually significantly more than in Southern or Eastern Europe.

- Taxes vary between different markets. For example, the rate of value added tax (or its equivalent sales tax) can be as high as 38 per cent in Italy compared to 17 per cent in the UK. There are also differences between markets in the manner in which sales taxes are expressed. In most markets, these are fully incorporated into price schedules, although on other occasions (such as in the USA) it is more usual to price a service exclusive of taxes.
- Local customs influence customers' expectations of the way in which they are charged for a service. While customers in the domestic market may expect to pay for bundles of services, in an overseas market consumers may expect a separate price for each component of the bundle. Also, in some countries, it is customary to expect customers to pay a tip to the front-line person providing a service, whereas other cultures expect to pay an all-inclusive price without the need subsequently to add a tip. Formal price lists for a service may be expected in some markets, but in others, the prevalence of bartering may put an operator who keeps to a fixed price list at a competitive disadvantage.
- Government regulations can limit price freedom in overseas markets. In addition to controls over prices charged by public utilities, many governments require 'fair' prices in a wide range of services—for example, tourism related—and for the prices charged to be clearly publicized.
- The price for a service can reflect the stage of development in a market. For a category of service which is already established in an overseas market a newcomer may be able to gain market share only by offering significant price incentives. In the early stages, discounting may have to be used to establish trial of the service until the brand is sufficiently strongly established that the company can charge a premium price.

It is worth noting that service organizations are generally much better able to sustain discriminatory pricing policies between countries compared to exporters of manufactured goods. If wide differences in the pre-tax price of goods emerge between countries, it is open to entrepreneurs to buy goods in the lower-priced market and sell them in the higher-priced one. The inseparability of production and consumption generally prevents this happening with services. A low-priced hotel room cannot be taken from the relatively cheap Spanish market and offered for sale in London.

13.9.3 Accessibility decisions

Where a service organization is launching into a new overseas market, intermediaries can have a vital role in making the service available to consumers. The selection of intermediaries to facilitate the introduction of a service to a new overseas market is considered in more detail below. Consideration is given briefly here to the place and manner in which a service will be made available.

The analysis of location decisions presented in Chapter 10 can be applied equally to overseas markets. However, a service provider must avoid assuming that a locational strategy that has worked in one market will work just as effectively overseas. A revised strategy may be required on account of differences in the geography of the overseas market, in consumer expectations, in current methods of making that type of service available and in legislative constraints:

- Geographical differences can be important where land-use patterns differ greatly in the target overseas market. As an example, the extensive nature of many urban areas within the

USA results in there being a series of suburban commercial areas rather than a clearly defined central business district. A European retail bank with a city-centre service format which had worked well in its domestic market may only be able to succeed in the USA by developing out-of-own formats of its branches.

- Consumer behaviour may differ significantly in overseas markets. What is a widely accepted outlet in one country may be regarded with suspicion in another. The idea of taking refreshments in a snack bar located within a clothing store may appear quite ordinary within the UK but may encounter resistance in more traditional markets. Also, the extensiveness of outlet networks will be influenced by customers' expectations about ease of access—for example, in relation to the availability of car-parking facilities or the distance that they are prepared to travel.
- Differences in the social, economic and technical environments of a market can be manifested in the existence of different patterns of intermediaries. As an example, the interrelatedness of wholesalers and retailers in Japan can make it much more difficult for an overseas retailer to get into that market compared to other overseas opportunities. In some markets, there may be no direct equivalent of a type of intermediary found in the domestic market. Estate agents on the UK model are not found in many markets where the work of transferring property may be handled entirely by a solicitor. The technological environment can also affect accessibility decisions. The relatively underdeveloped postal and telecommunications services of many Eastern European countries makes direct availability of some services to consumers difficult.
- What is a legal method of distributing a service in the domestic market may be against the law of an overseas country. Many countries restrict the sale of financial services, holidays and gambling services—among others—to a much narrower set of possible intermediaries than is the case in the domestic market.

13.9.4 People decisions

It has already been noted that the people element of the marketing mix is generally more important for services than for goods, therefore it is important that this element is appropriately formulated for an overseas market. Where overseas service delivery involves direct producer-consumer interaction, a decision must be made on whether to employ local or expatriate staff. The latter may be preferable where a service is highly specialized and may be useful in adding to the global uniformity of the service offering. In some circumstances, the presence of front-line expatriate serving staff can add to the appeal of a service. For example, a chain of traditional English pubs established on the Continent may add to their appeal by employing authentic English staff.

For relatively straightforward services a large proportion of staff would be recruited locally, leaving just senior management posts filled by expatriates. Sometimes an extensive staff-development programme may be required to ensure that locally recruited staff perform in a manner that is consistent with the company's global image. This can, in some circumstances, be quite a difficult task. A fast-food operator may have problems in developing values of speed and efficiency among its staff in countries where the pace of life is relatively slow.

Where staff are recruited locally, employment legislation can affect the short- and long-term flexibility of service provision. This can influence the ease with which staff can be laid off or dismissed should demand fall. For example, in Germany, the Dismissals Protection Law (*Kundigungsschutzgesetz*) gives considerable protection to salaried staff who have been in their job for more than 6 months, allowing dismissal only for a 'socially justified' reason. There are also differences between countries in the extent to which an employer can prevent an employee with valuable trade secrets leaving their employment to work for a competitor.

13.10   MARKET-ENTRY STRATEGIES

A new overseas market represents both a potential opportunity and a risk to an organization. A company's market-entry strategy should aim to balance these two elements.

The least risky method of developing an overseas service market is to supply that market from a domestic base, something which is often a possibility in the case of separable service offerings. A wide variety of financial and information services can be provided to overseas markets by post or telephone, avoiding the cost and risk of setting up local service outlets.

Where inseparability of service production and consumption occurs and the producer must go to the consumer, local outlets must be established. Risk can be minimized by gradually committing more resources to a market, based on experience to date. Temporary facilities could be established which have low start-up and close-down costs and where the principal physical and human assets can be transferred to another location. A good example of risk reduction through the use of temporary facilities is found in the pattern of retail development in Eastern Germany following reunification. West German retailers who initially entered East Germany in large numbers were reluctant to commit themselves to building stores in a part of the country that was still economically unstable and where patterns of land use were rapidly changing. The solution adopted by many retailers was to offer branches of their chain in temporary marquees or from mobile vehicles—these could move in response to the changing pattern of demand. While the location of retail outlets remained risky, this did not prevent retailers from establishing net works of distribution warehouses that could supply retail outlets, wherever they were eventually located.

Market-entry risk-reduction strategies also have a time dimension. While there may be long-term benefits arising from being the first company to develop a new category of service in an overseas market, there are also risks. If development is hurried and launched before service quality can be guaranteed to comply with an organization's international standards, the company's long-term image can be damaged, both in the new overseas market and in its wider world one. In the turbulent marketing environment of Eastern Europe in the late 1980s, two of the world's principal fast-food retailers—McDonald's and Burger King—pursued quite different strategies. The former waited until political, economic, social and technological conditions were capable of allowing it to launch a restaurant that met its global standards. In the case of Burger King, its desire to be first in the market led it to offer a very sub-standard service, giving it an image from which it will probably take a long while to recover.

Where the inseparability of a service offer makes it impossible for an organization to supply the service to an overseas market from its home base, an assessment of risk is required in deciding whether it should enter an overseas market on its own or in association with another organization. The former maximizes the strategic and operational control which the organization has over its overseas operations, but it exposes it to the greatest risk where the overseas market is relatively poorly understood. A range of entry possibilities are considered below.

13.10.1   Direct investment in overseas subsidiary

This option gives a service organization maximum control over its overseas operations, but can expose it to a high level of risk on account of the poor understanding that it may have of the overseas market. A company can either set up its own overseas subsidiary from scratch (as many UK hotel companies have done to develop hotels in overseas markets) or it can acquire control of a company which is already trading (such as the acquisition by Marks & Spencer of the US-based Brooks Brothers store group).

Where the nature of the service offer differs relatively little between national markets, or where it appeals to an international market (for example, hotels), the risks from creating a new subsidiary are reduced. Where there are barriers to entry and the service is aimed at an essentially local market with a culture different from the domestic market, the acquisition of an established subsidiary may be the preferred course of action. Even the latter course is not risk-free, as was illustrated by the problems encountered by Midland Bank following its acquisition of a substantial interest in the US-based Crocker Bank during the 1980s.

Direct investment in an overseas subsidiary may also be made difficult by legislation restricting ownership of certain services by foreigners. Civil aviation is a good example where many countries prevent foreigners owning a controlling interest in a domestic operator.

13.10.2   Management contracting

Rather than setting up its own service organization overseas, a company with a proven track record in a service area may seek to run other companies' businesses for them. For a fee, an overseas organization which seeks to develop a new service would contract a team to set up and run the facility. Usually, the management team would get the project started, and gradually hand over its running to a local management. This type of arrangement is useful for an expanding overseas organization where the required management and technical skills are difficult to obtain locally. In countries where the educational infrastructure offers less opportunity for management and technical training, a company (or, in many cases, overseas governments) can buy-in state-of-the-art management skills.

For the company supplying management skills under such contracts, the benefits are numerous. Risks are kept to a minimum as the company generally does not need to invest its own capital in the project. The company gathers overseas market knowledge which it may be able to use to its own advantage if it plans similar ventures of its own in other countries. For staff employed by the company, the challenge of working on an overseas project can offer career opportunities outside the mainstream domestic management route.

Management contracting has found many applications in the service sector. For UK companies, the demise of the British Empire resulted in most newly independent colonies seeking to establish their own service organizations, for which they were ill equipped to manage themselves. Most countries immediately set up their own airline, making use of management expertise bought-in from BOAC—a forerunner of British Airways. More recently, developments in Eastern Europe have resulted in many opportunities for UK-based service companies, including the management of hotels, airlines and educational establishments.

13.10.3   Licensing/franchising

Rather than setting up its own operations in an overseas market, a company can license a local company to provide a service. At its simplest, a licence allows an overseas company to sell a service on behalf of the principal. In the service sector, it can be difficult to define when a licence becomes a franchise. Licensing is more commonly associated with manufactured goods where the identity of the overseas licensee who manufactures the goods is not usually important to the customer, as long as quality control is adequate. The inseparability of service offers makes service producers an integral part of a service, requiring greater control over the whole process by which the overseas business operates. Therefore, while exporters of manufactured goods frequently license an overseas producer to manufacture and sell their products, a company developing a service overseas is more likely to establish a franchise relationship with its overseas producers.

Franchising in an overseas market can take a number of forms. In some cases, the organization seeking to develop overseas could enter into a direct franchising relationship with each individual franchisee. The problem of this approach is the difficulty in monitoring and controlling a possibly large number of franchisees in a country far from home. To alleviate some of these problems, the franchisor would normally establish its own subsidiary in the overseas territory which would negotiate and monitor franchisees locally or, alternatively, grant a master franchise for an area to a franchisee where the latter effectively becomes the franchisor in the overseas country. In between these options are a number of permutations of strategy. For example, a subsidiary could be set up as a joint venture with a local company in order to develop a franchise network.

As with the development of a domestic franchise service network, franchising can allow an organization to expand rapidly overseas with relatively low capital requirements. While a clearly defined business format and method of conducting business is critical to the success of an overseas franchise, things can still go wrong for a number of reasons. The service format could be poorly proven in the home market, making overseas expansion particularly difficult. Unrealistic expectations may be held about the amount of human and financial resources that need to be devoted to the operation of an overseas franchise. Problems in interpreting the spirit and letter of contractual agreements between the franchisor and franchisor can result in acrimonious misunderstanding. A good example of an overseas franchise failure is the breakdown of the agreement made in the 1970s between McDonald's and its Paris franchisee, which resulted in McDonald's successfully pursuing legal proceedings against the latter for failing to maintain the standards as specified.

CHOICE OF INTERNATIONAL MARKET-ENTRY OPTIONS

While franchising is no stranger to the service sector, the hotel industry in particular has been quick to recognize its advantages. A franchised hotel chain with a proven business format and favourable customer recognition is able to grow quite rapidly using capital introduced by its franchisees. Furthermore, in an industry which involves a lot of client contact and attention to detail, it can be easier to motivate relatively small-scale franchisees compared to salaried managers of a large corporation.

The existence of internationally branded chains can in itself offer many advantages over independent stand-alone hotels. For international travellers, brands allow rapid recognition of the standards of service which a hotel is likely to offer. A chain is also better able to support a worldwide sales operation than a single hotel, making the onward reservation of accommoda-tion relatively easy for travellers. Hotel chains have achieved such significance that, by the early 1990s, it has been estimated that about 70 per cent of 50 + bedroom hotels in the USA belonged to some form of chain, the majority as franchise operations. The comparable figure for the UK was just 15 per cent.

International expansion by hotel operators has often been achieved through franchising. This was the route chosen by Choice Hotels International, the largest hotel operator in the world (when measured by hotel numbers rather than rooms). The American-based company operates a total of 2300 hotels in 29 countries and of its 250 000 bedrooms, all but 5000 are operated on a franchise basis, the latter comprising a small number of company-operated or managed hotels. Its hotel chains are highly segmented, with Econo Lodge and Friendship Inns providing basic facilities at the lower end of the market and its Clarion and Quality brands having more up-market chains.

An analysis of Choice Hotels' European development strategy indicates some of the opportunities as well as the possible pitfalls of international franchising. Its strategic plan for Europe, developed during the late 1980s, envisaged having 300 hotels operating under the Choice umbrella by 1997 and 500 by 2000.

One of Choice's first moves into the UK market was to sign a franchise agreement with Scandic Crown Hotels UK, a small chain of five hotels. In return for paying franchise fees, the owners of Scandic Crown Hotels were able to benefit from the worldwide marketing effort of Choice Hotels. The chain was to operate under the brand name of Clarion—one of Choice Hotels' more up-market brands. However, on the point of developing an internationally recognized brand, this initial venture into UK franchising encountered a number of problems. While Choice sought to develop a strong brand which would stand for internationally consistent attributes, it encountered the loyalty of franchisees to their existing names. The latter insisted on giving primary emphasis to their own name and only secondary emphasis to the Clarion brand name, to the point where one typical hotel became known confusingly as the 'Clarion Scandic Crown Nelson Dock'. Choice hotels also became mindful of the variable efforts made by its franchisees in implementing service quality standards for which the Clarion brand stood.

Faced with the problem of establishing values for its franchisees to follow, the company resorted to developing its own small chain of branded hotels to hold up as an example to franchisees of the standards expected of the brand.

In this way, Quality Hotels Europe was founded with the aim of creating a chain of 30 Quality Hotel or Comfort Inn branded hotels throughout Europe, using $200 million of capital provided by the US parent company.

In seeking to expand into Europe, the company was careful not to Americanize the European hotel scene but to incorporate the local character and operating style of hotels to suit the needs of both domestic and international customers. For this reason, it decided not to bring the American-style Econo Lodge, Rodeway and Friendship brands to Europe, opting instead to develop the Clarion, Quality, Comfort and Sleep Inn brands. Of the latter, Quality and Comfort Inns form the focus of the company's effort

In the case of the Sleep Inn brand, Choice sold a franchise for exclusive UK development rights to an organization called Budgotel. Its first hotel opened in Nottingham in 1990, with planned openings soon following on new sites in Hull and Chesterfield. Meanwhile, the European subsidiary established by Choice continued to sell franchises for the Quality and Comfort brands. Unlike the completely new build which characterized new Sleep Inn openings, 75 per cent of Quality and Comfort franchises were conversions from existing hotels. Franchise fees typically worked out at an initial one-off fee of £120 per bedroom, a 1 per cent payment on sales turnover and reservation fees paid to Choice of £3.50 per booking. Franchise agreement were normally for an initial term of 20 years, with mutual rights to terminate after 3-, 6-, 10- and 15-year periods.

The initial poor performance of its European operations led Choice to impose much more stringent strictures on its franchisees with regard to branding. Existing franchisees were no longer allowed to use the corporate brand as secondary to its own name while new franchisees were required to be fully branded from the outset. Any hotel owners who failed to brand their hotels in this manner would lose their franchise. Plans to extend the range of Choice brands available in Europe for franchise was limited to the four core brands of Comfort, Quality, Sleep and Clarion.

For the longer term, the company recognized that opportunities existed in the more up-market luxury hotel sector which it currently did not adequately serve. In addition to the possibility of developing franchise links with existing well-respected hotel names, it has also investigated the possibility of acquiring an up-market European brand which already has a strong position in the luxury-hotel sector. Such a move may make a lot of sense for Choice, allowing its bed space to be sold through its world-wide sales network. The development of an additional brand for the Europe market in addition to its highly segmented range of American brands can be seen as a recognition of the need to adapt brands to meet the needs of overseas markets.

13.10.4 Joint ventures

An international joint venture is a partnership between a domestic company and an overseas organization or government. It can take a number of forms and is particularly attractive to a domestic firm seeking entry to an overseas market where:

- The initial capital requirement threshold is high, resulting in a high level of risk.
- Overseas governments restrict the rights of foreign companies to set up business on their own account, making a partnership with a local company—possibly involving a minority shareholding—the only means of entering the market.
- There may be significant barriers to entry which a company already based in the overseas market could help to overcome. For services, an important barrier is often posed by the availability of intermediaries. As an example, the UK mortgage market is dominated by banks and building societies, largely selling their own mortgages, and a number of foreign banks have taken the view that their best market-entry strategy would be to work in partnership with a smaller building society, providing them with funds and allowing them to sell mortgages under their own name through their established network of branches.
- There may be reluctance of consumers to deal with what appears to be a foreign company. A joint venture can allow the operation to be fronted by a domestic producer with whom customers can be familiar, while allowing the overseas partner to provide capital and management expertise.
- A good understanding of local market conditions is essential for success in an overseas market. It was noted above that the task of obtaining marketing research information can be significantly more difficult abroad compared to an organization's domestic market. A joint venture with an organization already based in the proposed overseas market makes the task of collecting information about a market, and responding sensitively to it, relatively easy.
- Taxation of company profits may favour a joint venture rather than owning an overseas subsidiary outright.

A distinction can be made between equity and non-equity joint ventures. The former involves two or more organizations joining together to invest in a 'child' organization which has its own separate identity. A non-equity joint venture involves agreement between partners

Table 13.2 Examples of UK financial service organizations' involvement in overseas joint ventures

Venture partners	Holding (%)	Subsidiary/purpose
Prudential	50	Creation of Prudential Assicurazione to
Inholding (Italy)	50	provide insurance services in Italy
Abbey National	92	Creation of Abbey National Mutui to offer
Diners Club (Italy)	0	mortgages in Italy
Winterthur (Switzerland)	8	
Gerard and National Caisse des	33	Creation of Trifutures to offer brokerage
Depôts et Consignations (France)	33	services on Paris futures exchange
Banque d'Escompte (France)	33	

Non-equity joint ventures		
Commercial Union	Agreement for CI to sell and distribute CU's life and
Credito Italiano (Italy)	non-life insurance policies in Italy
Hambros Merchant Bank	Cooperation agreement in cross-frontier merger and
Bayerische Vereinsbank (West Germany)	acquisition finance
Barclays Bank	Agreement gave Barclays Bank a banking licence to
Tokyo Trust (Japan)	operate in Japan to provide trust management and securities handling in collaboration with its partner

on such matters as marketing research, new-service development, promotion and distribution, without any agreement to jointly provide capital for a new organization.

Joint ventures are an important feature of many service sectors where the benefits listed above can be achieved. They have assumed particular importance in the hotels, airline and financial services sectors. Some recent examples of the latter are shown in Table 13.2.

Strategic alliances—whether involving joint equity or not—are becoming increasingly important within the service sector. These are agreements between two or more organizations where each partner seeks to add to its competencies by combining its resources with those of a partner. A strategic alliance generally involves cooperation between partners rather than joint ownership of a subsidiary set up for a specific purpose, although it may include agreement for collaborators to purchase shares in the businesses of other members of the alliance.

Strategic alliances can be very powerful within the service sector. They are frequently used to allow individual companies to build upon the relationship they have developed with their clients by allowing them to sell on services that are produced not by themselves but by another member of the alliance. This arrangement is reciprocated between members of that alliance. Strategic alliances have assumed great importance within the airline industry, where a domestic and an international operator can join together to offer new travel possibilities for their respective customers (see case study below).

International strategic alliances can involve a principal nominating a supplier in related service fields as a preferred supplier at its outlets worldwide. This strategy has been used by car-rental companies to secure a link with other transport principals to offer what the latter sees as a value-added service. An example is the agreement whereby Hertz Car Rental was appointed by British Airways as preferred supplier worldwide for a 5-year period from 1988. Under the arrangement, passengers could reserve a Hertz car at the same time as their air ticket and in some instances (for example, shuttle passengers) Hertz guaranteed that a car would be waiting for passengers at their destination airport even if no prior reservation had been made. Hertz gained additional custom for its car-rental business, while British Airways was able to add value to its service offer.

BRITISH AIRWAYS AND USAIR TO FORM WORLD'S LARGEST AIRLINE ALLIANCE

It is not economically feasible for airlines to operate direct flights between all airports they serve, just as a telephone company does not run a cable from each telephone to every other telephone in its network. Therefore during the 1970s and 1980s, airlines developed a series of 'hubs'—airports where passengers could fly in on one route (a 'spoke') and make a connection to another route. The development of hub-and-spoke systems potentially allows a very large range of origin–destination possibilities.

Against the improved journey potential brought by the development of a hub-and-spoke system, making connections at a hub airport can result in problems for transferring passengers. If the two connecting services are operated by completely independent carriers it may. be necessary to purchase two separate tickets and passengers may have to transfer their own baggage rather than checking it in through to their final destination. Should the incoming flight be delayed, the second carrier may show little sympathy in rescheduling a ticket on account of delay caused by another airline.

Because of these operational problems, competitive advantage at hub airports is gained by airlines that can offer the most comprehensive network of services. This can be achieved either by being very large or by forming strategic alliances with other airlines. The latter approach can make sense where a dom-estic operator with an intensive network of local routes from its hub and an overseas carrier operating into that hub come to an agreement for the through-ticketing of passengers between national and international routes. The benefit for passengers would be a 'seamless' journey, free of the dual ticketing and transfer problems described above. For the airlines, a strategic alliance brings mutual benefits. The domestic operator feeds passengers into its partner's international services while the latter provides its partner with additional domestic business.

During the late 1980s, British Airways had been watching with concern the growth of very large American carriers such as American, United and Delta, who were capable of offering a very comprehensive network of services. These were putting British Airways at a competitive disadvantage. For a number of years, British Airways had been seeking a strategic alliance with an airline that would allow it to compete with these large carriers by being able to provide 'seamless' transatlantic travel to a comprehensive range of American destinations. Discussions had been taking place with United Airlines to form a strategic alliance, but broke down following the failure of a proposed management buy-out for United. British Airways then pursued an alliance with the Dutch airline KLM, hoping that the alliance might have included the Dutch airline's stake in Northwest Airlines. Again, discussions broke down.

In July 1992 British Airways announced that it had reached agreement to acquire an interest in USAir for $750 million, creating an airline with a combined annual turnover of $16 billion. Due to statutory restrictions on the level of voting power that could be held by non-US citizens in US airlines, British Airways would only be able to cast 25 per cent of the votes at USAir shareholders' meetings, despite agreeing to purchase 44 per cent of the total shares. Nevertheless, its American competitors pointed out that the structure of the deal would give British Airways effective control over a number of crucial issues. As a result of strong lobbying by the large American airlines—who wanted permission for the takeover to be made conditional upon American airlines gaining greater access to the UK market—British Airways' attempted strategic alliance was initially blocked by the US government.

British Airways was anxious not to let the proposed alliance be lost and lobbied hard to win approval, both directly to the American government and indirectly through the UK government. Eventually, in March 1993, a modified strategic alliance was approved by the US government with a number of awkward caveats which prevented British Airways from taking too much control too quickly. Crucial to British Airways was approval of a 'code-sharing' agreement which allowed international flights to appear in USAir schedules as USAir-operated flights but in British Airways schedules as British Airways flights. The agreement with USAir meant that British Airways would be able to feed passengers from its transatlantic route network into USAir's hub airports for onward movement by the latter's network. Similarly, USAir's loyal domestic clientele would be fed into British Airways' European hub airports for onward connections. Both airlines would be able to significantly increase the range of 'seamless' journeys possible within their networks.

British Airways claimed that the alliance with USAir was a major step towards achieving its policy of globalization, paving the way for a comprehensive global airline group. Progress towards this had already been made by an agreement in 1990 with the Russian airline Aeroflot to form a new international airline, 'Air Russia', and with a German regional airline to form Deutsch BA.

REVIEW QUESTIONS

1. Examine the reasons why a UK-based general insurance company should seek to expand into continental Europe.
2. What cultural differences may cause problems for a hotel chain developing a location in India?
3. How might a bank go about researching market potential for business development loans in an overseas country?
4. In what circumstances is a global rather than a localized marketing strategy likely to be successful?
5. Suggest methods by which a firm of consulting engineers can minimize the risk of proposed overseas expansion.
6. What is meant by a strategic alliance and why are they of importance to the services sector? Give examples of strategic alliances.

GLOSSARY

Blueprint   A method of visually portraying the processes and participants involved in the production of a service.

Branding   The process of creating a distinctive identity for a service or service organization.

Competitive advantage   A firm has a marketing mix that the target market sees as meeting its needs better than the competitors' marketing mix.

Consumer services   Services that are finally used up in consumption by individuals and give rise to no further economic benefit.

Co-production of service   A service benefit can be realized only if more than one party contributes to its production, e.g. customer–producer co-production implies that customers take a role in producing service benefits.

Core service   The essential nature of a service, expressed in terms of the underlying need which it is designed to satisfy.

Critical incidents   Encounters between customers and service producers that can be especially satisfying or dissatisfying.

Culture   The whole set of beliefs, attitudes and customs common to a group of people.

Customer Charter   A statement by a service organization to its customers of the standards of service which it pledges to achieve.

Customer expectations   The standard of service against which actual service delivery is assessed.

Customer needs   The underlying forces that drive an individual to make a purchase and thereby satisfy his or her needs.

Customization   The deliberate and planned adaptation of a service to meet the specific requirements of individual customers.

Direct marketing   Direct communication between a seller and individual customers using a method of promotion other than face-to-face selling.

Discriminatory pricing   Selling a service at two or more prices, where the difference in prices is not based on the differences in costs.

External benefits   Service benefits for which the producer cannot appropriate value from recipients.

Franchise   An agreement where a franchisor develops a good service format and marketing strategy and sells the rights for other individuals or organizations ('franchisees') to use that format.

Functional quality   Customers' subjective judgements of the quality of service delivery.

High-contact services   Services in which the production process involves a high level of contact between an organization's employees and its customers.

Industrialization of services The process of de-skilling and simplifying service production processes with the aim of reducing variability in outcomes and processes.

Inseparability The production of most services cannot be spatially or temporally separated from their consumption.

Intangibility Pure services present no tangible cues which allow them to be assessed by the senses of sight, smell, sound, taste or touch.

Intermediaries Individuals or organizations involved in transferring service benefits from the producer to the final consumer. For services, this usually requires the intermediary to become a co-producer of the service.

Internal marketing The application of the principles and practices of marketing to an organization's dealings with its employees.

Just-in-Time (JIT) delivery Reliably getting products to the customer just before the customer needs them. An essential aspect of perishable service production processes.

Key clients Customers who are particularly important to an organization.

Management contracting Selling an organization's management expertise to manage another organization's facility on its behalf.

Marginal cost The addition to total cost resulting from the production of one additional unit of output.

Market A group of potential customers with similar needs who are willing to exchange something of value with sellers offering products that satisfy their needs.

Market segmentation A process of identifying groups of customers within a broad product market who share similar needs and respond similarly to a given marketing mix formulation.

Marketing mix The aspects of marketing strategy and tactics that marketing management use to gain a competitive advantage over its competitors. A conceptual framework which—for services—usually includes elements labelled the 'service offer', 'price', 'promotion', 'accessibility', 'people', 'physical evidence' and 'processes'.

Mission statement A means of reminding everyone within an organization of the essential purpose of the organization.

Multiplier Effect The addition to total income and expenditure within an area resulting from an initial injection of expenditure.

Mystery shopper A person employed by an organization to systematically record the standard of its service delivery.

Organizational image The way consumers see the organization providing a service, based on the consumers' set of beliefs and previous exposure to the organization.

Perishability Describes the way in which service capacity cannot be stored for sale in a future period—if capacity is not sold when it is produced, the chance to sell it is lost forever.

Positioning Developing a marketing mix which gives an organization a competitive advantage with its chosen target market.

Producer services Services that are sold to other businesses in order to assist them in producing something else of value. Often referred to as 'Business-to-business services'.

Product line A range of service offers that are related to each other.

Product mix The total range of services offered by an organization.

Productivity The efficiency with which inputs are turned into outputs. Difficult to measure for services as inseparability means that changes in production inputs often affect consumers' perceptions of the value of service outcomes.

Pure services Services which have none of the characteristics associated with goods, i.e. are intangible, inseparable, instantly perishable and incapable of ownership.

Quality of service The standard of service delivery, expressed in terms of the extent to which the customers' expectations are met.

Quality Circles Groups of employees formed to discuss methods of better meeting customers' expectations of quality.

Queuing system A system for handling temporal excesses of demand relative to capacity.

Relationship marketing A means by which an organization seeks to maintain an ongoing relationship between itself and its customers, based on continuous patterns of service delivery, rather than isolated and discrete transactions.

Roles Behaviour of an individual which is a result of his or her social conditioning, as distinct from innate predispositions.

Scripting Pursuing a pattern of behaviour that is tightly specified by another party.

Service agents Intermediaries who assist a service principal in making service benefits available to consumers. An agent is usually a co-producer of a service and acts on behalf of the service principal, with whom customers enter into legal relations.

Service encounter The period during which an organization's human and physical resources interact with a customer in order to create service benefits.

Service image The way consumers picture a service offer, based on their set of beliefs and previous experience of the service.

Service offer The complexity of tangible and intangible benefits that make up the total functional, psychological and social benefits of a service.

Service principal A relational term describing an organization which produces a service, but which makes some or all of the benefits available through intermediaries.

Service process The activities involved in producing a service which can be specified in the form of a blueprint.

SERVQUAL A method of researching service quality and the gaps between the expectations of customers and the perceptions of actual service delivery.

Substantive service The essential function of a service.

Tangible cues Physical elements of the service offer, brochures and adverts which provide tangible stimuli in the buying decision-making process.

Technical quality Objective measures of quality, not necessarily the measures that consumers consider to be important.

Variability The extent to which service processes or outcomes vary from a norm.

REFERENCES

Aaker, D. A. and J. G. Myers (1982), *Advertising Management*, Prentice-Hall, Englewood Cliffs, NJ.

Abell, D. F. and J. S. Hammond (1979), *Strategic Market Planning: Problems and Analytical Approaches*, Prentice-Hall, Englewood Cliffs, NJ.

Ackoff, R. L. (1970), *A Concept of Corporate Planning*, Wiley-Interscience, New York.

Adams, J. and J. K. V. Prichard (1987), *Franchising, Practice and Precedents in Business Format Franchising*, 2nd edn, Butterworths, London.

Alderson, W. (1982), *Marketing Behaviour and Executive Action*, Irwin, Homewood, IL.

Allen, J. (1988), 'Service Industries: Uneven Development and Uneven Knowledge', *Area*, **20**, pp. 15–22.

Anderson, P. (1982), 'Marketing, Strategic Planning and Theory', *Journal of Marketing*, Spring, pp. 15–26.

Ansoff, I. H. (1957), 'Strategies for Diversification', *Harvard Business Review*, September–October.

Ansoff, H. I. (1984), *Implementing Strategic Management*, Prentice-Hall, Englewood Cliffs, NJ.

Anthony, R. N. (1988), *Planning and Control Systems: A Framework for Analysis*, Harvard University Press, Cambridge, MA.

Arbratt, R. and D. Sacks (1988), 'Perceptions of the Societal Marketing Concept', *European Journal of Marketing*, **22**, pp. 25–33.

Arndt, J. (1977), 'A Critique of Marketing Concepts', in White, P. D. and Slater, C. (eds), *Macromarketing*, University of Colorado Press, Colorado.

Assael, H. (1990), *Marketing: Principles and Strategy*, 2nd edn, The Dryden Press, Fort Worth, TX.

Atkinson, J. (1984), 'Manpower Strategies for Flexible Organizations', *Personnel Management*, August.

Bagozzi, R. P. (1975), 'Marketing as Exchange', *Journal of Marketing*, **39**, No. 4, pp. 32–9.

Baker, M. J. (1979) *Marketing: An Introductory Text*, Macmillan, London.

Baker, M. J. (1985), *Marketing Strategy and Management*, Macmillan, London.

Barnes, I. and J. Campbell (1988), 'From Planners to Entrepreneurs: The Privatisation of Local Economic Assistance?' *Public Policy and Administration*, **3**, No. 3.

Bateson, J. E. G. (1977), 'Do We Need Service Marketing?' in *Marketing Consumer Services: New Insights*, Report 77–115, Marketing Science Institute, Boston, MA.

Bateson, J. E. G. (1979), 'Why We Need Service Marketing' in Ferrell O. C., Brown S. W. and

Lamb C. W. (eds), *Conceptual and Theoretical Developments in Marketing*, AMA, Chicago, IL.

Bayton, J. A. (1958), 'Motivation, Cognition, Learning-Basic Factors in Consumer Behaviour', *Journal of Marketing*, **22**, (Jan), pp. 282–89.

Beer, M. *et al.* (1984), *Managing Human Assets*, Free Press, New York.

Berry, L. L. (1980), 'Services Marketing is Different', *Business*, May-June, **30**, No. 3, pp. 24–9.

Berry, L. L. (1981), 'The Employee as Customer', *Journal of Retail Banking*, March.

Berry, L. L. (1983), 'Relationship Marketing', in Berry L. L. *et al.* (eds), *Emerging Perspectives of Services Marketing*, American Marketing Association, Chicago, IL.

Bitner, M. J. (1990), 'Evaluating Service Encounters: The Effects of Physical Surroundings and Employee Responses', *Journal of Marketing*, **51**, April, pp. 69–82.

Bitner, M. J., B. H. Booms, and M. S. Tetreault, (1990), 'The Service Encounter: Diagnosing Favorable and Unfavorable Incidents', *Journal of Marketing*, **54**, January, pp. 71–84.

Bolton, R. and J. Drew, (1991), 'A Multistage Model of Customers' Assessments of Service Quality and Value', *Journal of Consumer Research*, **17**, March, pp. 375–84.

Booms, B. H. and M. J. Bitner (1981), 'Marketing Strategies and Organisation Structures for Service Firms', in Donnelly, J. and George, W. R. (eds), *Marketing of Services*, American Marketing Association Chicago, pp. 51–67.

Borden, N. H. (1965), 'The Concept of the Marketing Mix', in Schwartz, G. (ed.), *Science in Marketing*, John Wiley, New York, pp. 386–97.

Bowden, D. E. and B. Scheider (1988), 'Services Marketing Management: Implications for Organisational Behaviour', *Research in Organisational Behaviour*, **10**, pp. 43–80.

Boxall, P. (1992), 'Strategic HRM: Beginnings of a New Theoretical Direction', *Human Resource Management Journal*, **2**, No. 3.

Bramwell, B. and G. Broom (1989), 'Tourism Development Programmes—An Approach to Local Authority Tourism Initiatives', *Tourism Intelligence Papers*, English Tourist Board, with subsequent updates.

British Franchise Association (1989), Spring National Franchise Exhibition, Official Catalogue, May.

Brooke, R. (1985), 'The Enabling Authority—Practical Consequences', *Local Government Studies*, September-October, pp. 55–63.

Brookes, R. (1988), *The New Marketing*, Gower Press, Aldershot.

Burchill, F. (1992), *Labour Relations*, Macmillan, London.

Bureau, J. R. (1981), *Brand Management*, Macmillan, London.

Campbell, N. C. G. (1985), 'An Interaction Approach to Organisational Buying Behaviour', *Journal of Business Research*, **13**, pp. 35–48.

Carlzon, J. (1987), *Moments of Truth*, Ballinger, Cambridge, MA.

Carman, J. M. (1990), 'Consumer Perceptions of Service Quality: An Assessment of the SERVQUAL Dimensions', *Journal of Retailing*, **66** (1), pp. 33–55.

Carman, J. M. and E. Langeard (1979), 'Growth Strategies for Service Firms', *Proceedings of the 8th Annual Meeting of the European Academy for Advanced Research in Marketing*, Gröningen.

Central Statistical Office (CSO) (1991), *Annual Abstract of Statistics*, HMSO, London.

Chandler, A. (1962), *Strategy and Structure*, MIT Press, Cambridge, MA.

Channon, D. F. (1978), *The Service Industries*, Macmillan, London.

Charter, R. E. J. and F. Fernique (1990), *The Financial Performance of the Top 100 UK Business Format Franchising Companies*, CAMC, Oxford.

Chartered Institute of Public Finance and Accountancy, (1991), *Leisure and Recreation Statistics, 1990–91 estimates*, London.

Chisnall, P. (1985), *Marketing: A Behavioural Analysis*, McGraw-Hill, Maidenhead.

Chisnall, P. M. (1986), *Marketing Research*, McGraw-Hill, Maidenhead.

Christopher, M. A. Payne, and M. Ballantyne, (1991), *Relationship Marketing*, Heinemann, London.

Churchill, G. and C. Suprenant, (1982), 'An Investigation into the Determinants of Customer Satisfaction', *Journal of Marketing Research*, **19**, November, pp. 491–504.

Cole, G. (1988), *Personnel Management*, DP Publications, London.

Colley, R. (1961), *Defining Advertising Goals for Measured Advertising Response*, Association of National Advertisers, New York, pp. 10–12.

Coulson-Thomas, C. T. (1985), *Marketing Communications*, Heincmann, London.

Cowell, D. (1984), *The Marketing of Services*, Heinemann, London.

Cowell, D. (1988), 'New Service Development', *Journal of Marketing Management*, **3**, p. 3.

Crimp, M. (1990), *The Marketing Research Process*, Prentice-Hall, Englewood Cliffs, NJ.

Cronin, J. J. and S. A. Taylor, (1992), 'Measuring Service Quality: A Re-examination and Extension', *Journal of Marketing*, **56**, July, pp. 55–68.

Crosby, L. A. (1989), 'Maintaining Quality in the Service Relationship', in Brown S. W., and Gummesson, E. (eds), *Quality in Services*, Lexington Books, Lexington, MA.

Crosby, L. A., K. R. Evans, and Cowles D. (1990), 'Relationship Quality in Services Selling: An Interpersonal Influence Perspective', *Journal of Marketing*, **54**, July, pp. 68–81.

Crosby, P. B. (1984), *Quality Without Tears*, New American Library, New York.

Cunningham, M. T. and P. W. Turnbull (1982) 'Inter-organisational Personal Contact Patterns', in Häkansson, H. (ed.), *International Marketing and Purchasing of Industrial Goods*, John Wiley, New York.

Cyert, R. M. and J. G. March, *A Behavioural Theory of the Firm*, Prentice-Hall, Englewood Cliffs, NJ.

Davis, D. L., J. P. Guiltinan and W. H. Jones (1979), 'Service Characteristics, Consumer Search and the Classification of Retail Services', *Journal of Retailing*, **55**, p. 3.

Day, G. S. and R. Wensley, (1983), 'Marketing Theory with a Strategic Orientation', *Journal of Marketing*, **47**, Fall, pp. 79–89.

Delozier, M. W. (1976), *Marketing Communication Process*, McGraw-Hill, Maidenhead.

Deshpandé, R. and G. Zaltman (1984), 'A Comparison of Factors Affecting Researcher and Manager Perceptions of Market Research Use', *Journal of Marketing Research*, 21 (February), pp. 32–38.

Demski, J. S. and S. Baiman (1980), 'Economically Optimal Performance Evaluation and Control Systems', *Journal of Accounting Research*, **18**, pp. 184–220.

Department of Transport (1991), *Transport Statistics*, HMSO, London.

Diffenbach, J. (1983), 'Corporate Environmental Analysis in US Corporations', *Long Range Planning*, **16**, No. 3, pp. 107–16.

Dolan, P. and I. Brierley, (1992), *A Tale of Two Bus Companies*, Partnership Research, London.

Donovan (1968) 'Trade Unions and Employers' Associations', Royal Commission, HMSO, London.

Drucker, P. F. (1973), *Management: Tasks, Responsibilities and Practices*, Harper & Row, New York.

Dwyer, F. R., P. H. Schurr, and S. Oh, (1987), 'Developing Buyer and Seller Relationships', *Journal of Marketing*, **51**, April, pp. 11–27.

Easingwood, C. J. (1986), 'New Product Development For Service Companies', *Journal of Product Innovation Management*, No. 4.

Eccles, R. G., (1983), 'Control with Fairness in Transfer Pricing', *Harvard Business Review*, Nov/Dec, pp. 149–56.

Eiglier, P. and E. Langeard (1977), 'A New Approach To Service Marketing' in *Marketing Consumer Services: New Insights*, Report 77–115, Marketing Science Institute, Boston, MA.

Ennew, C. P. Wong, and M. Wright (1992), 'Organisational Structures and the Boundaries of the Firm: Acquistions and Divestments in Financial Services', *The Services Industries Journal*, **12**, No. 4, pp. 478–97.

Firestone, S. H. (1983), 'Why Advertising a Service is Different' in Berry L. L., Shostack G. L. and Upah G. D. (eds), *Emerging Perspectives in Services Marketing*, American Marketing Association, Chicago, IL.

Fishbein, M. (1967), *Readings in Attitude Theory and Measurement*, John Wiley, New York.

Fisk, R. P. (1981), 'Toward a Consumption/evaluation Process Model for Services', in Donnelly, J. H. and George, W. R. (eds), *Marketing of Services*, American Marketing Association, Chicago, IL.

Frombrun, C. (1984), *Strategic Human Resource Management*, John Wiley, New York.

Fox, A. (1988) *Man Mismanagement*, IRRU, Warwick.

Frazier, G. L. (1983), 'Interorganisational Exchange Behaviour: A Broadened Perspective', *Journal of Marketing*, **47**, Fall, pp. 68–78.

Fuchs, V. (1968), *The Service Economy*, National Bureau of Economic Research, Columbia University Press, New York.

George, W. R. and L. L. Berry (1981), 'Guidelines for the Advertising of Services', *Business Horizons*, **24**, July-August.

George, W. R., J. P. Kelly and C. E. Marshall (1983), 'Personal Selling of Services', in Berry, L. L., Shostack, G. L. and Upah, G. D. (eds), *Emerging Perspectives in Services Marketing*, American Marketing Association, Chicago, IL.

George, W. R. and T. A. Myers (1981), 'Life Underwriters' Perceptions of Differences in Selling Goods and Services', *CLU Journal*, April.

Gershuny, J. (1978), *After Industrial Society? The Emerging Self-Service Economy*, Macmillan, London.

Giles, W. (1988), 'Marketing Planning for Maximum Growth', in Thomas, M. J. (ed.), *The Marketing Handbook*, Gower, Aldershot.

Golzen, G. and C. Barrow (1986), 'Taking Up a Franchise', *The Daily Telegraph Guide*, 3rd edn, London.

Goodchild, M. F. and V. T. Noronha (1987), 'Location Allocation and Impulsive Shopping: The Case of Gasoline Retailing, in Ghosh, A. and Rushton, G. (eds), *Spatial Analysis and Location Allocation Models*, Van Nostrand Reinhold, New York.

Govoni, N., Eng, R. Galpes and M. Galper (1986), *Promotional Management*, Prentice-Hall, Englewood Cliffs, NJ.

Greenley, G. E. and S. M. Matcham (1986), 'Marketing Orientation in the Service of Incoming Tourism', *European Journal of Marketing*, **20**, No. 7, pp. 64–73.

Gronroos, C. (1978), 'A Service Orientated Approach to the Marketing of Services', *European Journal of Marketing*, **12**, No. 8, pp. 588–601.

Gronroos, C. (1982), *Strategic Management and Marketing in the Service Sector*, Swedish School of Economics and Business Administration, Helsingfors, Finland.

Gronroos, C. (1984a), *Strategic Management and Marketing in the Service Sector*, Chartwell-Bratt, Bromley, Kent.

Gronroos, C. (1984b), 'A Service Quality Model and its Marketing Implications', *European Journal of Marketing*, **18**, No. 4, pp. 36–43.

Gronroos, C. (1989), 'Defining Marketing: A Market-Oriented Approach', *European Journal of Marketing*, **23**, No. 1, pp. 52–60.

Gronroos, C. (1990a), *Service Management and Marketing: Managing the Moments of Truth in Service Competition*, Lexington, Books, Lexington, MA.

Gronroos, C. (1990b), 'Relationship Approach to Marketing in Service Contexts: The Marketing and Organisational Interface,' *Journal of Business Research*, **20**, pp. 3–11.

Gronroos, C. (1990c), *Service Marketing and Management*, Lexington Books, Lexington, MA.

Gronroos, C. (1991), 'The Marketing Strategy Continuum: Towards a Marketing Concept for the 1990s', *Management Decision*, **29**, No. 1, pp. 7–13.

Guest, D. (1987), 'Human Resource Management and Industrial Relations', *Journal of Management Studies*, **24**, No. 5.

Guest, D. (1989), 'HRM and Personnel Management: Can you spot the difference?', *Personnel Management*, January.

Guest, D. (1991), 'Personnel Management: The End of Orthodoxy?', *British Journal of Industrial Relations*, **29**, No. 2.

Guest, D. (1992), 'HRM Current Trends and Future Prospects', Unpublished paper for the LSE Industrial Relations Trade Union Seminar.

Guiltinan, J. P. (1987), 'The Price Bundling of Services: A Normative Framework,' *Journal of Marketing*, **51**, April, pp. 74–85.

Gummesson, E. (1991), 'Marketing-orientation Revisited: The Crucial Role of the Part-time Marketer', *European Journal of Marketing*, **25**, No. 2, pp. 60–75.

Gurshuny, J. (1978), *After Industrial Society*, Macmillan, London.

Häkansson, H. (ed.) (1982) *International Marketing and Purchasing of Industrial Goods*, IMP Group, John Wiley, New York.

Handy, C. B. (1989), *The Age of Unreason*, Harvard Business School Press, Boston, MA.

Hart, S. (1988), 'The Causes of Product Deletion in British Manufacturing Companies', *Journal of Marketing Management*, **3**, p. 3.

Hendry, C. and A. Pettigrew (1986), 'The Practice of Strategic HRM', *Personnel Review*, **15**, No.5.

Hendry, C. and A. Pettigrew (1990), 'An Agenda for the 1990s', *International Journal of HRM*, **1**, No.1.

Henry, H, (1971), *Perspectives on Management Marketing and Research*, Crosby Lockwood, London.

Herzberg, F. (1966), *Work and the Nature of Man*, Staples Press, New York.

Hill, C. W. L. and J. F. Pickering (1986), 'Divisionalisation, Decentralisation and Performance of Large United Kingdom Companies', *Journal of Management Studies*, **23** (January), pp. 26–50.

Hise, R. T. (1977), *Product/Service Strategy*, Petrocelli/Charter, New York.

HMI (1991), *Higher Education in Further Education Colleges*, HMI Report, ref. 228/91/NS, Department of Education and Science, London.

Hoffer, C. W. and D. E. Schendel (1978), *Strategy Formulation: Analytical Concepts*, West, New York,

Hood, C. (1991), 'A Public Management for All Seasons', *Public Administration*, **69**, Spring, pp. 3–19.

Houston, F. S. and J. B. Gassenheimer (1987), 'Marketing and Exchange', *Journal of Marketing*, **51**, October, pp. 3–18.

Howard, J. A. and J. N. Sheth (1969), *The Theory of Buyer Behaviour*, John Wiley, New York.

Huff, D. L. (1966), 'A Programmed Solution for Approximating an Optimal Retail Location', *Land Economics*, **42**, pp. 293–303.

Hyman, H. H. (1960), 'Reflections on Reference Groups', *Public Opinion Quarterly*, Fall.

Ingham, H. (1991), 'Organisational Structure and Internal Control in the UK Insurance Industry', *The Services Industries Journal*, 11, No. 4, October, pp. 425–38.

International Labour Office (ILO) (1991), *Year Book of Labour Statistics*, Geneva.

Jackson, B. B. (1985a), 'Build Customer Relationships that Last', *Harvard Business Review*, November-December.

Jackson, B. B. (1985b), *Winning and Keeping Industrial Customers: The Dynamics of Customer Relations*, Lexington Books, Lexington, MA.

Jaworski, B. J. (1988), 'Toward a Theory of Marketing Control: Environmental Context, Control Types and Consequences', *Journal of Marketing*, 52, No. 3, pp. 23–39.

Jelinek, M., L. Smirich and P. Hirsch (1983), 'Introduction: A Code of Many Colours', *Administrative Science Quarterly*, 28, p. 337.

Johnson, E. M. (1970), 'The Selling of Services', in Buell, V. P. (ed.), *A Handbook of Modern Marketing*, McGraw-Hill, New York.

Johnson, G. and K. Scholes, (1988), *Exploring Corporate Strategy*, 2nd edn, Prentice-Hall, Hemel Hempstead.

Jones, G. (1992), 'Setting Measurable Standards in Customer Service', Paper presented at BEM seminar on the measurement of customer service. London, June.

Jones, K. G. and D. R. Mock (1984), 'Evaluating Retail Trading Performance', in Davies, R. L. and Rogers, D. S. (eds), *Store Location and Store Assessment Research*, John Wiley, Chichester.

Juran, J. M. (1982), *Upper Management and Quality*, Juran Institute, New York.

Karnani, A. (1984), 'The Value of Market Share and the Product Life Cycle—a Game Theoretic Model', *Management Science*, 6, June, pp. 696–712.

Keegan, W. J. (1989), *Global Marketing Management*, 4th edn, Prentice-Hall, Englewood Cliffs, NJ.

Kent, R. A. (1986), 'Faith in the Four Ps: An Alternative', *Journal of Marketing Management*, 2, No. 2, pp. 145–54.

Key Note (1987), 'Franchising. An Industry Sector Overview', London.

King, S. (1975), 'Practical Progress from a Theory of Advertisements, *ADMAP*, October.

Kinnear, T. and J. Taylor (1991), *Marketing Research: An Applied Approach*, McGraw-Hill, New York.

Kohli, A. K. and B. J. Jaworski, (1990), 'Market Orientation: The Construct, Research Propositions and Management Implications', *Journal of Marketing*, 54, April, pp. 1–18.

Kotler, P. (1991), *Marketing Management: Analysis, Planning, Implementation and Control*, Prentice-Hall, Englewood Cliffs, NJ.

Kotler, P. and A. Andreasen (1991), *Strategic Marketing for Non-Profit Organisations*, Prentice-Hall, Englewood Cliffs, NJ.

Kotler, P. and G. Armstrong (1991), *Principles of Marketing*, 5th edn, Prentice-Hall, Englewood Cliffs, NJ.

Lavidge, R. J. and G. A. Steiner (1961), 'A Model for Predictive Measurements of Advertising Effectiveness', *Journal of Marketing*, 25 (October), pp. 61–65.

Lazarsfeld, P. F., B. Berelson and H. Gaudet (1948), *The People's Choice*, Columbia University Press.

Levitt, T. (1960), 'Marketing Myopia', *Harvard Business Review*, July-August, pp. 45–56.

Levitt, T. (1972), 'Production Line Approach to Service', *Harvard Business Review*, September-October, pp. 41–52.

Levitt, T. (1976), 'Addendum on Marketing and the Post-industrial Society', *The Public Interest*, No. 44, Summer, pp. 69–103.

Levitt, T. (1981), 'Marketing Intangible Products and Product Tangibles', *Harvard Business Review*, **59**, May-June, pp. 95–102.

Levy, S. and G. Zaltman (1975), *Marketing, Society and Conflict*, Prentice-Hall, Englewood Cliffs, NJ.

Lewis, B. R. (1981), 'Restaurant Advertising: Appeals and Consumers' Intentions', *Journal of Advertising Research*, **21**, No. 5, pp. 69–74.

Lewis, B. R. (1991), 'Bank Service Quality', *Journal of Marketing Management*, **7**, No. 1, pp. 47–62.

Lewis, B. R. and V. W. Mitchell (1990), 'Defining and Measuring the Quality of Customer Service, *Marketing Intelligence and Planning*, **8**, No. 6.

Lovelock, C. H. (1981), 'Why Marketing Needs to be Different for Services', in Donnelly, J. H. and George, W. R. (eds), *Marketing of Services*, American Marketing Association, Chicago, IL.

Lovelock, C. H. (1983), 'Classifying Services to Gain Strategic Marketing Insight', *Journal of Marketing*, **47**, Summer, pp. 9–20.

Lovelock, C. H. (1984a), *Services Marketing, Text, Cases and Readings*, Prentice-Hall, Englewood Cliffs, NJ.

Lovelock, C. H. (1984b), 'Developing and Implementing New Services', in *Developing New Services*, American Marketing Association, Chicago, IL.

Lovelock, C. H. (1991), *Services Marketing*, Prentice-Hall, Englewood Cliffs, NJ.

Lunn, T. (1986), 'Segmenting and Constructing Markets', in Worcester, R. and Downham, J. (eds), *Consumer Market Research Handbook*, ESOMAR/McGraw-Hill, New York.

MacKay, S. and A. Conway (1992), 'A Network Approach to New Service Development', Working Paper for the Marketing Education Group Conference, Salford University.

Marchington, M. and P. Parker (1990), *Changing Patterns of Employee Relations*, Harvester Wheatsheaf, Hemel Hempstead.

Marginson, P. (1989), 'Employment Flexibility in Large Companies: Change and Continuity', *Industrial Relations Journal*, **20**.

Marshall, J. N. (1985), 'Business Services, the Regions and Regional Policy', *Regional Studies*, **19**, pp. 353–63.

Marshall, A. (1890), *Principle of Economics*, Macmillan, London.

Marshall, R. A. B., B. A. Palmer, and S. N. Weisbort, (1979), 'The Nature and Significance of Agent–Policyholder Relationships', *CLU Journal*, **33**, January, pp. 44–53.

Martin, Christopher (1986), *The Strategy of Distribution Management*, Heinemann, London.

Maslow, A. (1943), 'A Theory of Human Motivation', *Psychological Review*, **50**, July.

Maslow, A. (1954), *Motivation and Personality*, Harper and Row, New York.

Mayo, E. (1949), The Social Problems of Industrial Civilizations, RYP, London.

Mayo, E. J. and L. P. Jarvis (1981), *The Psychology of Leisure Travel*, CBI Publishing Co., Boston, MA.

McCarthy, J. E. (1960), *Basic Marketing: A Management Approach*, Irwin, Homewood, IL.

McDonald, M. H. B. (1984), *Marketing Plans: How to Prepare Them, How to Use Them*, Heinemann, London.

McGuire, W. J. (1969), 'The Nature of Attitude and Attitude Change', in Lindzey, G. and Aronson, E. (eds), *Handbook of Social Psychology*, Vol. 3, Addison-Wesley, Reading, MA.

McNair, M. P. (1958), 'Significant Trends and Developments in the Post-War Period', in

Smith, A. B. (ed.), *Competitive Distribution in a Free High Level Economy and its Implications for the University*, University of Pittsburgh Press, Pittsburgh, pp. 1–25.

McQuiston, D. H. (1989), 'Novelty, Complexity, and Importance as Causal Determinants of Industrial Buyer Behaviour,' *Journal of Business Research*, **53**, No. 2, pp. 66–79.

Melville-Ross, T. (1989), 'Marriage of Two Minds', *Management Today*, October.

Mesure, D. (1992), 'Marketing Services: Market Research', *Marketing*, 30 April.

Moorman, C. G. Zaltman and R. Deshpande, (1992), 'Relationships Between Providers and Users of Market Research: The Dynamics of Trust Within and Between Organisations', *Journal of Marketing Research*, **29**, August, pp. 314–28.

Morgan, N. (1991), *Professional Services Marketing*, Heinemann, London.

Morrison, A. and R. Wensley (1991), 'Boxing Up or Boxed In? A Short History of the BCG Share/Growth Matrix', *Journal of Marketing Management*, **7**, p. 2.

Moutinho, L. (1989), 'Goal Setting Process and Typologies: the Case of Professional Services', *Journal of Professional Services Marketing*, **4**, No. 2, pp. 3–100.

Moutinho, L. and M. Evans (1992), *Applied Marketing Research*, Addison-Wesley, Reading, MA.

Munting, R. (1989), 'Betting and Business: The Commercialisation of Gambling in Britain', *Business History*, **31**, No. 4.

Narver, J. C. and S. F. Slater (1990), 'The Effect of a Market Orientation on Business Profitability,' *Journal of Marketing*, October, pp. 20–35.

Newbould, G. D. (1982), 'Product Portfolio Diagnosis for US Universities,' in Kotler P., Ferrell O. C. and Lamb C. (eds), *Cases and Readings for Marketing of Non Profit Organisations*, Prentice-Hall, Englewood Cliffs, NJ.

Normann, R. (1983), *Service Management*, John Wiley, New York.

OECD (1984), 'The Contribution of Services to Employment,' *Employment Outlook*, September, pp. 9–54.

Oliver, G. (1990), *Marketing Today*, 3rd edn, Prentice-Hall International, Hemel Hempstead.

Palmer, A. J. (1992), 'Franchised Degree Teaching—What Can Educators Learn From Business?' *Journal of Further and Higher Education*, **16**, No. 3, pp. 71–80.

Palmer, A. J. (1993), 'Local Authority Tourism Development Strategies—The Role of Tourism Development Action Programmes', *Local Economy*, (7) No. 4, pp. 361–68.

Palmer, J. D. (1985), 'Consumer Service Industry Exports: New Attitudes and Concepts Needed for a Neglected Sector', *Columbia Journal of World Business*, **20**, No. 1, Spring, pp. 69–74

Parasuraman, A. (1991), *Marketing Research*, Addison-Wesley, Reading, MA.

Parasuraman, A., V. A. Zeithaml and L. Berry, (1985), 'A Conceptual Model of Service Quality and its Implications for Future Research', *Journal of Marketing*, **49**, Fall, pp. 41–50.

Parasuraman, A., V. A. Zeithaml and L. Berry (1988), 'Servqual: A Multiple-Item Scale for Measuring Consumer Perceptions of Service Quality', *Journal of Retailing*, **64**, p. 1.

Pascale, R. T. and A. Athos (1981), *The Art of Japanese Management*, Simon & Schuster, New York.

Peters, T. J. and R. H. Waterman, (1982), *In Search of Excellence: Lessons from America's Best Run Companies*, Harper & Row, New York.

Piercy, N. (1985), *Marketing Organisation: An Analysis of Information Processing, Power and Politics*, Allen and Unwin, London.

Piercy, N. (1990), 'Marketing Concepts and Actions: Implementing Marketing-led Strategic Change', *European Journal of Marketing*, **24**, No. 2, pp. 24–39.

Piercy, N. and M. Evans (1983), *Managing Marketing Information*, Croom Helm, London.

Pollert, A. (1988), 'The Flexible Firm; Fact or Fixation?' *Work, Employment and Society*, **1**, No. 1.

Porter, M. E. (1980), *Competitive Strategy: Techniques for Analysing Industries and Competitors*, Free Press, New York.

Porter, M. and V. Millar, (1985), 'How Information Gives You Competitive Advantage', *Harvard Business Review*, **85**, July-August, pp. 149–60.

Pride, W. M. and O. C. Ferrell, (1991), *Marketing: Basic Concepts and Decisions*, Houghton-Mifflin, Boston, MA.

Pruitt, D. G. (1981), *Negotiation Behaviour*, Academic Press, New York.

Rathmell, J. M. (1974), *Marketing in the Service Sector*, Winthrop Publishers Inc., Cambridge, MA.

Ries, A. and Trout, J. (1981), *Positioning*, McGraw-Hill, New York.

Rogers, E. M. (1962), *Diffusion of Innovation*, Free Press, New York.

Rumelt, R. P. (1974), *Strategy, Structure and Economic Performance*, Division of Research, Graduate School of Business Administration, Harvard University, Boston, MA.

Rushton, A. M. and D. J. Carson (1985), 'The Marketing of Services: Managing the Intangibles', *European Journal of Marketing*, **19**, No. 3, pp. 19–41.

Rushton, A. and J. Oxley (1989), *Handbook of Logistics and Distribution Management*, Kogan Page, London

Sasser, W. E., R. P. Olsen and D. D. Wyckoff (1978), *Management of Service Operations: Texts, Cases, Readings*, Allyn and Bacon, Boston, MA.

Scanzoni, J. (1979), 'Social Exchange and Behavioural Interdependence', in Burgess, R. L. and Huston, T. L. (eds) *Social Exchange in Developing Relationships*, Academic Press, New York.

Schurr, P. H. and J. L. Ozanne, (1985), 'Influences on Exchange Processes: Buyers' Preconceptions of a Seller's Trustworthiness and Bargaining Toughness', *Journal of Consumer Research*, **11**, March, pp. 939–53.

Shostack, G. L. (1977), 'Breaking Free From Product Marketing', *Journal of Marketing*, **41**, April.

Shostack, G. L. (1984), 'Designing Services that Deliver', *Harvard Business Review*, January–February, pp. 133–9.

Shostack, G. L. (1985), 'Planning the Service Encounter', in Czepiel, J. A., Solomon, M. R. and Suprenant, C. F. (eds.) *The Service Encounter*, Lexington Books, Lexington, MA, pp. 243–54.

Shostack, G. L. (1987), 'Service Positioning Through Structural Change', *Journal of Marketing*, **51**, pp. 34–43.

Sisson, K. (1989), *Personnel Management in Britain*, Blackwell, Oxford.

Smith, A. (1977), *The Wealth of Nations*, Penguin, Harmondsworth (first publication 1776).

Solomon, M. R. and S. J. Gould, (1991), 'Benefitting from Structural Similarities among Personal Services', *Journal of Services Marketing*, **5**, No. 2, Spring, pp. 23–32.

Solomon, M. R., C. F. Suprenant, J. A. Czepiel and E. G. Gutman (1985), 'A Role Theory Perspective on Dyadic Interactions: The Service Encounter, *Journal of Marketing*, **49**, Winter, pp. 99–111.

Stanton, W. J. (1981), *Fundamentals of Marketing*, McGraw-Hill, New York.

Storey, J. (1989), *New Perspective on Human Resource Management*, RKP, London.

Storey, J. (1992), *Developments in the Management of Human Resource*, Blackwell, Oxford.

Strong, E. K. (1925), *Psychology of Selling*, McGraw-Hill, New York.

Sullivan, J. and R. Peterson, (1982), 'Factors Associated with Trust in Japanese–American Joint Ventures,' *Management International Review*, **22**, pp. 33–40.

Swan, J. E. and L. J. Combs (1976), 'Product Performance and Consumer Satisfaction: A New Concept', *Journal of Marketing*, April.

Swan, J. E., I. F. Trawick and D. Silva, (1985), 'How Industrial Salespeople Gain Customer Trust', *Industrial Marketing Management*, **14**, August, pp. 203–11.

Symon I. and J. Arndt (1980), 'The Shape of the Advertising Response Function', *Journal of Advertising Research*, August.

Taylor, F. D. (1964), *Scientific Management*, Harper & Row, London.

Thomas, D. R. E. (1978), 'Strategy is Different in Service Businesses', *Harvard Business Review*, July-August.

Tull, D. S. and D. I. Hawkins (1984), *Marketing Research: Measurement and Method*, Macmillan, London.

Von Neumann, J and O. Morganstern (1944), *Theories of Games and Economic Behaviour*, Princeton University Press, Princeton, NJ.

Williamson, O. (1975), *Markets and Hierarchies: Analysis and Antitrust Implications*, Free Press, New York.

Wilson, A. (1972), *The Marketing of Professional Services*, McGraw-Hill, Maidenhead.

Wilson, D. T. and V. Mummalenen (1988), 'Bonding and Commitment in Buyer–Seller Relationships: A Preliminary Conceptualisation', *Industrial Marketing and Purchasing*, **1**, No. 3, pp. 44–58.

Wind, Y. J. (1982), *Product Policy: Concepts, Methods and Strategy*, Addison-Wesley, Reading, MA.

Wind, Y. J. (1986), 'Models for Marketing Planning and Decision Making', in Buell, V. P. (ed), *Handbook of Modern Marketing*, 2nd edn, McGraw-Hill, New York, pp. 49.1–49.12.

Wood, P. A. (1987), 'Producer Services and Economic Change, Some Canadian Evidence', in Chapman, K. and Humphreys, G. (eds), *Technological Change and Economic Policy*, Blackwell, London.

Wyckham, R. G. *et al.* (1975), 'Marketing of Services: An Evaluation of the Theory', *European Journal of Marketing*, **9**, No. 1, pp. 59–67.

Yorke, D. A. and P. Kitchen (1985), 'Channel Flickers and Video Speeders', *Journal of Advertising Research*, April-May.

Zeithaml, V. A. (1981), 'How Consumers Evaluation Processes Differ Between Goods and Services', in Donnelly, J. H. and George, W. R. (eds), *Marketing of Services*, American Marketing Association, Chicago, IL, pp. 186–90.

Zeithaml, V. A., L. L. Berry and A. Parasuraman, (1993), 'The Nature and Determinants of Customer Expectations of Service', *Journal of the Academy of Marketing Science*, **21**, No. 1, pp. 1–12.

Zeithaml, V. A., A. Parasuraman and L. L. Berry (1985), 'Problems and Strategies in Services Marketing', *Journal of Marketing*, **49**, Spring, pp. 33–46.

Zeithaml, V. A. Parasuraman, A. and Berry, L. L. (1990), *Delivering Quality Service*, Free Press, New York.

INDEX